Ann V. N

ArtScroll® Series

Rabbi Nosson Scherman / Rabbi Meir Zlotowitz
General Editors

To Ann,

May Hashem continue to bless you with wonderful years filled with health, happiness, success & holiness.

Your friend,
Aryeh Wolbe

Insights of Rav Shlomo Wolbe on the weekly Torah readings and the Festivals

Published by
ArtScroll®
Mesorah Publications, ltd

RAV WOLBE
on
CHUMASH

RABBI YITZCHOK CAPLAN

FIRST EDITION
First Impression ... October 2014

Published and Distributed by
MESORAH PUBLICATIONS, LTD.
4401 Second Avenue / Brooklyn, N.Y 11232

Distributed in Europe by
LEHMANNS
Unit E, Viking Business Park
Rolling Mill Road
Jarow, Tyne & Wear, NE32 3DP
England

Distributed in Australia and New Zealand
by **GOLDS WORLDS OF JUDAICA**
3-13 William Street
Balaclava, Melbourne 3183
Victoria, Australia

Distributed in Israel by
SIFRIATI / A. GITLER — BOOKS
Moshav Magshimim
Israel

Distributed in South Africa by
KOLLEL BOOKSHOP
Northfield Centre, 17 Northfield Avenue
Glenhazel 2192, Johannesburg, South Africa

ARTSCROLL® SERIES
RAV WOLBE ON CHUMASH
© Copyright 2014, by MESORAH PUBLICATIONS, Ltd.
4401 Second Avenue / Brooklyn, N.Y. 11232 / (718) 921-9000 / www.artscroll.com

---

ALL RIGHTS RESERVED
The text, prefatory and associated textual contents and introductions
— including the typographic layout, cover artwork and ornamental graphics —
have been designed, edited and revised as to content, form and style.

No part of this book may be reproduced
IN ANY FORM, PHOTOCOPYING, DIGITAL, OR COMPUTER RETRIEVAL SYSTEMS
— even for personal use without written permission from
the copyright holder, Mesorah Publications Ltd.
except by a reviewer who wishes to quote brief passages
in connection with a review written for inclusion in magazines or newspapers.

THE RIGHTS OF THE COPYRIGHT HOLDER WILL BE STRICTLY ENFORCED.

ISBN 10: 1-4226-1531-6 / ISBN 13: 978-1-4226-1531-7

Typography by CompuScribe at ArtScroll Studios, Ltd.
Printed in the United States of America by Noble Book Press Corp.
Bound by Sefercraft, Quality Bookbinders, Ltd., Brooklyn N.Y. 11232

Dedicated in loving memory of

Rabbi and Mrs. Jonah Caplan

לעילוי נשמת

הרב יונה אפרים בן הרב שלמה חיים זצ"ל
נפטר כב' כסלו תשמ"ח

לינה בת ר' שמריהו ע"ה
נפטרה יב' כסלו תשמ"ח

Spiritual architects who helped lay
the foundation for Torah Jewry in America,
and dedicated *talmidim* of Aharon Hakohen —
אהבו את הבריות וקירבן לתורה.

❊ ❊ ❊

לעילוי נשמת
ר' בנימין ביינוש ב"ר שלמה יוסף ז"ל
Who taught respect of a Rebbi

❊ ❊ ❊

לעילוי נשמת
הרב יצחק עמרם אליהו ב"ר אברהם אשי ז"ל

Table of Contents

Foreword	11
Introduction	15

ספר בראשית
Sefer Bereishis

פרשת בראשית / Parashas Bereishis	23
פרשת נח / Parashas Noach	31
פרשת לך לך / Parashas Lech Lecha	39
פרשת וירא / Parashas Vayeira	48
פרשת חיי שרה / Parashas Chayei Sarah	61
פרשת תולדות / Parashas Toldos	66
פרשת ויצא / Parashas Vayeitzei	72
פרשת וישלח / Parashas Vayishlach	82
פרשת וישב / Parashas Vayeishev	90
פרשת מקץ / Parashas Mikeitz	99
פרשת ויגש / Parashas Vayigash	103
פרשת ויחי / Parashas Vayechi	111

ספר שמות
Sefer Shemos

פרשת שמות / Parashas Shemos	121
פרשת וארא / Parashas Va'eira	131
פרשת בא / Parashas Bo	139
פרשת בשלח / Parashas Beshalach	147
פרשת יתרו / Parashas Yisro	158

פרשת משפטים / Parashas Mishpatim	167
פרשת תרומה / Parashas Terumah	176
פרשת תצוה / Parashas Tetzaveh	183
פרשת כי תשא / Parashas Ki Sisa	188
פרשת ויקהל-פקודי / Parashas Vayakhel-Pekudei	195

ספר ויקרא
Sefer Vayikra

פרשת ויקרא / Parashas Vayikra	207
פרשת צו / Parashas Tzav	211
פרשת שמיני / Parashas Shemini	214
פרשת תזריע-מצורע / Parashas Tazria-Metzora	222
פרשת קדושים / Parashas Kedoshim	230
פרשת אמור / Parashas Emor	239
פרשת בהר-בחקותי / Parashas Behar-Bechukosai	246

ספר במדבר
Sefer Bamidbar

פרשת במדבר / Parashas Bamidbar	255
פרשת נשא / Parashas Nasso	259
פרשת בהעלותך / Parashas Beha'alosecha	261
פרשת שלח / Parashas Shelach	270
פרשת קרח / Parashas Korach	279
פרשת חקת / Parashas Chukas	288
פרשת בלק / Parashas Balak	295
פרשת פנחס / Parashas Pinchas	301
פרשת מטות-מסעי / Parashas Matos-Masei	306

ספר דברים
Sefer Devarim

Mishneh Torah

פרשת דברים / Parashas Devarim	317
פרשת ואתחנן / Parashas Va'eschanan	319
פרשת עקב / Parashas Eikev	328
פרשת ראה / Parashas Re'eh	336
פרשת שופטים / Parashas Shoftim	343

פרשת כי תצא / Parashas Ki Seitzei	349
פרשת כי תבוא / Parashas Ki Savo	359
פרשת נצבים-וילך / Parashas Nitzavim-Vayeilech	365
פרשת האזינו / Parashas Ha'azinu	372
פרשת וזאת הברכה / Parashas V'Zos HaBerachah	374

מועדים
Festivals

אלול / Elul	379
ראש השנה / Rosh Hashanah	381
יום כפור / Yom Kippur	387
סוכות / Succos	394
שמחת תורה / Simchas Torah	398
חנוכה / Chanukah	400
פורים / Purim	404
פסח / Pesach	414
ספירת העומר / Sefiras HaOmer	424
שבועות / Shavuos	428
תשעה באב / Tishah B'Av	432
Glossary	439

Foreword

av Shlomo Wolbe *z"l* needs no introduction. He is known as the *Mashgiach* who took the *mussar* of the prewar European yeshivos and tailored it to our generation. His *sefarim* can be found in yeshivos the world over, and they grace the bookshelves of countless homes. Many consider him the final word on *chinuch*. However, Rav Wolbe did not write this book, and hence, the need for this introduction.

Rav Wolbe used to deliver a weekly *mussar shmuess* in the Bais HaMussar in Yerushalayim. These *shmuessen* were committed to paper by Rabbi Aryeh Tench in English and emailed to hundreds of people. After Rav Wolbe passed away, the Bais HaMussar was determined to keep his torch aflame. To this end, the Bais HaMussar began sending out a weekly *dvar Torah* gleaned from the many *sefarim* he left over as his legacy.

Each week, for the last nine years, the Bais HaMussar has sent out an email connected to the weekly *parashah* or pertinent to the time of year or a forthcoming Yom Tov. The email list has grown by over a thousand names, as more and more people wished to be inspired by the Torah and *mussar* of Rav Wolbe, which has made a lasting impact on so many people's lives.

While many *divrei Torah* in this book are based on his magnum opus, *Alei Shur*, and his numerous other *sefarim*, the largest portion of *divrei Torah* were taken from his *Shiurei Chumash*. *Shiurei Chumash* is a compilation of the *shiurim* that Rav Wolbe gave to help his *talmidim* better understand *Chumash, Rashi*, and the other commentators. These *vaadim* were given over the course of many years, first in Yeshivas Be'er Yaakov, later in the Bais HaMussar, and finally in Yeshivah Givat Shaul. The *Mashgiach's* family gathered his handwritten notes and the copious notes of his disciples. Armed with these notes, and with recordings of an entire cycle of *Chumash shiurim* given in the Bais HaMussar, they succeeded in producing *Shiurei Chumash*. This *sefer* was very well received by the public, as it is an indispensable resource for anyone interested in delving into the profundity of the *parshiyos*.

To date, however, *Shiurei Chumash* has only been published on *Sefer Bereishis* and *Sefer Shemos*, and only in Hebrew. Many have asked — or, more accurately, begged — Rav Wolbe's family to publish the *vaadim* on the rest of *Chumash*. Additionally, there are many who wish to gain from Rav Wolbe's wisdom, but are unable to study the Hebrew texts. These and other factors propelled me to publish some of the weekly *divrei Torah* in what might be called an English version of *Shiurei Chumash*, but this time on the entire Torah and with an additional section on the *Mo'adim*.

Yet there is a major difference between the Hebrew *Shiurei Chumash* and the book you now hold in your hands. The Hebrew version of *Shiurei Chumash* was culled from actual recordings and handwritten notes; the ideas and words are all Rav Wolbe's. That is not the case with this book. Although all the ideas are his, the words are not. I tried to remain as faithful as possible to what was already written in *Shiurei Chumash, Alei Shur*, and his other *sefarim*, but an exact translation would have been impossible; nor was it the intention behind the *divrei Torah*. Additionally, the practical application found at the end of most of the *divrei Torah* was almost always my personal addition. I have added the sources for the *divrei Torah* to allow the reader to refer to the original source for a more in-depth explanation of the topic at hand.

I would like to point out that this *sefer* should be viewed as a mere taste of Rav Wolbe's Torah, and cannot take the place of studying his *sefarim* in their original form. The true greatness and depth of his Torah cannot be captured or fully appreciated in a book of concise *divrei Torah*. My hope is that after tasting his clarity of thought, your appetite will be whetted to the point that you will decide to follow in the ways of countless others and designate a portion of your time to learning his *sefarim*.

I would like to thank a number of people without whom this book could have never been published:

Rabbi Aryeh Tench, who was the inspiration behind the weekly email, and whose email list formed the base of the many weekly recipients of Rav Wolbe's *divrei Torah*.

My father-in-law Reb Avrohom Wolbe, the *Mashgiach's* son and his truest *talmid*, who enlisted me to write the weekly *dvar Torah* after his father passed away. This adds one more item to the list of things for which I am very thankful to my in-laws.

My father, Rabbi Shlomo Caplan *shlita*, who, with his great Torah erudition, his sharp eye, and his keen sense of the way to successfully deliver a message, spent countless hours polishing the *divrei Torah*. Each week the *dvar Torah* would have to pass his scrutiny, and his (and my mother's) astute suggestions have been incorporated into every *dvar Torah*. A simple thank-you surely cannot suffice for all that my parents have done and continue to do for me and my family. In appreciation, I am dedicating this book in memory of my father's parents, Rabbi and Mrs. Jonah Caplan *z"l*.

Mrs. Miriam Jakubowicz, who sifted through the hundreds of *divrei Torah*, and then combined and refined them into their present state. It is due to her great expertise that this book made it to the publisher.

Shmuel Blitz and Mrs. Malky Heimowitz of the ArtScroll staff who took this project under their wing.

Finally, I would like to thank my wife, who really deserves all the credit (for this book and everything else I do). It is she who enables and encourages me to write the *divrei Torah* no matter what else is going on, and without her constant support, the weekly *divrei Torah* would have stopped a long time ago. שלי ושלכם שלה.

Most importantly, I would like to thank Hashem for all His tremendous kindness in general, and specifically, for giving me the opportunity to disseminate Rav Wolbe's words to the public.

בהודאה על העבר ותפילה על העתיד שאזכה ללמוד וללמד לשמור ולעשות ולקיים את כל דברי תלמוד תורתך באהבה.

Yitzchok Caplan

(To receive the weekly *dvar Torah* please send an email to <u>baishamussar@gmail.com</u>).

Introduction

THE PROPER APPROACH TO LEARNING CHUMASH

When learning *Tanach* we must bear in mind that we are light-years away from the spiritual level of the people we learn about. For example, the *navi* Yeshayah castigates his generation with extremely harsh accusations: "Woe, a sinful nation, a people laden with sin, evil offspring, destructive children; they have forsaken Hashem, angered the Holy One of Yisrael and turned their back toward Him" (*Yeshayah* 1:4). A superficial reading of this *passuk* might cause us to think that Yeshayah's generation was full of corrupt, depraved people.

> "The very fact that the generation of Yeshayah merited hearing the rebuke of a navi is the greatest testimony to their awesome spiritual level."

However, the very fact that they merited hearing the rebuke of a *navi* is the greatest testimony to their awesome spiritual level.

If Yeshayah's generation was truly great, how could they have been idol worshipers? We have no concept of the allure of idol worship, and we therefore cannot understand their behavior. We do know, however, that the drive toward idol worship was so immensely powerful that King Menashe came to one of the *Amora'im* in a dream and told him that had he lived in an earlier generation, he would have picked up the hem of his clothing in order to run even faster in the pursuit of idol worship (*Sanhedrin* 102b). The urge was so difficult to overcome that *Chazal* felt compelled to *daven* to Hashem to abolish this desire. Their wish was granted, and today we have no clue as to the challenge that previous generations grappled with.

In order to gain some inkling of the spiritual level of the people in *Tanach*, we must first try to understand the greatness of the intermediate generations between their era and ours. We can still partially relate to the *mussar* given by the Chofetz Chaim, but we are totally disconnected from the *mussar* of Rav Yisrael Salanter, who lived a generation earlier. When he rebuked those around him for their apathy during Elul, he was not referring to the acute indifference toward the *Yamim Nora'im* that abounds today. Similarly, Rav Yisrael's generation could not match the generation of Rav Chaim Volozhin, who also lamented the low spiritual level of his times. The same variance exists between the generations of Rav Chaim Volozhin and the Ramchal. One of the early *Rishonim*, Rabbeinu Tam, explained in the introduction to a *mussar sefer* he authored that he felt his generation could not relate to the concepts mentioned in the *Chovos HaLevavos*, which was written a number of years earlier. This trend continues back through the generations of *Geonim*, *Amorai'm*, *Tanna'im* and *Nevi'im*.

We cannot possibly comprehend the greatness of the people in *Tanach*. When Yeshayah called the nation "sinful" and accused them of forsaking Hashem, he was referring to a subtle laxity in their *dveikus* to Hashem. By way of illustration, think of how we typically feel after Rosh Hashanah, when we remember that tomorrow we will have to rise early for *Selichos*. After two days of lengthy and intense *davening*, do not we think to ourselves, if only for a moment, *More davening? Isn't it enough already?* Such a thought borders on "forsaking Hashem."

If the Torah relates the stories of Adam, the *Avos*, the *Shevatim*, and *Bnei Yisrael*, then even we, with our limited spiritual capacity, are expected to learn from those accounts. Yet at the same time, when we read of Adam's sin with the *Eitz Hadaas*, and similar transgressions that unfold in the *Chumash*, we must remember that the people being discussed were immeasurably greater than we could ever imagine.

Although there are stories of transgressions in the *Chumash*, there are also numerous accounts of our forefathers' greatness. Hashem told Avraham, "I will make you into a large nation, I will bless you, I will make your name great, and you will be a blessing" (*Bereishis* 12:2). Rashi explains that "I will make you into a large nation" refers to the words "*Elokei Avraham*" (that we say in *Shemoneh Esrei*); "I will bless you" refers to the words "*Elokei Yitzchak*"; and "I will make your name great" refers to "*Elokei Yaakov*." Finally, "and you will be a blessing" refers to the end of the first blessing of *Shemoneh Esrei*, where we mention Avraham a second time: "*Magen Avraham*."

Rav Yerucham Levovitz explains the significance of referring to Hashem in the context of our forefathers. If not for our illustrious ancestors, we would know nothing about our Creator, because we cannot begin to comprehend Hashem's greatness. We know that Avraham Avinu went to great lengths to perform kindness with all types of people and that Yitzchak was willing to sacrifice his life to fulfill the will of his Creator. We witness Yaakov Avinu's uncompromising adherence to truth throughout his tenure in Lavan's employ. By reflecting on the greatness of Hashem's servants, we can begin to recognize the greatness of their Master. Accordingly, while *davening Shemoneh Esrei*, the emphasis should be placed on the word "Avraham" and not on the

> "*While davening Shemoneh Esrei, the emphasis should be placed on the word 'Avraham' and not on the word 'Elokei,' because it is only through Avraham that we can begin to know Hashem.*"

word "*Elokei*," because it is only through Avraham that we can begin to know Hashem.

The Midrash (*Devarim Rabbah* 3:5) relates that Rav Shimon ben Shetach once bought a donkey from an Arab. Upon arriving home, he discovered that the animal had a precious stone hanging from its neck. Though his students claimed that it was a God-given present, he responded, "I bought a donkey, not a precious stone." He then set off to return the stone to its original owner. Upon receiving this unexpected gift, the Arab exclaimed, "Blessed is the God of Shimon ben Shetach." Although he had no prior connection to Hashem, the Arab now became aware of the greatness of Shimon ben Shetach, and after seeing how a servant of the Creator acts, he had some picture of how awesome and great the Creator Himself must be. Our patriarchs provide us with a similar frame of reference. By contemplating their greatness, we develop a starting point from which to recognize Hashem Himself.

There is yet another benefit in contemplating the great acts of our forefathers. Hashem tells Avraham (*Bereishis* 12:3), "And all the families of the earth will be blessed through you." Rashi explains that when a father wishes to bless his child, he says, "May you be like Avraham." Why does a parent specifically say that his child should be like our forefathers? Would it not suffice to bless the child that he be a good Jew?

Such a blessing would be very vague, leaving it to the child himself to figure out exactly what a "good Jew" does. However, when we specify, "You should be like Avraham," a child who has learned about Avraham has a clear picture of what he must strive to be. Likewise, when we bless our children, "You should be like Ephraim and Menashe," they understand that this blessing refers to Ephraim and Menashe's greatness and their unique ability to study and keep the entire Torah despite living in the depraved environment of Mitzrayim.

We cannot fathom the awesome potential of man. The Torah is referred to as "the book of mankind" (ibid. 5:1; see Ramban), since a person who lives his life in accordance with everything written in the Torah reveals the true essence of man. The Torah does not measure greatness by how many grandiose buildings one has built or how many lawsuits he has won. True greatness is measured by how successful a person is in overcoming the myriad temptations he encounters throughout his life.

The Alter of Slabodka spent his entire life teaching about the greatness of man in general and Adam HaRishon in particular. Numerous great leaders emerged from his yeshivah, among them Rav Aharon Kotler, Rav Avraham Grodzinski, Rav Yitzchak Hutner, Rav Isaac Sher, and Rav Meir Chadash. Learning about our remarkable forefathers will help us gain an appreciation for the great levels a person can reach.

(*Shiurei Chumash Bereishis* p. 2, *Parashas Lech Lecha* 12:1)

ספר בראשית
Sefer Bereishis

פרשת בראשית
Parashas Bereishis

IN PUBLIC, IN PRIVATE

וְלֹא יִתְבֹּשָׁשׁוּ
And they were not ashamed (2:25).

The Torah tells us that before Adam and Chavah ate from the *Eitz Hadaas* they were not embarrassed by their lack of clothing. Rashi explains that they were not aware of the concept of *tznius*, which enables a person to distinguish between good and bad. This explanation of Rashi reveals a novel approach to defining the term *tznius*: *Tznius* is the manner by which one determines whether his actions are good or bad.

How can a person know the true motivation underlying his actions? Rav Yerucham Levovitz would say that a person has to familiarize himself with the many faces and colors of the *yetzer hara*. Although one might feel a great desire to perform a specific mitzvah, he must be able to discern whether the surge of adrenaline is coming from his *yetzer tov* or his *yetzer hara*. Performing a mitzvah is commendable, but it should not come at the expense of a greater or more timely Torah obligation. Rav Yisrael Salanter would say, "The *yetzer hara* does not mind if one says *Tehillim* the entire day — as long as he does not sit down to study Torah in depth."

In this vein, we can understand the Gemara at the end of *Maseches Makkos* (24a), which discusses the *passuk* (Michah 6:8) "What does Hashem request of you but to do justice, love kindness, and walk modestly with Hashem?" The Gemara tells us that to "walk modestly with Hashem" refers to proper participation in funerals and marriages. The Gemara concludes that if these events — which are generally performed publicly — must be carried out in a modest manner, how much more so must we ensure that actions meant to be done privately are carried out modestly. In other words, the way to gauge whether the justice and kindness mentioned in the first part of the *passuk* are a true fulfillment of Hashem's commandment is to determine whether they would have been performed in the same manner had they been performed far from the eyes of any onlooker.

> "Tznius is not simply an inconspicuous manner of dress; it is an inconspicuous manner of living."

Tznius is not simply an inconspicuous manner of dress; it is an inconspicuous manner of living. If the actions that one performs publicly would be performed in the same way behind closed doors, then one can be confident that he has fulfilled his obligation.
(*Shiurei Chumash, Parashas Bereishis* 2:25)

❊ ❊ ❊

THE REAL PUNISHMENT

בְּעֶצֶב תֵּלְדִי בָנִים ... בְּזֵעַת אַפֶּיךָ תֹּאכַל לֶחֶם
With pain you will bear children ... by the sweat of your brow you will eat bread (3:16-19).

After eating from the *Eitz Hadaas*, Adam and Chavah were punished in numerous ways. Prior to his sin, Adam cleaved to Hashem and did not perceive "nature" at work in the creation because everything flowed easily, smoothly, and in a miraculous fashion. His food was available without any effort on his part. His children were born without delay and in a manner completely devoid of pain and difficulties. Hashem's presence in the creation was clear beyond any shadow of a doubt.

That all changed when he ate from the *Eitz Hadaas*. Sin brings in its wake a separation between man and Hashem, causing Hashem's presence to be hidden. This is the meaning behind Hashem's question to Adam (ibid. 3:9), "Where are you?" With his sin, Adam had in effect erected a barrier between himself and his Creator.

This concept provides us with a deeper understanding of reward and punishment. A person must strive to reach the level where he cleaves to Hashem, and reward is anything that eases the hardship involved in reaching this goal. Conversely, punishment is something that makes it harder to perceive Hashem's presence, thereby requiring effort on man's behalf to discern the Hand of Hashem.

Adam lost his clarity of Hashem's presence, and that was in and of itself his punishment. His newfound situation required that he invest time and effort to bring about the same results that were achieved so effortlessly prior to his sin. Such a situation leads a person to think that it is his own efforts that allow him to accomplish. "And you will think in your hearts, 'My strength and the power of my hand caused me to gain all this wealth'" (*Devarim* 8:17). Nevertheless, his assignment stays the same as it was before he sinned, although his job is many times harder: He must perceive Hashem's presence even though it is now hidden.

> *"It is a mistake to think that our material occupation is central to our existence, while serving Hashem is tangential."*

It is a mistake to think that our material occupation is central to our existence, while serving Hashem is tangential. In reality, the opposite is true. Our entire purpose in life is to recognize and be completely cognizant of Hashem's presence, in the creation and in our everyday lives. The punishment meted out to all of mankind was that we now have to discern His presence from within the framework of our own efforts and despite all the hardships we undergo. Although we must toil in order to achieve, the physical exertion is not an end unto itself.

Before one decides to spend all of his free time working, he should realize that instead of merely fulfilling the obligation of physical toil caused by Adam's sin, he is making it his life's goal. His real occupation is the service of Hashem, and that is how at least a portion of his free time should be spent.

(*Shiurei Chumash, Parashas Bereishis* 3:17-19)

❊ ❊ ❊

WHO ARE YOU REALLY?

וַיֹּאמֶר ה׳ אֱלֹקִים הֵן הָאָדָם הָיָה כְּאַחַד מִמֶּנּוּ לָדַעַת טוֹב וָרָע

And Hashem God said, "Behold Man has become like the Unique One among us, knowing good and bad" (3:22).

The *berachah* we recite daily in *Birchos Hashachar*, "Blessed are You, Hashem … Who clothes the naked," refers to the clothing that Hashem tailored for Adam and Chavah after they ate from the *Eitz Hadaas* and became cognizant of their nakedness. Before they transgressed Hashem's commandment, they were not embarrassed by their lack of clothing.

When Adam was created, his very essence was his *neshamah*. The physical body was created merely as "clothing" for the *neshamah*. (In fact, Rav Elya Lopian referred to the body as "pants of flesh.") Accordingly, his lack of clothing was no reason for shame, since he had a physical body that served that purpose. Once Adam sinned, however, he altered his very makeup, and his essence became a mixture of body and soul. The physical body no longer clothed Adam; it became part and parcel of his being and required its own covering. It was at this point that Hashem prepared clothing for Adam and Chavah.

We identify ourselves as, and associate ourselves with, our physical bodies. Though we are made up of both *guf* and *neshamah*, it is much easier for us to relate to the *berachah* of *Asher Yatzar* than to the *berachah* of *Elokai, Neshamah*. To the question "Who are you?" most people would give an answer that describes their physical appearance or occupation, while completely overlooking the spiritual aspect of who they are. This is one of the side effects of human sin.

Despite this confusion, it is incumbent upon each of us to familiarize ourselves with our *neshamah*. Who are you really? In what areas of *avodas Hashem* do you connect significantly with your Creator? What are your weaknesses, and, more importantly, what are your strengths? Make an appointment with yourself and get to really know yourself. *You are the most interesting person you will ever meet.* And with a solid understanding of your spiritual makeup, your *avodas Hashem* has the potential to improve greatly.

> "*You are the most interesting person you will ever meet.*"

(Shiurei Chumash, Parashas Bereishis 3:21)

* * *

PERSONALITY RENOVATION

זֶה סֵפֶר תּוֹלְדֹת אָדָם

This is the account of the descendants of Adam (5:1).

The end of *Parashas Bereishis* lists the generations from Adam until Noach. The Torah prefaces this list with the words "*Zeh sefer toldos Adam*" — This is the account of the descendants of Adam. The Ramban comments that the word "*sefer*" in this *passuk* does not refer merely to the genealogical account that follows; rather, it refers to the Book of Torah in its entirety.

Most people live their lives without much deliberation. Their thoughts, actions, and speech are "*hefker,*" executed at whim. In contrast, when one learns Torah, it affects his essence and changes his entire way of life. As the Rambam writes (*Hilchos Dei'os* 5:1), "A *talmid chacham* is distinguishable by his actions, his speech, and his manner of walking." The Torah is responsible for this personality renovation.

Some people are amazed by a person who founds a grandiose corporation or builds a colossal building, but the Torah teaches us that our amazement should be channeled in a different direction. A person who passes a test — conquering his *yetzer hara* or overcoming a negative *middah* — is the truly amazing person. Because the Torah teaches us how great a human being can become, it can aptly be described as "*sefer toldos adam*" — the book that describes the offspring (which means both "children" and "deeds") of man (*adam*).

Since man's true essence is defined by the Torah, every mitzvah or *aveirah* affects the makeup of his body. In fact, there were great people who were able to discern which *aveirah* another person had transgressed. The Arizal once told a disciple that he had transgressed the *aveirah* of causing pain to an animal. This disciple had eaten before feeding his animal, in violation of the halachah that requires a person to feed his animal before partaking of his own meal. When the disciple came before the Arizal again, the Arizal mentioned that it was noticeable that he had rectified his misdeed.

Rav Yerucham Levovitz gave yet another example of the greatness the Torah attributes to man. In *Parashas Matos* the Torah describes at length the halachos that pertain to one who makes a *neder*. It is incredible that a human has the ability to forbid something by way of his speech in a manner that is just as binding as any other mitzvah written in the Torah and commanded by Hashem Himself!

Every aspect of the Torah can and should effect a positive change in us. Slowly but surely, Torah will cause all of our mannerisms to change for the better, and people will declare (*Yoma* 86a),

"Praiseworthy is his father who taught him Torah; praiseworthy is his rabbi who taught him Torah!"
(*Shiurei Chumash, Parashas Bereishis* 5:1)

❊ ❊ ❊

WIELDING OUR INFLUENCE

וְנֹחַ מָצָא חֵן בְּעֵינֵי ה'
And Noach found favor in Hashem's eyes (6:8).

Sforno explains that it was not due to Noach's great merits that his children were saved from death, but rather because Noach found favor in Hashem's eyes. "And these three men — Noach, Daniel, and Iyov ... I swear, says Hashem, that they will not save their sons nor their daughters; only they themselves will be saved" (*Yechezkel* 14:14-16).

Noach, Daniel, and Iyov did not have the ability to protect others from punishment because, unlike Avraham, Moshe, and Shmuel, they did not teach their respective generations to recognize Hashem. Although Noach chastised the populace to abandon their decadent way of life, he did not teach them the spiritual values necessary to be truly cognizant of Hashem. Noach was completely righteous, but only those who extend themselves to others with the intention of helping them improve have the ability to save other people. It is worthwhile to save the evildoers because they might be influenced by the righteous to repent, but if the righteous do not wield their influence there is no point in saving the evildoers.

The *Chovos HaLevavos* (*Shaar HaBitachon*) writes that a person can look forward to a portion in the World to Come when he not only fulfills mitzvos himself, but also influences others to fulfill mitz-

> "*A person can look forward to a portion in the World to Come when he not only fulfills mitzvos himself, but also influences others to fulfill mitzvos.*"

vos. Elsewhere (*Shaar Ahavas Hashem*), the *Chovos HaLevavos* explains that those who simply study and perform mitzvos themselves, and those who perform mitzvos and also educate others, can be compared to two different businessmen. The first businessman sold his lone piece of merchandise and netted a profit. The second businessman had a variety of merchandise to sell, and although he sold each individual piece for less, at the end of the day he came out far ahead of his counterpart. So, too, a person who influences others to improve accrues the merits of all those whom he succeeded in helping, and his portion in the World to Come is far greater than one who cares only about himself.

We must bear this concept in mind, and also inculcate it into our children from a young age. Torah that is learned is not meant to be merely a personal acquisition, but rather one that will be imparted to others as well. Just as the halachah mandates that one set aside a portion of his wealth to help those who are monetarily less fortunate, we should also set aside a portion of our time to help those who are spiritually less fortunate. It is advisable that one-tenth of our learning time should be donated toward *kiruv rechokim*. But even fifteen minutes a week on the telephone can change not only another person's life, but ultimately our own lives as well.

(*Shiurei Chumash, Parashas Bereishis* 6:8)

פרשת נח

Parashas Noach

THE SUN IS THE YARDSTICK

נֹחַ אִישׁ צַדִּיק תָּמִים הָיָה בְּדֹרֹתָיו
*Noach was a righteous man,
perfect in his generations (6:9).*

Rashi writes that some commentators explain this *passuk* in a positive light: Had Noach lived in a generation with other righteous people he would have been an even greater *tzaddik*. However, others explain it derogatorily and say that Noach was only considered a *tzaddik* in his generation; had he lived in the generation of Avraham, he would not have been given even an "honorable mention."

Rav Yerucham Levovitz explains how the Torah perceives man's accomplishments. Though some commentators explain the Torah's accolade of Noach to be a true compliment and some interpret it only in relation to Noach's generation, all of them agree that a person is measured in comparison to the generation of the greatest stature. By way of illustration, one can measure the amount of light produced by a candle in comparison to a lightbulb or flashlight, or in comparison to the greatest source of light that exists: the light of the sun. The Torah gauges one's spiritual level in comparison to the light of the "sun": the founder of Judaism, Avraham Avinu.

"The Torah gauges one's spiritual level in comparison to the light of the 'sun': the founder of Judaism, Avraham Avinu."

A person might look around at his acquaintances and smugly reassure himself that he has surpassed his colleagues or friends in their spiritual ascent, and as a result he can slacken off a bit. However, this is not at all true. A person who has the ability to grow spiritually or accomplish more in his lifetime cannot rest on the laurels of his past accomplishments. He will not be judged in comparison to his family, his colleagues, his *kollel*, his city, or even his entire generation. The true test of a person's greatness is seeing how he measures up against his own vast potential.

(*Shiurei Chumash, Parashas Noach* 6:9)

❈ ❈ ❈

SUCCESSFUL REENTRY

וַיָּחֶל נֹחַ אִישׁ הָאֲדָמָה וַיִּטַּע כָּרֶם
And Noach made himself mundane and planted a vineyard (9:20).

Noach spent an entire year of total selflessness in the ark, where he sustained an untold number of animals and lived a truly spiritual life as a prophet of Hashem. Thereafter, the Torah tells us, "And Noach made himself *mundane* and planted a vineyard." Rashi explains that his initial choice should have been to plant something different, since wine has the ability to intoxicate (which is, in fact, what happened to Noach). When a person experiences a spiritual lift and then does something that is not on a par with his newfound level, he has in essence "made himself mundane."

For this reason, *Chazal* instituted that we begin building our *succah* immediately after Yom Kippur, thereby maintaining the spiritual level achieved on the holiest of days. After every mitzvah through which one attains a greater level of holiness, such as Shabbos or *tefillah*, he must be careful with regard to his subsequent actions lest he "make himself mundane."

The night following Yom Kippur can be compared to the return flight of a space shuttle. The most dangerous aspect of the flight is the reentry into the atmosphere. If the space shuttle does not enter at precisely the right angle, it will burn up from the friction caused by contact with the air. So, too, after Yom Kippur, when we reenter day-to-day living, it is possible that the entire "Yom Kippur" can get burned by the free-for-all atmosphere around us. It is not a simple task to reenter life at the correct angle and not lose all that we have gained on Yom Kippur.

The Gemara (*Berachos* 32b) tells us that early righteous Torah scholars would spend an hour in preparation for prayer, an hour praying, and another hour after prayers. The need for preparation is understandable, but why did they spend another hour of their precious time after they had already finished *davening*? The answer is that they knew how important it was to reenter the routine of their lives at the correct angle, and this took an additional hour of preparation.

The key to a successful year is the ability to take the feelings of spirituality one experienced during the *Yamim Nora'im* and "stretch" them to the subsequent days and weeks. Rav Wolbe once took leave of the Mirrer Yeshivah on the day after Yom Kippur and returned shortly before Chanukah. When he entered the yeshivah upon his return, he was immediately able to sense the atmosphere of the *Yamim Nora'im* that still permeated the air.

"The key to a successful year is the ability to take the feelings of spirituality one experienced during the Yamim Nora'im and 'stretch' them to the subsequent days and weeks."

Parashas Noach / 33

Our Sages instituted the idea of *Yom Kippur Katan* — a miniature Yom Kippur — before the beginning of each month. Such a day is supposed to be reminiscent of the "real" Yom Kippur, thereby allowing us to relive its spirituality to some degree. One day a month was set aside to take stock of the level we are on and how we have fared so far with the resolutions we made in the *Yamim Nora'im.* This is a wonderful way to extend the levels attained during the *Yamim Nora'im* to the rest of the year.

(*Shiurei Chumash, Parashas Noach* 9:20; *Maamarei Yemei Ratzon*, p. 105)

❊ ❊ ❊

THE MUSSAR TELESCOPE

גִּבֹּר־צַיִד לִפְנֵי ה׳

A mighty hunter before Hashem (10:9).

Chazal tell us that Nimrod "knew his Master and intentionally rebelled against Him" (Rashi, *Bereishis* 10:9). How could Nimrod acknowledge Hashem's omnipotence and nevertheless rebel against Him?

The concept of "knowing one's Master and rebelling against Him" was more prevalent in the earlier generations because they had a clear perception of Hashem. It was precisely because of his closeness to Hashem that Nimrod had a problem: It was difficult for him to maintain such a lofty level for an extended period. Had someone asked Nimrod if he believed in Hashem, he would have answered, "Absolutely!" Nevertheless, his impulses refused to act in keeping with this knowledge.

When a person ascends a rung on the spiritual ladder, there is an automatic feeling of resistance. Rav Eliyahu Dessler compares this concept to a spring. The harder one presses down on the spring, the harder it will bounce back toward him. The bigger the resolution one accepts upon himself, the more resistance he will feel and the harder it will be for him to maintain this new level.

When a person learns *mussar* and engages in serious introspection, he may be surprised to find that he, too, possesses some feelings of resistance toward *ruchniyus*. One such example is our behavior after Yom Kippur, when many people sing and dance. Is this happiness born of genuine feelings of gratitude to Hashem for pardoning our sins? A person who learns *mussar* will discover that it is more likely that this singing and dancing is an expression of joy and relief as no longer having to say so many *tefillos* and confessions; it is simply too difficult for us to maintain the lofty level of Yom Kippur. This is a subconscious act of rebellion against Hashem.

The Alter of Kelm writes that *Chazal's* statements can be compared to stars, and the way to properly "see" them is with a "telescope" — the study of *mussar*. Although *Chazal's* statement about Nimrod might seem difficult to understand, the study of *mussar* acts as a telescope, allowing us to discover the very same trait inside ourselves and appreciate the profundity of *Chazal's* words.

> *"It is imperative to progress spiritually with small steps, since doing so engenders less resistance."*

It is imperative to progress spiritually with small steps, since doing so engenders less resistance. Someone who decides to completely refrain from speaking for a day by accepting a *taanis dibbur*, in order to prevent himself from speaking *lashon hara* and other prohibited speech, may find that the resistance is too great. The next day he might end up speaking twice as much *lashon hara* as he did before his *taanis dibbur*!

One must make an effort to internalize his awareness of Hashem, for then it becomes more than "knowledge" — it is part and parcel of his very being. The result will be that he will act in consonance with this awareness instead of rebelling against Hashem.

(*Shiurei Chumash, Parashas Noach* 10:9)

❊ ❊ ❊

INGRATITUDE: AN ANCIENT TRADITION

וַיֵּרֶד ה' לִרְאֹת אֶת־הָעִיר וְאֶת־הַמִּגְדָּל אֲשֶׁר בָּנוּ בְּנֵי הָאָדָם

And Hashem descended to see the city and the tower that were built by the offspring of man (11:5).

It is evident from *Parashas Noach* that ingratitude has been ingrained in mankind since the time of creation. The Torah tells us that Hashem came down to observe the construction of the tower of Bavel: "And Hashem descended to see the city and the tower that were built by the offspring of man." Rashi, citing *Chazal*, asks why it is necessary for the Torah to inform us that the tower was built by the offspring of man. Would we have thought that it was built by the offspring of donkeys or camels?

Rashi explains that "man" (*adam*) mentioned in the *passuk* refers not to humans but to Adam HaRishon. The Torah is emphasizing that this generation emulated the behavior of their forefather. Just as Adam, after eating from the *Etz Hadaas*, displayed ingratitude by blaming Hashem for giving him a wife, the builders of the tower were ungrateful to Hashem, Who had saved them from the flood, and they wanted to fight against Him.

There are two fundamental reasons why people refrain from showing *hakaras hatov*. The first reason is that people simply think they deserve everything they receive and therefore there is no reason to thank their benefactor. A child is born without intelligence, and by the time he is old enough to comprehend what is going on, he is already used to being healthy, well fed, dressed, and taken care of. A person is born with a sense of egocentricity that places him in the center of the universe and causes him to believe that everyone around him has been placed there simply to serve him. Hand a child a candy, and he'll snatch it and run away without saying thank you.

It takes a lot of work for a person to free himself of these attitudes and come to a realization that absolutely nothing, including life itself, can be taken for granted. One who comes to such a realization lives in a bright and happy world, for he perceives everyone around him as cogs in a huge world of kindness. In contrast, his egocentric counterpart looks upon the doctor, the bus driver, and the storeowner as people who serve him for no reason other than to make some money, and he therefore sees no reason to thank them for their services.

The second reason people refrain from expressing gratitude is that they dislike feeling indebted to their benefactor. Acknowledging that one benefited from another person means that he owes him something in return, and no one likes to feel indebted.

Hakaras hatov might be a difficult *middah* to master, but it is well worth the investment, for it is the key to good interpersonal relationships and a real connection with the Creator.

(*Alei Shur,* Vol. II, p. 280)

> "*Hakaras hatov* is the key to good interpersonal relationships and a real connection with the Creator."

❋ ❋ ❋

CONSULTING THE UNDERLINGS

וַיֹּאמֶר ה׳... הָבָה נֵרְדָה וְנָבְלָה שָׁם שְׂפָתָם אֲשֶׁר לֹא יִשְׁמְעוּ אִישׁ שְׂפַת רֵעֵהוּ

And Hashem said, "… Let us descend and mix up their languages so that each one will not understand the language of his friend" (11:6-7).

Rashi explains that Hashem said, "Let us," in the plural form, because He was including His *beis din*. Hashem's great humility prompted Him to ask permission from the angels before He carried out what He deemed to be the proper course of action.

We find this idea in *Parashas Bereishis* as well. Before creating man, Hashem said, "Let us make man in our form and image" (*Bereishis* 1:26). There, too, Rashi explains that Hashem's *middah* of *anavah* prompted Him to consult with the angels. Since man would be fashioned in their form, He felt it was only right to present the idea to them. Although writing "Let us" might cause nonbelievers to mistakenly think that there is more than one Creator, the Torah took that risk in order to convey a vital lesson: *Derech eretz dictates that even a great person should ask the opinion of those smaller than himself.*

> "*Derech eretz dictates that even a great person should ask the opinion of those smaller than himself.*"

There are many lessons to be learned from these *pesukim*. For one thing, we see that one should not attribute his actions solely to himself; he should say "we" rather than "I." Furthermore, Hashem could have completely ignored anyone else's interests and done as He pleased. However, He chose to ask the angels' opinion, lest they feel bad about what He was going to do. Similarly, a person in a position of authority should not enact rules and regulations without asking the opinion of those under him. Harmony reigns only when everyone understands the need for the regulations imposed.

(*Shiurei Chumash, Parashas Bereishis* 1:26)

פרשת לך לך
Parashas Lech Lecha

ROOTS, SPROUTS, AND TREES

וַיַּעֲבֹר אַבְרָם בָּאָרֶץ
Abram passed into the land (12:6).

Many of the details mentioned in the stories recounted in *Sefer Bereishis* seem to be irrelevant or inconsequential. Why do we need to know how many wells were dug by our forefathers or exactly who prepared the food for the heavenly visitors to Avraham's tent? What is the significance of the Torah's telling us about Avraham's travels throughout the land of Canaan or where he went when there was a famine in the country?

Ramban (*Bereishis* 26:20) addresses this question: "I will explain to you a general rule regarding all of the upcoming *parshiyos* that deal with Avraham, Yitzchak, and Yaakov. Everything that happened to our forefathers is symbolic of what will occur to their children. Therefore, the Torah relates at great length the travels, the digging of the wells, and the other occurrences. One might think that these stories are unnecessary, while in reality they were all written to inform us of what will happen in the future." For example, Ramban explains that the three wells dug by Yitzchak symbolize the three *Batei Mikdash*.

In order for a tree to grow, a seed must be planted in the ground. The type of tree that will grow is determined by which seed was planted and how it took root. This concept is true in the spiritual realm as well. The *Avos* are not only our roots in a physical sense; they are also our spiritual roots. All of their actions were carried out with the intention of creating a spiritual nation. These actions were the seeds of the Jewish people, and the sprouts that grew out of those seeds can be perceived through what has occurred to the Jewish nation in the course of history.

When Bilam planned to curse *Bnei Yisrael*, his intention was to annihilate them by destroying their roots. For this reason, he had seven altars built, to rival the seven altars that were erected by our *Avos*. He was unsuccessful in his attempts, as he himself stated: "I look at their beginnings and their roots and I see that through the actions of the patriarchs and matriarchs their foundations are concrete like mountains and hills" (Rashi to *Bamidbar* 23:9).

Although the *Avos* succeeded greatly in their endeavors, they had the ability to do even more than they did. *Chazal* (*Bava Metzia* 85a) tell us regarding Avraham's hospitality toward the three angels that every action he performed personally garnered a reward that was delivered by Hashem Himself, while every action that he performed through an emissary garnered a reward that was delivered by an emissary of Hashem. Additionally, Ramban writes (*Bereishis* 12:10) that because Avraham did not place complete faith in Hashem that He would sustain him during the famine, and he left the country in which he had been commanded to reside, his offspring suffered the exile in Mitzrayim.

Chazal tell us (*Nedarim* 32a) that it was because Avraham took along *talmidei chachamim* when he waged war against the four kings that his descendants became slaves in Mitzrayim for 210 years. What should Avraham have done differently? How could he fight mighty armies with a handful of warriors? It seems that

Avraham, who was planting seeds with his every action, could have done even more, thereby influencing the events that would later "sprout" from his actions.

How does this apply to us? For one thing, it gives us a new appreciation of every single word written in the Torah. Additionally, there are instances when we, too, have the ability to plant seeds for the future. For instance, our actions on Rosh Hashanah plant seeds for the following year, and during those two days we must be extra careful with our behavior. Finally, this knowledge gives us an incentive to strive for greater heights. If the Torah tells us that even Avraham could have done more, then certainly we can do more.

> "If the Torah tells us that even Avraham could have done more, then certainly we can do more."

(Shiurei Chumash, Parashas Lech Lecha 12:6,12)

❊ ❊ ❊

A TIME TO PLANT

וַיָּרֶק אֶת־חֲנִיכָיו
And he armed his initiates (chanichav) (14:14).

After being informed of his nephew Lot's capture, Avraham galvanized his aides in pursuit of the captors. "And he armed his initiates (*chanichav*) ... and he gave chase until Dan" (14:14). Rashi comments that the root of the word "*chanichav*" is "*chaneich*," which means to initiate a person or tool into the craft in which it is destined to remain. Similarly, "*Chanoch lanaar al pi darko*" (*Mishlei* 22:6) should be translated as, "Initiate a child in accordance with his style." According to Rashi's explanation, *chinuch* (loosely translated as education) means proper initiation, ensuring that the child starts off on the right foot.

"You should teach your children Torah so that they should discuss its words" (*Devarim* 11:19). Rashi quotes *Chazal*: "When a child knows how to speak, his father must teach him '*Torah tzivah lanu*

Moshe.' From here we derive that when a child begins to speak, his father should converse with him in *Lashon Hakodesh* and teach him Torah. If he did not do this, it is as if he has buried his child." The harshness of our Sages' words derives from their understanding of the importance of perfect timing. If a father does not teach his son *"Torah tzivah lanu Moshe"* when the child starts communicating verbally, he has in a certain respect buried him.

Why is this moment so crucial? The first moments of speech are the time to "plant" *emunah* in a child. Agriculturally, there are specific times for planting; if a person waits until after the rains to plant, nothing will grow from all his labor. The opposite is also true. If he plants prematurely, the seeds will not sprout because the ground is not properly prepared to accept the seed. So, too, parents must "grab" each opportune moment during the course of their child's education and make the most of them. If they wait too long, they may very well have missed their chance. If they try too early, their child will most likely not be ready to absorb the lesson. However, if they catch the correct moment, then not only will lessons take root, they will continue to sprout and grow as the years go on.

> "Parents must 'grab' each opportune moment during the course of their child's education and make the most of them."

We must bear this concept in mind during the entire course of our children's development, and synchronize our expectations with our child's abilities. If we demand too much or too early, before the child understands what we want from him, then we might very well be causing serious damage to his educational growth. Such "seeds" cannot take root; a child cannot develop through demands that he does not understand. He must grow in stages and move up step-by-step through the different stages of childhood.

Some parents, for example, do not properly relate to their children's games. Rav Yisrael Salanter would say that if a child is playing with a piece of wood in the bathtub and he says it's a boat, taking away the wood from him is comparable to sinking the yacht of an adult. A person who disturbs a child's game is in essence stealing from him.

Additionally, one cannot expect a young child to sit quietly at the Shabbos table for the duration of the meal. A child needs to run around. Demanding that he sit still for an hour and a half is asking too much of him and can be harmful to him. Despite the parent's good intentions, a child cannot grow through expectations that are beyond his ability. On the other hand, if one properly adjusts his demands and his children's education in accordance with their abilities, with Hashem's help the rewards will sprout forth and only continue to grow with time.
(*Zeriyah U'Binyan B'Chinuch*, p. 13)

❋ ❋ ❋

SWEARING NOT TO FALTER

הֲרִמֹתִי יָדִי אֶל־ה'
I lift up my hand to Hashem (14:22).

After Avraham defeated the four kings in battle, the king of Sodom made a request: "Give me the people and take the spoils for yourself" (*Bereishis* 14:21). In response, Avraham swore not to take any of the bounty, lest someone claim that it was the king of Sodom who made Avraham wealthy. Ramban explains that the impetus for Avraham's oath was to keep his *yetzer hara* in check. He cites *Sifrei*, which states that we find such conduct on the part of all righteous men: they swear in order to prevent their *yetzer hara* from causing them to sin.

It is only the righteous who conduct themselves in such a manner. When they are concerned that their desires might get the best of them, they swear not to fall prey to their *yetzer hara*. This effectively erects a fence between them and the sin, for they will certainly not renege on a promise. Most of us, however, do not feel these concerns. We are often complacent and do not take the necessary precautions to avoid likely or imminent *aveiros*. The Torah teaches us that this is not the proper way. The righteous do not trust themselves, and when an opportunity for sin presents itself they immediately incapacitate their *yetzer hara* by swearing not to falter.

Practically speaking, we should not place ourselves in circumstances where we will be tested or tempted to sin. However, if we anticipate that we might come to such a situation or we already find ourselves in such a situation, the best ammunition against the yetzer hara is to create a barrier, by taking additional or exceptional precautions. Such conduct will give us the added dose of determination not to fall into the hands of the *yetzer hara*. If Avraham felt it necessary, shouldn't we?

> "The best ammunition against the yetzer hara is to create a barrier, by taking additional or exceptional precautions."

(*Shiurei Chumash, Parashas Lech Lecha* 14:22)

✻ ✻ ✻

ABSORBING THE MESSAGE

דַּמֶּשֶׂק אֱלִיעֶזֶר

Damascene Eliezer (15:2).

The Torah refers to Avraham's right-hand man as "*Damesek*" Eliezer. Rashi explains that "*Damesek*" is an acronym for "*doleh u'mashkeh*" — he draws forth and gives to drink — since Eliezer taught the Torah he learned from Avraham to others. We see from this appellation that Eliezer was not simply repeating Avraham's words verbatim. He delved into Avraham's lectures to understand their intent, he internalized their message, and he was then able to extract pearls of wisdom and teach them to other students.

The Alter of Kelm would write down his discourses and distribute them among his close disciples. They would then reciprocate by commenting on what he wrote. One *talmid* extracted from a single discourse nearly twenty fundamental ideas with regard to *chinuch*! Hearing or reading a *mussar* discourse sets the groundwork for character improvement. However, real change only happens as a result of reviewing and inculcating the message.

In Rav Wolbe's yeshivah a specific time was designated to review each *mussar* discourse. He would often say that feelings of spiritual arousal that one experiences after hearing a *mussar* discourse do absolutely nothing for a person in the long run. One must first review what was said; only after understanding its significance can he can build on it in a way that fits his personality.

This idea holds true not only with regard to parroting speeches, but also vis-à-vis imitating the actions of others. In the words of Rav Yerucham Levovitz, "Do not wear borrowed clothing": Do not copy other people's actions. Every individual has his own unique role in *avodas Hashem*, and only he was given the tools to actualize this potential. One must develop a plan of action that is appropriate for him and proceed accordingly.

> "A small amount of mussar that a person truly understands will go a lot further than a vast amount of mussar whose message was lost somewhere along the way."

The next time you hear or learn some *mussar*, take an extra minute to try to understand what the *mussar* is telling you. A small amount of *mussar* that a person truly understands will go a lot further than a vast amount of *mussar* whose message was lost somewhere along the way.

(*Shiurei Chumash, Parashas Lech Lecha* 15:2, 17:1)

❋ ❋ ❋

HASHEM'S CHERISHED PEOPLE

וְאֶתְּנָה בְרִיתִי בֵּינִי וּבֵינֶךָ

I will set My covenant between Me and you (17:2).

At the end of *Parashas Lech Lecha* the Torah describes Hashem's command to perform the mitzvah of *bris milah* and Avraham's subsequent fulfillment of this mitzvah. To truly appreciate the enormity of this event, we must take a few minutes to contemplate the implications of the Torah's account of this mitzvah.

The *parashah* begins with Hashem's instruction to Avraham to leave his land of residence for an unknown destination. We know that Avraham was seventy-five years old at the time, but the Torah does not tell us anything about the first years of his life. We are not told that he was thrown into a fiery furnace because of his staunch faith in Hashem; nor does the Torah describe the ten years he spent in jail, as related by *Chazal* (*Bava Basra* 91a). Rather, the Torah chose to begin its narrative about Avraham with an account of the first time Hashem spoke to him. This was such an important event that the Torah saw a need to record it for all future generations.

The *parashah* concludes with the mitzvah of *bris milah*. After circumcising himself, Avraham was on an even higher spiritual level and had an even greater connection to Hashem than described at the beginning of the *parashah*. Not only did the Creator speak with Avraham, He entered a covenant with him!

"Praise the Name of Hashem, for *His Name alone is exalted*" (*Tehillim* 148:13). Hashem is exalted beyond our comprehension. Nevertheless, the next *passuk* declares, "And He will raise the pride of His nation, causing praise for all His pious ones, *for the Jewish people, His intimate nation.*" Despite the awesome loftiness of the Creator, there is a nation on earth that He considers His cherished and intimate people and with whom He interacts!

This relationship began with the *Avos*, and specifically with Avraham Avinu. It is hard to comprehend how a human being was able to rise to such heights, to the point that he merited entering a covenant with Hashem.

> "One of the very foundations of our faith as Jews is the belief that a person has the ability to reach the level where Hashem will actually speak to him."

One of the very foundations of our faith as Jews is the belief that a person has the ability to reach the level where Hashem will actually speak to him. One who questions the veracity of the prophecies of our *Avos* or of Moshe Rabbeinu does not demonstrate a lack of belief in the Creator.

Rather, he shows that he does not believe such greatness is attainable by a human being.

(*Shiurei Chumash, Parashas Lech Lecha*, Introduction to 17:7)

We must believe in the awesome potential of *every* Jew to forge a relationship with Hashem. Let us not sacrifice this potential by becoming caught up in the petty things in life!

פרשת וירא
Parashas Vayeira

NOT JUST STORIES

וַיֵּרָא אֵלָיו ה' בְּאֵלֹנֵי מַמְרֵא וְהוּא יֹשֵׁב פֶּתַח־הָאֹהֶל כְּחֹם הַיּוֹם

Hashem appeared to Avraham in the plains of Mamrei, and he was sitting by the doorway in the heat of the day (18:1).

Rashi explains the true meaning behind this seemingly straightforward *passuk*:

"*Hashem appeared*" — to visit the sick. It was the third day after Avraham's *bris milah* and Hashem came to see how he was faring.

"*In the plains of Mamrei*" — Mamrei was the person who encouraged Avraham to perform a *bris*. He therefore merited that Hashem made His appearance on his property.

"*He was sitting*" — Since "*yosheiv*" (sitting) is written without a *vav*, it can be read as "*yashav*" (he sat), implying that he stood up and then sat down. Hashem told Avraham, "You sit and I will stand,

and this will be an indication that your children will sit while they judge, and I will stand in their assemblage."

"By the doorway" — Avraham was scanning the area for wayfarers to invite into his tent.

"In the heat of the day" — Hashem caused the sun to burn intensely so as not to bother Avraham with guests. However, when He saw that Avraham was distressed over his lack of guests, He sent him angels in the guise of men.

From this *parashah* we can understand the manner in which we must approach the entire Torah, and specifically its stories. Had Rashi not enlightened us, we might have perused this story like any other story we would read in a newspaper: "Hashem appeared to Avraham on a hot day while he was sitting in the town owned by Mamrei."

Rashi, on the other hand, dissects every word and reveals the pearls of wisdom found within. Why does the Torah merely state that Hashem appeared without relating what He said? What difference does it make in whose property Avraham was, and if he was standing or sitting? Do we need to know that he was sitting by the doorway or what the temperature was outside? If the Torah deemed it noteworthy to relate all these details, then surely there is something to glean from them, as nothing in the Torah is without special significance.

> *"If the Torah deemed it noteworthy to relate all these details, then surely there is something to glean from them."*

With this idea we can understand why we are not told anything about the first seventy years of Avraham's life. Everything that occurred before *Parashas Lech Lecha* is not pertinent to the Jewish people as a whole. *Parashas Lech Lecha* relates the origins and spiritual roots of our nation, and *Parashas Vayeira* begins by showing the extent of Avraham's kindness.

Such was the appreciation our Sages had for every word of Torah, and this is the way that we, too, should approach the stories recounted in the Torah.

(*Shiurei Chumash, Parashas Vayeira* 18:1)

❊ ❊ ❊

THE SHULCHAN ARUCH OF CHESSED

וַיֵּרָא אֵלָיו ה׳

Hashem appeared to him (18:1).

The Gra says that the 613 mitzvos are merely general commandments, while the specific details of each mitzvah are endless. He proves this idea from the fact that many *parshiyos* in the Torah contain not even one of the 613 mitzvos. If there is no mitzvah to be learned from them, why were these *parshiyos* written? It must be that there are aspects of the mitzvos that can be learned even from these *parshiyos*.

Parashas Vayeira is a case in point. Despite the fact that it contains not a single commandment, it is a veritable "*Shulchan Aruch*" with regard to *chessed*.

The *parashah* begins by recounting Avraham's extraordinary *hachnasas orchim*. Despite Avraham's very advanced age and weak state of health as he recovered from his circumcision, he nevertheless went out searching for guests in the scorching sun. When he finally spotted the God-sent angels in the guise of Arabs, he interrupted his conversation with Hashem so that he could tend to his guests. He told his guests he would give them only bread, but then proceeded to prepare them a gourmet meal, slaughtering three cows so that he could give each one the best cut of meat. Avraham did not wait until the entire meal was prepared; as each dish was ready, he hurried to bring the food to his hungry visitors. He waited on them as they ate, and personally escorted them after they finished their meal.

> "Despite the fact that this parashah contains not a single commandment, it is a veritable 'Shulchan Aruch' with regard to chessed."

The *chessed* modeled in this *parashah* is not limited to the host. The Torah tells us that the angels asked Avraham (18:9), "Where is your wife Sarah?" He answered that she could be found inside the tent. Rashi points out that although the angels knew Sarah's whereabouts, they posed this question to Avraham so that he would appreciate his wife's modesty. It did not make a difference that Avraham was nearly one hundred years old and had been married for over seventy years; a wife should always be endeared to her husband. This is *chessed* that pertains to a guest.

The Torah also reveals a *chessed* performed by Hashem Himself. After being informed that she would give birth to a child, Sarah laughed and questioned the possibility of such an event, in light of Avraham's old age. Hashem, the God of truth, repeated this conversation to Avraham, albeit with a small change intended to preserve the couple's marital harmony. Instead of relaying that Sarah had said, "*My husband* is old," Hashem quoted Sarah as having said, "*I* am old." *Chazal* derive from Hashem's words that it is permissible to deviate from the truth for the sake of peace. When the intention is *chessed*, an untruth is not considered deceit.

Our second encounter with the *chessed* performed by Avraham in this *parashah* takes place after he is informed of the imminent destruction of the cities of Sodom and Amorah. Though the inhabitants of those cities were wicked, he was nevertheless concerned about them, and extended himself on their behalf by praying fervently for their survival. He did not even know them, yet he did everything in his power to save them.

If we study this *Shulchan Aruch* of *chessed*, we will find many lessons that we can incorporate into our everyday lives: there is nothing loftier than helping another person; there is virtually no situation in which it is too difficult to perform *chessed*; it is not beneath one's dignity to personally perform a kindness; the beneficiary deserves the very best treatment, without delay; and every person is a potential beneficiary, regardless of age or social status.

We have much to gain from an in-depth study of the *parashah* — even one that contains none of the 613 commandments!

(*Shiurei Chumash, Parashas Vayeira* 18:1,9,13)

❅ ❅ ❅

HONOR BEFORE KINDNESS

וַיִּשָּׂא עֵינָיו **וַיַּרְא** וְהִנֵּה שְׁלֹשָׁה אֲנָשִׁים נִצָּבִים עָלָיו **וַיַּרְא** וַיָּרָץ לִקְרָאתָם מִפֶּתַח הָאֹהֶל וַיִּשְׁתַּחוּ אָרְצָה

*And he raised his eyes **and he saw**, behold there were three men standing before him, **and he saw** and he ran toward them from the doorway of the tent and he bowed to the ground (18:2).*

Rashi, explaining by the repetition in the *passuk*, says that the first "and he saw" is meant literally, while the second "and he saw" means that Avraham *understood*. He saw the angels standing still and he understood from their behavior that they did not want to trouble him. Despite the fact that the angels knew that Avraham would come to greet them, they did not walk in his direction. They did this to honor him, by demonstrating that they did not wish to impose on him.

Middas hachessed would dictate that the angels should not have troubled an elderly man to walk out of his tent into the sweltering heat to greet them outside. However, the angels opted to honor Avraham instead of performing a kindness for him. This teaches us an important lesson in interpersonal relations: When a person has the choice of either honoring someone else or performing an act of kindness for him, giving honor takes precedence over an act of kindness.

> *"When a person has the choice of either honoring someone else or performing an act of kindness for him, giving honor takes precedence over an act of kindness."*

Nevertheless, a few *pesukim* later we find that when the choice is between performing a kindness for others and promoting one's own honor, priority must be given to kindness for others. Ramban (18:7) explains why the Torah describes Avraham's preparations of the meal he served his guests: "To inform us of his great desire to do kindness for others. This great man, who had 318 able warriors in his house, and who was extremely old, and weak from his *bris milah*, went himself to Sarah's tent to urge her to quickly prepare the bread, and then afterward ran to the barn to select a choice tender animal to prepare for his guests, and he did not perform any of this through his servants."

With regard to returning a lost object *Chazal* tell us (*Bava Metzia* 30a) that if the finder is elderly, or it is beneath his dignity to deal with such an object, he is exempt from the mitzvah of *hashavas aveidah*. It is clear from the Ramban's statement, however, that this exemption does not apply to other types of *chessed*. Indeed, we often find that the greater the person, the greater the amount of effort he expends on performing acts of kindness for others.

We have many opportunities every day to not only perform kindness for others, but — more importantly — to honor them. Telling a colleague what an asset he is to the company or complimenting a spouse on a job well done can do wonders for the person, and the good feelings engendered will last far longer than a cup of coffee we might prepare for that person.

(*Shiurei Chumash, Parashas Vayeira* 18:2)

❖ ❖ ❖

LOVE YOUR NEIGHBOR — AND GET TO KNOW HIM

הַמְכַסֶּה אֲנִי מֵאַבְרָהָם ...

Shall I conceal from Avraham ... (18:17).

Before destroying Sodom, Hashem deemed it necessary to inform Avraham of the impending destruction. "Am I going to conceal from Avraham what I am doing ... For I have cherished him (*ki yedativ*)" (18:17-19). Rashi explains that although "*yedativ*" in this context is used as a term of affection, essentially the word "*yedativ*" means, "I have known him." This terminology is used to describe affectionate feelings because when one cherishes another person he draws him close and gets to know him.

> "When one cherishes another person he draws him close and gets to know him."

Rav Yerucham Levovitz once traveled by train from his hometown of Mir to Warsaw. In those days, Jewish passengers would typically congregate in a designated train car so that they could travel in a friendly atmosphere, and over the course of the trip, these passengers would become acquainted with one another. By the time Rav Yerucham reached his destination he had acquainted himself with each and every passenger. Not only did he inquire as to their hometown, destination, and occupation, he also attempted to alleviate any difficulties they were facing. To one person he mentioned a marriage prospect for his daughter, to another he suggested a possible partner for his business venture, and to others he offered advice in various areas. Rav Yerucham loved all Jews, and therefore tried his best to get to know them.

It is all too common for two people to sit beside each other on a daily basis and have no interaction other than a "Good morning" greeting or a slight nod of the head. It might be the person in the next seat at shul, the individual across the table during lunch break, or an employee at work. A person with *ahavas habriyos* will try to familiarize himself with the lives of those around him, not simply out of curiosity, but because he has a true desire to acquaint himself with them and possibly offer assistance should the need arise.

Take the initiative and strike up a friendly conversation with a person you would otherwise ignore. At the very least, you will have increased *ahavah* and *shalom* in *Klal Yisrael*, and in many instances you might even be able to do a *chessed* for the person.

(*Shiurei Chumash, Parashas Vayeira* 18:19)

JUDICIOUS CHINUCH

וַה' אָמָר הַמְכַסֶּה אֲנִי מֵאַבְרָהָם אֲשֶׁר אֲנִי עֹשֶׂה ... כִּי יְדַעְתִּיו לְמַעַן אֲשֶׁר יְצַוֶּה אֶת בָּנָיו וְאֶת בֵּיתוֹ אַחֲרָיו וְשָׁמְרוּ דֶּרֶךְ ה' לַעֲשׂוֹת צְדָקָה וּמִשְׁפָּט

> And Hashem said, "Will I conceal from Avraham that which I am going to do? ... For I am fond of him because he will educate his children and household to follow the ways of Hashem, to perform acts of charity and carry out judgment" (Rashi, 18:17–19).

It seems from this *passuk* that Avraham's righteousness and many acts of kindness were not a great enough source of merit to make him worthy of being privy to Hashem's plans. Only by educating his children to follow the ways of Hashem did he earn special endearment, which in turn led to Hashem's revealing His intentions with regard to the destruction of Sodom. From this we see the great importance of *chinuch* and the obligation to make sure we are properly educating our children and pupils.

Chinuch must be carried out judiciously, and the level of education must be appropriate for the child's age. *Chazal* tell us (*Avos* 5:24), "A five-year-old begins studying Torah, a ten-year-old begins studying *Mishnah*, a thirteen-year-old is required to keep the mitzvos ..." Specific ages were determined for all aspects of Torah study and mitzvah observance, in consonance with a child's natural growth process.

If this holds true for learning Torah and performing mitzvos, how much more so does it apply to behavior and *derech eretz*.

> *"A child might not be ready to understand that a particular action is forbidden, and one cannot demand that he behave in a way that is beyond his level of maturity."*

A child might not be ready to understand that a particular action is forbidden, and one cannot demand that he behave in a way that is beyond his level of maturity. Forethought is required during every stage of a child's development, in order to convey messages in a palatable manner. This is the key to ensuring a pleasant relationship between the educator and the child.

Although this idea might seem simple and self-evident, it is the underlying reason why many people do not succeed in *chinuch*. They do not pay attention to the child's stages of growth and therefore do not act in accordance with his level of maturity.

(*Alei Shur*, Vol. II, p. 339)

This idea is not only critical in *chinuch*; it is applicable to every person's own growth in *avodas Hashem*. One must be objective in assessing his own spiritual level and act accordingly. When a person demands more from himself than he can handle, he ruins the learning process and hinders his spiritual growth. By taking a good look at oneself and one's children, a person will be spurred to implement necessary changes, reaping many dividends in the long run.

❊ ❊ ❊

IN THE MERIT OF TEN RIGHTEOUS PEOPLE

אוּלַי יֵשׁ חֲמִשִּׁים...
What if there should be fifty... (18:24).

In *Parashas Vayeira* we read of how Avraham implored Hashem not to destroy Sodom, Amorah and their environs (18:23-32). Avraham claimed that it would be a grave injustice to wipe out the righteous together with the wicked, and he beseeched Hashem to save these five cities in the merit of the fifty righteous men who resided therein. Rashi explains that when Avraham requested that Hashem turn back His wrath for the sake of these fifty righteous people, he was requesting that all five of the cities be saved. When he asked that they be spared in the merit of forty righteous people, he was asking Hashem to spare four cities. In other words, Avraham saw it as axiomatic that ten righteous people have the ability to save an entire city.

It is crucial that people recognize the great merits that accrue to the entire Jewish nation through our Torah scholars. *Chazal* tell us

(*Sanhedrin* 99b) that the definition of a heretic is one who asks, "What benefit do Torah scholars provide for society?" It is only because of these scholars that protection is afforded to the entire community.

This concept holds true in our times as well. Rav Avraham Grodzinski, *Hy"d*, the *mashgiach* of the Slabodka Yeshivah, lived in the Kovno Ghetto during the first few years of World War II. Every Friday night he would gather his disciples and deliver a discourse. When he realized that the Germans intended to liquidate the ghetto, he gathered ten disciples and formed a "*mussar vaad.*" He learned from Avraham that ten truly righteous individuals have the ability to save an entire community, and he wished to create such an elite group, in which each member would accept upon himself to follow precisely the instructions given by Rav Grodzinski. He hoped that in this way they would be considered righteous in the eyes of Hashem, and that their merits would result in the salvation of the entire community.

> "Ten truly righteous individuals have the ability to save an entire community."

We might not see the connection between our *talmidei chachamim* and the protection of our communities. However, the Torah clearly informs us that in their merit the undeserving are protected. If so, is there a limit to the gratitude we should have toward Torah leaders and rabbanim?

(*Shiurei Chumash, Parashas Vayeira* 18:29)

❊ ❊ ❊

THE FIRST STEP TOWARD ACHIEVING ONE'S POTENTIAL

וַיַּעַן אַבְרָהָם וַיֹּאמַר הִנֵּה נָא הוֹאַלְתִּי לְדַבֵּר אֶל ה' וְאָנֹכִי עָפָר וָאֵפֶר

And Avraham responded and said, "Behold, now, I have begun speaking to Hashem, and I am dust and ashes" (18:27).

Avraham Avinu's humility is apparent from his dialogue with Hashem, in which he entreats Him to save the city of Sodom but adds that he is "dust and ashes." Rashi explains that Avraham was referring to two incidents that he had experienced: When Avraham heard that his nephew Lot was taken captive by the four kings, he gave chase to the kings despite the great danger involved. Avraham's statement "I am dust" was a declaration that had it not been for Hashem's kindness, he would have been "turned into dust" by the four kings. The other incident occurred after Avraham destroyed his father's idols and was brought before Nimrod, who threw him into a fiery furnace. With this scenario in mind, Avraham referred to himself as "ashes," for had Hashem not saved him, he would have been burned and only his ashes would have remained.

> "Disregarding one's good qualities is not humility, but foolishness."

What compelled Rashi to explain this *passuk* with an Aggadic interpretation? Why couldn't he simply explain that Avraham was stating that he was as insignificant as dust and ashes? The answer is that disregarding one's good qualities is not humility, but foolishness. True humility is when a person recognizes his positive qualities, yet realizes that they are not a result of his own deeds but rather a God-given present — and therefore there is no reason to be arrogant.

A person must be aware of his strengths so that he can utilize them to the maximum. Rav Yerucham Levovitz would say, "Woe to a person who is not aware of his [spiritual] deficiencies, since he does not know what he must rectify. But double woe to a person who is not aware of his positive qualities, since he does not know what tools he was given to achieve his potential."

Despite Avraham's disclaimer that he was "dust and ashes," he spoke with persistence to Hashem with the hope of saving five cities and their inhabitants. We do not find that Avraham was punished or reprimanded for speaking the way he did. Likewise, the Torah testifies that Moshe Rabbeinu was the humblest man to walk this earth (*Bamidbar* 12:3). Nevertheless, on numerous occasions, Moshe "demanded" that Hashem have compassion and redeem *Bnei Yisrael*. The humility of these great individuals did not cause them to disregard their positive qualities, but rather to capitalize on them for the sake of others.

Let us take a moment to reflect on our positive qualities. With this knowledge, we may be able to make a difference in someone else's life. At the very least, we will become cognizant of the tools we possess — which is the first step toward achieving our potential.
(*Shiurei Chumash, Parashas Vayeira* 18:27)

❋ ❋ ❋

RIDING ON THE DONKEY

וַיַּשְׁכֵּם אַבְרָהָם בַּבֹּקֶר וַיַּחֲבֹשׁ אֶת־חֲמֹרוֹ
*And Avraham rose early in the morning
and saddled his donkey (22:3).*

Chazal tell us that Moshe rode on the same donkey on his way to Egypt to redeem the Jewish people, and ultimately Mashiach will ride on this donkey at the time of the Final Redemption.

A lecturer in a prominent university mockingly questioned the veracity of *Chazal's* statement. "How could Mashiach bring redemption to our modern world while riding on an ancient donkey?" Despite this lecturer's erudition, he failed to see the depth behind *Chazal's* profound words.

Chazal by no means intended to profess that the donkey would live for thousands of years, until the Final Redemption. Rather, they wished to convey the idea that Avraham, Moshe, and Mashiach all reached similar spiritual heights.

Avraham taught the world about the Creator, and *Chazal* tell us that the entire populace convened and proclaimed Avraham king over them. Similarly, the Torah says with regard to Moshe, "See that I have given you dominion over Pharaoh" (*Shemos* 7:1), implying that he was given total authority over the most powerful empire in the world. Mashiach will bring the redemption, and will enjoy sovereignty over the entire world. From where does the unique power wielded by these great men stem? The answer is that all three of them were "*rocheiv al ha'chamor*" (riding on the donkey).

"*Rocheiv*" connotes complete control. We refer to Hashem as "*Rocheiv Shamayim*" — literally, One Who rides the Heavens, for He maintains complete control over the Heavens and everything beneath them. "*Chamor*" symbolizes *chumriyos* — the physical aspects of this world. The intention behind *Chazal's* words is that these three men succeeded in controlling their physical bodies to an extent unparalleled by any other human beings. Without any external kingly trappings, these men "ruled over" themselves to a degree that was discernible to all those around them. Consequently, the people around them acknowledged their greatness and unanimously proclaimed them king.

> "Without any external kingly trappings, these men 'ruled over' themselves to a degree that was discernible to all those around them."

We are put in this world to study and internalize the Torah. To the extent that one succeeds in using the spiritual to overcome the physical, one can influence those around him to change for the better.

(*Olam HaYedidus*, p. 91)

פרשת חיי שרה
Parashas Chayei Sarah

DERECH ERETZ: THE VESSEL FOR TORAH

וָאָבֹא הַיּוֹם
I came today (24:42).

*C*hazal tell us that the speech of our forefathers' servants is "superior" to the Torah given to later generations, as evidenced by the fact that the Torah gives two detailed accounts of how Eliezer found a wife for Yitzchak, while many fundamental halachos of the Torah are conveyed through a subtle hint (Rashi, 24:42). Why is such great importance attributed to the servants' speech?

The Torah uses the speech of our forefathers' servants as a way of transmitting the guidelines of *derech eretz*. Eliezer's every action and expression was rooted in *derech eretz*, and therefore constituted a crucial lesson for future generations. Yet, we may wonder, why is *derech eretz* so important?

Chazal say, "Derech eretz kadmah laTorah" — derech eretz precedes Torah (*Tanna D'vei Eliyahu* 1:1). When a person goes shopping, he needs a bag to hold the potatoes and a container to hold the eggs, because he cannot bring his purchases home without a proper receptacle. This concept holds true with regard to spirituality as well. Torah must be placed in a proper vessel, and that vessel is *derech eretz*.

> "*Derech eretz* can be defined as those actions and behaviors that every person should recognize as proper without being taught."

Derech eretz can be defined as those actions and behaviors that every person should recognize as proper without being taught. Before a person starts to learn Torah, he must first behave in accordance with the dictates of *seichel* and intuition. Once he does so, he has reached the level where he can be called a human being; indeed, one who lacks basic *derech eretz* is referred to by *Chazal* as worse than an animal's corpse (*Vayikra Rabbah* 1:15). Only once a person has reached the level of a human can he hope to internalize words of Torah, which elevate him above other human beings and bring him to a supernatural level.

There is yet another form of *derech eretz*. The Midrash (*Bamidbar Rabbah* 13:16) writes that Torah learning must be interspersed with acts of *chessed*, as the *mishnah* states (*Avos* 2:2), "It is good to learn Torah along with *derech eretz*, for the two together eliminate sin." We see from here that *chessed* is also included in *derech eretz*. If we pay close attention to the story of Eliezer's meeting with Rivkah, we can glean numerous insights into how to conduct our lives with both forms of *derech eretz*.

(*Shiurei Chumash, Parashas Chayei Sarah* 24:42)

❈ ❈ ❈

WHERE THE ANGELS APPEARED

בְּאֵר לַחַי רֹאִי

Be'er Lachai Ro'i (24:62).

When Eliezer returned with Rivkah they encountered Yitzchak, who had just arrived from Be'er Lachai Ro'i. In *Parashas Lech*

Lecha we read how Hagar fled to Be'er Lachai Ro'i when she felt persecuted by Sarah, and it was there that four angels appeared to her. Ramban writes (24:62) that it is possible that Yitzchak had designated Be'er Lachai Ro'i as an appropriate place for prayer, since angels had visited that site.

We know that angels were quite commonplace in Avraham's house. What, then, prompted Yitzchak to leave his home and travel to this site in the desert to pray?

The Gemara (*Berachos* 10a) mentions five ways in which the *neshamah* is similar to Hashem. One of these is, "Just as Hashem sees but cannot be seen, so, too, the *neshamah* sees but cannot be seen."

The difficulty in attaining a high level of *emunah* is due to the fact that Hashem cannot be seen. When we look out the window, all we perceive is the glamour and glitter of the physical world. This is all a facade that obstructs our view of "He Who cannot be seen." He sees all that we do, hears all that we speak, and knows all that we think, and it is from Him that all bounty and blessings emanate. In truth, the spiritual world is more of a reality than the physical world, and our efforts should reflect that. It is our failure to perceive the reality of the spiritual world that clouds our outlook on life and causes us to digress from the path we are meant to take.

When Hagar fled to the desert and was visited by the angels, she called Hashem "You are the God of seeing." The Torah continues, "Therefore the well was called 'Be'er Lachai Ro'i — the Well of the Living One Who appeared to Me'" (16:13-14). Yitzchak was accustomed to seeing angels regularly because he had reached the level where the *Shechinah* rested upon him, and the *Shechinah* is always accompanied by angels. However, it was unusual for angels to visit Hagar, a lowly maidservant. This incident demonstrated that although one cannot perceive Hashem, He is very much "alive" and involved in the lives of even the lowly and despondent. This recognition prompted Yitzchak to designate that particular site as his place of prayer, for there could be no better place to speak to Hashem than the location where He had shown His concern for and involvement in the life of a maidservant.

The Jewish people have experienced numerous revelations of Hashem's concern for us, beginning with the Ten Plagues, the Splitting of the Sea, and the Giving of the Torah. In the days of the *Shoftim*, the nation felt His presence whenever they sinned and subsequently when they did *teshuvah*. And throughout the long *galus*, we, too, recognize how He is very much "alive" and closely involved in our lives. Had this not been the case, our small nation could not have survived among "seventy wolves."

> "The more cognizant we are of the reality of Hashem's involvement in our lives, the easier it will be to believe in and relate to Him."

The more cognizant we are of the reality of Hashem's involvement in our lives, the easier it will be to believe in and relate to Him. If we succeed in perceiving how Hashem is "alive" in our own lives, our *tefillos* will gain a special quality similar to Yitzchak's *tefillos* when he prayed at Be'er Lachai Ro'i.

(*Alei Shur*, Vol. II, p. 650)

❊ ❊ ❊

וַיְבִאֶהָ יִצְחָק הָאֹהֱלָה שָׂרָה אִמּוֹ

And Yitzchak brought her into the tent of Sarah his mother (24:67).

After Eliezer returned with Rivkah, the Torah tells us, "And Yitzchak brought her into the tent of Sarah his mother; and he took Rivkah as his wife." Targum Onkelos explains that Yitzchak saw that Rivkah's behavior paralleled his mother's, and only then did he take her as his wife.

In the previous *passuk* the Torah states that Eliezer told Yitzchak everything that had happened to him. Rashi explains that Eliezer recounted the numerous miracles that occurred in the course of his finding a mate for Yitzchak: the earth contracted to allow him to arrive at his desired destination quickly, and immediately after the conclusion of his *tefillah*, he was answered in an astonishing way. If so, what more was needed to prove that Yitzchak and Rivkah were literally a match made in heaven? After hearing about the miracles that brought him his prospective match, why did Yitzchak feel compelled to examine Rivkah's actions before agreeing to marry her?

The answer is that even if there are earth-shattering events that all point in the direction of a specific match, the deciding factor must still be the person's *middos*. At the beginning of the *parashah*, when Eliezer wished to find a proper wife for Yitzchak, he prepared a test to assess her *middos*. The Torah-true way of checking into a *shidduch* is by investigating how the prospective spouse conducts himself or herself.

> "Even if there are earth-shattering events that all point in the direction of a specific match, the deciding factor must still be the person's middos."

Like many other things, miracles may make us lose sight of what is truly important. We must always bear in mind that "*Derech eretz kadmah laTorah*" — good *middos* precede and are the foundation of the Torah. They are the foundation of the entire Jewish nation as well, which is why our *Avos* sought good *middos* when looking for a mate with whom to build their families and all future generations.

(*Shiurei Chumash, Parashas Chayei Sarah* 24:66, quoting the Brisker Rav)

פרשת תולדות
Parashas Toldos

SPIRITUAL EQUILIBRIUM

וְאֵלֶּה תּוֹלְדֹת יִצְחָק בֶּן־אַבְרָהָם אַבְרָהָם הוֹלִיד אֶת־יִצְחָק

These are the offspring of Yitzchak the son of Avraham; Avraham begot Yitzchak (25:19).

Addressing the redundancy in this *passuk*, Rashi explains that the scoffers in Avraham's generation claimed that Sarah conceived during the night she spent in Avimelech's palace. After all, she was married to Avraham for many years and never conceived, yet shortly after the incident with Avimelech she gave birth to a child. To squelch these claims, Hashem made Yitzchak's face strikingly similar to Avraham's, dispelling any doubt that it was Avraham who fathered Yitzchak. Accordingly, the *passuk* is to be understood as follows: These are the offspring of Yitzchak, [who was clearly] the son of Avraham, [since his facial features bore testimony to the fact that] Avraham begot Yitzchak.

It is astounding that although Avraham Avinu was one of the greatest people in history, there were still scoffers who mocked him. But this phenomenon is rooted in the very creation of the world. Wherever Hashem created holiness, He created the potential for its opposite. Every generation has spiritual giants, and every generation has scoffers to counteract the holiness of these giants. The Maharal writes (*Gevuros Hashem*, Chapter 19) that even in the generation of Moshe and Aharon there existed a Dasan and Aviram, who were there to ensure spiritual equilibrium. This balance is imperative in facilitating man's free will. If the integrity and goodness of the righteous would be blatantly obvious, there would be no possibility of choosing a different way of life. Therefore, there are always scoffers who claim that the righteous are not as righteous as they seem to be, and their way of life is not necessarily the proper path to follow.

> "Every generation has spiritual giants, and every generation has scoffers to counteract the holiness of these giants."

Our generation is no different in this respect. There are the righteous and there are the scoffers, and there are those of us in the middle who have the responsibility to utilize our free will to determine which side is right. However, one thing should be abundantly clear: The faction that holds tenaciously to the Torah and mitzvos is the group we are to join and whose lead we are to follow.

(*Shiurei Chumash, Parashas Toldos* 25:19)

❋ ❋ ❋

WHEN ONE NATION RISES, THE OTHER WILL FALL

שְׁנֵי גיים [גוֹיִם] בְּבִטְנֵךְ
Two nations are in your womb (25:23).

Chazal tell us that during Rivkah's pregnancy she felt conflicting movements inside her womb. When she passed a *beis midrash* the baby would kick, indicating a desire to leave the womb in order to study Torah. When she passed a house of idol worship, however, she once again felt the kicking, indicating the appeal of a drastically different way of life. This uncertainty with regard to the future of her child compelled her to ask the prophet Shem to unravel the mystery. His answer is recorded in the Torah: "Two nations are in your womb, and two regimes from your innards will be separated; *the might will pass from one regime to the other*, and the elder will serve the younger" (25:23).

Rashi explains that the two nations will not attain greatness simultaneously; when one nation rises, the other will fall. This *passuk* encapsulates the last few thousand years of world history. The many wars fought and the numerous conflicts between countries all revolve around the Jewish nation. Even when two gentile nations fight between themselves, it ultimately results in the Jewish people being affected on some level. *Chazal* stated unequivocally, "All calamity that befalls the world is because of Yisrael" (*Yevamos* 63a).

This idea is apparent even in our day and age. The Arab countries are in constant conflict with all of Western culture, but it is Israel that is at the crux of this hostility. The goal of Zionism was to solve "the Jewish problem" by founding a Jewish state, yet we are witness to the fact that "the Jewish problem" has not been settled even after the establishment of the State of Israel.

> *"The Arab countries are in constant conflict with all of Western culture, but it is Israel that is at the crux of this hostility."*

It is in our hands to determine the outcome of this continuous discord. "When the voice is the voice of Yaakov, the hands no longer belong to Esav" (*Bereishis Rabbah* 65:20). When *Bnei Yisrael* study Torah, the entire nation rises. The automatic result is that our enemies will fall!

(*Shiurei Chumash, Parashas Toldos* 25:23)

❋ ❋ ❋

MASTER OVER THE MITZVOS

וַיִּבֶז עֵשָׂו אֶת־הַבְּכֹרָה
Esav scorned the birthright (25:34).

After Esav sold his birthright, the Torah adds (25:34), "He ate and drank, stood up and left; and Esav scorned the birthright." Ramban quotes the *passuk* in *Mishlei* (13:13) that states, "One who scorns a thing will be injured by it." There is a dispute among the commentators whether the sale of the birthright was valid, for it might not be possible to sell something as intangible as one's spiritual status. However, one thing is certain: he who scorns a spiritual level forfeits that level. Even if the sale was not valid, the very act of belittling the birthright caused Esav to lose the spiritual level that the birthright afforded him.

> "One thing is certain: he who scorns a spiritual level forfeits that level."

The respect that one must accord Torah and mitzvos surpasses the importance of the Torah and mitzvos themselves. *Chazal* tell us that although the study of Torah can at times be superseded by certain mitzvos, the respect one owes the Torah can never be minimized (see *Megillah* 3b). Additionally, our Sages relate that every generation prior to Moshe's argued that they should be the ones to receive the Torah. Hashem countered each generation's claim to the Torah by pointing out that they had sinned in one way or another and were therefore unworthy of accepting this precious treasure. In order to be worthy of receiving the Torah, one must be 100 percent committed to fulfilling its precepts, without showing disrespect for any of them. Those who lack this commitment also lack the ability to be a proper receptacle for the Torah.

Rav Yerucham Levovitz noted that people tend to believe that they are the master over their mitzvos; they decide whether they want to perform them or not. The truth is that the mitzvos are master over themselves. If a person does not show proper respect for mitzvos and willingness to sacrifice for them, he loses the ability to perform them. Rav Yerucham expressed this idea at a time when the Polish government was planning to forbid the ritual slaughter of animals. Because the Jewish people were not *moser nefesh* for the mitzvah of *shechitah*, they faced the possibility of losing the privilege of performing it at all.

This concept can help us understand why the Israeli government at one time was bent on drafting women into the army. Since the Jewish community did not show the proper respect for the mitzvah of *tznius*, the mitzvah was being removed from them forcibly.

The only way to truly become a "master" over the mitzvos is by subjugating oneself to them and demonstrating one's commitment to fulfilling them regardless of the circumstances.

(*Shiurei Chumash, Parashas Toldos* 25:34)

❈ ❈ ❈

THE TRUE REASON REMAINS A SECRET

שְׁמַע בְּקֹלִי

Heed my voice (27:43).

After Yaakov succeeded in obtaining the *berachos* that Yitzchak had intended for Esav, Esav began to plot his revenge. The Torah tells us, "When Rivkah was told of the words of her older son Esav, she sent and summoned her younger son Yaakov and told him, 'Esav intends to kill you'" (27:42). Rashi explains that Rivkah was informed of Esav's plans through *ruach hakodesh*. Nevertheless, when Rivkah wished to send Yaakov to safer pastures, she told Yitzchak that the reason she wished to send him off was because it was time for him to get married, and she was disgusted by the local girls. She made no mention of the Divine revelation that was the real impetus for her actions.

This incident unmasks the remarkable *tznius* that characterized Rivkah's actions. She had attained a level of spirituality that few others in history even came close to, yet she did not let anyone in on the secret — even Yitzchak.

We also see in Rivkah's words another practice that is characteristic of great people. Though the real reason she sent away Yaakov was for his own safety, she gave Yitzchak an entirely different reason.

Similarly, a *gadol* will often mention one reason for a specific decision, while in reality many factors contributed to his decision. Moreover, the reason given by the *gadol* may not even be the main reason. Yet some people decide that the reason given by the *gadol* does not strike their fancy or does not apply to them. Had they been privy to the *gadol*'s true rationale, however, they would not have been so quick to reject his decision. This is one of the reasons for the concept of *emunas chachamim*. We act in accordance with what our *gedolim* tell us, regardless of whether we understand their rationale.

> "A gadol will often mention one reason for a specific decision, while in reality many factors contributed to his decision."

A *talmid* once asked Rav Yerucham Levovitz for permission to leave yeshivah to travel elsewhere. That day was Wednesday, and Rav Yerucham told him there is a principle that one is not supposed to start something new on Monday or Wednesday (*Shulchan Aruch, Yoreh Dei'ah* 179:2). Some time later, when Rav Yerucham was giving a *Chumash shiur*, he mentioned that the above principle does not apply to traveling. Rav Wolbe deduced from this incident that the explanation Rav Yerucham had given the *talmid* who requested permission was not the true reason for his decision. Either he did not wish to reveal his true motive, or he was concerned that the *talmid* would travel regardless of what he said. Since he did not want his *talmid* to be guilty of defying his rebbi, he gave him a reason that involved no personal element.

Some people think they know better than our leaders. However, as we see in *Parashas Toldos, emunas chachamim* dictates that we listen to our *gedolim* even when we fail to understand the rationale behind their words.

(*Shiurei Chumash, Parashas Toldos* 27:42)

פרשת ויצא
Parashas Vayeitzei

THE TORAH, OUR HELPMATE

מַלְאֲכֵי אֱלֹקִים עֹלִים וְיֹרְדִים בּוֹ

Angels of God were ascending and descending on it (28:12).

*P*arashas *Vayeitzei* recounts Yaakov's prophetic dream, in which he had a vision of Hashem standing over him. The Gemara (*Chullin* 91b) explains that when the angels perceived Yaakov's image etched into Hashem's throne, they became jealous and wished to harm Yaakov. Hashem therefore stood above Yaakov in order to protect him. This incident reveals to us the awesome potential of man: He can reach a spiritual level greater than that of the angels, to the extent that his image can become etched into the Throne of Glory.

Rav Wolbe writes in his introduction to the second volume of *Alei Shur* that his *sefer* is based upon the concept of *adam* — man. He then proceeds to ask the following question: Since Torah and mitzvos are the manifestation of Hashem's will and therefore the essence of Judaism, why does Hashem place such an emphasis on the person himself? What is the most fundamental aspect of Judaism: the Torah or the person who upholds the laws of the Torah? The answer can be found in the following passage from *Tanna D'vei Eliyahu* (14):

> I [Eliyahu HaNavi] was once walking and a man approached me with a question: "I have two things in this world that I love totally and completely: the Torah and Yisrael. Which one deserves preference?"
>
> I answered him, "My child, most people would say that the Torah deserves preference, for it is written, 'Hashem acquired me [the Torah] — the *first* of His ways.' However, I say that Yisrael deserves preference, for it is written, 'Holy are Yisrael to Hashem — the *first* of His crop.'"
>
> This is comparable to a king whose wife and child were living in a certain residence. The king wrote to the others living there, "If not for my wife and child who are also living in that house, I would have destroyed the entire place." Likewise, if not for *Bnei Yisrael*, the world would not have been created.

The king's wife, whom he "acquired," represents the Torah, which was acquired by Hashem. The king's child, the "first of his crop," represents *Bnei Yisrael*, the firstborn of Hashem. Of course, both the Torah and *Bnei Yisrael* are important and are deemed "the first." However, the purpose, "the cream of the crop" of Creation, is **Bnei Yisrael**. The purpose of the Torah is to enable *Bnei Yisrael* in general and each person in particular to reach the highest possible level of perfection.

The Torah states (*Devarim* 33:4), "Moshe taught us the Torah, an inheritance (*morashah*) for the congregations of Yaakov." Our Sages write (*Pesachim* 49b) that the Torah is likened to a betrothed woman: "Do not read the word '*morashah*' (an inheritance) as it is written, but rather '*me'orasah*' (betrothed)."

Why is the Torah described as the wife of the person who studies its laws? Would it not be more appropriate to describe it as the crown that adorns the head of the scholar who studies it? The answer is that the Torah is the "*eizer k'negdo,*" the helpmate of the *talmid chacham*. The Torah, like one's wife, can help a person reach infinite spiritual heights. The goal toward which we strive is perfection — to the best of our ability.

> "*The Torah, like one's wife, can help a person reach infinite spiritual heights.*"

Adam HaRishon had extraordinary abilities. His spiritual perfection allowed him to perceive what was occurring in the far corners of the earth and up to the heights of the heavens. After he sinned he lost this ability, but he retained the capability to regain his previous level of perfection. Slowly but surely, beginning with Avraham Avinu and culminating with *Matan Torah*, *Bnei Yisrael* regained their former glorious status. This awesome spiritual level lasted a mere few days, after which they once again forfeited it with the sin of the golden calf. The purpose of the Torah and the second set of *Luchos* was to help them reclaim the magnificent level they had briefly attained.

Shleimus ha'adam is what we aim for, and Torah is the conduit through which we can actualize this goal. However, perfunctory performance of the mitzvos will not lead us to perfection. In the service of Hashem nothing comes automatically. Every mitzvah earns reward, but perfection comes only if one puts his heart into the performance of mitzvos and works on achieving *shleimus*. Although this requires much effort, the realization that a human being can attain such magnificent levels should encourage us to take the time to work our way up to the summit.

(*Alei Shur,* Vol. II, p. 19)

❀ ❀ ❀

THE ROAD OF ONE'S DESIRES

בֵּית אֱלֹקִים
The abode of God (28:17).

When Yaakov Avinu arrived at Charan he said, "Is it possible that I passed by the place where my fathers prayed [Har HaMoriah — the place where the *Beis HaMikdash* stood] and I did not pray there?" (Rashi, 28:17). Yaakov Avinu decided to turn back toward Har HaMoriah, and immediately Hashem caused the earth to contract, bringing Har HaMoriah toward Yaakov. Why did Hashem not stop Yaakov when he originally passed the site of the *Beis HaMikdash*, so he could pray there? Rashi answers that if Yaakov himself did not feel that he should pray there, Heaven would not intervene to stop him.

This teaches an important lesson. If a person does not find it within himself to do something, no matter how important it is, he will not have *siyatta diShmaya* in completing the task. The promise of the continuity of the Jewish people was revealed to Yaakov only after he returned to Har HaMoriah. Had he not found it within himself to return, he and all future generations would have lost this great promise.

"One who comes to purify is granted Divine assistance" (*Yoma* 38b). The first step in receiving this assistance is creating the will inside of us. If a person has a strong desire to improve, he will be helped immediately. This, too, we see from Yaakov Avinu. As soon as he decided to return to Har HaMoriah, Hashem caused the earth to contract, and Har HaMoriah was brought toward him.

"By observing where a person stands spiritually at the end of his life, we can determine what his true desires were."

By observing where a person stands spiritually at the end of his life, we can determine what his true desires were. If someone has the will to grow and accomplish, he will be helped to bring these desires to fruition. However, the opposite is also true. "The door is opened

Parashas Vayeitzei

for one who comes to defile" (ibid.). A person should not think that if everything is going smoothly for him it means that Hashem obviously approves of the path he chose. Hashem allows each person to travel the road of his desires.

In our climb to self-perfection, we need to take small steps and make small resolutions. For example, when a person who is learning starts to feel tired, he typically closes his *sefer* and goes to sleep. But when it gets hard, we have to push ourselves; we have to learn for another three minutes. If we do not give ourselves the first push, we might remain stationary our entire lives. When we do push ourselves, though, the reward can usually be sensed immediately. Let us try to clarify for ourselves what our real desires are, and thereby merit the abundant help of the Almighty.

(*Shiurei Chumash, Parshas Vayeitzei* 28:17; *Alei Shur,* Vol. II, p. 437)

❈ ❈ ❈

HASHEM IS OUR SHADOW

וַיִּדַּר יַעֲקֹב נֶדֶר לֵאמֹר אִם יִהְיֶה אֱלֹקִים עִמָּדִי וּשְׁמָרַנִי בַּדֶּרֶךְ הַזֶּה אֲשֶׁר אָנֹכִי הוֹלֵךְ וְנָתַן־לִי לֶחֶם לֶאֱכֹל וּבֶגֶד לִלְבֹּשׁ: וְשַׁבְתִּי בְשָׁלוֹם אֶל־בֵּית אָבִי וְהָיָה ה' לִי לֵאלֹקִים: וְהָאֶבֶן הַזֹּאת אֲשֶׁר שַׂמְתִּי מַצֵּבָה יִהְיֶה בֵּית אֱלֹקִים

> And Yaakov made a promise saying, "If Hashem will be with me and watch over me on the path I will take and give me food to eat and clothing to wear; and if I will return to my father's house in peace and Hashem will be for me a God; then this stone that I have placed as a monument will be a house for Hashem" (28:20-22).

It seems that Yaakov was asking Hashem to watch over him with an extremely high level of *Hashgachah Pratis*. What justification did Yaakov have to ask for such special treatment from the Almighty?

Hashgachah Pratis works measure for measure, in accordance with the amount of effort a person invests into his *avodas Hashem*.

The closer one grows to Hashem, the more intense the Divine Providence. Yaakov was not merely asking for a free handout; he realized that he would need to reach a lofty level of spirituality in order to merit the ultimate *Hashgachah Pratis* — that Hashem dwell in an abode on earth (i.e., upon the stones that he placed as a monument). He was declaring that if he succeeded in reaching a high level of spirituality, Hashem would then reciprocate and "be with him" — He would watch over him and take care of his physical needs. If this would indeed happen, then Yaakov would know that he had succeeded. He would then be able to build his monument into a house for Hashem, because by perfecting himself, he would have created a proper resting place to accommodate Hashem's *Shechinah* here on earth.

Our forefathers merited constant *Hashgachah Pratis* in all of their dealings, because they endeavored to serve Hashem in their every action. Moreover, they earned the ultimate *Hashgachah Pratis* when Hashem's *Shechinah* rested upon them. They subjugated themselves entirely to Hashem and thereby merited that thrice daily we refer to Hashem as, "The God of Avraham, the God of Yitzchak, and the God of Yaakov."

This level of *Hashgachah Pratis* is not limited to our *Avos*; it is attainable by every one of us. As *Chazal* teach, Hashem leads a person on the path he wishes to follow. For example, if one is extremely cautious with regard to his speech or his thoughts, Hashem will assist him not to transgress in that area. The more effort one puts into his Divine service, the more Divine Providence he merits.

> *"If one is extremely cautious with regard to his speech or his thoughts, Hashem will assist him not to transgress in that area."*

We say in *Tehillim* (121:5), "Hashem is your shadow." He is our shadow because He mimics our behavior. If we are vigilant in a certain area of *avodas Hashem*, Hashem will help us in that area.

A man once decided to take upon himself to be careful not to miss hearing the *haftarah* on Shabbos. One week he had to step out of shul, and he missed hearing the *haftarah*. On his way home he was called into a *minyan* that needed a tenth man, because someone had left in the middle. He entered to find the *minyan* just about to begin the reading of the *haftarah*. As they finished, the original tenth man reappeared, and the man was free to go home.

The *Hashgachah Pratis* was clear.

(Shiurei Chumash, Parashas Vayeitzei 28:20)

❊ ❊ ❊

GIVING UP ETERNITY, TO SPARE SOMEONE EMBARRASSMENT

וַיְהִי בַבֹּקֶר וְהִנֵּה־הִוא לֵאָה

And it was in the morning and behold she was Leah (29:25).

After Yaakov Avinu married the bride he thought was Rachel, the Torah tells us, "And it was in the morning and behold she was Leah." Rashi notes that at night he was not able to distinguish that his bride was Leah. Yaakov had given Rachel signs, in case Lavan would try to switch her with another girl. When Rachel realized that Lavan was planning to substitute Leah for her, Rachel gave the signs to Leah so she should not be embarrassed.

We should take a minute to appreciate Rachel's greatness. She knew that Yaakov would father all the *shevatim* and subsequently the entire Jewish nation. Besides, she had no idea that Lavan would agree to marry her off to Yaakov as well, or that Yaakov would agree to marry another wife. By giving the signs to Leah, Rachel was in essence giving up an eternity that was rightfully hers. She was giving up the chance to mother the chosen nation: the purpose behind the creation of the world.

Although *Chazal* (*Sotah* 10b) tell us that it is better for a person to throw himself into a fiery furnace than to publicly embarrass his friend, this refers to one who actively embarrasses his friend. This was not the case with Rachel, who would merely have played a passive role in Leah's embarrassment. Therefore, Rachel was in no way obligated to give Leah the signs. But she nevertheless mustered the superhuman strength to save her sister from disgrace. While Rachel understood the enormity of the significance of giving birth to the Jewish nation, she also understood the impossibility of building upon someone else's humiliation.

Later in the *parashah* we find a similar level of consideration on Leah's part. "Afterward she [Leah] had a child and named her Dinah" (30:21). Rashi tells us that Dinah was so named because Leah, so to speak, made a "judgment" (*din*) with herself. She calculated that if she would have a seventh son, Rachel would not have as many sons as each of the two maidservants. Leah prayed to Hashem, and He changed the child into a girl.

> "While Rachel understood the enormity of the significance of giving birth to the Jewish nation, she also understood the impossibility of building upon someone else's humiliation."

Leah wanted to mother as many *shevatim* as possible. However, since her intentions were entirely *l'shem Shamayim*, when this desire would have contributed to someone else's embarrassment, she did everything in her power to prevent her ambition from materializing.

In order to determine if one's actions are truly *l'shem Shamayim*, a person must consider whether his actions might hurt another person's feelings. If he subsequently refrains from his desired course of action, not only has he proven that he acts truly for the sake of Heaven, he has also emulated our matriarchs by conquering his negative *middos* in superhuman fashion.

(*Shiurei Chumash, Parshas Vayeitzei* 29:25)

❊ ❊ ❊

IT WON'T HELP TO TALK LOGIC

הַבָּנוֹת בְּנֹתַי וְהַבָּנִים בָּנַי וְהַצֹּאן צֹאנִי וְכֹל אֲשֶׁר־אַתָּה רֹאֶה לִי־הוּא

The daughters are my daughters, the sons are my sons, and the flock is my flock, and all that you see is mine (31:43).

When Yaakov Avinu fled with his family and possessions without telling Lavan, Lavan gathered a few of his men and proceeded to chase after Yaakov. When he caught up with Yaakov, an interesting conversation ensued. Lavan accused Yaakov of stealing his idols; Yaakov denied the accusation and allowed Lavan to search all of his possessions. When the search proved futile, Yaakov vehemently protested Lavan's unscrupulous behavior (31:37-41):

"You have searched all of my possessions; what have you found from the possessions of your house? Place them between my brothers and your brothers, and they will decide between the two of us. I have been with you for twenty years; your sheep and goats did not miscarry, and I did not eat any rams of your flock. I did not bring you killed animals; rather, I took the loss. You claimed it from my hand whether it was stolen by day or by night. During the day the heat devoured me as did the ice by night, and sleep was held back from my eyes. I have spent the past twenty years in your house: fourteen years I worked for your two daughters and six years for your sheep, and you changed my wages one hundred times!"

To which Lavan responded, "The daughters are my daughters, the sons are my sons, the flock is my flock, and all that you see is mine."

One cannot help but be amazed at Lavan's response. Yaakov just gave a lengthy explanation of how everything he owned was rightfully his, down to the last penny, yet Lavan did not acknowledge anything Yaakov said. He simply stated that everything in sight belonged to him and not to Yaakov!

At times, a conflict arises between the dictates of a person's *seichel* and the desires that stem from his bad *middos*. In such a situation, it is useless to argue logically with this person. Explanations aimed at the *seichel* will not succeed in changing preconceived notions that are a product of the person's faulty *middos*. Lavan simply "did not hear" what Yaakov said, because he did not want to hear. His lust for money would not allow him to absorb the fact that all of Yaakov's possessions were rightfully his.

This is the danger of bad *middos*. When a person is entrenched in a mindset born of his base desires, even a completely logical argument might not succeed in causing him to change that mindset.

(*Shiurei Chumash, Parashas Vayeitzei* 31:43)

> "*Explanations aimed at the seichel will not succeed in changing preconceived notions that are a product of the person's faulty middos.*"

פָּרָשַׁת וַיִּשְׁלַח
Parashas Vayishlach

EFFORT AND PRAYER: A NECESSARY COMBINATION

וַיִּשְׁלַח יַעֲקֹב מַלְאָכִים
And Yaakov sent angels (32:4).

Ramban, in his introduction to *Parashas Vayishlach*, enumerates a number of lessons to be learned from the stories recounted in the *parashah*: "This *parashah* was written to publicize that Hashem saved His servant and redeemed him from a power mightier than he and sent an angel who rescued him. Additionally, it teaches us that Yaakov did not rely on his righteousness but rather attempted to save himself, with all his resources."

Hashem created the world to run in accordance with the laws of nature. The *Avos* understood that if He willed the world to operate in such a manner, they, too, must act in accordance with these laws. Therefore, all of their dealings with others were within the framework of nature.

Yaakov did not merely say, "Hashem, You're in charge. Please save us!" Instead, he did everything in his power to save himself and his family: He sent presents to his brother in an attempt to appease him, while preparing for war and for the possibility that he might be overwhelmed and be forced to flee. He realized that it was incumbent upon him to do his *hishtadlus*, and that this, too, is an aspect of *avodas Hashem*.

> "*Yaakov did not merely say, 'Hashem, You're in charge. Please save us!' Instead, he did everything in his power to save himself and his family.*"

Toward the beginning of World War II, Rav Leib Malin urged all of the *bachurim* in the Mirrer Yeshivah to flee to Japan, despite the fact that many great people felt differently. Rav Yerucham Levovitz had impressed upon him that a person must not rely upon miracles, but must rather do all that is possible to save himself by conventional means. Rav Leib's advice was responsible for the survival of the Mirrer Yeshivah; those who fled to Japan were spared the horrors of the Holocaust.

Yaakov also *davened* to Hashem to save him from his angry brother. His practical attempts to save his family were intertwined with his prayer to Hashem. Likewise, we find in *Parashas Mikeitz* that Yaakov told his sons to prepare a present for the viceroy of Egypt in an attempt to appease him, so that he would free Shimon and Binyamin. He also added a prayer on their behalf: "And may Hashem grant you compassion" (43:14). All of one's endeavors must be accompanied by *tefillah* to Hashem. Even when a person takes medication he is supposed to pray, "May it be [Your] will that this endeavor provide a cure for me" (*Shulchan Aruch, Orach Chaim* 230:4).

Hashem created the world in a way that requires us to abide by the laws of nature. Inherent in this system, however, is the danger that a successful person might begin to think that it was his brains and brawn that brought him success. Although we must invest whatever effort is necessary in a particular endeavor, we should never lose sight of Who is really in charge. Along with our efforts, we must

Parashas Vayishlach / 83

also pray to Hashem to help us succeed, because *hishtadlus* and *tefillah* go hand in hand.

(*Shiurei Chumash, Parashas Vayishlach,* Introduction, 32:9)

❊ ❊ ❊

A GUEST IN A FOREIGN LAND

עִם־לָבָן גַּרְתִּי

I have sojourned with Lavan (32:5).

The *parashah* begins with Yaakov sending a message to his brother Esav: "So says your servant Yaakov: I have sojourned with Lavan and was detained until now" (32:5). Rashi writes that the word "*garti*" — I lived — has the numerical value of 613. Yaakov was implying that although he lived with Lavan, he kept all 613 mitzvos and did not learn from Lavan's evil ways.

It was only because Yaakov felt like a sojourner — *garti* — that he succeeded in keeping all the mitzvos of the Torah. Charan had its own culture and ideology, which were absorbed by all the people in its midst. Nevertheless, even after twenty years, Yaakov did not acclimate to his surroundings in the least. It was only because he viewed himself as a guest and clung steadfastly to his roots that he succeeded in withstanding the negative influence of Charan.

There is some truth to the claim that assimilation is a natural process. If a person behaves like the gentiles around him, that will automatically lead to assimilation. Rav Wolbe resided in Sweden for eight years, during and after World War II, and he had numerous occasions to observe Swedish customs. On the twentieth of December, the local residents would dance around a roasted pig, and on the longest day of the summer, the entire populace — men, women, and children — would dance around a tall tree and sing children's songs. Even if there is nothing intrinsically wrong with the customs of one's host country, there is great danger in adopting them. A person who possesses a heightened spiritual sensitivity can perceive how the observance of gentile customs — even seemingly innocuous ones — distances a person from the Torah.

The Torah tells us that there is a prohibition of "*B'chukoseihem lo seileichu* — Do not follow their statutes" (*Vayikra* 18:3). The root of the word "*chok*" (statute) is "*cheik*" (chest), because a country's customs stem from the "heart" of the nation. A person who joins in the customs of his host country has, to a certain extent, already drifted from the Torah. However, one who perceives himself as a "*ger*" in a foreign land will merit the *siyatta diShmaya* to hold onto the Torah without swaying from its precepts even one iota.

> "A person who joins in the customs of his host country has, to a certain extent, already drifted from the Torah."

(*Shiurei Chumash, Parashas Vayishlach* 32:5)

❊ ❊ ❊

MUSSAR IS HALACHAH, TOO

וַיְחַבְּקֵהוּ וַיִּפֹּל עַל־צַוָּארָו וַיִּשָּׁקֵהוּ וַיִּבְכּוּ

And he embraced him, and he fell upon his neck, and he kissed him; then they wept (33:4).

The Torah describes Yaakov's encounter with Esav: "And Esav ran to greet him and he embraced him, and he fell on his neck, and he kissed him; then they wept" (33:4). Rashi cites an opinion in *Chazal* that this was a true display of Esav's emotions. "Rabbi Shimon bar Yochai said, 'It is a halachah that Esav hates Yaakov. Nevertheless, his compassion was aroused at that time and he kissed him wholeheartedly.'"

Why do *Chazal* refer to Esav's hatred of Yaakov (i.e., the Jewish people) as a halachah? Would it not it be more accurate to describe this phenomenon as *aggadah* (a term used to describe the non-halachic teachings of *Chazal*)? The answer is that *aggadah* and *mussar* are also halachos. Rav Avraham Grodzinski brought a beautiful "proof" to this idea. The Rif (one of the first *Rishonim*) wrote a *sefer* dedicated solely to summarizing all of the halachos that are found in the Gemara. However, he included many *aggados* in his *sefer*. The same can be said of the Rambam, who wrote a similar type of *sefer*.

It is a mistake to classify the mitzvos that involve our hearts and *middos* strictly as "*mussar*." The above *Rishonim* understood that even *aggadah* and *mussar* fall under the banner of halachah. As a matter of fact, the constant mitzvos such as loving, fearing, and cleaving to Hashem, which are the very fundamentals of the Torah, all relate to the duties of our hearts.

> "Even aggadah and mussar fall under the banner of halachah."

The *Mishnah Berurah* writes (1:12) that everyone is obligated to learn *mussar* every day. A person who had only ten minutes a day to dedicate to learning once asked Rav Yisrael Salanter how that slot should be filled. Rav Yisrael answered that the person should spend the time studying *mussar*, and then he might realize that in fact he has more than ten minutes a day to learn.

Many people perceive *mussar* as "extra credit." It's a nice thing to learn and to live by, they think, but it isn't as important as the study and performance of the "real" mitzvos. This mindset was what prompted Rabbeinu Bachya to write his renowned *sefer*, *Chovos HaLevavos* — *Duties of the Heart*. In his introduction he proves that the duties of the heart are just as obligatory as the duties of the body. Moreover, proper performance of the mitzvos involving the body is contingent on the proper performance of the mitzvos involving the heart!

(*Shiurei Chumash, Parashas Vayishlach* 33:4)

❊ ❊ ❊

SAVORING WHAT WE HAVE

יֶשׁ־לִי־כֹל

I have everything (33:11).

In an attempt to appease his brother Esav, Yaakov Avinu sends him an impressive gift in advance of their encounter. Later, when the two meet, Esav tells Yaakov to take back all that he sent, because "I have plenty" (33:9). Yaakov answers, "Please accept my gift, for Hashem has shown me grace and I have everything" (ibid. v. 11).

Esav, whose entire life revolved around pleasures and materialistic acquisitions, only allowed himself to say that he owns *plenty*. Despite continuously acquiring things, such a person will never feel that he has everything, because there are always additional things that can be acquired. *Chazal* tell us, "He who has one hundred wants two hundred, and he who has two hundred wants four hundred." As a result, "A person does not leave this world with even half of what he desires" (*Koheles Rabbah* 1:34).

Yaakov Avinu, on the other hand, whose life was rooted in spirituality, was not only completely content with what he owned, but had no interest in acquiring more possessions. He was therefore able to declare, "I have everything." Yaakov realized that being content with what one has does not stem from a feeling of resignation: "I have to make do with what I have." Rather, it is a positive frame of mind: "I have one hundred and I am perfectly fine without two hundred."

> "Being content with what one has does not stem from a feeling of resignation ... Rather, it is a positive frame of mind."

A person who is obsessed with buying the latest fashions and home furnishings will never feel that he has everything that he desires.

There are fringe benefits to being content with what one has. *Chazal* tell us (*Bava Basra* 16b), "Three people were given a taste of the next world while still in this world: Avraham, Yitzchak, and Yaakov ... Yaakov, as it is written, 'And I have everything (*kol*).' Three people were not ruled by their *yetzer hara*: Avraham, Yitzchak, and Yaakov, as it is written [about each of them, respectively] *bakol, mikol,* and *kol*."

The *yetzer hara* is the driving force behind the craving to acquire more possessions and indulge in bigger and better pleasures. Someone who works on being content with what he has and cultivates the feeling of "I have everything" has reined in his *yetzer hara*, to some extent. A lifestyle centered around materialistic acquisitions is one that expresses itself as a quest for quantity. In contrast, someone who is satisfied with what he has leads his life in pursuit of quality. By focusing on the quality of what Hashem bestowed upon him, Yaakov Avinu was able to savor a spiritual, otherworldly taste in his materialistic acquisitions and pleasures.

How can we introduce such feelings into our daily lives? A possible first step is to make a point of concentrating on the *berachah* of *"She'asah li kol tzorki* — He has provided me with all my needs." If we truly believe what we are saying, then we will begin to appreciate that which we do have, thereby setting us on a course to reach the level attained by Yaakov Avinu.

(*Alei Shur*, Vol. II, p. 327)

❈ ❈ ❈

JEWISH SOLITUDE IS WORTH DYING FOR

וְיָשַׁבְנוּ אִתְּכֶם וְהָיִינוּ לְעַם אֶחָד

We will dwell with you and become a single people (34:16).

After Dinah was abducted by Shechem, his father, Chamor, approached Yaakov and his sons and requested that they allow Shechem to marry Dinah. Yaakov's sons responded that it would be a disgrace for them to give their sister to an uncircumcised man. However, if every male in the city would circumcise himself, *Bnei Yisrael* would give their daughters to the people of Shechem and would likewise marry their daughters. Chamor and Shechem agreed at once and succeeded in convincing the rest of the local populace to follow suit.

On the third day after the mass circumcision, Shimon and Levi entered the city of Shechem and killed every male. They then took their sister Dinah and left. The Torah relates Yaakov's response to Shimon and Levi's actions (34:30): "You have sullied me, making me disgusting among the inhabitants of the land, and I am few in number; should they band together and attack me, they will destroy me and my household." To this, his sons responded, "Should our sister be treated like a harlot?" (v. 31).

What type of answer was this? Yaakov was understandably worried for the safety of his family, and his sons seemingly disregarded this concern.

Their response can be explained as follows. *Bnei Yisrael* are, at their core, "a nation that dwells in solitude" (*Bamidbar* 23:9); they cannot assimilate with the other nations of the world. The abduction of Dinah was the first time another nation attempted to mingle with *Bnei Yisrael* and their daughters. Shimon and Levi's answer to Yaakov was that it is completely unacceptable to abandon a Jewish girl and let her live with a gentile. They could not remain silent in the face of this atrocity, and it was worthwhile to annihilate the city even if it would cost them their lives.

> *"Bnei Yisrael are, at their core, 'a nation that dwells in solitude.'"*

This was the first historical attempt at assimilating the Jewish people, but it was certainly not the last. The story of Chanukah was another such attempt made by both the Greeks and the Hellenists. Once again, the leaders of *Bnei Yisrael* decided that they could not remain silent — even if it would cost them their lives. A handful of *tzaddikim* risked their lives to fight the mighty Greek army, and Hashem recognized the efforts of these righteous men by granting them a miraculous victory. *Yiddishkeit* does not allow for any assimilation; it is worthwhile for us to give up our lives rather than forfeit our ability to "dwell in solitude."

(*Shiurei Chumash, Parashas Vayishlach* 34:31)

פרשת וישב
Parashas Vayeishev

NO RECLINERS IN A FACTORY

וַיֵּשֶׁב יַעֲקֹב
Yaakov settled (37:1).

Immediately after the Torah relates that Yaakov settled in the land of Canaan, it launches into the narrative of the dreams and the subsequent sale of Yosef. Rashi explains that Yaakov yearned to settle down and live without distress, but shortly after his "settling" in Eretz Yisrael he suffered the tragedy of Yosef's disappearance (37:2ff). *Chazal* tell us that when righteous people seek to live in peace and tranquility, Hashem counters, "Is it not sufficient what awaits them in the World to Come? Do they also want to live in this world without difficulties?"

When Yaakov sought serenity, his intention was not to relax in a recliner with a cigar. Yaakov Avinu, the embodiment of perpetual Torah study, felt that if his life were tranquil he would be better able to delve into Torah study. Why, then, was Yaakov not granted his request?

Rav Yerucham Levovitz said, "You will never find a recliner in a factory." Since everyone in a factory is busy working, there is no time to sit back and relax. Likewise, we are not meant to amble through a utopian life in this world. That state of tranquility is reserved for the next world.

Yaakov Avinu had an extremely difficult life. His brother, Esav, was bent on killing him, and he fled to his uncle Lavan, who cheated him incessantly. On his way back to his parents' home, he experienced the kidnapping and violation of his daughter Dinah. When he finally arrived home, his beloved son Yosef was sold by his brothers — eventually leading to Yaakov's exile to Egypt. All of the distress he experienced was meted out to him in order that he realize that in this world he must rise above adversity and perform to the best of his ability.

Often, a person feels that his circumstances make it impossible for him to focus on his spiritual obligations. After all, how can he possibly concentrate on Torah study or *davening* when his life is in such turmoil? However, it is specifically in these situations that we are expected to rise above the external factors that were placed in our paths to test us.

Rav Chaim Soloveitchik once asked his son (who later became known as the Brisker Rav) to bring him a specific *sefer*. After completing the task, Rav Chaim asked his son what he was thinking. His son told him that he had encountered a difficulty in the Rambam that he was trying to resolve. Rav Chaim stated that he could have gotten the *sefer* himself, but he wanted to habituate his son to think in Torah even when he was preoccupied with other matters.

Rav Wolbe commented that sometimes, when he had quiet time to study, he could not arrive at a *chiddush*. However, *chiddushim* would often occur to him when the phone was ringing, or students needed attention, or things had to be organized, or there was someplace he had to go. It is specifically during busy times that we can reap the boundless rewards of fulfilling our spiritual obligations despite adversity.

(*Shiurei Chumash, Parashas Vayeishev* 37:2)

> "It is specifically during busy times that we can reap the boundless rewards of fulfilling our spiritual obligations despite adversity."

❈ ❈ ❈

THERE IS NOTHING WORSE THAN CAUSING ANOTHER JEW TO SUFFER

הִוא מוּצֵאת וְהִיא שָׁלְחָה אֶל־חָמִיהָ לֵאמֹר לְאִישׁ אֲשֶׁר־אֵלֶּה לּוֹ אָנֹכִי הָרָה וַתֹּאמֶר הַכֶּר־נָא לְמִי הַחֹתֶמֶת וְהַפְּתִילִים וְהַמַּטֶּה הָאֵלֶּה

And she [Tamar] was being taken out [to be killed] and she sent to her father-in-law saying, "By the man to whom these objects belong, I have become pregnant." And she said, 'Please identify to whom this signet ring, garment, and staff belong" (38:25).

Rashi explains that Tamar did not want to explicitly inform her father-in-law, Yehudah, that she had conceived from him, because she did not want to embarrass him publicly. Instead, she conveyed the message in such a manner that she would be saved from death only if he would voluntarily admit his involvement. From this incident *Chazal* deduce that it is better for a person to throw himself into a fiery furnace than to embarrass someone publicly (*Sotah* 10b).

Why did Tamar have to give up her life to save Yehudah from embarrassment? Even if embarrassing another person publicly is tantamount to murder, halachah mandates that if a person is being pursued by a would-be murderer he may kill his pursuer to save his own life. If so, why couldn't Tamar save her own life by embarrassing Yehudah?

Chazal did not say that one is *obligated* to give up his own life to save another person from embarrassment; they said it is *better* for one to give up his life. Such an act would not be considered suicide.

Tamar did not have to give up her life; she *wanted* to give up her life in order not act with a bad *middah*. This idea is reinforced by another statement of *Chazal* (*Bava Metzia* 59a): "A person who embarrasses his friend publicly loses his portion in the World to Come." Even murder does not incur such a harsh punishment.

In a similar vein, Rabbeinu Yonah writes (*Shaarei Teshuvah*, Chapter 3:188) that one must place himself in mortal danger rather than flatter a wicked person (see *Sotah* 41a). This begs the obvious question: We know that a person is only obligated to give up his life in order to avoid transgressing the three cardinal sins. Why, then, must he endanger his life to avoid flattering a wicked person?

So dangerous is it for a person to acquire a negative trait that it is better for him to risk his life rather than perform an act motivated by a bad *middah*. Life is a precious commodity, yet it is preferable for someone to give up his life rather than embarrass another person publicly, because there is nothing worse than causing another Jew to suffer.

> "*It is preferable for someone to give up his life rather than embarrass another person publicly, because there is nothing worse than causing another Jew to suffer.*"

(*Shiurei Chumash, Parashas Vayeishev* 38:25)

❊ ❊ ❊

BRINGING HASHEM WITH US

ה' אִתּוֹ

Hashem was with him (39:3).

No matter where Yosef found himself, he acted as if he were in the presence of Hashem. Even when he was a slave to an Egyptian master, the Torah tells us, "And his master saw that Hashem was with him" (39:3). Rashi explains that his master was able to perceive that Hashem was with him because Yosef constantly mentioned the Name of Hashem.

We might wonder: Why was Yosef HaTzaddik so exceptional? Do we not also say "*baruch Hashem*" and "*im yirtzeh Hashem*" constantly? Haven't we also reached the level of "*shem Shamayim shagur b'fiv*" (the name of Heaven was always on his lips)?

The answer is that Yosef was in a different league altogether. When he said, "*im yirtzeh Hashem,*" he truly felt that the outcome of his actions was completely dependent on Hashem's will. He was able to say *b'ezras Hashem* because he perceived Hashem's involvement clearly. The expressions of his mouth bore witness to the feeling that "Hashem was with him."

We are very generous with our use of these phrases. We might say "*im yirtzeh Hashem*" without Hashem even crossing our minds. Often people write *BS"D* (with the help of Heaven) at the top of their papers, and then proceed to pen a letter that contains *lashon hara* or other foolishness.

Rav Wolbe was once speaking to a *gadol* when the latter observed, "Look at this street that is bustling with so many people, and not even one of them is thinking about Hashem!"

Rav Wolbe once asked Rav Yechezkel Levenstein how he was doing. Rav Yechezkel simply answered, "Well." He felt that it was meaningless to say *baruch Hashem* without thinking about the words that left his mouth.

There is yet another lesson to be learned from this *passuk*, one that is applicable even to a person who has already accustomed himself to thinking about Hashem while mentioning His Name. Even among secular people, he should speak the same way he would among friends. If one is in the habit of saying "*b'ezras Hashem*" or "*im yirtzeh Hashem*" — with Hashem's help — he should use these phrases regardless of his surroundings.

> "If one is in the habit of saying 'b'ezras Hashem' or 'im yirtzeh Hashem,' he should use these phrases regardless of his surroundings."

We should make an effort to think about Hashem when mentioning His Name. This was the *middah* of Yosef HaTzaddik, and this is the way to bring Hashem "with us" wherever we might find ourselves.

(*Shiurei Chumash, Parashas Vayeishev* 39:3)

❈ ❈ ❈

NOT EVEN A LINGUISTIC CONNECTION

וְחָטָאתִי לֵאלֹקִים

And I will have sinned against God (39:9).

When Potiphar's wife attempted to seduce Yosef, Yosef countered, "There is no one greater than I in this house, and [Potiphar] did not withhold anything from me except you, since you are his wife; how then can I commit this terrible act, and I will have sinned against God?" (39:9).

Yosef stated that if he would comply with her advances, then *he* would have sinned before Hashem. Would not it have been more accurate to state that if they would sin together, then they both would have sinned against Hashem? The Kotzker Rebbe offers an enlightening explanation. Had Yosef said "*we* would have sinned," then he would have already been guilty of uniting himself, on some level, with his master's wife. Yosef wanted nothing to do with her — not even a linguistic connection. This highlights the concept that the Jewish people are a nation that "dwells in solitude." We do not desire — in any way, shape, or form — to blend with the nations around us.

> "*Yosef wanted nothing to do with his master's wife — not even a linguistic connection.*"

Yosef's response also reflected his profound fear of sin. A few *pesukim* later, we find another example of his fear of sin. When Potiphar's wife grabbed him, he left his garment in her hands and ran out. *Sforno* (39:12) explains that he ran out of the room lest his *yetzer hara* overwhelm him. Had we found ourselves in a similar situation, we likely would have been confident in our ability to overcome our *yetzer hara* and not succumb to temptation. Yosef's fear of sin was so great, however, that he would not take any chances. If Yosef HaTzaddik took such precautions, shouldn't we?

(*Shiurei Chumash, Parashas Vayeishev* 39:9, 12)

❋ ❋ ❋

THE ACT DOES NOT END HERE

וַיְהִי כְּדַבְּרָהּ אֶל־יוֹסֵף יוֹם יוֹם וְלֹא־שָׁמַע אֵלֶיהָ לִשְׁכַּב אֶצְלָהּ לִהְיוֹת עִמָּהּ

And she spoke to Yosef day after day, and he did not listen to her to lie next to her, to be with her (39:10).

Despite the continuous attempts by Potiphar's wife to seduce Yosef, he maintained his righteousness and did not sin with her. Rashi explains the seemingly redundant language of the *passuk*, "to lie next to her, to be with her." "To lie next to her" refers to this world, while "to be with her" refers to the World to Come. Had Yosef sinned with Potiphar's wife, he would have ultimately ended up together with her in the next world. What is the meaning of this ambiguous statement?

> "An action performed in this world does not end with the completion of the action. Rather, it creates a spiritual reality that continues into the World to Come."

An action performed in this world does not end with the completion of the action. Rather, it creates a spiritual reality that continues into the World to Come. This spiritual reality is the reward or punishment one receives in *Olam Haba*.

Each mitzvah or *aveirah* performed in this world comprises two parts: the physical action, and the spirituality that the mitzvah produces. When a person reaches the next world and is able to perceive the spiritual component of his actions, he becomes cognizant of the magnitude of those actions. Recognizing the enormity of the positive spirituality produced by a mitzvah is in and of itself the reward for that mitzvah, while perceiving the magnitude of an *aveirah* is itself the punishment. This is what *Chazal* meant when they said (*Avos* 4:2), "The reward for a mitzvah is a mitzvah, and the reward for an *aveirah* is an *aveirah*." Had Yosef sinned with Potiphar's wife, the *aveirah* would have accompanied him to the next world, where its enormity would have been plainly evident.

An *aveirah* is not "over" upon the conclusion of the transgression. *Chazal* tell us (*Sotah* 3b) that an *aveirah* surrounds the transgressor and cleaves to him like a dog until the World to Come, where it turns into the punishment for that very *aveirah*. If this is true with regard to *aveiros*, how much more does it apply to mitzvos!
(*Shiurei Chumash, Parashas Vayeishev* 39:10)

❋ ❋ ❋

FINDING HASHEM IN THE DAILY HEADLINES

בַּאֲשֶׁר ה׳ אִתּוֹ
For Hashem was with him (39:23).

Toward the end of *Parashas Vayeishev* the Torah relates how Yosef was falsely accused of improper behavior and consequently thrown into jail. He found favor in the eyes of the jail warden, and he was accorded preferential treatment. In an exact repetition of what occurred when he was in Potiphar's house, his superior entrusted him with the day-to-day management of the jail, and Yosef took complete charge over his fellow inmates. The *passuk* tells us, "The officer of the jail did not supervise anything *for Hashem was with him*, and whatever he did Hashem granted him success" (39:23).

We should take note of the simple explanation of this *passuk*: It is possible for Hashem to live with a person. No matter where a person finds himself, even if he is in a secular or antagonistic environment, he must realize that Hashem is with him. Yosef was in a forlorn dungeon together with a group of gentiles, in the basest, most immoral land, and nevertheless the Torah tells us clearly that "Hashem was with him."

One cannot blame his environment for causing him to slacken off in his commitment to Torah and mitzvos, because Hashem can be found everywhere.

Rav Wolbe once attended a lecture in Sweden. In the middle of the speech the speaker mentioned that "the very atmosphere of Sweden is *treif*." Rav Wolbe felt a strong desire to vehemently protest such a statement, since it implied that Hashem is not to be found in Sweden! We know that "His glory fills the entire world" (*Yeshayah* 6:3) and that He can be found in the most far-flung and desolate places. We simply have to look for Him, but if we make the effort, His presence will be clear beyond a shadow of a doubt.

This can be seen from the subsequent *pesukim* in the *parashah*. The Torah relates that shortly after Yosef was thrown into jail, two officers of the king were also imprisoned for their respective offenses. Rashi tells us (40:1) that the accusations leveled at Yosef by Potiphar's wife generated much negative talk about Yosef. Hashem therefore brought about the indictment of the king's officers so that attention should be shifted away from him.

Rav Yerucham Levovitz once said that if we would have the "eyes of the Torah," we would be able to see *Hashgachah* evident even in the newspapers. To this day, Hashem continues to act in the same manner. When the media starts attacking religious Jews, Hashem reveals some scandal and the spotlight is shifted away from the Jews.

> "Hashem can be found in the ashrams of India, in the subways of Manhattan, and even in the North Pole."

Our surroundings do not always support our *avodas Hashem*, but we can choose whether or not to live with Hashem. He can be found in the ashrams of India, in the subways of Manhattan, and even in the North Pole. We simply have to look for Him, and if we do, we will find Him everywhere — even in the daily headlines!

(*Shiurei Chumash, Parashas Vayeishev* 39:23, 40:1-2)

פרשת מקץ
Parashas Mikeitz

A GLIMPSE OF WHAT WILL HAPPEN WHEN MASHIACH COMES

וַיְרִיצֻהוּ מִן־הַבּוֹר
They rushed him from the dungeon (41:14).

In *Parashas Mikeitz* we are given a small glimpse of what will happen when Mashiach comes. When Pharaoh failed to find a suitable interpretation for his dreams, he was told that Yosef had correctly interpreted dreams in the past and that he might be able to help. Immediately, Yosef was hurried out of prison, given a haircut and a change of clothing, and brought before Pharaoh.

Hashem decreed that Yosef should spend an additional two years in prison (aside from the original ten years), but as soon as those two years were up, he was immediately freed from bondage. *Sforno* (41:14) writes that Yosef's salvation happened instantaneously, like all of Hashem's salvations, as it is written (*Yeshayah* 56:1), "For My salvation is close by." This is what happened in Mitzrayim, as the Torah describes (*Shemos* 12:39), "For they were *chased out* of Mitzrayim," and this is what will occur in the future, when Mashiach arrives, as it is written (*Malachi* 3:1), "And *suddenly* the Master will come to His Sanctuary." *Gedolim* of past generations would describe how they might be sitting down to learn, when suddenly they will hear a newspaper boy outside, toting a just-printed special edition announcing Mashiach's arrival. His sudden appearance will take us by surprise.

An additional preview of the coming of Mashiach can be found later in the *parashah*. When Yosef's brothers were brought before him, he seated them according to age order and served them food, giving Binyamin the largest portion. It is astounding that despite all these clues to the true identity of the ruler who stood before them, the brothers failed to realize that he was, in fact, their brother Yosef. It was only after Yosef revealed himself that everything fell into place, in hindsight. Rav Yerucham Levovitz commented that we, too, are confused by everything that goes on around us. Yet when Mashiach will come and reveal himself, we will suddenly understand everything, in hindsight.

> "When Mashiach will come and reveal himself, we will suddenly understand everything, in hindsight."

May we be *zocheh* to the coming of Mashiach speedily, in our days! (*Shiurei Chumash*, *Parashas Vayeishev* 41:14, 43:33)

❊ ❊ ❊

DO NOT FORGET

וַיִּקְרָא יוֹסֵף אֶת־שֵׁם הַבְּכוֹר מְנַשֶּׁה כִּי־נַשַּׁנִי אֱלֹקִים אֶת־כָּל־עֲמָלִי וְאֵת כָּל־בֵּית אָבִי

> Yosef named his firstborn Menashe — "ki nashani Elokim — for Hashem caused me to forget all my hardships and my father's household" (41:51).

When Yosef revealed his identity to his brothers, he requested that they inform their father of his whereabouts. Rashi tells us that

Yosef sent wagons to Yaakov as an allusion to the last topic they had studied together, twenty-two years earlier. Additionally, when Yosef was on the verge of sinning with Potiphar's wife, Rashi tells us that his father's image suddenly appeared before him. This could only have occurred if Yosef kept his father at the forefront of his thoughts. What, then, did Yosef mean when he said that he had forgotten his father's house?

The Torah's definition of forgetting is much more demanding than ours. We define forgetting as having no recollection whatsoever, while the Torah defines it as even a slight neglect of the topic of discussion. Yosef felt that in some way he had forgotten his father's house, and he alluded to that when he named his son Menashe.

The phrase recited on Chanukah in *Al Hanissim*, "when the Greeks attempted to cause them to forget their Torah," can be understood in

> "We define forgetting as having no recollection whatsoever, while the Torah defines it as even a slight neglect of the topic of discussion."

a similar fashion. The objective of the Greeks was not to cause us to forget the Torah entirely; instead, they aimed to integrate Greek philosophy into the Torah outlook, adulterating pure Torah study with foreign ideas.

How does Greek knowledge differ from Torah knowledge? Greek knowledge revolves around the study and understanding of nature, while Torah knowledge — namely, the Oral Torah — revolves around the study and understanding of the Written Torah. What the two bodies of knowledge have in common is that Torah and nature are different means through which Hashem reveals Himself. But there is a fundamental difference between the two.

Nature is controlled by forces that cause it to act in a certain manner. Be it the movements of the sun, moon, and stars, or the natural tendencies of a human being, all of these forces are continuously compelled to follow a course charted by their Creator. Those individuals who are completely engrossed in researching the laws of nature may feel that they, too, are compelled by nature to act in a certain way. This feeling absolves them of all moral obli-

Parashas Mikeitz / 101

gations, for how can they be expected to overcome their natural tendencies?

Torah study, on the other hand, not only causes a person to acknowledge his obligation to overcome the animalistic aspects of his nature, it also gives him the capacity to accomplish such a feat. "No one is truly free except he who toils in Torah" (*Avos* 6:2). Torah study elevates a person to levels that no other wisdom can, enabling him to rise above his natural tendencies. In contrast, the Greeks' ultimate goal was "to compel them to stray from the statutes of Your will," and constrain them within the limitations of human nature. This miracle, in which the Jewish spirit prevailed over the Hellenistic culture, is what we celebrate on Chanukah.

(*Shiurei Chumash, Parashas Miketz* 41:51; *Alei Shur,* Vol. II, p. 459)

פרשת ויגש
Parashas Vayigash

NO REVENGE

וְלֹא־עָמַד אִישׁ אִתּוֹ בְּהִתְוַדַּע יוֹסֵף אֶל־אֶחָיו

And no one remained with him when Yosef revealed his identity to his brothers (45:1).

After Yosef revealed his identity to his brothers, the Torah tells us, "And he kissed all his brothers and wept upon them, and afterward his brothers spoke to him" (45:15). Rashi explains that after Yosef revealed his identity, the brothers were too embarrassed to speak to him. Only after he calmed them down and kissed each of them were they able to bring themselves to speak to him.

Yosef's inner fortitude is astounding. Not only did he not harbor any ill feelings toward his brothers, he did whatever he could to ease their feelings of guilt. He told them, "It was not you who sent me here; rather, it was Hashem, and He has made me an adviser to

Pharaoh, a master over his house, and the ruler of the entire land of Mitzrayim" (45:8).

This interaction could easily have looked very different. Many people, when they feel wronged, wish to get even with the offender, and the intensity of their revenge is directly proportional to how high they have climbed on the ladder of success. If the offended person were to become a monarch, the offender would probably pay with his life. This was not the case with Yosef, who, despite his position as viceroy, did not exact any revenge at all. Moreover, the Torah tells us that Yosef's only consideration when revealing his identity was that his brothers should not be embarrassed. For this reason, before he identified himself he insisted that all the Egyptians present leave the room — even though this request put him in mortal danger, at the mercy of his brothers.

> "Yosef's only consideration when revealing his identity was that his brothers should not be embarrassed."

Avodas hamiddos, rectifying our character traits, is the most difficult challenge we face. We have excellent role models to emulate, however, since the Torah's stories of the *Avos* and the *Shevatim* depict for us the levels we must strive for. Although the spiritual greatness of our forefathers was on an entirely different plane, *Chazal* tell us (*Tanna D'vei Eliyahu* 25), "A person must say, 'When will my actions reach the actions of my forefathers?'"

(*Shiurei Chumash, Parashas Vayigash* 45:15)

❇ ❇ ❇

CRYSTAL CLEAR

וְלֹא־יָכְלוּ אֶחָיו לַעֲנוֹת אֹתוֹ כִּי נִבְהֲלוּ מִפָּנָיו

And his brothers could not answer him because they were astounded (45:3).

When Yosef revealed his true identity to his brothers, the Torah tells us, "And his brothers could not answer him because they were astounded." They were astounded because at that moment, they were able to comprehend everything that had occurred throughout the past twenty-two years.

What happened to their brother whom they had sold so many years earlier? Why was the viceroy in Egypt dealing with them so harshly? Why was the money they had spent on their food returned to them? Why was the viceroy so adamant that Binyamin be brought to Egypt? What was the viceroy's goblet doing in Binyamin's sack? Yosef's revelation dispelled all these mysteries, answering all of their questions with a few revealing words: "I am Yosef." Immediately everything became crystal clear.

The brother they had sold into slavery was now the viceroy standing before them. He was dealing with them harshly because he wanted to be sure they had done complete *teshuvah* and would not repeat their mistake. The goblet was placed in Binyamin's sack as the ultimate test: Would they abandon Binyamin in Egypt, displaying the same lack of concern they had exhibited to Yosef years earlier, or would they stand by him in his time of need? The brothers withstood the test and merited to see the entire picture, which had been shrouded behind a bizarre sequence of events.

Rav Yerucham Levovitz described the coming of Mashiach in similar terms. When Mashiach arrives, Hashem will proclaim, "I am Hashem," and everything will become crystal clear. Suddenly, all of our questions will be answered: Why do bad things happen to good people? What is the meaning behind the financial meltdown? Why are we continuously being attacked by our enemies? We will be able to view the entire picture at once, and we will finally understand that the very things we thought were detrimental were actually the source of our redemption.

> "When Mashiach arrives, Hashem will proclaim, 'I am Hashem,' and everything will become crystal clear."

(*Shiurei Chumash, Parashas Vayigash* 45:3)

❖ ❖ ❖

PREORDAINED FREE WILL

וְעַתָּה לֹא־אַתֶּם שְׁלַחְתֶּם אֹתִי הֵנָּה כִּי הָאֱלֹקִים וַיְשִׂימֵנִי לְאָב לְפַרְעֹה וּלְאָדוֹן לְכָל־בֵּיתוֹ וּמֹשֵׁל בְּכָל־אֶרֶץ מִצְרָיִם

It was not you who sent me here; rather, it was Hashem, and He has made me as an adviser to Pharaoh, a master to his entire house, and a ruler over the entire land of Egypt (45:8).

Yosef recognized that the entire sequence of events leading up to this phenomenal moment was a product of Hashem's *Hashgachah Pratis*, and not a result of his brothers' decision to sell him. By selling him, his brothers had intended to rid themselves of Yosef and his far-fetched dreams. In reality, however, their actions were the catalyst for the fulfillment of those dreams, and it was clear that the hand of Hashem had orchestrated all that had transpired.

Many people are confused as to what exactly *bechirah* is. Does Hashem allow events to unfold in accordance with people's free will, or is everything preordained from Heaven, regardless of people's choices? The answer can be found in *Chovos HaLevavos* (*Avodas Elokim*, Chapter 8), which writes that both are true: everything is dependent on our *bechirah*, and at the same time everything is preordained by Hashem. In other words, we must make decisions as if we are solely responsible for the outcome of our actions. However, in the final analysis, Hashem will arrange things the way He sees fit.

When making a decision, one should not simply take a shot in the dark while rationalizing that whatever Hashem has in mind will happen regardless of one's actions. Rather, he must analyze the issue at hand from all angles, consult with knowledgeable individuals, and come to a sensible conclusion. At the end of the day, Hashem might make things turn out differently than expected, but that does not exempt us from our obligation to act rationally.

Hashem judges us by our actions, not by the ensuing results.

We cannot know what Hashem's plans are, but He gave us *seichel* to calclulate what is best for us and make decisions that seem right for us. Yet even if things turn out differently from the way we envision, we can be sure that what happens is what Hashem wants — and that it is truly what is best for us.

(*Shiurei Chumash, Parashas Vayeishev* 37:14)

> "Even if things turn out differently from the way we envision, we can be sure that what happens is what Hashem wants — and that it is truly what is best for us."

❊ ❊ ❊

THE QUEST FOR MENUCHAH

וַיִּפֹּל עַל־צַוָּארָיו וַיֵּבְךְּ עַל־צַוָּארָיו עוֹד

And Yosef fell on his [Yaakov's] neck and he cried on his neck again (46:29).

The Torah describes the emotional encounter between Yaakov and Yosef when they meet after many years of separation. Rashi notes that the Torah only recounts how Yosef reacted; it does not tell us how Yaakov reacted. He explains that Yaakov did not fall on Yosef's neck, nor did he kiss Yosef, since he was occupied in reciting *Shema*.

Such behavior demonstrates Yaakov's incredible *menuchas hanefesh*. Despite not having seen his son for more than twenty years, and having been under the impression that his beloved son had died many years earlier, when they were finally reunited he did not lose his composure.

Nowadays, we have all but lost this *middah* of *menuchas hanefesh*. People are constantly busy, and many of them are mired in feelings of depression. Some people behave differently when they are together with their friends; they seem to change hats with their surroundings. They lack the *menuchah* needed to define who they are without worrying what people will say about them. Others simply cannot come to terms with their faults and are always worried that people will discover that they are lacking. Such behavior negates the possibility of being satisfied with their lot and acquiring *menuchas hanefesh*.

Menuchas hanefesh is an important *middah* in *avodas Hashem*. The yeshivah in Kelm, which produced countless *gedolim* and *baalei mussar*, centered its *avodah* around the *middah* of *menuchas hanefesh*. Incorporating this *middah* into one's life is imperative to achieving *shleimus*, since it allows one to act in accordance with the Torah regardless of the situation in which he finds himself.

> "The least we can do in our quest to attain menuchas hanefesh is to focus primarily on our good qualities instead of our flaws."

Yaakov Avinu exemplified this *middah*, and he therefore succeeded in perfecting himself. Although we are far from such *shleimus*, the least we can do in our quest to attain *menuchas hanefesh* is to focus primarily on our good qualities instead of our flaws. This will bring us to an awareness that we are not as bad as we thought we were, and our newfound confidence will help us to improve our *avodas Hashem*.

(*Shiurei Chumash, Parashas Vayigash* 46:29)

❊ ❊ ❊

FILLING OUR DAYS WITH LIFE

יְמֵי שְׁנֵי מְגוּרַי שְׁלֹשִׁים וּמְאַת שָׁנָה מְעַט וְרָעִים הָיוּ יְמֵי שְׁנֵי חַיַּי

The years of my dwelling are 130; few and terrible were the years of my life (47:9).

Yaakov Avinu traveled to Mitzrayim and stood before Pharaoh. In response to Pharaoh's question of "How old are you?" Yaakov answers, "The years of my *dwelling* are 130; few and terrible were the years of my *life*." Why did not Yaakov simply answer that he was 130 years old? Why did he give such a long-winded answer?

Yaakov was telling Pharaoh that *dwelling* in the world and *living* in it are two different things. If Pharaoh wanted to know how long Yaakov had been walking the face of this earth, then the answer was 130 years. However, this period cannot be considered his *life*, because the years were "few and terrible."

Yaakov continues, "And they did not reach the years of *life* of my ancestors in the days of their dwelling." Regarding Avraham Avinu the Torah says (25:7), "And these are the days of life of Avraham that he lived (*asher chai*)." Similarly, the Torah writes regarding Adam (5:5), "And all the days of Adam that he lived (*asher chai*)." Avraham's 175 years were filled from beginning to end with "life," as were Adam's. In his answer to Pharaoh, Yaakov was saying that the years of his life did not equal the years he actually dwelled on earth.

To Yaakov Avinu, true life was living with *ruach hakodesh* and *hashraas haShechinah*. Yaakov felt that he had not truly lived during the many years that he was deprived of *ruach hakodesh*. Although we do not have *ruach hakodesh*, we can define true life as utilizing our days to their fullest.

A story is told of a man who went to a certain town and was shown the cemetery. He perused the tombstones and was astonished to find that everyone in the town had died young. One tombstone said that the deceased had lived for twelve years; on another was engraved that the deceased had lived for ten years, and so on. The man was baffled, because he had met the townspeople and they did not appear to be that young. When he asked one of the natives for an explanation, the person answered that in that town, the duration of a person's life was not measured by how many years a person actually lived, but by how many of his days were used productively. Many of the people buried in that cemetery had died when they were eighty, ninety, or even a hundred years old, but they had not made the most of all the years of their life.

Hashem said to the Jewish people (*Shemos Rabbah* 25:13): "I will deal with you measure for measure. I gave you the Torah in order that you should engage in it each and every day (*yom yom*), as it states, 'Praiseworthy is the one who listens to Me, diligently frequenting My door *yom yom*.' Therefore, I will satisfy your hunger with the heavenly *mann yom yom*, as it states, 'And the nation went out and collected *dvar yom b'yomo*.'"

The days of our lives were not given to us as a means to learn and master the Torah; rather, the days themselves are the purpose.

> "Our goal is not to gain knowledge of the entire Shas as much as it is to learn Torah on a daily basis."

Our goal is not to gain knowledge of the entire *Shas* as much as it is to learn Torah on a daily basis. Each and every day of our lives must be spent productively.

It is imperative that we make a *cheshbon hanefesh*, and scrutinize one area in particular: How did we spend our days? Were they spent constructively and in the service of Hashem, or did we neglect them and waste our time?

With this approach, we can succeed in not merely residing in this world, but in truly *living*.

(*Shiurei Chumash, Parashas Vayigash* 47:9; *Maamarei Yemei Ratzon*, p. 26)

פרשת ויחי
Parashas Vayechi

CLOSED BY BONDAGE

וַיְחִי יַעֲקֹב
Yaakov lived (47:28).

At the beginning of *Parashas Vayechi* Rashi notes that the space usually left in the *sefer Torah* between *parshiyos* is missing between *Parashas Vayigash* and *Parashas Vayechi*. He cites *Chazal*'s explanation that once Yaakov Avinu passed away, the eyes and hearts of *Bnei Yisrael* became "closed" due to the burden of the Egyptian bondage. Therefore, the Torah symbolically "closed" *Parashas Vayechi*.

We know that the bondage in Egypt did not begin after Yaakov died; it began only after the last of the *Shevatim* passed away, which was many years after Yaakov's passing. If so, what did *Chazal* mean when they said that after Yaakov died, the eyes and hearts of *Bnei Yisrael* became closed due to the burden of bondage?

The bondage *Chazal* refer to is not a physical enslavement, but rather a spiritual one. It was at this point that *Bnei Yisrael* began to be influenced by the Egyptian culture. As long as Yaakov Avinu was alive, he succeeded in ensuring that *Bnei Yisrael* maintained the spiritual level they had achieved in their homeland of Canaan. When Yaakov passed away, however, *Bnei Yisrael* lost their protection against the prevailing cultural winds.

> "The bondage Chazal refer to is not a physical enslavement, but rather a spiritual one."

Although those living in *chutz la'aretz* might be more susceptible to the influence of non-Jewish culture than those living in Eretz Yisrael, we are all affected in one way or another by the lifestyle of the nations around us. If, however, we connect to a *gadol baTorah* or a *talmid chacham*, we will certainly be more successful in warding off the influence of trends and fashions that are antithetical to the Torah way of life.

(*Shiurei Chumash, Parashas Vayechi* 47:28)

❊ ❊ ❊

INVERSE PROPORTION

וַיִּשְׁתַּחוּ יִשְׂרָאֵל עַל־רֹאשׁ הַמִּטָּה

Yisrael prostrated himself toward the head of the bed (47:31).

Shortly before Yaakov Avinu passed away, he requested that Yosef swear to bury him in *Me'aras Hamachpeilah*. After Yosef complied with his father's wish, Yaakov Avinu prostrated himself toward the head of the bed. Rashi comments that he bowed specifically toward the head of the bed because the *Shechinah* rests above the head of someone who is ill.

Why is the *Shechinah* located above the head of an ill person? Hashem's closeness to a person is inversely proportional to the extent that the person feels he can depend on himself. The more a person feels that he can manage on his own, the farther he is from Hashem. Someone who is ill, however, recognizes his lack of strength and is much less confident in his own power. He subjugates himself before his Creator, thereby meriting a special closeness to Hashem. *Chazal* (*Bereishis Rabbah* 53:14) further tell us that an ill person's prayers are more effective in bringing about his recovery than the prayers of others on his behalf. It is because he is more cognizant of his dependence on Hashem that Hashem favors his *tefillos*.

When Yitzchak and Rivkah prayed for children, the Torah stresses that Hashem answered Yitzchak's prayers, as opposed to Rivkah's. Rashi explains that the prayers of someone whose parents are wicked cannot be compared to the prayers of someone whose parents are righteous (25:21). The Alter of Kelm explains that someone whose ancestors were wicked knows that he cannot depend on their merits. However, someone whose ancestors were righteous might feel that he need not pray so intensely, since he has abundant merits on which to rely. If he nonetheless subjugates himself before Hashem and prays with the proper intensity, that means he has worked on his *tefillos* to a greater degree than someone who lacks ancestral merit. Hashem accepts this type of *tefillah* in a special way.

Rabbeinu Yonah writes that someone who is haughty does not merit Heavenly assistance (*Shaarei Teshuvah* 1:27). An arrogant person thinks that he can rely on his own abilities, and therefore does not subjugate himself before Hashem. Similarly, the Gra writes that young children merit special providence because they realize that they are completely dependent on others. Their lack of self-reliance is their key to receiving Divine assistance.

"Our closeness to Hashem, and the efficacy of our prayers, mirror the extent to which we subjugate ourselves before Him."

"Hashem is close to all those who call out to Him — to all who call out to Him sincerely" (*Tehillim* 145:18). Hashem listens to every single prayer without regard to the supplicant's spiritual level. However, when a person prays, he must realize that he is completely dependent on Hashem, and that only He has the ability to help him. Our closeness to Hashem, and the efficacy of our prayers, mirror the extent to which we subjugate ourselves before Him.

(*Shiurei Chumash, Parashas Vayechi* 47:31, *Parashas Toldos* 25:21)

❄ ❄ ❄

THE ARROW IN OUR MOUTHS

בְּחַרְבִּי וּבְקַשְׁתִּי
With my sword and my bow (48:22).

Prior to Yaakov's passing, he told Yosef, "I have given you Shechem as an additional portion … which I captured from the Emori with my sword and my bow." Rashi offers an enigmatic explanation: "my sword" refers to Yaakov's wisdom, while "my bow" refers to his *tefillos*. What is the connection between a sword and wisdom, and between a bow and *tefillos*?

A sword is sharp and slim, and is an apt metaphor for wisdom, since words of wisdom are clear and concise. A bow is the tool that propels an arrow to great lengths, and is similar to a mouth, which propels our *tefillos* toward Hashem. We do not need philosophical proofs that there is a Creator; the very fact that we *daven* "into the air" and our *tefillos* are answered is clear proof of the Omnipresent!

A Russian convert once shared an amazing story with Rav Wolbe. He recounted that when he was a student in university he was plagued by many questions and doubts with regard to religion. He was a truth seeker, and these issues troubled him to the extent that he would pray, cry, and fast, with the hope of unraveling these mysteries. During one of his tearful prayers, he fell asleep and he had a dream in which the answers to his many questions were revealed to him. This was the impetus for his eventual conversion to Judaism. *Tefillah* has the quality of an arrow: a true prayer hits its mark and is answered.

> "*Tefillah* has the quality of an arrow: a true prayer hits its mark and is answered."

Yaakov Avinu felt that his victory over the people of Shechem was due to his Torah study and his *tefillos*. Yes, he had to pick up a sword and fight (see third comment of Rashi, ibid.), but the ultimate decisor of victory was his prayer.

Today, when Jews — particularly those in Israel — are under constant threat, it is incumbent upon each one of us to make use of the "ammunition" we possess. If the situation truly troubles us, we will be driven to pray in a manner that will give our *tefillos* the potency of an arrow.

(*Shiurei Chumash, Parashas Vayechi* 48:22)

❊ ❊ ❊

HASTE MAKES WASTE

רְאוּבֵן בְּכֹרִי אַתָּה כֹּחִי וְרֵאשִׁית אוֹנִי יֶתֶר שְׂאֵת וְיֶתֶר עָז. פַּחַז כַּמַּיִם אַל־תּוֹתַר כִּי עָלִיתָ מִשְׁכְּבֵי אָבִיךָ

> *Reuven, you are my firstborn, my might and my first strength; you were destined to be greater [than your brothers] in priesthood and kingship. [Since you were] hasty like water, you will not be foremost; because you ascended your father's bed"* (49:3-4).

Before Yaakov Avinu passed away, he gathered all of his sons and blessed each of them. Reuven, the eldest and the rightful heir to the privileges of the firstborn, was the first to receive his father's blessing. But because he had acted hastily when he removed Yaakov's bed from Bilhah's tent, he lost his rights to *kehunah* and *malchus*.

A person who acts out of haste cannot possibly be a king, for a king must remain composed in all circumstances, and not respond impulsively to sudden and disturbing news. If he reacts in haste, he is liable to bring destruction upon the citizens for whom he is responsible.

The same holds true for *kehunah*: a person who behaves rashly cannot serve in the *Beis HaMikdash*.

Yet the Gemara (*Pesachim* 65a) tells us that *Chazal* did not institute Rabbinic restrictions in the *Beis HaMikdash* because the *Kohanim* acted with *zerizus*, and there was therefore no need for extra safeguards. What does this mean? Isn't someone who acts with *zerizus* more prone to making mistakes?

> "*Zerizus* is not found in the feet, but in the head."

Rav Avraham Grodzinski explains that *zerizus* is not found in the feet, but in the head. *Zerizus* is not haste — which makes waste. Instead, it is a zeal and a fastidiousness that ensures that a person does not deviate an iota from his assignment.

Reuven, who exhibited the trait of haste, was not a candidate for either of the above positions.

At first glance, it is hard to understand how Yaakov's rebuke to Reuven can be called a blessing. In truth, however, it was one of the greatest blessings possible. In the course of his rebuke, Yaakov revealed to Reuven his underlying character trait. Such a piece of information is worth far more than gold! It is a spiritual treasure that can set a person on the proper path for the rest of his life by attuning him to the *middah* that is liable to destroy his *avodas Hashem* if left unchecked.

Rav Yerucham Levovitz would say that just as a person has an underlying negative *middah* that can derail his *avodas Hashem*, a person also has an underlying positive *middah* that can be used to rectify all of his faulty *middos*. We might need someone else to identify this *middah* for us, but once we do find out what it is, we should cherish this piece of information as we would a precious gem, for it is the key to our success in *avodas Hashem*.

(*Shiurei Chumash, Parashas Vayechi* 49:4)

❋ ❋ ❋

CREDITING YOUR ACCOUNT

זְבוּלֻן לְחוֹף יַמִּים יִשְׁכֹּן ... יִשָּׂשכָר חֲמֹר גָּרֶם רֹבֵץ בֵּין הַמִּשְׁפְּתָיִם

Zevulun will dwell on the shores of the sea …
Yissachar is a bony donkey that crouches between the borders (49:13-14).

Sforno notes that the blessing of Zevulun, who spends his days in the workplace, precedes the blessing of Yissachar, who spends his days toiling in Torah. He explains that this is because a person must be provided with his material needs in order to toil in Torah, as *Chazal* state (*Avos* 3:21), "If there is no flour, there is no Torah." If one provides for his friend's material needs, thereby enabling him to learn Torah (as Zevulun did for Yissachar), the *avodas Hashem* that is a product of this financial assistance is credited to both the learner and his benefactor.

The mitzvah to study Torah is one that is incumbent upon every individual. But this mitzvah is one that can be carried out indirectly, by supporting another person's learning. With regard to the mitzvah of *davening*, for example, another person's *tefillah* will not exempt you from your personal obligation even if you support him. But if a person provides financial backing so that his friend can learn Torah, he is a partner in all the Torah that his friend learns!

Similarly, the Gemara (*Kiddushin* 29b) asks what one should do if he has the means to provide for either himself or his son to learn Torah, but not for both of them. Should he learn Torah himself, or should he support his son? The Gemara answers that if his son is more intellectually proficient, he should send his son. How will the father fulfill his own obligation to learn Torah? By sending his son in his place, thereby enabling him to learn Torah.

If one is able to learn, he does not have to rely on others to fulfill his obligation.

> *"If one is unable to learn a full day, he can still have much Torah study credited to his account if he supports those who spend their days and nights engrossed in Torah study."*

However, if one is unable to learn a full day, he can still have much Torah study credited to his account if he supports those who spend their days and nights engrossed in Torah study.

(*Shiurei Chumash, Parashas Vayechi* 49:13)

ספר שמות
Sefer Shemos

פרשת שמות

Parashas Shemos

THE CLASP ON THE NECKLACE

וְיוֹסֵף הָיָה בְמִצְרָיִם
And Yosef was in Mitzrayim (1:5).

Parashas Shemos begins with a brief synopsis of the last few *parshiyos*: "And the descendants of Yaakov numbered seventy; and Yosef was in Mitzrayim" (1:5). Do not we already know that Yosef was in Mitzrayim? What is this *passuk* teaching us? Rashi answers that the Torah is alluding to Yosef's greatness. Yosef, who was the shepherd of his father's flock, who was sold to Mitzrayim, and who was eventually crowned king, maintained his righteousness in these varying situations.

As a shepherd, Yosef was far from the limelight, and sheltered from the outside world. Then, without warning, he was uprooted and deposited in Mitzrayim, the seat of immorality in the world at that time. However, Yosef rose to the challenges of his new environment and position, remaining steadfast in his adherence to all that was sacred to him.

We see in Yosef the quintessential embodiment of the *middah* of *seder*, orderliness. Many people are set in their ways and adhere to a rigorous daily schedule, but cannot maintain it when confronted by something out of the ordinary. But Yosef's *seder* was internal, independent of his external situation.

How can we put our lives into an order that will endure even when our circumstances change unexpectedly? First and foremost, an orderly external appearance promotes an internal orderliness. Additionally, we must ask ourselves two questions: What do I want to accomplish in my service of Hashem? And what can I do, in my present situation, to actualize these goals? Orderliness bears witness to a person's true will, and one's true will must be expressed through orderliness.

With the answers to these two questions in mind, we should be able to build a schedule for ourselves that includes ample time for eating, sleeping, and relaxation, while ensuring that times set aside for praying, learning, and doing mitzvos are immutable. The answers to these questions must not be too ambitious, however, for if we take on more than we can handle, we will end up throwing away the entire regimen.

> "A person may possess a wealth of talents and good qualities, but without seder, all of his virtues are liable to scatter."

Once we establish a schedule for ourselves, it is imperative that we abide by it. The Alter of Kelm said that *seder* can be compared to the clasp on a pearl necklace. No one can deny that the pearls are more important than the clasp, but without the clasp the pearls will scatter, and the owner of the necklace will be left with only the string. Similarly, a person may possess a wealth of talents and good qualities, but without *seder*, all of his virtues are liable to scatter, leaving him with nothing.

If we can organize our day in a way that reflects our true priorities, then we can hope that no matter what circumstances we find ourselves in, our priorities will remain priorities.

(*Alei Shur,* Vol. I, p. 68; Vol. II, pp. 319-320)

❋ ❋ ❋

BUILDING OUR OWN HOUSES

וַתִּירֶאןָ הַמְיַלְּדֹת אֶת־הָאֱלֹקִים

But the midwives feared Hashem (1:17).

We find that one way to gauge a person's greatness is by his level of *yirah*, generally understood as Fear of Hashem, as we see in the following examples. Avraham Avinu referred to Sarah as his sister (*Bereishis* 20:11), "For I said there is no *fear of Hashem* in this place and they will kill me because of my wife." After *Akeidas Yitzchak* Hashem told Avraham (ibid. 22:12), "Now I know that you *fear Hashem*." The Torah writes about Amalek (*Devarim* 25:18), "And he did not *fear Hashem*." These are but a few of the numerous instances.

In *Parashas Shemos* we are told that the Jewish midwives, Shifrah and Puah (also known as Yocheved and Miriam), did not heed Pharaoh's command to kill the Jewish baby boys. On the contrary, they did everything in their power to keep them alive and healthy. The Torah tells us, "But the midwives *feared Hashem* and did not do as the king of Mitzrayim told them" (1:17). Additionally, the Torah relates that they were rewarded for their *yiras Shamayim*: "Because the midwives *feared Hashem*, He made for them houses" (1:21). Rashi explains that the "houses" mentioned in the *passuk* refer to the "house of *kehunah*" (Aharon, who descended from Yocheved) and the "house of kingship" (David, who descended from Miriam).

Chazal (*Shemos Rabbah* 1:16) add that in this merit, Yocheved gave birth to Moshe, and from Miriam came Betzalel, who built the *Mishkan*. In that sense, the *yiras Shamayim* of these two women laid the groundwork for the entire *Sefer Shemos*. *Shemos* describes the redemption of *Bnei Yisrael* and the receiving of the Torah — both of which were accomplished through Moshe — and the building of the Mishkan, which was directed by Betzalel.

Yiras Shamayim can be described as the ability to withstand the trials that Hashem places before a person. It is the *middah* by which a person builds his spiritual stature from start to finish. The midwives "built" themselves to the point that they were able to withstand the greatest test: they put their lives on the line to save Jewish children. And Hashem rewarded them measure for measure.

Reward in the Torah is not given as compensation for something that a person does, like a candy given to a child for good behavior. Rather, the reward is the very fruit of the person's actions. By building themselves, Yocheved and Miriam merited the "houses" that were built for them.

> *"Reward in the Torah is not given as compensation for something that a person does, like a candy given to a child for good behavior."*

Not a day goes by that we are not tested in one way or another: Should we hurry through *davening*? How should we spend our time? Should we bring this newspaper or that magazine into our house? The list is endless. Each time we withstand a test, we build our spiritual stature — and reap the fruit of our efforts.

(*Alei Shur,* Vol. II, pp. 339-342)

❊ ❊ ❊

THE SECRET OF THE REDEMPTION

וַיֵּלֶךְ אִישׁ מִבֵּית לֵוִי וַיִּקַּח אֶת־בַּת־לֵוִי

And a man went from the house of Levi and took a daughter [from the house] of Levi (2:1).

Why does the Torah not tell us the names of the individuals mentioned in the above *passuk*? *Chazal* (*Pesachim* 54b) say that seven things are hidden from people, one of which is the day of redemption. Redemption originates from the higher worlds, a realm that we cannot comprehend at all. Matters concerning the redemption are a secret, and the birth of the redeemer of *Bnei Yisrael* is completely shrouded in secrecy. Until the redemption actually materializes, the Torah does not even reveal the names of his parents.

This concept can help us understand another *passuk* in *Parashas Shemos*. After smiting the Egyptian, Moshe saw a Jew about to hit his fellow Jew, and when he chastised the would-be offender, the latter retorted, "Are you going to kill me as you killed the Egyptian?" The *passuk* then states, "And Moshe was afraid and he said, 'Behold, the thing has become known'" (2:14). Rashi explains that Moshe was worried that *Bnei Yisrael* might not be worthy of redemption, since there were gossipmongers among them. The presence of gossipmongers could thwart the redemption because the redemption is a secret matter, and those who cannot keep a secret cannot be redeemed.

Moshe had wondered why specifically the Jews, of all the nations, were subjected to *galus* — and now the reason became known. *Bnei Yisrael* were punished with *galus* because of the gossipmongers. The Jewish nation's uniqueness stems from *penimiyus*, while the other nations of the world are focused on *chitzoniyus*. If a Jew cannot keep a secret, then he lacks basic *penimiyus* and his place will be in *galus* among the other nations of the world.

> "If a Jew cannot keep a secret, then he lacks basic penimiyus and his place will be in galus among the other nations of the world."

To maintain our *penimiyus* and preserve our uniqueness as a nation, we must ensure that secrets remain secret, thereby distancing ourselves from *lashon hara*.

(Shiurei Chumash, Parashas Shemos 2:1, 2:14)

❋ ❋ ❋

SIXTH SENSE FOR HOLINESS

הַאֵלֵךְ וְקָרָאתִי לָךְ אִשָּׁה מֵינֶקֶת מִן הָעִבְרִיֹּת

Shall I go summon for you a wet nurse from the Hebrew women? (2:7).

When Moshe was born, his mother put him inside a basket and placed it among the reeds on the riverbank, while his sister, Miriam, stood at a distance to see what would happen. The Torah relates that Pharaoh's daughter went to bathe in the river and discovered the Jewish child in the basket. Miriam then asked if she should call a Jewish wet nurse to feed the child. Rashi tells us that this inquiry came after Pharaoh's daughter brought Moshe to a number of Egyptian women, and he refused to nurse from them, since he would ultimately use his mouth to speak with Hashem.

How did Moshe, who was merely three months old, know that there was something wrong with nursing from a non-Jewish woman? A person imbued with *kedushah* can sense when something is not appropriate. At times, even animals can detect when something is amiss. *Chazal* relate (*Chullin* 7a) that Rabbi Pinchas ben Yair's donkey refused to eat from food that had not been tithed. Rabbi Pinchas ben Yair was on such a high spiritual level that even his animals were able to sense that the food was forbidden.

Rav Yerucham Levovitz would say that everything that is true regarding *kedushah* has a parallel in the realm of *tumah*. If we have trouble comprehending a concept of *kedushah* because of our distance from that spiritual level, we might, unfortunately, have an easier time comprehending the concept in the context of *tumah*. Sometimes, while walking in the street, a person might suddenly glance in a certain direction and unwittingly behold an indecent sight. His psyche sensed the *tumah* and drew him to turn his gaze in that direction.

The ability to foster a sense of *kedushah* is not limited to those who lived in the times of *Chazal*. Shortly before Rav Yerucham passed away, when his health was failing, his doctor instructed that he eat meat that had not been salted to remove the blood. When Rav Yerucham was served this meat, he placed it in his mouth and immediately spit it out, declaring that it was non-Jewish meat. His sense of *kedushah* enabled him to detect that the meat was not kosher.

> "Kedushah and tumah are not merely abstract concepts; they are a reality."

Kedushah and *tumah* are not merely abstract concepts; they are a reality. Rav Wolbe once commented to a group of former *talmi-*

dim that the main goal of his discourses was to convey the idea that *ruchniyus* is a reality!

(*Shiurei Chumash, Parashas Shemos* 2:7)

❊ ❊ ❊

ZERO TOLERANCE FOR INJUSTICE

וַיִּגְדַּל מֹשֶׁה
And Moshe grew up (2:11).

Parashas Shemos provides a short biographical sketch of Moshe Rabbeinu, before he was chosen to become the leader of *Bnei Yisrael*. Specifically, the Torah describes the following three incidents:

First, Moshe left his palatial surroundings to see how his brethren were faring. Upon witnessing an Egyptian beating a fellow Jew, he was distressed to such a degree that he smote the Egyptian. Ramban (2:23) comments that Moshe was merely twelve years old at the time of this incident.

The second incident occurred the following day, when Moshe again sought out his brothers' welfare. This time Moshe observed one Jew poised to hit a fellow Jew and called out, "Why do you hit your friend?" In response, the aggressor asked rhetorically (13-14), "Who made you a judge over us? Are you going to kill me just as you killed the Egyptian?"

The third incident happened as a direct result of the previous one. After realizing that his act of slaying the Egyptian had become public knowledge and that Pharaoh wanted to execute him, Moshe was forced to flee for his life. He escaped to Midyan and chanced upon a distressing scene taking place at the local well. Seven girls were trying to fill their troughs with water, but were chased away by other shepherds. Upon witnessing this injustice, Moshe was galvanized into action; he protected the girls and gave water to their sheep.

The Alter of Kelm comments that if the Torah chose to highlight these three incidents in Moshe's life, we can deduce that these stories personify him. The common thread that runs through them is Moshe's intolerance of injustice. It did not matter that he was only twelve years old or that he was a stranger in Midyan; Moshe could not tolerate wrongdoing.

The closer a person is to holiness, the more sensitive he is to transgression and injustice. Moshe could have thought to himself that it was not his concern if the Midyanites were fighting with one another. However, his innate holiness did not allow him to ignore the situation.

The *parashah* continues with a dialogue between Hashem and Moshe. For seven days Hashem tried to convince Moshe to lead Bnei Yisrael out of Egypt, and Moshe repeatedly declined. What compelled Moshe to so adamantly refuse this vital mission?

> "It did not matter that he was only twelve years old or that he was a stranger in Midyan; Moshe could not tolerate wrongdoing."

It was this same sensitivity to injustice. *Chazal* (*Shemos Rabbah* 3:16) tell us that Moshe felt it was wrong for him to accept a leadership position when he had an older brother who was fit for the assignment. Moshe's intolerance of wrongdoing was all encompassing, and extended to himself as well.

It is easy to criticize others, but not as easy to turn our critical eye inward. Not only should we protest injustices perpetrated by others, we must also take a good look at ourselves to make sure that we live up to the same standards we demand from others.

(*Shiurei Chumash, Parashas Shemos* 2:17, 4:10; *Alei Shur,* Vol. I, p. 164)

❊ ❊ ❊

THE HARDEST MIDDAH TO MASTER

מִתּוֹךְ הַסְּנֶה

From amid the bush (3:2).

The first time Hashem spoke to Moshe, He revealed Himself in a burning bush. Rashi (3:2) explains that Hashem specifically chose to reveal Himself in a bush, as opposed to a more impressive tree, because He too "feels anguish" when the Jewish people suffer. Even when Hashem hides His presence from the Jewish people, so to speak, and allows them to suffer, He still feels their pain.

The Gemara (*Berachos* 3a) tells us that every time *Bnei Yisrael* answer, "*Amen, Yehei Shmeih Rabba*," Hashem exclaims, "Woe unto My children, for I have destroyed their *Beis HaMikdash* and exiled them among the nations." Moreover, Hashem does not merely feel the suffering of the entire Jewish nation as a whole; He feels the aches and pains of every individual. The *mishnah* (*Sanhedrin* 6:5) states that when a person has a headache, or a pain in his arm, Hashem says, "My head is heavy; My arm is heavy."

Hashem desires to be connected to His creations, and being *nosei b'ol* — sharing people's burdens

> "Since nesiah b'ol is the ultimate manner of emulating Hashem, it is also the most difficult middah to master."

— is perhaps the way He most commonly connects to them. This is why being *nosei b'ol* is such a fundamental attribute. We are commanded to emulate all of Hashem's attributes, and because His primary attribute is *nesiah b'ol*, we must make every effort to acquire this trait. However, since *nesiah b'ol* is the ultimate manner of emulating Hashem, it is also the most difficult *middah* to master.

The very first story the Torah tells us about Moshe revolves around his *nesiah b'ol chaveiro*. Moshe left Pharaoh's palace to see how his enslaved brethren were faring. Rashi (2:11) tells us that he "placed his eyes and heart [toward them] to feel their pain." He saw what was happening to them and internalized it in his own heart. He did not merely say, "It must be so hard for you"; he felt his fellow Jews' pain as if it were his own. Moshe Rabbeinu, the quintessential embodiment of Hashem's attributes, personified this trait of *nosei b'ol*.

One can and should be *nosei b'ol* with every Jew in need. Whether rich or poor, healthy or ill, when a person is suffering he needs someone with whom he can share his burden. Let us emulate our Creator and truly empathize with our brethren, thereby bringing ourselves and the entire world closer to perfection.

(*Shiurei Chumash, Parashas Shemos* 2:11, 3:2)

פרשת וארא

Parashas Va'eira

LIVING BY THE PROMISE

וָאֵרָא אֶל־אַבְרָהָם אֶל־יִצְחָק וְאֶל־יַעֲקֹב בְּאֵל שַׁדָּי וּשְׁמִי ה' לֹא נוֹדַעְתִּי לָהֶם

And I appeared to Avraham, Yitzchak, and Yaakov with the Name "Kel Shakai," and My Name "Yud-Hei-Vav-Hei" I did not make known to them" (6:3).

Rashi notes that Hashem did not say that He did not mention the Name *Yud-Hei-Vav-Hei* to the *Avos*. Rather, Hashem said that He did not *make Himself known* to them by that Name. The *Avos* never saw the manifestation of the *middah* connoted by this Name of Hashem, which represents the fulfillment of Hashem's previous guarantee. Hashem was telling Moshe that He made numerous promises, and He also made a covenant with Avraham that He would give Eretz Yisrael to his children, but the *Avos* never saw the realization of this promise.

Now, He would reveal Himself with the Name *Yud-Hei-Vav-Hei*, and fulfill to Moshe and his generation what He had promised the *Avos*.

According to Rashi's explanation, the Torah is letting us know that Hashem has two distinct Names: *Kel Shakai*, which connotes a promise that will be fulfilled in the future, and *Yud-Hei-Vav-Hei*, which connotes the fulfillment of a previous promise. Why do a promise and its fulfillment need two separate Names? Are they not in reality one extended process?

A "*havtachah*," a promise for the future, is not merely a means of actualizing an intended goal; it is a *middah* by which Hashem runs the world. Our *Avos* were promised great things in the future, and they had to live with total faith that Hashem would ultimately fulfill what He promised. Their *avodah* was to live in a way that showed their belief and complete reliance on Hashem's word.

> "Our avodah is actually very similar to that of the Avos, for we must live with complete faith that all of our actions will be duly rewarded in the next world."

Our *avodah* is actually very similar to that of the *Avos*, for we must live with complete faith that all of our actions will be duly rewarded in the next world. We cannot see the reward or the punishment that awaits those who perform the mitzvos or neglect them, but we must nevertheless believe in Hashem's *havtachah* that we will ultimately be paid in full for all that we have done. We live in this world with the Name *Kel Shakai* — the promise of future compensation, and in the next world we will be able to perceive the manifestation of the Name *Yud-Hei-Vav-Hei*.

(*Shiurei Chumash, Parashas Va'eira* 6:3)

❊ ❊ ❊

THE TRUE MEANING OF TOLERANCE

וַיְדַבֵּר ה' אֶל־מֹשֶׁה וְאֶל־אַהֲרֹן וַיְצַוֵּם אֶל־בְּנֵי יִשְׂרָאֵל

Hashem spoke to Moshe and Aharon and commanded them regarding Bnei Yisrael (6:13).

Rashi explains that Hashem was commanding Moshe and Aharon to lead the Jewish people calmly and with *savlanus*, tolerance. The Midrash (*Shemos Rabbah* 7:3) adds that Hashem told them, "My children are stubborn and frustrating, and you are accepting this position with the knowledge that they might curse you and throw stones at you."

> *"A person who is tolerant of others is similar to a porter who hauls a heavy load and perseveres despite the burden."*

A person who does not have the ability to act patiently and tolerantly toward those around him cannot be a leader, nor should he hold any public office. Without patience, one cannot succeed in any communal position, be it as a rabbi, teacher, manager, or *gabbai*.

Yet *savlanus* is an essential *middah* even for those who do not occupy public positions, for all of us frequently come into contact with other human beings. The Alter of Kelm writes, "We should make great efforts to accustom ourselves to acting with tolerance, for it is the root of all *middos* and serenity" (*Chochmah U'Mussar*, p. 432). No two people have identical characteristics, upbringings, habits, pastimes, or idiosyncrasies. Therefore, if a person wishes to get along with his spouse, friends, colleagues, neighbors, roommates, or learning partners, he must be tolerant of their actions and words.

What is *savlanus*? The root of the word is "*sovel*," to bear (a heavy load). A person who is tolerant of others is similar to a porter who hauls a heavy load and perseveres despite the burden. Likewise, every day we hear and see numerous things that we do not agree with or that irritate us. Many times, people act in a way that is insulting or even downright nasty. Rather than being wounded or daunted, a *savlan* simply bears the burden of people's offensive actions or words.

It must be stressed that *savlanus* is *not* indifference. It is not a feeling of, "Who cares what he does? Let him live his life and do not get me involved." Rather, when someone behaves in an offensive manner, a *savlan* retains his composure and responds calmly, instead of erupting in a frenzy or ignoring the incident completely. He rebukes, when necessary, and refuses improper demands, but with love and serenity and without anger.

Tolerance is an aspect of the *middah* of humility that everyone must endeavor to master. We should designate fifteen minutes a day for acting with tolerance, at a time when we know we will be in contact with other people. During these fifteen minutes we should make an effort to bear whatever the people around us do or say, without responding rashly. This does not mean that we should remain silent for those fifteen minutes. Rather, we should remain composed, and any response we make should emanate from a place of serenity, not indignation.

(*Alei Shur,* Vol. II, pp. 214-220)

❊ ❊ ❊

RESPECT IS FOR A PERSON'S OWN SAKE

אֱמֹר אֶל־אַהֲרֹן קַח מַטְּךָ ...
Say to Aharon, take your staff ... (7:19).

The Torah tells us that the first three *makkos* happened as a result of Aharon hitting specific objects with his staff. The plagues of blood and frogs involved hitting the water, and the plague of lice involved hitting the sand. *Chazal* tell us (*Shemos Rabbah* 9:9) that Moshe did not strike the water and sand himself because he felt indebted to the water for protecting him when he was placed in the Nile River as a baby, and he felt indebted to the sand for covering up the Egyptian he slayed.

The obvious question is, since both water and sand are inanimate and have no feelings, what difference would it make if Moshe was the one to smite them? Moshe refrained from taking an active role in these *makkos* not because of any damage that he would cause the water and sand, but because of the damage he would cause to his own character. A refined person maintains a certain level of respect toward anything he comes in contact with, regardless of what it is.

We find a similar idea with regard to the halachah of *bizui ochlin* — disgracing food. There are several actions that may not be done with food because they constitute a disgrace to the food (see *Orach Chaim* 171). Although food has no feelings, we must refrain from degrading it *for our own sake*, because as human beings, we must behave in a consistently dignified manner. In a similar vein, when Rav Dessler would don his hat, he would not grab it with one hand and place it on his head; he would respectfully pick it up with both hands.

> "Although food has no feelings, we must refrain from degrading it for our own sake, because as human beings, we must behave in a consistently dignified manner."

We might not be on the level of picking up our hat with both hands, but there are definitely things we treat cavalierly that might deserve a bit more respect. Moreover, if we accustom ourselves to treating inanimate objects with respect, we will certainly not be careless with the respect owed to our family, friends, neighbors, and colleagues.

(*Shiurei Chumash, Parashas Va'eira* 7:19)

❃ ❃ ❃

TAKING PHARAOH'S LESSON TO HEART

וְהַכְבֵּד אֶת־לִבּוֹ

He made his heart stubborn (8:11).

Pharaoh's reaction to the plagues is hard to believe. He suffered through a week without water, only blood. Then came another week of frogs invading every possible space, followed by a third week of terrible lice. Nevertheless, when these punishments passed, he hardened his heart. In return for his stubbornness, he endured a week of ferocious animals wreaking havoc upon his kingdom and then a week of livestock dying with their rotting carcasses filling his country. Yet when these weeks finally passed, Pharaoh hardened his heart once again. He was suffering terribly, and he simply ignored the pain! How can we understand such madness?

The entire *Shema* revolves around this idea that a person's "heart" plays a pivotal role in *avodas Hashem*. In the first paragraph of *Shema* we say, "And you shall love Hashem with all your *heart*... And you shall place these words upon your *heart*." In the second paragraph we continue, "and to serve Him with all your *hearts*."

Later in the second paragraph we are warned, "Be careful lest your *hearts* be swayed and you deviate and serve other gods." Such behavior brings exile in its wake. The only way out of this exile is, "And you shall place these words upon your *hearts*" — we must rebuild our hearts, which deviated from the service of Hashem. In the last paragraph we are warned once again, "Do not stray after your *hearts* and after your *eyes*." Once we have experienced the destruction wrought by our wayward hearts, we must make an extra effort not to stray after our hearts.

The key to success in *avodas Hashem* is the ability to have our Torah and *avodah* penetrate our hearts. It is not enough to learn and perform the mitzvos; Hashem's words must be firmly implanted in our hearts.

This is where Pharaoh failed. He suffered through every one of the plagues, and was as miserable as all of the other Egyptians. However, he put up a tough front and simply did not allow the pain and misery to penetrate his heart. As soon as the danger passed, he reverted to his old ways. He was cognizant of what was happening, but the knowledge remained in his head and did not reach to his heart. In response, Hashem told Moshe, "This time I am sending all My plagues to his *heart*" (9:14). The only way to change Pharaoh was to ensure that the suffering penetrated his heart.

It is incredible to see how a human being can block out the most earth-shattering events and remain unaffected. What is even more unbelievable is that we ourselves do this all the time! Often, we know what we should be doing, but we simply ignore this knowledge and act on impulse. We might even be receiving "messages" from Hashem, yet we do whatever we can to prevent these messages from penetrating our hearts. Sometimes we have to take a lesson from Pharaoh. We need to stop closing our eyes to what we know is true and begin serving Hashem with heartfelt *avodah*.

(*Shiurei Chumash*, Va'eira 9:7)

❋ ❋ ❋

ACTIVE OR PASSIVE AGENTS

בַּעֲבוּר הַרְאֹתְךָ אֶת־כֹּחִי וּלְמַעַן סַפֵּר שְׁמִי בְּכָל־הָאָרֶץ

So that you may behold My strength and recount [the greatness of] My Name throughout the land (9:16).

Before the plague of hail, Hashem commanded Moshe to add a few words of admonishment when he warned Pharaoh about the impending plague. "*For I could have now sent out My hand and smitten you along with the [animals during the plague of] pestilence and you would have been wiped out from the earth. However, it is for this reason that I have kept you alive; so that you may behold My strength and recount [the greatness of] My Name throughout the land*" (9:15-16).

Chazal relate (*Shemos Rabbah* 7:4) that Hashem was asked why wicked people were created, and He answered that fruit trees were created to provide fruit, and non-fruit-bearing trees were created to provide wood for building and heat. Likewise, the good deeds of the righteous, who fulfill the Torah, provide the world with "fruit." The wicked do not provide the world with fruit, but they serve another important purpose: They are agents through whom Hashem's glory is revealed to the world.

> "Both the righteous and the wicked reveal Hashem's glory to the world. The righteous accomplish this actively, through their good deeds, while the wicked accomplish it passively, through the punishments meted out to them."

Both the righteous and the wicked reveal Hashem's glory to the world. The righteous accomplish this actively, through their good deeds, while the wicked accomplish it passively, through the punishments meted out to them. A person is given numerous tools — his body, his house, his money, and so on — to serve Hashem and glorify His Name. If he uses these tools toward this end, then he fulfills his purpose in life. If he does not, then he and everything he owns become a tool in the hands of Hashem to reveal the glory of Heaven. This is why Pharaoh was kept alive: "To behold My strength and recount [the greatness of My Name] throughout the land."

The Third Reich, which was meant to last a thousand years, endured for a mere eleven years, in fulfillment of the verse "When the wicked bloom like grass and all the doers of iniquity blossom, it is to destroy them forever" (*Tehillim* 92:8). In contrast, "the righteous will flourish like a date palm and will grow tall like a cedar … to show that the ways of Hashem are just" (ibid. 92:13-16). Both the destruction of the wicked and the flourishing of the righteous demonstrate that Hashem's ways are just.

The decision to utilize the tools at our disposal in the service of Hashem or for the opposite purpose is one that we make on a continual basis. Should I help my neighbor or read the newspaper instead? Should I give money to *tzedakah* or spend it on trivial things? Every situation gives us an opportunity to actively glorify Hashem's Name, and fulfill the purpose for which we were placed here on earth.

(*Shiurei Chumash, Parashas Va'eira* 9:16)

פרשת בא

Parashas Bo

AVOIDING SYSTEM FAILURE

כִּי כָּל־אֹכֵל מַחְמֶצֶת וְנִכְרְתָה הַנֶּפֶשׁ הַהִוא מֵעֲדַת יִשְׂרָאֵל

For anyone who eats leavening — that soul shall be cut off from the Jewish nation (12:19).

While every transgression carries some sort of repercussion, some are more severe than others. Regarding one who eats *chametz* on Pesach, the Torah tells us, "Seven days sourdough shall not be found in your homes, for anyone who eats leavening — that soul shall be cut off from the Jewish nation" (12:19). One who is guilty of this transgression has severed his spiritual connection to *Bnei Yisrael*.

Physical existence is dependent on a specific set of conditions. A person cannot survive if he deprives himself of food, drink, or sleep. Similarly, spiritual existence is only possible when certain conditions — the mitzvos — are present. One who fails to put on *tefillin* or sit in a *succah* has not merely lost an invaluable opportunity; he has deprived himself of an integral part of his spiritual makeup. Every mitzvah can be compared to a limb in the spiritual body, and the lack of a limb is a handicap that inhibits proper spiritual existence.

Refraining from eating *chametz* on Pesach is so vital that one who fails to do so has caused a "system failure." He has not properly provided for his spiritual body, and in its present state it can no longer survive. In the words of the Torah, he has been cut off from *Bnei Yisrael*.

> "While some mitzvos are critical, all mitzvos are necessary, and must be performed in order to ensure a healthy spiritual existence."

Many people have predispositions to certain mitzvos. Some love learning Torah, while others enjoy performing *chessed*. For some, Shabbos is in their blood, while others connect with mitzvos performed during the Yamim Tovim. However, while some mitzvos are critical, all mitzvos are necessary, and must be performed in order to ensure a healthy spiritual existence. The same applies to refraining from transgressions. Some *aveiros* are easier to abstain from than others, but the effort must be made to refrain from them all. Performance of all the mitzvos of the Torah is the key to spiritual well-being.

(*Shiurei Chumash, Parashas Bo* 12:19)

✻ ✻ ✻

DIFFICULT BEGINNINGS

וַיֵּלְכוּ וַיַּעֲשׂוּ בְּנֵי יִשְׂרָאֵל כַּאֲשֶׁר צִוָּה ה' אֶת־מֹשֶׁה וְאַהֲרֹן

And Bnei Yisrael went and did as Hashem commanded Moshe and Aharon (12:28).

Immediately after Moshe instructed *Bnei Yisrael* regarding the *Korban Pesach*, the Torah tells us, "And *Bnei Yisrael* went and did as Hashem commanded Moshe and Aharon" (12:28). This communication took place on Rosh Chodesh Nissan, two weeks before the

Korban Pesach was to be slaughtered. If so, how could they have performed the mitzvah immediately upon being instructed? Rashi explains that although *Bnei Yisrael* had not yet actually performed the mitzvah, since they had accepted upon themselves to do so, the Torah considered it as if the mitzvah had already been completed. A firm decision to comply is akin to the actual performance of the commandment.

Therefore, *Chazal* tell us (*Berachos* 6a) that a person who resolved to perform a mitzvah but was unable to bring his intentions to fruition, due to circumstances beyond his control, is considered to have fulfilled the mitzvah. This demonstrates the significance of *kabbalah* — accepting upon oneself to comply with Hashem's will.

Elsewhere, we find another aspect of the magnitude of *kabbalah*. Prior to *Matan Torah* Hashem told *Bnei Yisrael*, "And now, if you will surely listen to My voice and guard My covenant, you will be for Me a treasure among all the nations" (19:5). Rashi, troubled by the seemingly superfluous introduction "And now," explains that Hashem was conveying to *Bnei Yisrael* that if *now* they overcome the difficulties inherent in accepting the Torah, it will be pleasant for them from now on, since all beginnings are difficult.

Entering the world of Torah study constitutes a transition from a materialistic world to a spiritual one, and that transition is not always smooth. Many people find that just when they open a *sefer* to learn, they are inundated by a barrage of mental distractions: past memories, future worries, current obligations, and all sorts of fantasies. The *yetzer hara* succeeds in convincing us that concentrating on these thoughts and fantasies is more important and pleasurable than focusing on the *divrei Torah* before us.

> "Many people find that just when they open a sefer to learn, they are inundated by a barrage of mental distractions."

How does one combat these unwelcome thoughts? He must make an ironclad *kabbalah* to devote himself to learning Torah. Once he does that, he will begin to experience the true pleasure associated with Torah learning and a Torah life.

Often, when a person encounters difficulties in his *avodas Hashem*, he becomes discouraged and gives up. If he would be cognizant of *Chazal*'s axiom that all beginnings are difficult, he would be able to muster the commitment necessary to persevere, and would subsequently experience smooth (and pleasurable) sailing.
(*Shiurei Chumash, Parashas Bo* 12:28; *Alei Shur,* Vol. I, p. 23)

✻ ✻ ✻

HOLINESS: THE REWARD FOR FAITH

וְגַם־צֵדָה לֹא־עָשׂוּ לָהֶם
Nor had they made provisions for themselves (12:39).

The Torah tells us that *Bnei Yisrael* left Mitzrayim in a hurry and did not even prepare any provisions for the way. Rashi (12:39) comments that from here we see *Bnei Yisrael*'s greatness; they followed Hashem into the wilderness without an inkling as to how they would procure food for themselves. Referring to this display of loyalty, Hashem declared (*Yirmiyahu* 2:2-3), "I recalled for you the kindness of your youth, the love of your nuptials, your following Me into the desert, into an unsown land." Rashi adds that the reward for this blind faith is mentioned in the following *passuk*: "Yisrael is holy to Hashem."

It seems from the *passuk* that because *Bnei Yisrael* had *bitachon* they were rewarded with *kedushah*. We tend to think that *bitachon* and *kedushah* are two unrelated concepts. However, the *navi* is enlightening us to the fact that these two *middos* are interdependent, and *Bnei Yisrael* merited becoming holy due to their complete *bitachon* in Hashem.

We can explain the connection between *bitachon* and *kedushah* as follows. *Kedushah* means to be devoted in an absolute manner. The Torah refers to one who is dedicated entirely to Hashem as a *kadosh*, while a man who is devoted to promiscuous activity is referred to as a *kadeish* (*Devarim* 23:18). In a similar vein, Hashem is described as *Kadosh* because He is totally set apart from humanity. We are therefore commanded (*Vayikra* 19:2), "And you shall be holy (*kedoshim*) because I am Holy (*Kadosh*)." Just as Hashem is completely set apart, *Bnei Yisrael* should set themselves apart from the rest of mankind and be absolutely dedicated to Hashem.

How does one reach this level of *kedushah*? Through *bitachon*. A person who has absolute faith in Hashem devotes himself to Him entirely and does not place his trust in any human being. *Bnei Yisrael*, with their *bitachon*, followed Hashem blindly into the wilderness and showed that they were utterly devoted to Him. This complete devotion raised them to the level of *kedoshim*.

Kedushah is not as difficult to attain as one might think. A few minutes a day spent studying *Shaar HaBitachon* in the *Sefer Chovos HaLevavos* can contribute greatly not only to one's *menuchas hanefesh*, but also to one's level of *kedushah*.

(Shiurei Chumash, Parashas Bo 12:39)

> "Just as Hashem is completely set apart, Bnei Yisrael should set themselves apart from the rest of mankind and be absolutely dedicated to Hashem."

❋ ❋ ❋

WHO IS THE WICKED SON?

וְהָיָה כִּי־יִשְׁאָלְךָ בִנְךָ מָחָר לֵאמֹר מַה־זֹּאת וְאָמַרְתָּ אֵלָיו בְּחֹזֶק יָד הוֹצִיאָנוּ ה׳ מִמִּצְרַיִם מִבֵּית עֲבָדִים

And when your son will ask you tomorrow, saying, "What is this?" and you will answer him, "It was with a mighty hand that Hashem took us out of Egypt, from the house of bondage" (13:14).

Rashi notes that in four different places the Torah mentions the son's question with regard to the Exodus. He explains that the Torah is referring to four different personalities: the wise son, the wicked son, the simple son, and the one who does not even know how to ask.

If the Torah deemed it imperative to write four separate *pesukim* to parallel the four different sons, that implies that every child must be spoken to in a language that he can understand. Even the wicked son must be answered with a response that is tailored to his personality.

The wickedness of this son lies in the way he phrases his question regarding the *Korban Pesach*: "What is this service for *you*?" The *Haggadah* explains that he is emphasizing "for *you*" — and not for *him*. He inquires, but does not identify with the topic of his question. This is a "wickedness" that many of us are guilty of: We learn Torah, but do not necessarily allow its lessons to impact our personal lives. With regard to the spies who were sent to Eretz Yisrael and returned with a derogatory report, *Chazal* tell us, "These *wicked* men saw [what happened to Miriam, who spoke derogatorily about Moshe] and did not derive *mussar* from it" (*Bamidbar* 13:2; Rashi). *Mussar* is the ability to integrate the lessons we learn into our day-to-day lives. A person who does not derive *mussar* from what he learns — no matter how great his stature — is considered by *Chazal* to be wicked in this respect.

> "A person who does not derive mussar from what he learns — no matter how great his stature — is considered by Chazal to be wicked in this respect."

The study of *mussar* is not simply opening a *Mesilas Yesharim* and perusing what is written therein. When Miriam was afflicted with *tzaraas*, surely the entire nation studied *hilchos shemiras halashon*. The problem was that their learning did not impact the way they acted, as evidenced by the subsequent sin of the *meraglim*. True study of *mussar* involves taking a line of the *Mesilas Yesharim*, measuring what it says against our own personality, and, in the event that the two do not match up, working to change ourselves to meet the *Mesilas Yesharim*'s standard.

(*Shiurei Chumash, Parashas Bo* 13:14)

❊ ❊ ❊

THE POWER OF "AMEN"

"*All the gates of Gan Eden are opened for he who answers amen with all his might … What is amen? R' Chanina says, ['Amen' is an acronym for] **A**il **M**elech **N**e'eman*" (*Shabbos* 119b).

Chazal often unveil remarkable and lofty concepts that are encapsulated in a small action. One of these is the power of the word *amen*, which is an affirmation of our faith in Hashem. By answering *amen* — a small act of *emunah* — a person succeeds in unlocking *all* the gates of Gan Eden.

Chazal's choice of words was not coincidental. They specifically state, "The gates of Gan Eden are opened," as opposed to the more familiar, "He is guaranteed a portion in the World to Come." Gan Eden was home to Adam HaRishon before he sinned, a place where the forces of evil had not yet separated man from his Creator. After Adam's sin, Hashem became "hidden" behind the veil of nature, and Adam could no longer live in Gan Eden, the place where Hashem's presence was openly manifest. It became possible to perceive the world as a self-contained system, to look at all of history as a chain of random occurrences, and to view all personal successes as a direct outcome of the actions that preceded them. If one's actions did not engender the desired results, his failure could be blamed on bad luck and a twist of fate. But each time a person entertains such thoughts, he unwittingly erects a barrier between himself and Hashem.

Emunah is the tool that allows one to break down that barrier and thereby perceive Hashem despite His being hidden by the facade of nature. A person who answers *amen* with all of his might — with complete belief in Hashem — has unlocked the gates of Gan Eden. He himself stands in a world of obscurity, but he is nevertheless connected to a world of clarity. His *emunah* allows him to see past "Mother Nature" to the true "Master of Ceremonies." He recognizes every occurrence in history as a manifestation of Hashem's Omnipotent control, and acknowledges that

> "*Emunah allows one to see past "Mother Nature" to the true "Master of Ceremonies."*"

his successes are not the result of his own blood, sweat, and tears, but rather the product of Hashem's guiding hand. In essence, he has built for himself a spiritual oasis within this very materialistic world.

Ramban (13:16) writes that *emunah* is the purpose of the entire Creation and the foundation of every mitzvah: *"Therefore [Chazal] said, 'One should be careful with a simple mitzvah just as he would with a difficult mitzvah,' because all mitzvos are extremely precious, since through them a person acknowledges his Creator. The intention of all the mitzvos is that we should believe in Hashem and acknowledge that He is our Creator, and this is the purpose of the Creation. For we have no other reason in the original Creation, and Hashem has no interest in this world, other than that a person know his God and acknowledge that He is his Creator …"*

A person who is missing *emunah* in his life is missing the essence of life. Every person should know this Ramban by heart, for it is one of the basic foundations of Judaism.

(*Alei Shur,* Vol. I, pp. 98-99)

פרשת בשלח
Parashas Beshalach

OUR NATIONAL PROFESSION

וַיְהִי בְּשַׁלַּח פַּרְעֹה...
It happened when Pharaoh sent out ... (13:17).

If we had to find a theme for *Parashas Beshalach*, it would be the importance and power of *tefillah*. The *parashah* begins with *Bnei Yisrael*'s leaving Mitzrayim. When the Egyptians realized that *Bnei Yisrael* had no intention of returning, they set out in hot pursuit of their former slaves. The Jewish people were terrified, "and *Bnei Yisrael* cried out to Hashem" (14:10). After all *Bnei Yisrael* had gone through, why did Hashem put them in such a frightening situation?

The Midrash (*Shemos Rabbah* 21:5) answers this question: "Hashem desired to hear their *tefillos*. Rabbi Yehoshua ben Levi said that this can be compared to a king who was traveling and heard a princess call out to him, 'Save me from these bandits!' The king saved her, and some time later he asked for her hand in marriage. He desired to hear her voice, but she would not comply.

"What did the king do? He had bandits attack her once again so she would cry out. When the bandits attacked her she began to cry out to the king. The king responded, 'This is exactly what I wanted — to hear your voice!'

"Similarly, when *Bnei Yisrael* were subjugated in Mitzrayim, they began lifting their eyes and calling out to Hashem. Hashem saved them with a strong hand, and He desired to hear their voice once again, but *Bnei Yisrael* did not comply. What did Hashem do? He had Pharaoh chase after them and they immediately called out to Him. To which Hashem said, 'This is exactly what I wished to hear!'"

Despite the fact that Hashem has no needs, He "desires" to hear our voice. If we comply, He will not have to resort to extreme tactics to get us to call out to Him.

Rashi (14:19) states that when *Bnei Yisrael* were put through this terrifying ordeal, "they seized the profession of their forefathers" and began to *daven*. *Chazal* choose to describe *tefillah* as a "profession" because a person's job becomes his second nature. If a doctor is awakened in the middle of the night to perform surgery, he will get up and operate without any preparation. Similarly, when *Bnei Yisrael* were threatened by Pharaoh's army, they immediately began to *daven*. They did not need any preparation, and they did not look for other ways out of their predicament; they simply began doing what came naturally to them.

"What did these secular Israelis know about Hashem? Not much. But all Jews have an innate attachment to tefillah."

One of Rav Wolbe's students was on a boat with several other Israeli soldiers, most of them secular, when the boat was hit by a torpedo and started to sink. The soldiers began to call out, "Hashem, help us!" What did these secular Israelis know about Hashem? Not much. But all Jews have an innate attachment to *tefillah*.

At the end of the *parashah*, we learn that *Bnei Yisrael* were attacked by Amalek, and Moshe ascended the mountain and raised his hands in prayer. "When Moshe raised his hand *Bnei Yisrael* were stronger, and when he lowered his hand Amalek was stronger" (17:11). Rashi cites the *mishnah* (*Rosh Hashanah* 29a), which asks how Moshe's hands could be the deciding factor in the war. The *mishnah* explains that when his hands were raised, *Bnei Yisrael* would look heavenward and subjugate their hearts to Hashem, and He would assist them. Their *tefillos* were heard, and the effectiveness of those *tefillos* was immediately reflected in the battlefield.

Hashem desires our *tefillos*. Turning to Him is second nature to us, and the response is often (although not always) immediate. When Moshe asked Hashem for a Name (i.e., a sign) to convey to *Bnei Yisrael*, Hashem responded that they need no other sign than the reality that people call out in prayer and Hashem answers them (see Ramban to 3:13). Do we need any other incentive to turn to Hashem in whatever situation we find ourselves?

(*Shiurei Chumash, Parashas Beshalach* 14:10, 17:11)

❊ ❊ ❊

THE SNAKE WITHIN US

וַיֵּהָפֵךְ לְבַב פַּרְעֹה וַעֲבָדָיו

And the heart of Pharaoh and his servants became transformed (14:5).

The beginning of *Parashas Beshalach* describes how, after *Bnei Yisrael* were drive out of Egypt, the Egyptians had a change of heart and set out in pursuit of their former slaves. The Torah tells us that Pharaoh took "six hundred elite chariots and all the [rest of the] chariots of Egypt" and pursued *Bnei Yisrael* (14:7).

Where did the Egyptians obtain the horses for these chariots? They could not have used their own horses, since their animals had died in the plagues of pestilence and hail. Nor could they have used Jewish-owned animals, since *Bnei Yisrael* took all of their livestock along with them when they left Egypt. Rashi, citing the Midrash, answers that the animals belonged to the God-fearing Egyptians who had gathered their animals into their houses when they were warned about the impending plague of hail. These animals survived the hail, and were later mobilized to chase after *Bnei Yisrael*. Regarding this incident Rabbi Shimon commented, "Kill [even] the upright among the Egyptians; smash the head of [even] the best snake."

Despite the fact that these Egyptians had demonstrated their fear of God by gathering in their animals, they remained inherently deficient in *yiras Shamayim*. In this way, the Egyptians were similar to a snake: Although it is possible to tame a snake and train it to act docile, the Mishnah (*Bava Kamma* 1:4) tells us that a snake is always considered a *mu'ad* — an animal that is intrinsically dangerous.

Every person is created with positive and negative *middos*. Our *avodah* is to rectify our negative traits so that they should not be reflected in our actions. However, even if we succeed in doing so, we have not completely uprooted the negative trait; we have merely suppressed it or channeled it toward a positive outlet. We must always be on guard to ensure that these negative *middos* do not rear their ugly heads at a later point.

> *"If we would have the ability to entirely uproot our negative middos, we would upset the balance and lose our bechirah."*

Why cannot we rid ourselves entirely of our negative traits? *Bechirah* requires that there always be a negative force to counteract the positive. If we would have the ability to entirely uproot our negative *middos*, we would upset this balance and lose our *bechirah*. Because the roots of these *middos* remain, we are constantly required to exercise our *bechirah* by controlling our *middos*.

If people would pay more attention, they would notice that they have specific negative *middos* that surface regularly. It is these *middos* that are their battleground. The *middos* cannot be uprooted entirely, but if an effort is made, they can be restrained or even channeled positively.

(*Shiurei Chumash, Parashas Beshalach* 14:7; *Alei Shur,* Vol. I, p. 145)

❊ ❊ ❊

THE SPIRITUAL THERMOS

אָז יָשִׁיר־מֹשֶׁה וּבְנֵי יִשְׂרָאֵל

Then Moshe and Bnei Yisrael chose to sing (15:1).

The climax of the splitting of the Yam Suf occurred when *Bnei Yisrael* sang "*Az Yashir.*" There is an interesting theme found through the entire song. Toward the beginning of the song *Bnei Yisrael* proclaimed (15:2), "*Zeh Keli v'anveihu*" — This is my God and I will build a *Beis HaMikdash* for Him. In the middle of the song they stated (v. 13), "*Neihalta b'azcha el nevei kadshecha*" — With Your strength You led them to Your *Beis HaMikdash*. In conclusion they sang (v. 17), "*Mikdash Hashem konenu yadecha*" — Your hands formed Your *Beis HaMikdash*.

What is the correlation between the splitting of the Yam Suf and the *Beis HaMikdash*? Why, after experiencing such a miracle, did *Bnei Yisrael* dedicate their entire song of praise to the *Beis HaMikdash*?

Rav Wolbe was frequently asked, "How can I keep feelings of spiritual uplift from dying out?" He would answer that this "high" will inevitably die out by itself; these feelings are intangible, and it is impossible to hold onto them for extended periods. However, by transforming these feelings into action and giving them a practical expression, we can preserve our spiritual "highs," because we will always retain the ability to hold onto the action it engendered.

After experiencing a Divine revelation of remarkable proportions, where a simple maidservant perceived Hashem with more clarity than the greatest future prophets, *Bnei Yisrael* felt they needed a way to preserve their newfound spiritual level (*Mechilta, Parashas Beshalach*). Building a *Beis HaMikdash* — the ultimate House of Hashem — would help them maintain this momentum and integrate it into their daily lives. Therefore, their song revolved around the practical application of their miraculous experience.

This insight also sheds light on the incident immediately following *Krias Yam Suf*. After walking for three days in a parched desert, *Bnei Yisrael* complained to Moshe (15:24), "What should we drink?" Regarding the location of their request, the Torah writes (v.

25), "There He gave the nation portions of the Torah and there He tested them."

Rashi explains that *Bnei Yisrael* were tested to see if they would respectfully request that Moshe Rabbeinu *daven* for them. Would they ask in a fashion befitting people on their level? They failed this test, and instead of making a proper request, they complained.

In essence, this was a test to see if they had truly integrated the spiritual level they so much desired into their daily lives. It might very well be that they failed the test because they had not yet transformed their feelings into actions. Therefore, Hashem gave them portions of the Torah to toil in, since toiling in Torah is the ultimate practical application for lofty feelings.

> "The Torah was given to us to serve as a 'thermos': by studying its precepts, we are able to keep the revelation experienced at Har Sinai warm."

On Pesach we say in the *Haggadah*, "Had Hashem brought us to Har Sinai and not given us the Torah, it would have been enough." What would we have gained by standing at Har Sinai without receiving the Torah? The answer is that the revelation at Har Sinai constituted the pinnacle of spirituality for the Jewish people, since there they became intimately familiar with Hashem. What, then, was the purpose of receiving the Torah? The Torah was given to us to serve as a "thermos": by studying its precepts, we are able to keep the revelation experienced at Har Sinai warm.

The "thermos" that keeps Har Sinai warm is not limited to Torah study. Even great Torah leaders would make small resolutions such as concentrating while saying a specific *Amen* or *Amen, Yehei Shmeih Rabbah*. Bearing this in mind, we, too, can succeed in keeping the flame ignited by Yom Kippur, *Shovavim*, or a *mussar sefer* from flickering and going out.

(*Shiurei Chumash, Parashas Beshalach* 15:2,25)

❋ ❋ ❋

SECURITY FENCE

עַד־אָנָה מֵאַנְתֶּם לִשְׁמֹר מִצְוֹתַי וְתוֹרֹתָי

How long will you refuse to observe My commandments and My teachings? (16:28).

On the first Friday after Hashem gave *Bnei Yisrael* the *mann*, they noticed that everyone had gathered twice as much as they had gathered on previous days. When they asked the reason for this, Moshe informed them that *mann* would not fall on Shabbos and therefore they received a double portion on Friday. Nevertheless, on Shabbos morning there were those who left their tents to gather *mann*. In response to this incident, Hashem told Moshe, "Until when will you [plural form] refrain from performing My commandments and Torah? See that Hashem has given you the Shabbos, [and] therefore on Friday He gives you a double portion of bread — every man should stay put; no man should leave his place on the seventh day" (16:28-29).

Rashi explains that despite the fact that Moshe was in no way involved in collecting *mann* on Shabbos, he was blamed along with the evildoers: "As people say, 'The cabbage is destroyed along with the weeds' — i.e., the righteous are shamed along with the wicked." Why do the righteous have to suffer because of the sins of the wicked?

> *"If the majority fastidiously refrains from a given aveirah, they create a 'security fence' that does not allow others to be derelict in this area."*

When the wicked sin, the righteous are held accountable to a certain extent, for *Chazal* tell us that all Jews are responsible for one another. The entire nation is interconnected, and each person has the ability to prevent others from sinning. If the majority fastidiously refrains from a given *aveirah*, they create a "security fence" that does not allow others to be derelict in this area. Therefore, a breach by one person demands that everyone perform some self-introspection.

A case in point is the story of Achan (*Yehoshua* Ch. 7). After conquering Yericho, the Jewish people consecrated all of the items found inside the city, but Achan secretly appropriated a handful of valuables from the booty. Hashem told Yehoshua, "Yisrael sinned; they transgressed the covenant that I commanded them; they also took from the consecrated items; and they have also stolen, and also denied it, and also placed it in their utensils." A simple reading of the *pesukim* would lead us to think that the majority of *Bnei Yisrael* had sinned terribly, when in reality it was a lone man who perpetrated the crime. Why, then, do the *pesukim* make it sound as if the whole nation was guilty? The answer is as we have explained: If a single person could commit such a crime, then the rest of *Bnei Yisrael* were also somewhat to blame.

Sometimes, when hearing about another Jew's egregious act, we think to ourselves, *How could he have done such a terrible thing?* Our reaction should be different, however. We should turn around the question and ask ourselves, "Where have *I* gone wrong in this area?"

(*Shiurei Chumash, Parashas Beshalach* 16:28)

❊ ❊ ❊

DO NOT SPEAK THAT WAY ABOUT MY CHILDREN

עֲבֹר לִפְנֵי הָעָם
Pass before the nation (17:5).

Toward the end of *Parashas Beshalach* the Torah describes *Bnei Yisrael*'s dire lack of water in the wilderness (17:3): "There the nation thirsted for water and they complained to Moshe, 'Why have you brought us out of Mitzrayim, to kill me, my children, and my animals through thirst?'" Consequently, Moshe turned to Hashem for help: "What should I do for this nation? A bit more and they will stone me!" Hashem instructed him to "pass in front of the nation" with his staff in hand and hit the rock, and water would pour forth. Rashi (17:5) tells us that Hashem responded, "Why have you falsely accused My children?" He then told Moshe specifically to "pass in front of the nation" to prove that *Bnei Yisrael* would not stone him.

Moshe certainly was not exaggerating. If he said that *Bnei Yisrael* were going to stone him, then he must have felt that they were enraged to the point where it would be only a matter of time before they would kill their leader. Nevertheless, Hashem rebuked Moshe, "Why have you falsely accused My children?"

In a similar vein, the Midrash (*Mechilta, Parashas Bo*) contrasts the actions of three prophets: one defended the honor of the father while neglecting the honor of the son, one defended the honor of the son while neglecting the honor of the father, and one defended the honor of both the father and the son. Eliyahu defended the honor of Hashem (the Father) when he stated, "I have been zealous for the sake of Hashem." Yonah defended the honor of *Bnei Yisrael* (the son) when he ran away to avoid delivering the prophecy to the city of Nineveh lest their *teshuvah* constitute an indictment against *Bnei Yisrael*, who had repeatedly failed to do *teshuvah* despite hearing numerous prophecies. As a result, both of them were punished, and Hashem terminated their role as *neviim* to *Klal Yisrael*. In contrast, Yirmiyahu defended both Hashem and *Bnei Yisrael* when he declared, "*We* have sinned and rebelled, and *You* have not forgiven us." He was duly rewarded by having his *nevuah* doubled. Once again we see how careful one must be when speaking not only about Hashem Himself, but about his children as well.

> *"If neviim were taken to task for the way they spoke about Bnei Yisrael, how careful must we be when referring to any of our brethren."*

If *neviim* were taken to task for the way they spoke about *Bnei Yisrael*, how careful must we be when referring to any of our brethren. They are not only our brothers; they are the children of the Creator. Even a derogatory word about a single Jew is inexcusable; all the more so when the subject of negative speech is an entire group in *Klal Yisrael*! On the positive side, words are powerful, and if used properly they can garner immense rewards — even to the extent of doubling a prophet's *nevuah*.

(*Shiurei Chumash, Parashas Beshalach* 17:5)

❃ ❃ ❃

THE CHALLENGE OF HONORING OTHERS

בְּחַר־לָנוּ אֲנָשִׁים
Choose men for us (17:9).

In preparation for war with Amalek, Moshe instructed his trusted disciple Yehoshua, "Choose men for *us*." Rashi comments that in the task of finding the proper recruits to fight the war, Moshe was equating Yehoshua with himself. *Chazal* deduce from this gesture that "The honor of your disciple should be as dear to you as your own" (*Avos* 4:15). Moreover, they state, "the honor of your colleague should be like the reverence for your teacher, and the reverence for your teacher should be like the reverence of Heaven."

Rav Yerucham Levovitz asks, Why must one elevate each individual to a level that is beyond what he rightfully deserves? Why should one honor a disciple as he would a colleague? He answers that it is extremely difficult to confer upon another person the honor he deserves. Therefore, if one strives to honor each person with the honor appropriate for someone greater, hopefully he will succeed in at least giving him his due honor.

Why is honoring others so difficult? The prohibitions against scorning others have definitive guidelines: One is not allowed to embarrass or deride another person, nor may he call him by an offensive nickname, and so forth. Giving honor, on the other hand, is a positive act that not only varies according to the beneficiary, but also lacks any specific rules. With the exception of a teacher, parent, and spouse, it is left to our discretion to decide how to honor the people with whom we come in contact, and that is extremely difficult.

Although the general way to train ourselves in any good quality is to take a specific act and work on perfecting it for a set amount of time, with regard to giving honor we must digress from this norm. Every person and every situation calls for a unique display of *kavod*, which should arise from the feelings of respect engendered by the encounter.

What makes giving honor even more difficult is that the closer we are to the other person, the harder it is to honor him properly.

Two friends who meet after a long interval will find it much easier to accord appropriate respect than two co-workers who meet on a daily basis — not to mention spouses who live in the same house for many years. To train ourselves to accord people their due honor, we should take some time each week to find a way to honor someone with whom we will come in contact.

Rav Yerucham says that the mitzvos between man and his fellow are no less important than the mitzvah of *esrog*, regarding which we are told (*Succah* 11b), "Beautify mitzvos before Him." When writing a note to a friend, for example, we should make sure that it is written clearly, on a nice piece of paper, and in a manner that will bring pleasure to the person reading it. An act like this takes the recipient into account and is not done merely to discharge an obligation. This is the key to giving proper *kavod*.

(*Alei Shur,* Vol. II, pp. 228-229)

> "*The mitzvos between man and his fellow are no less important than the mitzvah of esrog, regarding which we are told (Succah 11b), 'Beautify mitzvos before Him.'*"

פרשת יתרו

Parashas Yisro

PRELUDE TO TORAH

יִתְרוֹ
Yisro (18:1).

Why is *Parashas Yisro* named after a gentile? Would not it have been more appropriate to name the *parashah* that describes *Matan Torah* after Moshe Rabbeinu, who brought the Torah down from the Heavens? Moreover, according to those who are of the opinion that Yisro arrived only after the giving of the Torah, why did the Torah deem it appropriate to reverse the chronological order of events and relate the story of Yisro's arrival before the account of *Matan Torah*?

The Torah wanted to give an introduction to *Matan Torah*, and the stories about Yisro constitute that introduction. What is it that we are supposed to glean from what we know about Yisro?

Picture for a moment a person reading in a newspaper that somewhere in the Middle East a "splitting of the sea" occurred. He would likely continue drinking his coffee and shrug off the news with, "A nice story, what else is going on?" However, as the Torah tells us (18:1), "Yisro heard" and he immediately came to find out what was happening. This is the first concept that prefaces the receiving of the Torah: the ability to hear.

The ability to *truly* hear is no simple feat. When Hashem told Shlomo HaMelech that He would grant him a wish, he requested, "Give Your servant a heart that hears (*lev shomeia*)" (*Melachim I* 3:9). We tend to think that we hear solely with our ears, but Shlomo HaMelech enlightened us that we must also hear with our hearts. If what we hear merely enters our ears, it might go into one ear and straight out the other. However, if we allow what we hear to sink into our hearts, it will achieve its intended effect.

Subsequently we are informed that Yisro left his prestigious position and headed out to the desert in search of *Bnei Yisrael*. Only someone who sincerely seeks the truth has what it takes to leave everything behind in pursuit of this goal. In a similar vein, Rashi tells us that Yisro had worshipped every idol in the entire world before he recognized his Creator. It was his drive for truth, coupled with a critical assessment of his findings, that propelled him to join *Bnei Yisrael* in the desert. Had he set off in search of the truth without the capability to properly assess what he found, he might easily have fallen for the first idol or religion that he encountered.

> "Only someone who sincerely seeks the truth has what it takes to leave everything behind in pursuit of this goal."

The Torah places the story of Yisro before *Matan Torah*, prompting us to deduce that these two traits are a necessary prelude to Torah. In order to receive the Torah, one needs to hear with his heart, not only his ears. And an astute person in pursuit of the truth will undoubtedly arrive at the truth.

An intelligent newcomer to Yeshivas Be'er Yaakov could not understand why time was set aside to review the discourses that Rav Wolbe delivered. Hadn't they just heard the discourse a few minutes earlier? However, after he spent time reviewing the material presented, he realized that although he had listened to the discourse, he had not heard — inculcated — what was said.

If we take a few minutes to review and scrutinize a Torah or *mussar* thought that we recently heard, it could make an indelible impression on us — one that might otherwise have been lost on us.

(*Shiurei Chumash, Parashas Yisro* 18:1)

❈ ❈ ❈

MEASURE FOR MEASURE: BUILT INTO THE MECHANICS OF THE WORLD

וַיִּשְׁמַע יִתְרוֹ כֹהֵן מִדְיָן חֹתֵן מֹשֶׁה אֵת כָּל־אֲשֶׁר עָשָׂה אֱלֹקִים
לְמֹשֶׁה וּלְיִשְׂרָאֵל עַמּוֹ כִּי־הוֹצִיא ה׳ אֶת־יִשְׂרָאֵל מִמִּצְרָיִם

Yisro, the priest of Midyan, the father-in-law of Moshe, heard everything that Hashem had done for Moshe and Bnei Yisrael; how He redeemed them from Mitzrayim (18:1).

Rashi (ibid.) lists the numerous miracles that prompted Yisro to leave his prestigious position in Midyan and travel out to the desert to meet the Jewish people: *Krias Yam Suf*, the war against Amalek, the daily *mann* that fell from Heaven, and the rock that provided drinking water.

However, from a conversation that took place after Yisro met Moshe, it seems that there was yet another impetus for his conversion to Judaism. Yisro exclaimed, "Now I know that Hashem is greater than all other gods, *for their scheming turned against them*" (18:11). Rashi, citing the Targum, explains that Yisro was awed by the fact that the Egyptians schemed to destroy the Jewish people by drowning their sons in water, and they themselves ended up drowning in water. This phenomenon clinched Yisro's decision to convert. What was so unique about this incident that it succeeded in convincing Yisro in a way that the other miracles had not?

The drowning of the Egyptians symbolized exact judgment, and this was the first time that Yisro encountered the attribute of *middah k'neged middah*. For him, this was an altogether new level of

Hashgachah Pratis, and it affected him in a way that the other miracles had not.

The concept of *middah k'neged middah* has been manifest throughout the generations. The *mishnah* (*Sotah* 9a) enumerates a number of punishments and rewards mentioned in *Tanach,* and shows how each one was meted out measure for measure. Additionally, the Gemara (*Berachos* 5a) tells us that one who is suffering should analyze his actions to try to ascertain the cause of his suffering. He should be able to deduce from his punishment exactly where he was negligent in his *avodas Hashem.* For example, if his foot hurts, perhaps that is an indication that he went to a place he should have avoided.

In 1844 there was an assembly of Reform Jews in Germany. They abolished many of the mitzvos, in effect creating for themselves a "new Torah." (The Malbim, in his introduction to *Sefer Vayikra,* writes that this gathering was the impetus for his writing a commentary on *Tanach.*) When Rav Yisrael Salanter heard about this gathering he declared, "They made a new '*Shulchan Aruch*' and permitted marriage to a non-Jew; there will come a time when the gentiles will make a new '*Shulchan Aruch*' and make marriage to a Jew a transgression punishable by death." Ninety years later, right there in Germany, the Nuremberg Laws were instituted, making it a capital offense for a Jew to live with a gentile. *Middah k'neged middah* is built into the mechanics of the world, which enables great people to foresee what will happen in the future.

> "Hashem is constantly sending us messages, and these messages are specifically tailored to their recipients."

Hashem is constantly sending us messages, and these messages are specifically tailored to their recipients. Of course, we might not always be able to figure out what Hashem wants from us. However, if we can identify a related issue that needs to be rectified, then even if we did not fully understand Hashem's intention, we have successfully taken His message to heart.

(*Shiurei Chumash, Parashas Yisro* 18:11)

❈ ❈ ❈

BEGINNINGS COUNT

וַיִּסְעוּ מֵרְפִידִים וַיָּבֹאוּ מִדְבַּר סִינַי
They traveled from Refidim and they arrived at Midbar Sinai (19:2).

When *Bnei Yisrael* were on their way to *Kabbalas HaTorah*, the Torah tells us, "They traveled from Refidim and they arrived at Midbar Sinai." Rashi comments that the juxtaposition of these two places teaches us that just as their arrival in Midbar Sinai was accompanied by *teshuvah*, so, too, their departure from Refidim was accompanied by *teshuvah*.

Why is it important for us to know that they left Refidim after doing *teshuvah*? The answer is that this act of *teshuvah* represents the concept of *hachanah* — preparation. It is of utmost importance that things start on the right foot.

The Torah places great emphasis on beginnings. Each year begins with Rosh Hashanah; each month begins with Rosh Chodesh; and immediately upon awakening at the beginning of each day we say *Modeh Ani*. It is the beginning that determines the success of whatever one is setting out to accomplish.

Chazal tell us (*Berachos* 6b), "Whoever designates a specific place for *davening* will be helped by Hashem just as He helped Avraham." Merely designating a *place* for prayer brings tremendous reward, even though the person has not yet begun to *daven*. The fact that he started off in the right direction already connects him to "*Elokei Avraham*" — Hashem Who protected Avraham.

> "When a person wants to strengthen his service of Hashem in any area, the first thing he must do is to bolster his first step."

When a person wants to strengthen his service of Hashem in any area, the first thing he must do is to bolster his first step. For example, if he thinks about his upcoming *tefillah* while on his way to shul in the morning instead of focusing on other thoughts, his *tefillah* will be greatly enhanced. Similarly, it was imperative that *Bnei Yisrael*'s first step, their departure from Refidim, be a preparation for *Kabbalas HaTorah*.

Since our success in mitzvos is directly linked to the preparation preceding them, we find many mitzvos that require preparation. Thirty days before each Yom Tov we begin studying the laws pertaining to that particular festival. The month of Elul prepares us for Rosh Hashanah; the *Aseres Yemei Teshuvah* prepare us for Yom Kippur; and the days of *Sefiras HaOmer* are a preparation for *Kabbalas HaTorah*.

Even negative commandments require preparation. *Chazal* tell us (*Kiddushin* 30b) that if the *yetzer hara* is hindering one's spiritual growth, he should "drag him to the *beis midrash*." Rav Yisrael Salanter explains that one should drag him to the *yetzer hara's* own *beis midrash* — i.e., the laws pertaining to that particular area (*Iggeres HaMussar*). If a person feels he is lax in guarding his tongue or not meticulous with regard to the laws pertaining to Shabbos or money matters, the way to combat these laxities is through studying the laws pertinent to those very areas. This is the preparation required when dealing with negative commandments. The more one involves himself in these laws, the more successful he will be in combating his *yetzer hara*.

(*Shiurei Chumash, Parashas Yisro* 19:2; *Alei Shur,* Vol. I, pp. 213-215)

❊ ❊ ❊

ELEVATED AND PRESTIGIOUS

וְאַתֶּם תִּהְיוּ־לִי מַמְלֶכֶת כֹּהֲנִים וְגוֹי קָדוֹשׁ

You will be unto Me a kingdom of kohanim and a holy nation" (19:6).

In preparation for *Matan Torah*, Hashem tells *Bnei Yisrael*, "If you listen to My voice and you guard My covenant …You will be unto Me a kingdom of *kohanim* and a holy nation" (19:5-6). Rashi tells us that *kohanim* in this context does not refer to priests but rather to dignitaries. By accepting the Torah, *Bnei Yisrael* would attain a loftier stature. Likewise, after *Matan Torah*, when *Bnei Yisrael* begged Moshe to act as an intermediary between Hashem and themselves, Moshe responded: "Do not fear, because it is for the purpose of exalting you (*l'nasos*) that Hashem has come" (20:17). Rashi explains that *l'nasos* is a term that describes elevation and greatness.

It appears from Rashi that the purpose of *maamad Har Sinai* was to elevate *Bnei Yisrael*. Could it be that the awesome revelations experienced at Har Sinai were intended solely to elevate them?

The Alter of Slabodka said, "Do not look to become better; rather, look to become higher." When one elevates himself to a higher standard, petty issues and obsessions automatically fall away. After experiencing the revelations of *Matan Torah*, *Bnei Yisrael* would gain an entirely new perception of themselves and of life in general.

We are an exalted nation, and each individual Jew is a dignitary. But this does not mean that we should act as if we are on a spiritual level we have not truly attained, for such behavior is doomed to failure from the start. This idea surfaces earlier in the *parashah*: "And also the *kohanim* who serve Hashem should prepare themselves" (19:22). Rashi explains that they should be prepared to stand in their designated places and not rush forward to get even closer to Hashem.

> "A person who gets caught up in the momentum of spiritual ascent and begins skipping rungs of the ladder will end up falling."

One of the hardest aspects of *avodas Hashem* is acknowledging where one stands and not biting off more than one can chew. A person who gets caught up in the momentum of spiritual ascent and begins skipping rungs of the ladder will end up falling.

Our true *avodah* is to recognize that regardless of our personal spiritual level, as the *mamleches kohanim* who received the Torah from Hashem, we are indeed elevated and prestigious. This perception will cause the insignificant issues in our lives to fade away, allowing us to focus on our real mission.

(*Shiurei Chumash, Parashas Yisro* 19:22, 20:17)

✽ ✽ ✽

EACH INDIVIDUAL'S DECISION

כֹּל אֲשֶׁר־דִּבֶּר ה׳ נַעֲשֶׂה
All that Hashem has spoken we shall do (19:8).

Before *Matan Torah*, Hashem asked Moshe to determine whether *Bnei Yisrael* wished to accept the Torah. Their immediate response is recorded in the Torah: "And the entire nation answered *as one* and they said, 'All that Hashem has spoken we shall do'" (19:8). The Mechilta explains the seemingly superfluous phrase "as one" as follows: These words were added so one should not think that all of *Bnei Yisrael* answered in a similar fashion due to *chanufah*, because they felt pressured to conform. The Torah informs us that the agreement to accept the Torah was an individual decision made by each and every member of the nation.

Often, when a poll is taken in a public forum, the majority feels one way, and the dissenting minority are too embarrassed to voice their opinion, so they concede to the majority. The Mechilta refers to such consent as an act of *chanufah*. The minority group does not truly agree, but they cannot bring themselves to disagree.

A group of people acting together create a powerful force. If a *tzibbur* learns Torah or does mitzvos together, that fosters an atmosphere that can strengthen each individual's Torah observance. It is easier to apply oneself when there are numerous people striving toward a similar goal. However, there is also a disadvantage to being part of a group, since a person might be deterred from developing his own individuality. He is concerned with what everyone else thinks and wonders how others regard him, which causes him to act or conform in ways that might not be appropriate for him.

"Often, when a poll is taken in a public forum, the majority feels one way, and the dissenting minority are too embarrassed to voice their opinion, so they concede to the majority."

There are certainly instances that require one to conform to the opinion of the majority. However, as in all other situations, one must be careful not to merely copy others. Rather, he should determine which course of action will best promote his individual growth, and act accordingly.

(*Shiurei Chumash, Parashas Yisro* 19:8)

פרשת משפטים
Parashas Mishpatim

HATE THE ACTIONS, NOT THE PERSON

כִּי תִקְנֶה עֶבֶד עִבְרִי
When you acquire a Jewish slave (21:2).

Parashas Mishpatim begins, "When you acquire a Jewish slave. ..." Rashi tells us that these *pesukim* are discussing a thief who was caught and does not have the means to pay back what he stole. He is therefore sold as a slave by *beis din*.

Rav Itzele Blazer (commonly referred to as Rav Itzaleh Peterburger) points out that in the Torah's view, even a thief has to be dealt with in a respectable manner. If he has the money to repay what he stole, he must make restitution, and no one will know what occurred. It is only when he does not have the ability to repay that he must be sold, and even then, it is not as a punishment but as a means of repaying his debt. This differs greatly from the way thieves are dealt with in contemporary society: As soon as someone is caught, his crime is publicized, which may ruin his life.

Later in the *parashah*, the Torah tells us, "If you should see the donkey of your enemy collapsing under its load . . . you shall surely help him" (23:5). The *Gemara* (*Bava Metzia* 21b) explains that "your enemy" refers to a person who has transgressed an *aveirah* that permits another Jew to hate him. Nevertheless, we are commanded to help the transgressor, "to subdue our *yetzer hara*." Tosafos (*Pesachim* 113b) ask the obvious question: If the Torah permits one to hate the sinner, why does the Torah command us to overcome our feelings and assist him? He explains that when a person hates someone, the other person will sense this and reciprocate the hatred, causing "a complete hatred between the two of them." In other words, the hatred will have turned into a personal quarrel not ordained by the Torah; therefore, he is commanded to overcome that hatred and help the transgressor.

We see how careful one must be when hating those who flagrantly transgress Torah prohibitions. One must despise the evil actions, but not the evil person. A Jew who sins remains a Jew and we must love him, even though we must hate his actions at the same time. Rav Yerucham Levovitz would say that only very great people have the ability to separate the actions from the perpetrator so they can hate only his actions.

> "A Jew who sins remains a Jew and we must love him, even though we must hate his actions at the same time."

We might look down upon certain people because they do not conform to our level of religious observance. But the Torah tells us that even a thief or a flagrant transgressor must be helped and loved, for it is only his actions that must be despised. Let us take a minute to think about someone who rubs us the wrong way, and undertake to do something positive for him, thus increasing our *ahavas Yisrael*.

(*Shiurei Chumash, Parashas Mishpatim* 21:2, 23:5)

❊ ❊ ❊

THE SLAVERY OF CONFORMITY

וְהִגִּישׁוֹ אֲדֹנָיו אֶל־הָאֱלֹהִים וְהִגִּישׁוֹ אֶל־הַדֶּלֶת אוֹ אֶל־הַמְּזוּזָה

And [he] shall bring him to the door or to the doorpost (21:6).

Rashi (21:6) at the beginning of *Parashas Mishpatim* quotes a fascinating statement of *Chazal*. The Torah mandates that a Jew who was sold into slavery must be set free after six years. If the slave chooses, he may remain enslaved for an extended period — until the *Yovel*. However, prior to this extension his master must bring him to *beis din*, stand him near the door or doorpost, and pierce his ear with an awl.

Why were the door and doorpost specifically chosen for this procedure? Rashi explains that they were witnesses in Mitzrayim when Hashem passed over *Bnei Yisrael*'s doors and doorposts and said, "*Bnei Yisrael* are servants solely to Me." Therefore, says Rashi, "He who acquires a different master for himself should have his ear pierced in their presence."

The essence of Torah observance is freedom from bondage to outside forces. Servitude to Hashem does not tolerate servitude to any other master, to the extent that a worker is allowed to renege in the middle of a workday (*Bava Metzia* 10a).

When Rav Wolbe would recite the *berachah* "... that You did not make me a slave," he would ask himself, "Am I truly not a slave?" A person who is obsessed with what others will think of him and tailors his actions to fit their ideals is the very embodiment of what slavery represents. He neglects what he knows is right in order to conform to social pressures.

> "A person who is obsessed with what others will think of him and tailors his actions to fit their ideals is the very embodiment of what slavery represents."

The Gemara (*Avodah Zarah* 18a) relates an intriguing incident. During the era following the destruction of the second *Beis*

HaMikdash, R' Chanina ben Tradyon defied orders and publicly gathered large groups of people in order to teach them Torah. Once, while talking to his *rebbi*, R' Yose ben Kisma, the latter berated him for endangering his life through his lectures. R' Chanina then proceeded to ask his *rebbi*, "Am I destined for the World to Come?"

"Did you ever do anything to merit such a portion?" R' Yose replied.

"Yes," R' Chanina answered. "I accidentally mixed up money set aside for *tzedakah* with some of my personal money, and I distributed the entire sum to the needy."

"If so," R' Yose said, "may my portion match your portion."

This entire dialogue is perplexing. Why was R' Chanina unsure whether he deserved a share in the World to Come? After all, what could be greater than risking one's life to ensure the perpetuation of Torah? Even more puzzling is R' Yose's question, "Did you ever do anything to merit such a portion?" What more could R' Chanina do than that which he had already done?

The explanation lies in the words of the *Chovos HaLevavos* (*Shaar Yichud Hamaaseh*), which explains that it is possible for all of a person's actions to be dictated by what others will think. No one can be certain that even his greatest actions are not tinged with thoughts of, *Now they'll think of me differently.* A person may buy an expensive *esrog*, *daven* a lengthy *Shemoneh Esrei*, or build a beautiful *succah*, thinking that he is acting purely for the sake of Heaven, while his real intention is to impress those around him. Only a small action that others might not know about, and which might pale in significance to other, greater accomplishments, can act as the true gauge of a person's spiritual level.

(*Shiurei Chumash, Parashas Mishpatim* 21:6; *Alei Shur,* Vol. I, p. 274; Vol. II, p. 501)

❃ ❃ ❃

IMMEDIATE RECOMPENSE

כָּל־אַלְמָנָה וְיָתוֹם לֹא תְעַנּוּן . . . כִּי אִם־צָעֹק יִצְעַק אֵלַי שָׁמֹעַ אֶשְׁמַע צַעֲקָתוֹ

"Do not oppress any widow or orphan. . . for if he shall cry out to Me I will listen to his cry" (22:21-22).

Ramban explains that there is a tendency to harass widows or orphans because they have no one to turn to for help, and the tormentor is not concerned about reprisal for his actions. Therefore, the Torah warns, if you oppress a widow or an orphan because they are helpless, know that all they have to do is cry out to Me and I will immediately come to their assistance.

In reality, then, they are better off than everyone else. When a regular person is tormented, he must ask someone else to come to his rescue, and even then, there is a possibility that his rescuer's endeavors will fail. In contrast, a widow or an orphan merely needs to cry out to Hashem and He will immediately come to their aid — and there is no chance that He will fail in meting out punishment to the tormentor.

The punishment for transgressions *bein adam lachaveiro* is meted out more swiftly and harshly than punishment for *aveiros bein adam laMakom*. We find an example of this phenomenon with Rachel and Leah, Yaakov's wives. The Torah tells us, "And Hashem saw that Leah was hated and He opened her womb; and Rachel was barren" (*Bereishis* 29:31). It is understandable why Hashem caused Leah to conceive, but why was Rachel barren? Why was she to blame for the fact that her sister was hated?

Yaakov's love for Rachel was the cause of his lesser love for Leah, and for that reason Rachel was barren. Even a minute infraction in the area of *bein adam lachaveiro* can have serious consequences.

> "Even a minute infraction in the area of bein adam lachaveiro can have serious consequences."

Parashas Mishpatim / 171

The opposite is true as well. There is a general rule that there is no reward in this world for the mitzvos we perform (*Kiddushin* 39b), since a mitzvah, which is spiritual and infinite, cannot be properly rewarded in this finite world. Nevertheless, the performance of certain mitzvos garners reward not only in the World to Come but also immediately in this world. The *Mishnah* (*Shabbos* 127) lists ten mitzvos in this category, almost all of which are *bein adam lachaveiro*: honoring one's parents, performing kindness, hospitality, visiting the sick, marrying off a bride, accompanying the deceased, concentrating on the meaning of the prayers (this is included in kindness — see *Rashi*), and making peace between man and his fellow.

There is great and immediate recompense for the mitzvos *bein adam lachaveiro*. One who neglects them will, God forbid, suffer dire consequences immediately, while one who performs them will be rewarded doubly — not only in the World to Come, but here in this world as well.

(*Shiurei Chumash, Parashas Mishpatim* 22:22, *Parashas Vayeitzei* 29:31)

❋ ❋ ❋

HASHEM LISTENS TO OUR PRAYERS, GRATIS

אִם־חָבֹל תַּחְבֹּל שַׂלְמַת רֵעֶךָ עַד־בֹּא הַשֶּׁמֶשׁ תְּשִׁיבֶנּוּ לוֹ. כִּי הִוא כְסוּתֹה לְבַדָּהּ הִוא שִׂמְלָתוֹ לְעֹרוֹ בַּמֶּה יִשְׁכָּב וְהָיָה כִּי־יִצְעַק אֵלַי וְשָׁמַעְתִּי כִּי־חַנּוּן אָנִי

> *If you take your friend's garment as a security you shall return it to him before sunset. For it alone is his clothing; it is his garment for his skin, and in what should he lie down? If he will cry out to Me I will listen, for I am compassionate (22:25-26).*

Ramban explains that Hashem is cautioning those who think they can take a garment belonging to a person who is not righteous as a security because even if the borrower cries out, Hashem will not heed his prayers. Therefore, the *passuk* stresses that He will listen because He is compassionate. Since Hashem is compassionate, He accepts the prayers of even those who are not righteous or deserving.

According to this explanation of Ramban, the *passuk* explicitly informs us that acceptance of *tefillah* is not entirely dependent on one's level of righteousness. One cannot be sure that the *tefillah* of a *tzaddik* will be accepted while that of a *rasha* will remain unanswered. As we see in *Tehillim* (145:18), there is only one prerequisite to *tefillah*: "Hashem is close to all those who call upon Him — to all who call upon him truthfully." In other words, one must not delude himself when *davening*. When praying to Hashem, a *rasha* must acknowledge that he is wicked, but he should nevertheless plead to Hashem to help him in his time of distress. He should be aware of where he stands spiritually, but still recognize that Hashem is the only One Who can truly help him.

> "When praying to Hashem, a rasha must acknowledge that he is wicked, but he should nevertheless plead to Hashem to help him in his time of distress."

Additionally, "true" prayer implies that there must be a possibility the prayer can be fulfilled. If a person prays that he should know the entire *Shas* by the next morning, there is a lack of truth in his prayer because such a feat is impossible.

Despite our shortcomings, Hashem takes an interest in our prayers and accepts them. One must never think, *Why should I daven? After all, who am I that Hashem should listen to my prayers?* The Torah tells us that Hashem is "*chanun*," compassionate. Ramban writes that "*chanun*" stems from the root word "*chinam*," gratis. Hashem listens to our prayers for free — even though we have nothing to offer in the way of righteousness.

(*Shiurei Chumash, Parashas Mishpatim* 22:26)

❈ ❈ ❈

TRUE AND ABSOLUTE VALUE

וּבְכֹל אֲשֶׁר־אָמַרְתִּי אֲלֵיכֶם תִּשָּׁמֵרוּ וְשֵׁם אֱלֹהִים אֲחֵרִים לֹא תַזְכִּירוּ

And you shall guard everything that I have said to you, and the names of other gods you shall not mention (23:13).

After enumerating many of the mitzvos, the Torah writes, "And you shall guard everything that I have said to you, and the names of other gods you shall not mention." What is the connection between the first and second halves of the *passuk*? Rashi explains that the Torah is implying that worshiping other gods is tantamount to transgressing all of the mitzvos; conversely, refraining from idol worship is equivalent to fulfilling all of the mitzvos.

It is understandable why a person who worships idols is akin to one who has transgressed all of the mitzvos. Ramban (*Bamidbar* 15:22) explains this idea succinctly: "Once one acknowledges another god, he has invalidated everything that Hashem commanded — both positive and negative commandments — for if there is another god, then there is absolutely no need to fear Hashem and heed His commandments." The flip side is much more difficult to understand, however. Why is it that when one refrains from *avodah zarah*, he is automatically considered to have fulfilled all of the mitzvos? Is it not possible that a person might realize the futility of idol worship but still have no interest in keeping the mitzvos?

We say in the Shabbos morning prayers, "There is nothing like Your value in this world." Every person has a set of values, some of lesser importance and some of greater importance. Usually there is one value that is of utmost importance to a person: that might be money, honor, or even collecting stamps. Yet the only true and absolute value is Hashem. Rambam writes (*Shemoneh Perakim*, Chapter 5) that everything a person does — his eating, drinking, health-promoting activities, and so on — should be carried out with one intention in mind: the service of Hashem. Eating and drinking often become a value in and of themselves, however, and many view health-promoting activities (e.g., sports) as a supreme value. Even wisdom can become an end unto itself. Taking anything of value that should be used in the service of Hashem and assigning it importance outside the realm of *avodas Hashem* is to a certain extent the creation of an *avodah zarah*.

We can now understand why a person who refrains from *avodah zarah* is akin to one who has performed all of the mitzvos. By refraining from *avodah zarah*, the person demonstrates that he views everything in the world as a means of serving Hashem, and acknowledges that nothing has intrinsic value unless it is used in His service. Such a person can certainly be considered to have observed all the mitzvos, since everything he does and values is for a single purpose: the fulfillment of Hashem's commandments.

(*HaMitzvos HaShekulos*, p. 7)

> "Taking anything of value that should be used in the service of Hashem and assigning it importance outside the realm of avodas Hashem is to a certain extent the creation of an avodah zarah."

פרשת תרומה
Parashas Terumah

RETURNING TO OUR PLACE

וְעָשׂוּ לִי מִקְדָּשׁ
They shall make a Sanctuary for Me (25:8).

The second half of *Sefer Shemos*, from *Parashas Terumah* and onward, describes the building of the *Mishkan*. The placement of this portion of the Torah is described by Ramban in his introduction to *Sefer Shemos*, where he outlines the contents of the *sefer*:

"The Torah finished Sefer Bereishis, which described the creation of the world and the events of the forefathers . . . and Sefer Shemos was designated to describe the first exile and the ensuing redemption . . . [which] was not complete **until they returned to their proper place** and to the level of their forefathers. When they left Mitzrayim, even though they had left the house of bondage, they were still considered exiled since they were not in their homeland, but wanderers in the desert. When they came to Har Sinai and built the Mishkan and Hashem rested His Shechinah upon them, they finally returned once again to the level of their forefathers, who were the 'Chariot' of Hashem, and then they were considered redeemed."

We might have understood from Ramban's statement that the redemption was not complete "until they returned to their proper place" to mean that in order to be considered redeemed, *Bnei Yisrael* had to enter Eretz Yisrael. However, it is clear from his subsequent words that this was not the case. Redemption did not occur when they left Mitzrayim, since they were still in exile, nor did it occur when they entered Eretz Yisrael, for by that point they had already been redeemed. Rather, the redemption occurred when Hashem placed His *Shechinah* upon *Bnei Yisrael* in the desert.

Chazal say (*Avos* 6:6), "Whoever repeats something in the name of the one who originally said it brings redemption to the world, as it is written, 'And Esther repeated it to the king in the name of Mordechai.'" Repeating a statement in the name of the speaker demonstrates one's ability to connect something to its source — i.e., the spoken word to the person who originally said it. This is the defining characteristic of redemption. Our world is disconnected from the Creator, and redemption is what reunites the world with the Creator — its original Source.

> "Our world is disconnected from the Creator, and redemption is what reunites the world with the Creator — its original Source."

When Hashem placed His *Shechinah* on *Bnei Yisrael*, they experienced true redemption, since the world was reconnected to its Source.

Ramban describes Hashem's *Shechinah* resting upon *Bnei Yisrael* as *Bnei Yisrael*'s "returning to their place." In other words, the very nature of *Klal Yisrael* is to envelop Hashem's *Shechinah* in its midst.

This is true not only of *Klal Yisrael* as a whole, but of each individual as well. Hashem said (25:8), "Make for Me a *Mikdash* and I will dwell among *you*," which teaches us that every person has the ability to turn himself into an abode for the *Shechinah*.

(*Daas Shlomo, Geulah,* p. 30)

❃ ❃ ❃

"TAKING" A DONATION

דַּבֵּר אֶל־בְּנֵי יִשְׂרָאֵל וְיִקְחוּ־לִי תְּרוּמָה מֵאֵת כָּל־אִישׁ אֲשֶׁר יִדְּבֶנּוּ לִבּוֹ תִּקְחוּ אֶת־תְּרוּמָתִי

"Speak to Bnei Yisrael and they shall take for Me a donation; from every man whose heart motivates him you shall take My donation (25:2)."

The question is obvious: Why did the Torah say that *Bnei Yisrael* should "take" a donation for Hashem? Would it not be more correct to say that they should "give" a donation to Hashem?

The Gemara (*Kiddushin* 7a) helps to answer this question. Halachah mandates that in order to perform *kiddushin* (part of the marriage ceremony), a man must give a woman something of value. (Today, a ring is used to fulfill this requirement.) However, there is one instance where the *kiddushin* can be accomplished by way of the woman giving the man something of value. When the man accepting the gift is someone who is held in high regard, then the fact that he accepted the woman's gift gives her pleasure. This pleasure is considered to have monetary value and therefore fulfills the halachic requirement to perform *kiddushin* with something of value. Similarly, the Torah is implying that when one gives a donation and it is accepted by Hashem, the real recipient is the donor. He has indeed "taken" a donation!

"Hashem does not need our Torah or mitzvos; He gives us the opportunity to learn and daven for our benefit."

When we *daven*, learn Torah, or perform a mitzvah, we tend to think that we have done Hashem a favor. Such an outlook is incorrect, for Hashem does not need our Torah or mitzvos; He gives us the opportunity to learn and *daven* for *our* benefit. David HaMelech declares (*Tehillim* 5:8), "And I, in Your abundant kindness, will enter Your Sanctuary." It is due to Hashem's great kindness that He allows us to serve Him. The benefit is solely ours.

(*Shiurei Chumash, Parashas Terumah* 25:2)

❊ ❊ ❊

INSIDE, OUTSIDE

וְצִפִּיתָ אֹתוֹ
You shall cover it (25:11).

The *Aron* in the Mishkan was made of wood, but it was covered on the inside and outside with gold. *Chazal* (*Yoma* 72b) tell us that a true *talmid chacham* must resemble the *Aron*; his inside must mirror his outside. Rambam writes (*Hilchos Dei'os* 2:6), "It is forbidden for one to smooth-talk and cajole. He should not say one thing with his mouth while intending something else in his heart; rather, his inside should be like his outside." A *talmid chacham* must say what he means and mean what he says.

It is interesting to note the importance that *Chazal* attributed to this quality. The Gemara (*Berachos* 28b) relates that Rabban Gamliel placed a guard at the door of the *beis midrash* and instructed him not to let in anyone whose outer conduct did not mirror his inner feelings. Even Rabbi Elazar ben Azariah, who subsequently removed the guard, did not disagree with Rabban Gamliel's restrictions; rather, he felt that everyone should be considered innocent until proven guilty. However, had he known with certainty that a specific person did not meet this criterion, he, too, would not have allowed such a student to enter the *beis midrash*.

We can deduce from this that the first step in becoming a *talmid chacham* is being meticulous with one's speech. Rambam continues, "And even a *single word* of wheedling or deceit is forbidden — only true speech, an accurate spirit, and a pure heart devoid of any treachery and deception."

> "The first step in becoming a talmid chacham is being meticulous with one's speech."

The two things that set humans apart from all other living creatures are intelligence and the ability to talk. A person must be careful to use this powerful tool of speech in the proper manner, thereby manifesting that superiority.

(*Alei Shur*, Vol. II, p. 36)

❈ ❈ ❈

THE CORE OF BLESSING

וְעָשִׂיתָ שֻׁלְחָן
You shall make a Table (25:23).

Parashas Terumah discusses the vessels of the *Mishkan*. With regard to the *Shulchan*, Rashi explains that the crown surrounding it symbolizes the crown of kingship, because we find the word "*shulchan*" used in reference to affluence and greatness. Ramban (25:24) elaborates that the *Shulchan* was the conduit through which *Bnei Yisrael* received their bounty and material blessings. After the creation of the world, Hashem ceased to create *ex nihilo*; everything that subsequently developed had a core that enabled its formation. Only once there is a core to act as a receptacle can the blessings of Hashem flourish and multiply.

This concept is illustrated by a story involving the prophet Elisha. With the intention of helping a woman in dire financial straits, he asked her what she had in her house, and she answered that the only thing she owned was a jug of oil. At Elisha's behest, she took the jug in her hand and poured continuously from it until she had filled the many vessels she had borrowed. The minute amount of oil she had in her house was enough of a receptacle for Hashem's blessing to rest on, causing it to multiply in a most astonishing manner. Similarly, the bread on the *Shulchan* contained Hashem's blessing, and a *kohen* who ate even a small amount, equivalent to the size of a bean, would feel satiated. This was the affluence symbolized by the *Shulchan*.

> "One cannot pray to master Shas or to perform a mitzvah if he does not take the initiative to accomplish his objectives."

This idea has ramifications in our everyday lives as well. Halachah dictates that one should not remove the bread from the table before he recites *Bircas Hamazon*, in order that there should be a receptacle for blessing on his table (*Orach Chaim* 180:1).

Similarly, when we pray for something, we have to provide a receptacle for our requests to come to fruition. One cannot pray to master *Shas* or to perform a mitzvah if he does not take the initiative to accomplish his objectives. Likewise, if a person does not take any steps to achieve his financial goals, he cannot pray to be blessed with wealth.

The concept of blessing requiring a receptacle can also be a source of encouragement. At times when a person feels that he is in a downward spiral or a spiritual rut, he should know that inside him is a core upon which Hashem's blessings can descend, for within every Jew there is a spiritual spark that is never extinguished.

(*Shiurei Chumash, Parashas Terumah* 25:24; *Alei Shur,* Vol. I, pp. 233-234)

❊ ❊ ❊

THE MISHKAN: A MINIATURE PERFECT WORLD

Before the sin of the golden calf, *Bnei Yisrael* were allowed to build a *mizbei'ach* wherever they desired. Hashem's glory filled the world, and one was therefore allowed to offer a sacrifice wherever he wished, as the *passuk* states, "Build for Me a *mizbei'ach* . . . any place where you mention My Name I will come to you and bless you" (20:21). This changed after the sin of the golden calf; Hashem decreed that His glory would have to be concentrated in a specific place. We were commanded to build the *Mishkan* to serve as that abode, and from then on sacrifices could only be offered in the *Mishkan,* or later the *Beis HaMikdash*.

The *Mishkan* was to act as a virtual world, a microcosm of the entire universe. *Chazal* tell us that the hooks holding together the *yeri'os* twinkled like the stars, the beams of the *Mishkan* paralleled the angels on high, and each of the utensils mirrored a different aspect of the universe.

When the world was first created it was pure, but it became tainted shortly thereafter when Adam sinned by eating from the *Eitz Hadaas*. After *Bnei Yisrael* heard the *Aseres Hadibros* at Har Sinai, they regained the purity of Adam before he sinned, but they lost that status with the sin of the golden calf. The *Mishkan* was intended to fill this void and serve as a miniature world devoid of sin.

It was for this reason that people who were ritually impure were not permitted to enter the *Mishkan*. As the *Kuzari* explains, all forms of ritual impurity are in some way connected to death. Ritual impurity associated with death comes as a result of sin, for as *Chazal* tell us, "It is not [the bite of] the snake that causes death; rather, it is the sin that causes death" (*Berachos* 33a). If there were no sin, there would be no death. Sins, and therefore death and ritual impurity, have no place in the utopian world where Hashem's *Shechinah* resided.

> *"Sins, and therefore death and ritual impurity, have no place in the utopian world where Hashem's Shechinah resided."*

The commandment to build the *Mishkan* can be explained homiletically. "Build for Me a *Mikdash*, and I will dwell within *each and every one of you*" (25:8). If the world around us is filled with decadence, each of us must attempt to create an environment that resembles the *Mishkan*, thereby enabling our homes to serve as an oasis for Hashem's *Shechinah*.

(*Shiurei Chumash, Parashas Mishpatim* 25:9)

פרשת תצוה
Parashas Tetzaveh

THE PERFECT CHESSED

לְהַעֲלֹת נֵר תָּמִיד
To kindle the lamp continually (27:20).

Parashas Tetzaveh begins with the commandment to light the *Menorah* in the Beis *HaMikdash* each evening. What is the purpose of this mitzvah? Does Hashem need us to illuminate the darkness for Him?

The Midrash (*Shemos Rabbah* 36:2) answers this question with a *mashal*:

A blind man was once walking with a friend. The friend turned to the blind man and said, "Hold on to me and I will lead you." Once they entered the house, the friend asked the blind man to light a torch for illumination, "so that you will not feel indebted to me for leading you."

The friend symbolizes Hashem, and the blind man represents *Bnei Yisrael*, who "groped in darkness" when they committed the sin of the golden calf. Despite their transgression, Hashem continued to lead them through the desert with the pillar of fire. Once *Bnei Yisrael* began building the *Mishkan*, Hashem commanded Moshe to light the *Menorah*. This way, *Bnei Yisrael* would, so to speak, illuminate the *Mishkan* for Hashem just as He illuminated the way in the desert for them.

Rav Yerucham Levovitz commented that we learn from this Midrash how to perform a perfect act of *chessed*. After helping another person, the benefactor should ask the beneficiary for a small favor. No one likes to feel indebted, and asking for a small favor will prevent the beneficiary from feeling indebted to the one who performed the *chessed*.

> "After helping another person, the benefactor should ask the beneficiary for a small favor, since no one likes to feel indebted."

Often, we assist others and decline any remuneration. Whether or not we accept the payment, we have performed the mitzvah of *gemilus chassadim*. At times, a complete *chessed* entails not accepting money, while at other times a complete *chessed* necessitates accepting payment. By accepting a person's money or favor in return for the *chessed* you have done, you are allowing him to express *hakaras hatov*, and freeing him from the burden of feeling indebted to you.

(*Alei Shur,* Vol. II, p. 281)

❋ ❋ ❋

CLARITY IN BOTH WORLDS

וְעָשִׂיתָ חֹשֶׁן מִשְׁפָּט

You shall make a Breastplate of Judgment (28:15).

"'Darkness descends and it is night.' This refers to *Olam Hazeh*, which is comparable to night" (*Bava Metzia* 83b).

Mesilas Yesharim (Ch. 3) elucidates this interesting analogy in a brilliant manner. Darkness causes two distinct problems: it either completely obscures objects from sight, or causes a person to falsely perceive an object — for instance, he might mistake a person for a pillar or a pillar for a person. Similarly, this physical, materialistic world does not allow a person to distinguish the pitfalls inherent in life. Moreover, it fools one into perceiving the good as bad and the bad as good.

The Torah is the light that dispels all confusion, and guides the Jewish people through the darkness of *Olam Hazeh*.

The Midrash tells us (*Devarim Rabbah* 5:7) that Hashem said, "Of all the nations that were created, I love only Yisrael ... Of all that was created I love only justice, as it is written, 'For I am Hashem Who loves justice (*mishpat*).' I will give that which I love to the nation I love." What is this "*mishpat*" that is so dear to the Creator?

In *Parashas Tetzaveh*, *Bnei Yisrael* are commanded to make a "*choshen mishpat*," breastplate (28:15). Rashi explains that the breastplate was called *mishpat* because it clarified its words through the *Urim V'Tumim*, similar to the concept of justice. This is the purpose of the Torah's laws: to provide clarity in every situation and every interaction with one's fellow man, leaving no room for doubt.

The Gemara (*Pesachim* 50a) relates that R' Yosef the son of R' Yehoshua ben Levi became ill and his soul temporarily left his body. When he "returned" from the world above, his father asked him what he had seen.

"I saw an inverted world," he answered. "Those who are high in this world are low in the next world, while those who are low in this world are high in the next world!"

His father responded, "My son, you have seen a world of clarity [undistorted by the biased appraisals of human beings]. Where do we [who study the Torah] stand in the next world?"

"Exactly where we stand in this world is where we stand in the next world," answered R' Yosef. "In addition, I heard them say, 'Praiseworthy is he who comes to this world with his Torah in hand.'"

"Those who study the Torah and are guided by its light live with clarity even in this world."

The World to Come is the world of true clarity. Yet those who study the Torah and are guided by its light live with a similar clarity even in this world. They are respected in the next world just as they are respected here in this world, for their Torah has granted them clarity even during their lifetime.

"Praiseworthy is he who comes with his Torah *in hand.*" It is not enough for a person to know what the Torah expects of him; he must also translate this knowledge into action. There is no new circumstance or invention that cannot be clarified halachically by the Torah's statutes. This is the clarity we must strive for in this world, which will in turn assure us a similar clarity in the World to Come.

(*Alei Shur,* Vol. II, p. 86)

❈ ❈ ❈

SPIRITUAL CLIMATE CHANGE

וְשָׁכַנְתִּי בְּתוֹךְ בְּנֵי יִשְׂרָאֵל

And I will dwell among Bnei Yisrael (29:45).

The *Mishkan* was built so that Hashem would have an abode in which to "reside" down here on Earth. However, the Torah tells us that His glory fills the entire world. If so, what was unique about the *Mishkan* that earned it the designation of Hashem's residence on Earth? Isn't Hashem found *everywhere*?

There are ten different levels of holiness in the land of Israel. The levels of holiness in the rest of the world cannot compare to the holiness of Eretz Yisrael, for prophecy could not be received outside of Eretz Yisrael. The difference in holiness is not a reflection of Hashem's proximity; the difference reflects how deeply His presence is felt. Although His glory fills the entire world, in some locations on Earth His presence is more manifest, while in others it is more hidden. Just as certain areas are conducive to growing specific vegetation, so, too, certain places on Earth are conducive to sensing Hashem's presence.

This idea is essential for those who have moved from *chutz la'aretz* to Eretz Yisrael. A person must recognize that the spiritual climate is different in Eretz Yisrael, and must adjust his lifestyle accordingly. However, even those who have not made such a move must bear this idea in mind. A person who lives in Eretz Yisrael and wishes to *daven* at the Kosel must prepare himself so that he can utilize the opportunity to its fullest.

When a person goes to a *shiur* or enters a shul or yeshivah anywhere in the world, he should realize that he has entered a place that is conducive to feeling Hashem's presence. However, if he does not prepare himself accordingly, he will have difficulty gaining from the experience. If he wishes to stay connected to his phone while entering a *mikdash me'at*, he might find himself leaving with no more *kedushah* than when he entered. A small amount of preparation will allow us to make the most of every spiritual opportunity.

(*Alei Shur*, Vol. II, p. 52)

"*If a person wishes to stay connected to his phone while entering a mikdash me'at, he might find himself leaving with no more kedushah than when he entered.*"

פרשת כי תשא

Parashas Ki Sisa

UNVEILING THE WORLD OF TORAH

When Moshe ascended Har Sinai, Yehoshua accompanied him as far as he was permitted and remained there for the entire forty days that Moshe spent atop the mountain. Since Yehoshua knew that Moshe would not come back for forty days, why did not he return to his tent and come back when the forty days were over?

Yehoshua personified the concept of *shimush talmidei chachamim* — serving Torah leaders — and he therefore remained there for the duration of Moshe's absence. He wanted to stay as close to his mentor as possible.

Many people, even if they spend all of their time engrossed in Torah study, still do not experience a true taste of Torah. It is as if they are standing outside the "world of Torah," because they never truly entered. What are they are lacking? The trait of *shimush talmidei chachamim*.

Chazal tell us (*Berachos* 7b), "Serving Torah leaders is greater than studying the Torah itself." Why is it imperative to have a mentor from whom to learn?

We say in *davening*, "They [the angels] accept upon themselves the yoke of Heavenly Kingship." From whom do they accept the yoke of Heavenly Kingship? The Vilna Gaon explains that each angel accepts it from the angel loftier than he, and in turn passes it on to a lower-level angel. The same holds true for a human being's acceptance of the yoke of Heaven: he can only accept it from one greater than himself.

True *shimush talmidei chachamim* is possible only if a person desires truth. It entails subjugating himself to his mentor, all the while being prepared to accept criticism. One should not merely imitate his *rebbi* or listen to his classes and discourses. Rather, he must strive to understand why his *rebbi* acted in a particular manner, and analyze exactly what he meant in his speech and what message he wished to impart. The stronger a person's relationship with his *rebbi*, the more he incorporates Torah values. As a result, he channels his thoughts in the manner the Torah desires.

A person can be compared to a tall building in which every story contains more treasures than the one beneath it. A person who lives on the bottom floor has no idea of the fortune above his head. Similarly, a person might live in the "basement" of his own strengths and attributes without having an inkling of the wealth of possibilities in his reach. Having a *rebbi* is the key to unlocking these hidden talents. Through the *rebbi*'s actions and guidance, an entirely new world opens before the student's eyes: a world of profundity and spiritual elevation, a world that is internal rather than external. This is the "world of Torah" that is opened by the "key" of *shimush talmidei chachamim*.

> *"A person might live in the 'basement' of his own strengths and attributes without having an inkling of the wealth of possibilities in his reach."*

The Midrash (*Bamidbar Rabbah* 14:4) states that when a person hears a Torah thought even from someone of small stature he should consider it as if he heard it from a wise man, from the Sanhedrin, from Moshe Rabbeinu, and even from Hashem Himself, as the *passuk* states, "The words which *I* am teaching you today should be upon your hearts" (*Devarim* 6:6).

This represents another dimension of *shimush talmidei chachamim*. By relating to a Torah thought it as if we heard it from Hashem, we can create a virtual situation of *shimush talmidei chachamim* — the transmission of Torah from God Himself — and unveil for ourselves the true "world of Torah."

(*Shiurei Chumash, Parashas Ki Sisa* 32:17; Introduction to *Alei Shur*, Vol. I)

❋ ❋ ❋

TAILORING THE MESSAGE

שְׁנֵי־לֻחֹת אֲבָנִים כָּרִאשֹׁנִים
Two stone Luchos like the first ones (34:1).

When Moshe Rabbeinu beheld *Bnei Yisrael* worshiping the golden calf, he threw down the *Luchos* and smashed them. *Chazal* tell us (*Shabbos* 88a) that afterward Hashem thanked Moshe for breaking the *Luchos*. Eighty days later, on Yom Kippur, Moshe descended from Har Sinai with a second set of *Luchos*, containing the same contents.

What was the impetus for Moshe's decision to break the *Luchos*? In addition, if he felt *Bnei Yisrael* were not worthy of receiving the Torah, what changed eighty days later when he returned with a similar set of *Luchos*?

The Gemara (*Avodah Zarah* 5a) states that the second set of *Luchos* differed from the first set. Had they merited the first set, *Bnei Yisrael* would have been free from the dominion of the *yetzer hara* and would never have been oppressed by foreign nations. They would have achieved a level of existence without sin. Prior to their sin, the Torah (i.e., the first set of *Luchos*) was tailored to the needs of a nation that had reached the pinnacle of spiritual ascent. When Moshe saw that the nation had sinned, thereby falling from their newfound spiritual plateau, he understood that the Torah in its present form was not suitable for *Bnei Yisrael*. They would need a new set of *Luchos*, tailored to a nation that had tasted sin. The actual Torah would remain unchanged, but the manner in which it would be conveyed to *Bnei Yisrael* would be different.

Every generation has a specific manner in which it can, and does, relate to the Torah. Those responsible for transmitting the Torah must understand the particularities of their specific generation and transmit the Torah accordingly. The Torah remains the same; it is merely the language that changes.

Chazal say (*Rosh Hashanah* 25b), "Yiftach in his generation paralleled Shmuel in his generation." What does this mean? Shmuel was a prophet who was compared to Moshe and Aharon, while Yiftach did not even merit prophecy. Rav Tzadok HaKohen explains that just as Shmuel succeeded in transmitting the Torah to his generation, Yiftach succeeded in transmitting the Torah to his. The difference in the spiritual levels of their respective generations was immense, but the mission remained the same. Like Shmuel, Yiftach found an appropriate means of conveying the Torah's eternal message.

Rav Yechezkel Levenstein commented that his *rebbeim* in the yeshivah of Kelm would say that speaking about the terrible punishments in *Gehinnom* in order to motivate people to improve is not the proper approach for our generation. The Alter of Slabodka would always stress *gadlus ha'adam* — the greatness of man. He understood that our era required a softer, more optimistic approach, and he tailored his discourses accordingly.

"We all have the ability to help others in their Torah growth; we need only find the right language."

Whatever the means of transmission, the beauty of the Torah remains constant. We all have the ability to help others in their Torah growth; we need only find the right language. What spoke to the last generation might not speak to our generation, and what speaks to our generation might not speak to our children's generation. If we bear this in mind when delivering Hashem's eternal message, we will, *be'ezras Hashem*, succeed in imbuing others with a true Torah outlook, in a manner that rivals the pedagogy of Shmuel HaNavi.

(*Shiurei Chumash, Parashas Ki Sisa*, p. 258)

❃ ❃ ❃

MATURITY THROUGH TORAH

שְׁנֵי־לֻחֹת אֲבָנִים כָּרִאשֹׁנִים
Two stone Luchos lke the first ones (34:1)

Ramban (34:27) writes that the second set of *Luchos* differed from the first set of *Luchos*, and the giving of the second set was tantamount to a new *Matan Torah* after the sin of the golden calf. Had *Bnei Yisrael* merited to keep the first set of *Luchos*, the world would look much different today. None of the Torah ever learned would have been forgotten, and neither the Angel of Death nor the nations of the world would have dominion over *Bnei Yisrael*.

Even the purpose of Torah study changed in the aftermath of the sin of the golden calf. After receiving the second set of *Luchos*, "Hashem dwelled among them in their impurity" (*Vayikra* 16:16). Before the sin, *Bnei Yisrael* had risen to a level where they had no *yetzer hara*, but they became impure due to their sin and thereafter had to contend with the *yetzer hara*.

The Torah is the weapon we were given to help us overcome the *yetzer hara*. As *Chazal* tell us (*Kiddushin* 30b), Hashem said, "I created the *yetzer hara* and I created the Torah as its spice" (through which the *yetzer hara* can be refined to become a positive force).

Chazal mention numerous methods of battling the *yetzer hara*: "*yargiz*" — get angry at him; "*misgaber*" — overcome him; "*rodeh*" — subjugate him; and "*mefatpeit*" — belittle him. All of these methods involve a direct confrontation with the *yetzer hara*. The study of Torah, on the other hand, functions in an entirely different manner. As Rashi (ibid.) explains, it elevates a person *above* his *yetzer hara*. A child might ride on a stick and claim that it is his horse, but as he grows older he will comprehend that a stick is not a horse. He does not have to fight with himself or convince himself not to ride on the stick; his new understanding is a function of maturity. The Torah works in a similar fashion. Once a person delves into the Torah, he matures to a level where he is simply not interested in what the *yetzer hara* previously offered him.

> "In our battle with the yetzer hara the optimal approach is not to fight him head-on, but to rise above him and make him irrelevant through the study of Torah."

In our battle with the *yetzer hara* the optimal approach is not to fight him head-on, but to rise above him and make him irrelevant through the study of Torah.

(*Alei Shur,* Vol. II, p. 109)

✻ ✻ ✻

HE CLEANSES, HE DOES NOT CLEANSE

וְנַקֵּה לֹא יְנַקֶּה

Who cleanses, but does not cleanse (34:7).

The last of Hashem's thirteen attributes is "*v'nakei lo yenakeh*" (34:7). The literal translation, "Who cleanses, but does not cleanse," is quite obscure, and the Targum adds a few words to elucidate the *passuk*: "He cleanses those who return to the Torah, and does not cleanse those who do not return to the Torah."

The Targum is introducing a new way of understanding the concept of *teshuvah*. The prevalent perception of *teshuvah* is not "returning to the Torah," but rather returning to Hashem. We find this idea of returning to the Torah in *Shemoneh Esrei* as well. In the fourth *berachah* we ask Hashem, "Return us, our Father, to Your Torah." Why is the emphasis placed on returning to the Torah, and not on returning to Hashem?

All *aveiros* are rooted in a laxity in the area of *limud haTorah*, and each individual must contemplate the exact area of Torah in which he was lax. One's *aveiros* might be attributed to a disregard for his fixed times for Torah study, or to learning without the proper depth. Maybe he could have learned more but opted to settle for less, or perhaps he neglected his obligations because he failed to review what he learned. Perhaps he did not take the time to study *mussar*, or even if he did, maybe he did not internalize what he learned. Whatever the case, had one not slackened off in his Torah study, he would not have sinned. *Teshuvah*, therefore, must entail returning to the proper study of Torah.

This concept can be applied in a very practical way. Everyone must study the halachos that apply to his daily life, such as Shabbos and kashrus. Additionally, the *Mishnah Berurah* writes that one must study *mussar* every day. Learning halachah and *mussar* arms one with knowledge of what is permissible and what is forbidden and gives him the ability to keep his *yetzer hara* in check.

An investment in Torah study is not only a great mitzvah in and of itself, it is also a means of facilitating the mitzvah of *teshuvah*.

(*Alei Shur*, Vol. I, p. 237)

פרשת ויקהל-פקודי
Parashas Vayakhel-Pekudei

THE GIFT OF SHABBOS

וּבַיּוֹם הַשְּׁבִיעִי יִהְיֶה לָכֶם קֹדֶשׁ שַׁבַּת שַׁבָּתוֹן לַה'
But the seventh day shall be holy for you, a day of rest of Hashem (35:2).

Although both *Parashas Vayakhel* and *Parashas Pekudei* deal entirely with the *Mishkan* and its vessels, the Torah prefaces these *parshiyos* with Moshe's warning to *Bnei Yisrael* to guard the Shabbos. Rashi (35:2) explains that although they were building a *Mishkan* for Hashem's *Shechinah*, they still had to be careful not to desecrate the Shabbos.

"*Shabbos differs from all other mitzvos in that it is not only a commandment, but also a gift.*"

Shabbos differs from all other mitzvos in that it is not only a commandment, but also a gift. *Chazal* (*Shabbos* 10b) tell us, "Hashem said to Moshe, 'I have a wonderful gift in My treasury called Shabbos; go tell *Bnei Yisrael* that I wish to give it to them.'" Likewise, we find that the *berachah* recited during *Kiddush* differs from the *berachos* recited when performing other mitzvos. Generally we say, "Blessed are You, Hashem, Who sanctified us with His mitzvos and *commanded* us," while on Shabbos we say, "Who sanctified us with His mitzvos and *desired* us, and He gave us His holy Shabbos with love and graciousness *as an inheritance.*" Shabbos is a treasured inheritance, not merely a set of obligations.

Some unique individuals were able to sense when Shabbos began without having to look at the clock. Throughout the week, the Alter of Kelm's face was white as a sheet, but on Shabbos his cheeks took on a reddish hue. Similarly, Rav Yerucham Levovitz's appearance on Shabbos changed to such a degree that a new student who saw him on Shabbos after meeting him earlier in the week thought that a new *Mashgiach* had come to the yeshivah.

"Hashem blessed the seventh day and sanctified it" (*Bereishis* 2:3), turning it into an entity of holiness that can be felt and experienced.

By resting on Shabbos we bear witness to the fact that Hashem created the world. The Torah writes, "For in six days Hashem made the heavens and earth, …and He rested on the seventh day" (20:11). Ramban explains that through Shabbos we remember Creation and thereby acknowledge that there is a Creator. Rav Samson Raphael Hirsch writes that the thirty-nine *melachos* forbidden on Shabbos demonstrate that Hashem, Who created the world, is the sole Master, and on this day man has no permission to perform any action that is a form of creation.

The *kedushah* of Shabbos is palpable, if we put in the effort to sense it. We should welcome Shabbos the way we would a guest, as we say in *Lechah Dodi*, "Come, O bride, come, O bride, the Shabbos queen." By reflecting on Hashem's wonderful gift to us as we usher in Shabbos each week, we can truly experience the holiness it brings with it.

(*Alei Shur,* Vol. II, p. 382)

❃ ❃ ❃

NOBLE INTENTIONS DO NOT JUSTIFY INCONSIDERATE ACTIONS

וּבַיּוֹם הַשְּׁבִיעִי יִהְיֶה לָכֶם קֹדֶשׁ שַׁבַּת שַׁבָּתוֹן לַה׳
*But the seventh day shall be holy for you,
a day of rest of Hashem (35:2).*

It is difficult to understand why *Bnei Yisrael* would have even entertained the notion that the building of the *Mishkan* should override the prohibition of performing *melachah* on Shabbos. We do not find the Torah warning us that even though there is a mitzvah to write a *sefer Torah*, we should bear in mind that it is forbidden to write on Shabbos. Moreover, we know that a special *passuk* is always required in order to allow any mitzvah to override the prohibition of performing *melachah* on Shabbos. Why would *Bnei Yisrael* think that the mitzvah of building the *Mishkan* was any different?

In *Parashas Ki Sisa*, which directly precedes *Parashas Vayakhel*, *Bnei Yisrael* sinned by making the golden calf. Ramban explains (32:1) that their transgression was the result of a mistake. Moshe Rabbeinu was the leader and guiding light of *Bnei Yisrael*. When forty days passed and he had not yet returned, they were thrown into a panic. Who would guide them and connect them with their Creator? In their fright, they created the golden calf to fill that role. Their intentions were noble, but that did not justify their actions, which could be termed a *mitzvah habaah b'aveirah* — a mitzvah that came about through sin. Therefore, the Torah warns *Bnei Yisrael*: Even though you are commanded to build a *Mishkan*, which is to act as an abode for Hashem and a means of connecting with Him, it should not be built on Shabbos, for this would constitute a *mitzvah habaah b'aveirah*.

This concept formed one of the focal points of Rav Yisrael Salanter's teachings. A person must ensure that his mitzvos are not performed by way of *aveiros*. Rav Yisrael would depict a scene in which a *maggid* came to town to deliver a *mussar shmuess*.

Everyone in the town was interested in hearing his words of wisdom, and they rushed to the shul where the speech was being held. In their haste, one person knocked over a passerby, another got angry because someone cut him off, and so on. Yes, they were running to perform a mitzvah — to hear words that would help them improve their *avodas Hashem* — but at what cost?

> "Yes, they were running to perform a mitzvah — to hear words that would help them improve their avodas Hashem — but at what cost?"

There is another well-known story about Rav Yisrael Salanter that illustrates this point. One morning before *Shacharis*, a man put on his *tallis* and wrapped his face in its folds. However, as he threw the *tzitzis* over his shoulder the strings slapped Rav Yisrael in the face! Here, too, the man's mitzvah came about through a flaw in his *bein adam lachaveiro*.

A modern-day application of Rav Yisrael Salanter's principle would be double-parking in order to come on time to *Minchah*. No matter how noble the goal, trampling on other people is never the way to achieve it.

(*Shiurei Chumash, Parashas Vayakhel* 35:2)

❊ ❊ ❊

ACQUISITION THROUGH SELF-SACRIFICE

וְלַחֹשֶׁן
And for the breastplate (35:27).

The *parshiyos* of *Vayakhel* and *Pekudei* revolve around the many different aspects of the *Mishkan*, among them the *choshen* worn on the chest of the *kohen gadol*. Rashi (4:14) tells us how Aharon, the first *kohen gadol*, merited this special adornment. Hashem told Moshe he should return to Mitzrayim, where he would become the redeemer of *Bnei Yisrael*, and Moshe declined because he feared that his older brother, Aharon, would feel slighted. After a weeklong dialogue, Hashem told Moshe not to fear because "he [Aharon] is coming out to greet you and he will see you and be glad in his heart." Rashi comments that it was due to these feelings of happiness that Aharon later merited to wear the *choshen* over his heart.

We can deduce from Rashi that the attainment of spiritual acquisitions differs from the attainment of material acquisitions. Material acquisitions are obtained through the work that we invest on our own behalf, while spiritual acquisitions are obtained through actions done on behalf of others. Aharon not only removed all feelings of jealousy from his heart, he also felt true happiness regarding his brother's rise to greatness. It was these feelings that "bought" him the merit of wearing the *choshen* over his heart.

This idea is reflected in many different stories related in the Torah. Shem's descendants merited the mitzvah of *tzitzis* due to the consideration he displayed in covering his father Noach. Both Sarah and Rachel overcame the natural feelings of jealousy that are generated by the presence of a rival, and allowed their maidservants to marry their husbands in the hopes that they would bear children in the merit of this self-sacrifice.

Similarly, the Jewish taskmasters in Mitzrayim were later chosen to form the Sanhedrin, an appointment that came as a reward for their selflessness. When the Jews under their supervision could not complete their daily quota of bricks, the taskmasters themselves accepted the beatings meant for their workers. It might seem that in order to merit an appointment as a judge on the Sanhedrin one would need to have studied the laws of the Torah for many years. However, the Torah tells us otherwise: The way to acquire a spiritual appointment is by giving of oneself for another person's benefit.

> *"The way to acquire a spiritual appointment is by giving of oneself for another person's benefit."*

In *Parashas Vayeira*, Avraham *davened* for the household of Avimelech to recover from their temporary state of barrenness. Immediately afterward, the Torah informs us of the birth of Yitzchak,

Avraham's son. *Chazal* deduce from the juxtaposition of these two events that one who prays for another person when he himself is lacking in that exact area merits salvation first (*Bereishis* 21:1; see Rashi).

When a person overlooks his own needs, and puts his heart and soul into praying for another's needs, he demonstrates the self-sacrifice necessary to obtain that which he himself lacks.

(*Shiurei Chumash, Parashas Vayeira* 21:1; *Shiurei Chumash, Parashas Lech Lecha* 16:2)

❖ ❖ ❖

YOU GET WHAT YOU PAY FOR

וַיַּעַשׂ בְּצַלְאֵל
Betzalel made (37:1).

While the *parshiyos* of *Terumah* and *Tetzaveh* recount Hashem's commandment to build the *Mishkan*, the *parshiyos* of *Vayakhel* and *Pekudei* describe the actual construction of the *Mishkan*. Regarding each aspect of the *Mishkan* the Torah simply writes (37:1), "And he made. . . ." However, when describing the construction of the *Aron*, the Torah writes, "And Betzalel made the *Aron*." Rashi explains that because Betzalel invested great effort in building the *Aron*, it was "called by his name."

We find this idea in several other places. Shimon and Levi are described as "Dinah's brothers" (*Bereishis* 34:25) since they risked their lives to save her from the clutches of Shechem. Miriam is referred to as "Moshe's sister" (15:20) because she was *moser nefesh* for him when he was placed in the Nile. The very last prophecy recorded in *Tanach*, "Remember the Torah of Moshe My servant" (*Malachi* 3:22), refers to the Torah as belonging to Moshe because he was *moser nefesh* on behalf of the Torah.

We might add that while the Torah is specifically referred to as belonging to Moshe, *Chazal* tell us that the Torah becomes the personal acquisition of anyone who expends effort and toils in its study. "Rava said, 'Initially the Torah is ascribed to Hashem, and eventually it is ascribed to *him*'" (*Avodah Zarah* 19a). Rashi explains that "him" refers to the student who toiled in the study of Torah. This acquisition is not external, for the Torah changes the very essence of a person who toils in its precepts.

Nevertheless, we can learn Torah, *daven*, and perform numerous mitzvos without their having a profound effect upon us. If we want the Torah and mitzvos to be truly ours, to change our essence and create a real connection to Hashem, then we must put effort into them. This might translate into an extra five minutes of learning after one has decided that he is ready to close the Gemara, or making an added effort to concentrate during *Shema* or the first *berachah* in *Shemoneh Esrei*. In the realm of *chessed* it might mean helping someone at the expense of personal comfort or making a difficult phone call that might help someone with a *shidduch*. The opportunities are endless, and many of them can be found in one's very own home!

> "If we want the Torah and mitzvos to be truly ours, to change our essence and create a real connection to Hashem, then we must put effort into them."

People often say, "You get what you pay for." Similarly, the spiritual reward in this world is directly proportionate to the effort expended in the performance of Hashem's will.

(*Shiurei Chumash, Parashas Vayakhel* 37:1)

❈ ❈ ❈

GREATER THAN ANY SPIRITUAL REVELATION

אֵלֶּה פְקוּדֵי הַמִּשְׁכָּן

These are the accountings of the Mishkan (38:21).

Both *Parashas Vayakhel* and *Parashas Pekudei* recap the many donations and utensils that were required for the building of the *Mishkan* — the place where Hashem's *Shechinah* dwelled here on Earth. Basking in the *Shechinah*'s presence would seem to be the pinnacle of spirituality attainable in this world. However, *Chazal* tell us that the mitzvah of *hachnasas orchim* takes precedence over receiving the *Shechinah*. This astounding idea is derived from Avraham Avinu, who, in the midst of a conversation with Hashem, excused himself to care for wayfarers.

What is so extraordinary about providing hospitality? Why did Avraham choose to tend to his guests and thus relinquish an opportunity to speak to God Himself? The *mishnah* tells us (*Avos* 4:22), "One hour of repentance and good deeds in this world is worth more than a life of eternity in the World to Come." We are placed in this world to serve Hashem, and that is greater than any spiritual revelations that can be attained in this world or even in the next.

> "We are placed in this world to serve Hashem, and that is greater than any spiritual revelations that can be attained in this world or even in the next."

If an opportunity to fulfill a mitzvah presents itself when a person is studying Torah, or reflecting on Hashem's greatness, or even receiving the *Shechinah*, he must stop what he is doing and run to perform the mitzvah.

Rav Yisrael Salanter was once reciting *Shema* when he overheard two people arguing over whose obligation it was to bury someone who had passed away. Immediately, Rav Yisrael took off his *tefillin* and ran to bury the man. It did not matter that he was in the middle of praying or that it was not his responsibility to bury the unfortunate man. He was a man of action, and he did not hesitate for even a moment when it came to the performance of a mitzvah.

One Yom Kippur when Rav Wolbe was studying in the Mirrer Yeshivah in Europe, before *Mussaf* the *chazzan* sent a number of students to check on the welfare of one of the boys who was ill. "This is the obligation of the day," the *chazzan* explained. Our obligation in this world is to perform mitzvos, and that takes precedence over *davening Mussaf* on the holiest day of the year.

Often we hear a speech, read a story, or study a passage of Torah that enlightens us to the spiritual levels we can attain. However, these revelations alone are not our ultimate goal. We must take these feelings and turn them into actions, thereby accomplishing more than one who has the awesome opportunity to speak to the *Shechinah*!

(*Shiurei Chumash, Parashas Vayeira* 18:3)

❈ ❈ ❈

DOWN TO THE LAST PENNY

אֵלֶּה פְקוּדֵי הַמִּשְׁכָּן

These are the accountings of the Mishkan (38:21).

The first *Rashi* in *Pekudei* (38:21) explains why there is yet another *parashah* dealing with the *Mishkan* and its *keilim*. This *parashah* enumerates all the donations to the *Mishkan* and shows how they were used.

The Midrash (*Shemos Rabbah* 51:1) explains the *passuk* (*Mishlei* 28:20) "An honest man will increase blessings" as referring to Moshe. Moshe was able to account for *every* donation given toward the building of the *Mishkan*, down to the last penny. Due to his unwavering integrity, the money he was entrusted with benefited from Hashem's blessing, and it was exactly sufficient for the needs of the *Mishkan*.

It is interesting to note that *Sefer Shemos* ends with the monetary integrity of Moshe Rabbeinu and begins with the monetary integrity of his mother Yocheved. When Moshe was three months old and his mother could no longer hide him, she put him in a bassinet and placed it in the reeds on the banks of the river. The Torah tells us that the bassinet was made out of *gomeh* — cane. Since Yocheved was trying to protect her son, it would have made more sense to build the bassinet out of strong, sturdy cedar wood as opposed to cheap, soft cane. The Gemara (*Sotah* 12a) infers from this incident that righteous people show more care about their money than about their bodies.

Why do the righteous care so much about their monetary possessions? They are careful with their money because they earned every penny honestly (ibid.). They do not steal or cheat, and therefore every dollar they receive is Heavenly ordained. If Hashem decided to entrust them with the money, then obviously it was given to them for a purpose. Since Yocheved was extremely careful with how she earned her money, she was also extremely careful with how she used it. Once she determined that a bassinet made out of cane would suffice, she did not want to spend Heaven-sent money on unnecessarily expensive material.

Many of us have lost this sensitivity toward money, to a certain extent. We might leave one of our possessions somewhere and not bother to retrieve it. If Yaakov Avinu expended the effort to retrieve some small bottles, should not we at least be careful with expensive items that we left behind? After all, if it was bought with the money that Hashem entrusted to us, we should do our best to protect it.

If a person is careless with his money, says Rav Wolbe, it might be an indication that it was not earned honestly, and he therefore does not appreciate that the money comes from Hashem. The realization that our money was given to us to be used in our *avodas Hashem* might revolutionize the way we spend it.

(*Shiurei Chumash, Parashas Pekudei* 38:21; *Shiurei Chumash, Parashas Shemos* 2:3)

ספר ויקרא
Sefer Vayikra

פרשת ויקרא
Parashas Vayikra

DAAS: FOCUSED THOUGHT

וַיִּקְרָא אֶל־מֹשֶׁה וַיְדַבֵּר ה' אֵלָיו מֵאֹהֶל מוֹעֵד לֵאמֹר

And He called to Moshe; and Hashem spoke to Moshe from the Ohel Moed (1:1).

The Midrash (1:15) deduces from this *passuk* that Moshe did not enter the *Mishkan* until Hashem specifically invited him inside. This attribute was a manifestation of *daas*. The Midrash goes on to say that a *talmid chacham* who lacks this attribute of *daas* is inferior to an animal carcass.

What exactly is *daas* and why is it so important? *Daas* is an awareness of what one is doing, as opposed to performing actions out of habit or mechanically. With regard to *davening*, *daas* is referred to as "*kavanah*." It is quite possible to recite the entire *Shemoneh Esrei* while our minds are preoccupied with thoughts that have nothing to do with *tefillah*. This is a *tefillah* recited without *daas*.

The same holds true for everything that we do and say. People converse with others freely, without thinking about what should be said and what should not be said. In fact, an entire day filled with events, conversations, and mitzvos can pass without one ever paying attention to what he has said or done!

> "An entire day filled with events, conversations, and mitzvos can pass without one ever paying attention to what he has said or done."

"*Yishuv hadaas*" describes actions performed with an awareness of what one is doing. A person who possesses *yishuv hadaas* lives an entirely different life than one who is lacking this quality. His *davening* and fulfillment of mitzvos create a connection with Hashem, his conversations are meaningful, and his actions show the thought lying behind them.

Moshe Rabbeinu possessed this quality of *daas*, and everyone must strive to attain it as well. A little focused thought can go a long way.

(*Pirkei Kinyan Daas*, p. 77)

❖ ❖ ❖

HIGHER CALLING

וַיִּקְרָא אֶל־מֹשֶׁה וַיְדַבֵּר ה' אֵלָיו

He called to Moshe, and Hashem spoke to him (1:1).

Sefer Vayikra begins, "He *called* to Moshe, and Hashem *spoke* to him from the *Ohel Moed,* saying" (1:1). Rashi explains that the numerous times Hashem spoke to Moshe or commanded him were all prefaced by a "calling" — i.e., a manner of speech that expresses affection. Rashi continues with a very interesting statement of *Chazal*: "One might think that even the breaks [between the parshiyos] were prefaced by a special calling; therefore, the Torah writes, 'And Hashem **spoke** to him,' which implies that only Hashem's speech was prefaced by a calling, and not the breaks. And what purpose did these breaks serve? They were there to enable [Moshe] to contemplate between the parshiyos and between the topics. How much more so must a simple person learning from a simple person [take time to contemplate between parshiyos and topics]."

The fact that *Chazal* even entertained the possibility that a special calling prefaced each break in the Torah proves that the breaks themselves are an integral facet of Torah. They, too, are Torah because they were put there to enable one who studies the Torah to take some time to contemplate, understand, and incorporate that which he has just learned. However, since it differs from the rest of the Torah, it did not necessitate a calling.

Chazal stress the importance of these breaks by concluding, "How much more so must a simple person learning from a simple person [take time to contemplate between *parshiyos* and topics]." If we would appreciate the importance of these breaks, everything we learn would take on an entirely new significance. Understandably, our *limud haTorah* would be more meaningful and on a much higher level.

> "If we would appreciate the importance of the breaks in the Torah, everything we learn would take on an entirely new significance."

This idea is the rationale behind *bein hazmanim*. These intermediate days were specifically designated as days that are free from the regular learning schedule to allow a person to contemplate what he has gained during the past months and prepare himself accordingly for the future months. Cognizance of the purpose behind *bein hazmanim* can prevent many of the problems that people encounter during this period.

(*Shiurei Chumash, Parashas Vayikra* 1:1)

❈ ❈ ❈

THE COMPLETE NAME ON A COMPLETE WORLD

קָרְבָּן לַה׳
An offering to Hashem (1:2).

Ramban (1:9), in his explanation of the commandment to bring *korbanos*, cites Chapter 50 in *Tehillim*, which discusses *korbanos*. The first *passuk* states, "The Almighty God, Hashem, spoke and called to the earth from the rising of the sun to its setting." Ramban writes that the *passuk* mentions "the complete Name on a complete world."

> "*Korbanos are a means of creating a complete world, thereby allowing the complete Name of Hashem to rest upon it.*"

Korbanos are a means of creating a complete world, thereby allowing the complete Name of Hashem to rest upon it. They bridge the huge chasm that divides the body and the soul: the division between the physical world and the Creator. When a person consecrates an animal, he brings *kedushah* upon the animal, enabling it to be brought on the *Mizbei'ach*. He has taken the basest creature and transformed it into something appropriate to be offered to the Creator Himself.

These *korbanos* were offered to Hashem in the *Mishkan*, a veritable spiritual haven in a turbulent world. It was there that the physical was transformed into the spiritual, and the *Mishkan* was therefore deemed a "complete world." Consequently, it was there that the *Shechinah*, "the complete Name," resided.

Despite the fact that we lack the ability to offer *korbanos*, the lesson we learn from the *korbanos* still holds true. We must make an effort to transform our physical bodies into spiritual entities. A person's body should be part and parcel of his *avodas Hashem*, along with the thoughts and intentions that accompany a mitzvah. When he succeeds in this endeavor, he has created a "complete world" that allows for "the complete Name" to reside therein.

(*Daas Shlomo*, unpublished manuscript)

פרשת צו
Parashas Tzav

ATTENTION TO DETAIL

זֹאת תּוֹרַת...
This is the law (Torah) of... (6:2).

Although both *Parashas Vayikra* and *Parashas Tzav* mention the *korbanos*, only in *Tzav* does the Torah preface the description of each of the *korbanos* with "This is the *Torah* of the *olah* [*shelamim, minchah*]." The difference between the two *parshiyos* can be explained with a Gemara in *Sanhedrin* (26b): Rav Chanan said, "Why is the Torah referred to as '*Toshiah*'? Because it weakens (*mateshes*) a person's strength."

The wisdom of Torah is unique in that it focuses more on the details than on the general rules. The primary goal of Torah study is to break down each mitzvah into the myriad practical halachos and *middos* that are encapsulated within it.

The importance the Torah lends to detail is apparent in a halachah of the *Shulchan Aruch* (*Orach Chaim* 211:7). If a person sits down to a meal and is served two kinds of food, one that requires the *berachah* of *shehakol* and one that requires a *borei pri ha'eitz*, the food that requires *borei pri ha'eitz* takes precedence because this *berachah* is recited on only one category of food (fruit). The *Mishnah Berurah* explains that because *borei pri ha'eitz* is more specific, it is considered a more important *berachah* than *shehakol*, which is a general *berachah* that includes many types of food. It is the attention to detail that is important in the eyes of the Torah.

> "It is specifically detail-oriented Torah study that has the ability to smash the yetzer hara to smithereens."

It is specifically detail-oriented Torah study that weakens a person and detracts from the vitality of the *yetzer hara*. Rav Yisrael Salanter writes that if one is overcome by his *yetzer hara*, he should "drag it to its *beis midrash*" (see *Kiddushin* 30b). In other words, he should study in depth the laws and many details relevant to the specific area where he is deficient. It is this form of Torah study that has the ability to "smash the *yetzer hara* to smithereens" (ibid.)

In *Parashas Tzav*, the Torah describes the *korbanos* in greater detail, and therefore prefaces its description with "This is the *Torah* of . . ." The details are referred to as Torah, and they give us the strength we need to battle our *yetzer hara*.

(*Daas Shlomo*, unpublished manuscript)

❊ ❊ ❊

WHAT DOES IT HAVE TO DO WITH ME?

וְהָאֵשׁ עַל־הַמִּזְבֵּחַ תּוּקַד־בּוֹ לֹא תִכְבֶּה
*The fire on the Mizbei'ach shall be kept burning on it,
it shall not be extinguished (6:5).*

While all other fields of study answer the question, "What is it?", the Torah answers the question, "What does it have to do with me?"

If we were to ask a scientist, "What is fire?" we would receive a detailed explanation of fire's properties: how a fire is started, what fuels it, etc. The Torah, on the other hand, enlightens us regarding the relationship we should have with fire: Fire is one of the four main things that cause damage, and one must therefore watch over his coals and compensate for any damage caused by a fire that he started. There are also mitzvos that must be performed with fire, such as the one mentioned in this *parashah*: "*The fire on the Mizbei'ach shall be kept burning on it, it shall not be extinguished.*"

This idea also holds true with regard to Hashem. The Torah does not tell us Who Hashem is, yet it does inform us of the relationship He has with us. *Chazal* tell us that Hashem wrapped Himself in a *tallis*, so to speak, and told Moshe that whenever *Bnei Yisrael* recite His thirteen attributes of mercy, Hashem will forgive them (*Rosh Hashanah* 17b). The Shelah quotes the *Geonim* who explain that reciting the thirteen attributes of mercy does not mean merely stating the attributes, but rather emulating them. We create a relationship with Hashem when we follow in His ways.

> "Reciting the thirteen attributes of mercy does not mean merely stating the attributes, but rather emulating them."

The Maharal writes that the word "*Torah*" comes from the same root as the word "*horaah*," which means "instruction." The Torah instructs a person as to the proper way to relate to everything in creation.

The Torah teaches us much more than how to relate to things, however. The *mishnah* (*Avos* 6:1) states, "It [Torah study] makes him great and elevates him above *all things*." The Torah exalts a person and gives him reign over everything, because it delineates the proper course of action in any situation that could possibly arise.

(*Daas Shlomo*, unpublished manuscript)

פרשת שמיני
Parashas Shemini

KNOWING ONE'S WORTH:
THE FIRST GATEWAY TO AVODAS HASHEM

קְרַב אֶל־הַמִּזְבֵּחַ
Come near to the Mizbei'ach (9:7).

The *parashah* begins with Moshe Rabbeinu cajoling Aharon to enter the *Mishkan* in order to perform the *avodah*: "Come near to the *Mizbei'ach* and perform the service of your sin offering and your burnt offering and the sacrifices of the nation" (9:7). Rashi explains that Aharon was too embarrassed to enter the *Mishkan*, and Moshe had to cajole him to enter: "Why are you embarrassed? You were specifically chosen to perform this *avodah*." Ramban adds that Aharon's shame and hesitation to enter the *Mishkan* stemmed from the role that he played in making the golden calf. Moshe responded, "Have a proud spirit, and come perform the *avodah*."

In *Pirkei Avos* (4:4), the *mishnah* says that a person should be exceedingly (*me'od me'od*) humble. With this in mind, we can understand Aharon's uneasiness in accepting the position assigned to him. He felt that he was unworthy of the lofty task of bringing sacrifices before the Creator of the world. If so, why did Moshe tell Aharon to be proud and perform the *avodah*, against the dictates of *Chazal*? The answer is that although one must be exceedingly humble (the terminology of *me'od me'od* is found almost nowhere else in *Chazal*), there is a limit to the extent that one should exercise this trait. If one's humility inhibits his *avodas Hashem*, then he has overstepped the proper parameters of this *middah*. Moshe was telling Aharon that if he was specifically chosen for this position, then this was not the time or place for humility.

This idea is relevant to every one of us. Many people shy away from learning *mussar* because they have no interest in highlighting their deficiencies. Even those who do learn *mussar* often fall into depression after discovering how many negative traits they possess. The truth is that *mussar* study is only effective for a person who is already cognizant of his abundance of positive traits and awesome innate greatness. Rabbeinu Yonah makes this clear at the beginning of his *sefer Shaarei Avodah*:

> "*Mussar study is only effective for a person who is already cognizant of his abundance of positive traits and awesome innate greatness.*"

"*The very first gateway [into avodas Hashem] is that one who wishes to serve Hashem must know his own worth; and be cognizant of his caliber and the caliber of his forefathers, and their greatness and importance, and how beloved they were to their Creator. He must constantly strive and strengthen himself to maintain this caliber, and he should think to himself, 'A great and important person like myself, who has lofty and awesome positive attributes, and who is the son of great people — the son of kings from the past — how can I do such a terrible thing and sin before Hashem?'*" Humility would only be detrimental to such a person, as he would recoil at the thought of serving the Creator in his lowly

state. This would send him down the ladder of *avodah* instead of up.
(*Alei Shur,* Vol. II, p. 160)

Mussar study is imperative for our self-improvement. However, knowing and believing in our positive traits takes precedence over studying *mussar*. Take a piece of paper and write down *at least 20 positive traits that you possess.* Only then should you proceed to the *Mesilas Yesharim* for a healthy dose of *mussar*.
(*Shiurei Chumash, Parashas Shemini* 9:7)

❋ ❋ ❋

SECRET TO SUCCESS

וַיָּבֹא מֹשֶׁה וְאַהֲרֹן אֶל־אֹהֶל מוֹעֵד

Moshe and Aharon came to the Ohel Moed (9:23).

Parashas Shemini describes the eighth and final day of the inauguration of the *Mishkan*. On that day, Aharon made his first appearance as the *kohen gadol*. Although hesitant at first, at Moshe's prodding he agreed to assume his new role. He brought the appropriate *korbanos*, performed the related *avodah*, and blessed *Bnei Yisrael*. Nevertheless, he did not succeed in bringing the *Shechinah* down to the abode that had been created for this purpose.

Rashi (9:23) tells us that Aharon was sure that it was his involvement in the making of the golden calf that was preventing the *Shechinah* from descending on the *Mishkan*. He expressed his disappointment to Moshe, whereupon he and Moshe entered the *Mishkan* and *davened*, causing the *Shechinah* to descend.

This incident carries a lesson that applies to each of us on a daily basis. *Bnei Yisrael* spent many days and months building the *Mishkan* and crafting its vessels, and after the construction was complete, the *kohanim* spent eight consecutive days inaugurating it. Yet they were not successful in these lofty endeavors until their actions were accompanied by *tefillah*. Likewise, even when we toil greatly and invest much effort in our spiritual growth, our *avodah* must be accompanied by *tefillah*.

The Gemara (*Niddah* 70b) relates that people asked Rabbi Yehoshua ben Chananya, "What is the proper way to acquire wisdom?" He answered, "One should devote much time to Torah study and limit the time he devotes to his work." They countered that many have followed this advice, and nevertheless have not succeeded. He responded, "One should ask for compassion from the One Who is the source of all wisdom." The Gemara asks: If acquiring wisdom is dependent entirely on prayer, why did Rabbi Yehoshua originally answer that wisdom is acquired through devoting much time to Torah study? The Gemara answers that one without the other is not sufficient.

We can understand that one who fails to open a *sefer* but spends the entire day praying that he succeed in learning will not acquire wisdom. However, it is harder to understand that one who spends the entire day immersed in learning will not succeed because he did not pray for Divine assistance. Yet the Gemara seems to imply that the actual learning is secondary to the *tefillah*! And if *Chazal* say so, then it is absolutely true. Yes, one must learn, but the main ingredient for success in Torah study is *tefillah*.

In this vein, the Chazon Ish said that on certain days he toiled more in his *tefillah* than he did in his study of Torah!

Rabbi Yehonason Eibeshutz, who was known as a genius, wrote that he found that on days when he *davened* with *kavanah* he succeeded in his learning, while the opposite was true when his *tefillos* lacked *kavanah*. He continues, "Therefore, do not say that one person is greater than another because of his intelligence or awesome wisdom and understanding. This is not the case! It is a falsehood! Rather, it is a gift from Hashem, when one anticipates His abundant goodness and compassion by means of abundant prayer and pleading. There is nothing that grants a person proper understanding and helps decipher difficulties like a tearful *tefillah* that He have compassion, for Hashem listens to all those who call out to Him truthfully" (*Ya'aros Devash*). (See also *Alei Shur*, Vol. II, pp. 124-127.)

We know that all material pursuits must be accompanied by a prayer for success. However, it is not as obvious that the same applies to our spiritual endeavors. We could accomplish so much in that realm if we added a heartfelt *tefillah*!
(*Shiurei Chumash, Parashas Shemini* 9:23)

❊ ❊ ❊

THE OCCUPATION OF SILENCE

וַיִּדֹּם אַהֲרֹן

And Aharon was silent (10:3).

Chazal (*Bereishis Rabbah* 71:8) tell us that Rochel Imeinu engaged in the "occupation" of silence, and her offspring engaged in the same "occupation." Her son Binyamin was privy to the sale of Yosef, but did not reveal this knowledge to Yaakov. Shaul HaMelech, her descendant, was anointed king, and chose not to share this wonderful news with others. Esther, another descendant, did not reveal her nationality to anyone in Achashveirosh's palace.

Sometimes silence is more expressive than words. In this *parashah* we read how Aharon's two sons, Nadav and Avihu, were consumed by a Heavenly fire when they brought an unauthorized incense offering. Thereafter we are told, "And Aharon was silent." His silence was an expression of his total acceptance of this Divine — albeit very painful — decree, and *Chazal* tell us that he was rewarded for his silence.

In contrast, a person who has difficulty remaining silent will never fully appreciate anything that he experiences. When he is awed or shaken by something that he has heard or seen, he feels compelled to categorize the occurrence with a verbal description: "Amazing!" or "Very nice!" If he would remain silent and allow what he has seen or heard to seep in and be internalized, it would have a much greater impression on him.

Silence goes hand in hand with solitude. A person who enjoys a quiet moment gets to know himself and his internal world, and will make an effort to find time for solitude. On the other hand, a person who does not know how to remain silent flees from solitude.

A moment of solitude affords him a private audience with himself — and he has no interest in getting to know himself.

If not for nighttime, we would not know that there are stars. Only after the sun sets are the stars revealed, and along with them new and almost endless expanses. Likewise, during the day a person is busy with a multitude of people and tasks. Only after the day concludes and he isolates himself from all the commotion does he have the ability to connect with his internal world and the spiritual yearnings that accompany it.

> "If not for nighttime, we would not know that there are stars."

We run from work to home, from the company of people to the radio, from our cell phone to our iPod, and we do not have a minute to get to know ourselves. Even if we would have a quiet minute, we would not know what to do with it. There is no one in the entire world more interesting than *you*. Take some time to discover the innermost yearnings of that unique personality!

(*Alei Shur,* Vol. I, p. 178)

❈ ❈ ❈

SPIRITUAL MAKEOVER

כִּי אֲנִי ה׳ הַמַּעֲלֶה אֶתְכֶם מֵאֶרֶץ מִצְרַיִם ... וִהְיִיתֶם קְדֹשִׁים
For I am Hashem Who brought you up from the land of Egypt ... and you shall be holy" (11:45).

In the *Aseres Hadibros* we read, "I am Hashem your God who *took you out* of the land of Egypt" (*Shemos* 20:2). In this *parashah* it appears that besides the actual Exodus, there was yet another aspect to *Yetzias Mitzrayim*: "For I am Hashem Who *brought you up* from the land of Egypt ... and you shall be holy" (11:45). We know that being "taken out of Egypt" refers to the Exodus, which was carried out amid much fanfare and with many miracles. But what is the significance of the fact that *Bnei Yisrael* were also "brought up" from the land of Egypt?

Rashi (*Shemos* 12:6) tells us that when Hashem came to redeem *Bnei Yisrael* from Mitzrayim, they were devoid of mitzvos, and had no merit through which to be redeemed. Hashem gave them two mitzvos to perform: *bris milah* and the *Korban Pesach*. If *Yetzias Mitzrayim* merely entailed leaving the land of their bondage, they would not have had to prepare themselves in a way that involved risking their lives, by performing a circumcision just before they left Egypt. The required acts of preparation prove that *Yetzias Mitzrayim* was much more than freedom from enslavement.

Yetzias Mitzrayim occurred in stages. The first stage was not the actual Exodus, but the spiritual redemption from the influences of Egyptian society, to which they had been subjected for 210 years. This cleansing process gave birth to a new nation.

The second stage was Hashem's revelation at midnight, which caused the Jewish people to realize their ultimate calling: that of a nation that acts as bearers of the *Shechinah*. It was the Jewish nation's "spiritual awakening" caused by the performance of these two mitzvos that effected a "spiritual awakening" in Heaven, manifesting itself in the form of this great revelation.

The third and final stage occurred when the very bodies of *Bnei Yisrael* became holy. The Gemara (*Bava Metzia* 61b) asks, why does the Torah write, "[Who] brought you up [from the land of Egypt]," in the section that deals with refraining from eating insects? The Gemara answers that the mere fact that *Bnei Yisrael* do not defile themselves by eating disgusting insects and vermin would have been sufficient reason to bring them up from Egypt. When the Torah writes that they were "brought up" from Egypt, it means that their bodies were elevated to a plane of holiness.

> "When the Jewish people left Egypt, they underwent a spiritual makeover, in which their very bodies became refined and more inclined toward spirituality."

David HaMelech says (*Tehillim* 40:9), "And Your Torah is in my innards." Why was the Torah in his innards? Would not it suffice if the Torah were in his head and heart? This statement depicts the holiness of a Jew's body. When the Jewish people left Egypt, they underwent a spiritual makeover, in which their very bodies became refined and more inclined toward spirituality. Thereafter, they were unable to tolerate coarse behavior and concepts.

Our obligation is not only to feel as if we ourselves left Egypt, but also to be cognizant that we were "brought up" from Egypt and elevated to the point that our bodies became permeated with holiness.

פרשת תזריע-מצורע
Parashas Tazria-Metzora

PRECIOUS DEPOSIT

אִשָּׁה כִּי תַזְרִיעַ וְיָלְדָה זָכָר
When a woman conceives and gives birth to a son (12:2).

The birth of any child is an entrustment from Hashem. David HaMelech says (*Tehillim* 8:5), "What is a person that You should remember him, and a man that You should be mindful of him (*ki sifkidenu*)?" The words "*ki sifkidenu*" can be translated homiletically, "that You entrust him with a deposit (*pikadon*)." The birth of a child is an expression of Hashem's trust in a person, to the extent that He has deposited a human in his care.

Children are not given to a person to tend to him in his old age, or as an object in which to take pride. They are a deposit from Hashem, one that must be cared for responsibly. What does one have to do to properly care for this most precious deposit?

Ramban notes that in the first *parashah* of *Krias Shema* we say (*Devarim* 6:7), "And you shall teach [Torah] to your children, and *you* shall speak [in Torah]." However, in the second *parashah* of *Krias Shema* we say, "And you shall teach [Torah] to your children so that *they* shall speak in them" (ibid. 11:19). He explains that the first step in teaching a child is invariably accomplished by way of the father speaking to the child. But the ultimate goal is that the child should be able to speak in Torah *on his own*.

Parents are obligated to teach their children Torah and guide them in a way that will enable them to grow properly. However, the ultimate goal is that the child should want to take initiative in his life and develop a *personal* desire to grow in Torah and mitzvos. It is a sad sight to behold "*chinuch*" that stifles the individual ambition of a child.

> "Children are not merely a privilege; they are a great responsibility."

Children are not merely a privilege; they are a great responsibility. They are not *our* children, but rather Hashem's children whom He has deposited with us, for a purpose and with a mission.

(*Zeriyah U'Binyan Bechinuch*, p. 32)

❊ ❊ ❊

LIVING WITH HASHEM

וְהָיָה בְעוֹר־בְּשָׂרוֹ לְנֶגַע צָרָעַת

And it will become a tzaraas affliction on the skin of his flesh (13:2).

Ramban (13:47) writes that *tzaraas* is a completely supernatural phenomenon. It occurs only in the chosen land of Eretz Yisrael, and afflicts only the Jewish people — and only when they maintain an elevated level of spirituality. When an *aveirah* is committed in such a spiritually charged environment, Hashem causes *tzaraas* to appear on the sinner's house, clothing, or body to indicate that He has distanced Himself from the offender as a result of the transgression.

In such an era, *Bnei Yisrael* lived with an incredible level of *Hashgachah Pratis*. A person who spoke *lashon hara* would immediately be punished with *tzaraas*. It was as if Hashem were literally speaking to him, as two friends would speak to each other. Even so, Ramban writes that people were afflicted with *tzaraas* only after *Bnei Yisrael* conquered and divided Eretz Yisrael, because only after they were settled would they have the peace of mind to fully recognize Hashem and His *Hashgachah Pratis*.

The essence of the Torah is to help us reach such a level of *Hashgachah Pratis*. Ramban writes that the purpose of the mitzvos is to divert our thoughts from the mundane and enable us to live with Hashem, so to speak, and be enveloped in *Hashgachah Pratis*. The very birth of the Jewish nation occurred through Hashem demonstrating that "I am Hashem *in the midst of the land*" (*Shemos* 8:18) — i.e., constant Divine Providence.

The Pesach *Seder* is designed to help us fulfill the dictum, "In every generation a person is obligated to feel as if *he* left Mitzrayim" (*Pesachim* 116b). We eat *maror* and *charoses* so that we can "taste" the bitterness of bondage and relate to the servitude that the Jews experienced. We eat matzah and drink the four cups of wine while reclining so that our bodies can sense the exhilaration of freedom. Why must we reexperience the Exodus? Would not retelling the wonders and miracles of *Yetzias Mitzrayim* be sufficient to build our *emunah*? The answer is that we are striving to achieve more than just cementing our belief in Hashem. We are trying to bring ourselves to a state where we, too, are enveloped in Hashem's *Hashgachah Pratis*. We are meant to come to the realization that "Originally our forefathers worshiped idols and *now* Hashem has brought us into His service." On the *Seder* night, Hashem takes us by the hand and guides us. This is the ultimate *Hashgachah Pratis*.

Unfortunately, *Hashgachah Pratis* is an abstract concept for many of us; we acknowledge it in our minds but it never makes its way into our hearts. What is a practical application of *Hashgachah Pratis* to which we can relate? Many people experience jealousy — of another person's superior *middos*, perhaps, or of someone else's greater intellectual capabilities. Some gifted individuals might wish they could forgo their talents so that they need not answer to all those who expect more from them. The solution to these problems is internalizing the concept of *Hashgachah Pratis*. Every person was put in his particular situation with a plethora of external and internal factors tailored to his unique purpose in life. It will not help to be like your neighbor or friend, because you will never accomplish what *you* have to accomplish.

Rav Naftali Amsterdam once commented to his *rebbi*, Rav Yisrael Salanter, that if he would have the intellectual capacity of the Shaagas Aryeh (a renowned genius), the heart

"With your mind, with your heart, and with your middos, you can become the true oveid Hashem you are meant to be."

of the Yesod V'shoresh HaAvodah, and the *middos* of Rav Yisrael Salanter, he would be able to serve Hashem properly. Rav Yisrael responded, "Rav Naftali, with *your* mind, with *your* heart, and with *your middos*, you can become the true *oveid Hashem* you are meant to be."

(*Daas Shlomo*, unpublished manuscript)

❊ ❊ ❊

WHEN IDEOLOGIES CRUMBLE

כֻּלּוֹ הָפַךְ לָבָן טָהוֹר הוּא

Having turned completely white, it is pure (13:13).

There is a fascinating halachah mentioned in this week's *parashah* with regard to *tzaraas*. Even a small patch of *tzaraas* can make a person *tamei*. Yet if the *tzaraas* spreads to the entire body and covers the person from head to toe, the Torah tells us that the person is *tahor* (see 13:13).

While it seems that this is an enigmatic spiritual law, it is clear from *Chazal* that we can extrapolate from this concept to other areas of life. The Gemara (*Sanhedrin* 97a) states, "Rabbi Yitzchak said, 'Mashiach will not arrive until the **entire** government turns to heresy.' Said Rava, 'Where is this mentioned in the Torah? *The entire [affliction of tzaraas] has turned white; it is pure.*'" When the entire government turns corrupt, one can be sure that purity (i.e., Mashiach) is on its way. How are we to understand this concept, which seems to conflict with logic? How can it be that the worse something gets, the better it really is?

Rav Wolbe explains as follows. We relate to good and evil as two entities that have different values: good is positive while evil is negative. However, it is clear that the Torah does not relate to evil in the same way that we do. In many places the Torah equates good with life and evil with death. The Torah views good as a reality, while evil is not real at all. As we perceive the world today, it is hard for us to digest such a concept. Evil seems to be all too much of a reality, greatly overshadowing the good. It takes a perceptive eye to be able to discern the truth behind this facade.

When the spies returned from scouting out the Land of Israel, they prefaced their negative appraisal of the land with some positive aspects: "We have seen the land, and indeed it flows with milk and honey" (*Bamidbar* 13:27). Rashi tells us that they deliberately added some truth to their false account because "a falsehood cannot endure unless it begins with a little bit of truth."

> "*Every evil regime places either freedom or justice on its ideological platform, because it is this virtue that affords them some degree of continuity.*"

Evil cannot exist unless it attaches itself to good. Every evil regime places either freedom or justice on its ideological platform, because it is this virtue that affords them some degree of continuity. Consequently, when that aspect of good disappears, the entire ideology crumbles along with the regime, because evil by itself has no continuity.

Thus, *Chazal* tell us that when the *entire* government turns to heresy, Mashiach will come. It was the minute amount of *emunah* that gave this regime its foundation, and when they lose that last bit of *emunah* the government will automatically self-destruct, making way for the ultimate dominion of Mashiach. Rava finds proof for this concept from the halachah that when *tzaraas* covers the entire body it is *tahor*. Impurity cannot exist unless there is some purity for it to latch onto.

This concept sheds light on the *baal teshuvah* movement of the past few decades. When ideologies lose any semblance of righteousness and crumble one after another, people begin to realize that all that is left is the truth and immortality of the Torah.

This is the key to understanding the Torah's guarantee that *Klal Yisrael* will do *teshuvah* in the "End of Days" (see *Devarim* 30:1). When society loses all its morals, the glamour of the outside world evaporates and the truth shines in all its glory, which prompts people to do *teshuvah*. We have definitely reached that point.

(*Maamarei Yemei Ratzon*, p. 443)

❊ ❊ ❊

SPEECH: THE VEHICLE OF CONNECTION

וְלָקַח לַמִּטַּהֵר שְׁתֵּי־צִפֳּרִים חַיּוֹת טְהֹרוֹת

And for the person being purified there shall be taken two live, clean birds (14:4).

Rashi notes that birds are part of the purification process of the *metzora* because *tzaraas* comes as a result of *lashon hara,* and this man, like birds, twittered.

On the *passuk* "Hashem blew into his nostrils a soul of life and man became a living being" (*Bereishis* 2:7), Rashi explains that although the Torah also refers to animals as "living beings," man is still superior, for he was endowed with the ability to think and speak. Speech is the tool that gives a person the ability to connect with others and makes him a "social creature," as philosophers describe. It is also the means by which we can connect with the Creator Himself. Halachah dictates that one must enunciate the words of *Shema* and *Shemoneh Esrei*; we can talk directly to Hashem, but only if we articulate our thoughts with words.

With regard to Torah study, the *mishnah* in *Pirkei Avos* (3:3) tells us, "Two who sit together and there are *words* of Torah between them, the Divine Presence rests upon them ... How do we know that Hashem gives a reward even to one person who sits and studies Torah? The *passuk* states, 'He will sit in solitude and be silent, for he will have received [a reward] for it.'" The Maharal notes that although a person who studies Torah alone is rewarded, the Divine Presence does not rest upon him. Only when two people study together is there a give-and-take, in which words of Torah are articulated. Such Torah study is considered "complete," causing Hashem's presence to rest upon them. This is not the case when one studies alone, for he has no one with whom to converse. His Torah is in some way deficient, for it lacks the connection to Hashem that is made possible by the power of speech.

One of the basic components of *teshuvah* is reciting *viduy*. *Chazal* (*Vayikra Rabbah* 3:3) compare the recitation of *viduy* to the soldering of two pieces of a rod back together. An *aveirah* distances a person from his Creator, and the process of *teshuvah* is what brings him back to his previous spiritual level. However, the actual connection — the soldering — only comes as a result of *viduy*. Speech is the unique tool that creates a bond between man and God through *tefillah*, Torah, and *teshuvah*.

> "Speech is the unique tool that creates a bond between man and God through tefillah, Torah, and teshuvah."

Understanding this concept will help us understand the severity of *lashon hara*. Hashem created speech, and He intended it to create a connection and closeness between man and his fellow man and between man and his Creator. A person who speaks *lashon hara* is utilizing this powerful tool for the opposite purpose: he is creating division and causing hatred between friends. Therefore, "A person who speaks *lashon hara* banishes the Divine Presence into the Heavens" (*Devarim Rabbah* 8:10). The *Shechinah's* presence is the ultimate manifestation of closeness and love, but there is no place for Him in this world when people use their power of speech to achieve the opposite result.

The Torah writes, "For Hashem your God walks in the midst of your camp to save you and deliver your enemies before you, and your camp shall be holy, and He should not observe any *ervas davar* causing Him to turn away from you" (*Devarim* 23:15). The Targum translates "*ervas davar*" as "sinful words." Sinful words — *lashon hara* — cause Hashem to turn away from *Bnei Yisrael*. Conversely, refraining from *lashon hara* brings down the Divine Presence and gives *Bnei Yisrael* the protection they so desperately need.

(*Alei Shur,* Vol. II, p. 34)

פרשת קדושים
Parashas Kedoshim

SMALL ACTIONS ARE THE KEY TO HOLINESS

קְדֹשִׁים תִּהְיוּ כִּי קָדוֹשׁ אֲנִי ה׳ אֱלֹקֵיכֶם
You should be holy, for holy am I, Hashem your God (19:2).

The numerous commandments in *Parashas Kedoshim* were specifically placed there in order that we recognize that they all fall under the heading of this *passuk*. Even the seemingly trivial mitzvos found in this *parashah* are the foundation for acquiring this trait of holiness. For instance, the obligation to leave a small portion of one's crop for the poor (19:9) might appear to be an inconsequential gesture of kindness, but it is the starting point for those striving for holiness.

> "What might appear to be an inconsequential gesture of kindness is the starting point for those striving for holiness."

In a similar vein, the Raavad makes a suggestion to those who are interested in repenting, but lack the physical stamina to fast: "One should not finish his meal in its entirety; instead, he should leave over a small portion on his plate" (*Shaar Hakedushah*). At first glance this seems to be a simple action that anyone can do. Only after attempting to follow this directive does one realize why this apparently insignificant action is the key to controlling his desires and achieving holiness.

Although this exercise involves no physical distress, it may prove more difficult than fasting. When food is especially appetizing or a dessert is particularly enticing, it can be extremely difficult to leave over a portion and not indulge one's desires by finishing the delicacy to the last crumb. One has to subdue his cravings and fight the tendency to give in to his "needs." He might even be tempted to rationalize that the Torah forbids one to waste perfectly good food (*bal tashchis*). To combat these thoughts, a person must clarify for himself that this exercise is not an act of destroying food, but part of a process of improving his character.

How does not giving into one's desires bring the person to holiness? By way of illustration, magnetic fields surround all the heavenly bodies. When a star passes through the magnetic field of the sun, the gravitational force causes it to veer ever so slightly from its course. Similarly, spiritual forces have "magnetic fields" that surround them. The *yetzer hara* exerts a powerful pull on us, in the form of cravings that seem irresistible. Our *neshamah* and *seichel* (the positive spiritual forces) have a corresponding "magnetic field," but it is not as powerful as the field surrounding our *yetzer hara*. When a person resists his desires, he draws himself away from the "pull" of the *yetzer hara*, and is no longer under the influence of its magnetic field. This enables him to enter the field of his *neshamah* and *seichel*, which is the core of *kedushah*.

If we can make even an occasional habit of leaving over a small portion on our plates, we will merit an impressive portion not only in this world but in the next world as well.

(*Shiurei Chumash, Parashas Kedoshim* 19:9; *Alei Shur*, Vol. II, p. 250; *Alei Shur*, Vol. II, pp. 43-46)

❋ ❋ ❋

YIRAS SHAMAYIM: THE TRUE DEFINITION

וְיָרֵאתָ מֵאֱלֹקֶיךָ אֲנִי ה'
You shall fear your God, I am Hashem (19:14).

If we were to take a poll of how people define *yiras Shamayim*, we would probably receive various answers. Some would claim that *yirah* means being meticulous in the performance of mitzvos. Others would opine that *yirah* is the performance of mitzvos with the proper intentions, or that *yirah* is the fear of *Gehinnom*. Although each of these answers touches on some aspect of *yirah*, none of them truly reveals the depth of this concept.

Rashi in *Parashas Kedoshim* enlightens us with a deeper understanding of *yirah*. "Do not curse a deaf man, and before a blind man do not place a stumbling block; you shall fear your God — I am Hashem" (19:14). Rashi explains that the *passuk* is referring to a figurative stumbling block: Do not give advice that serves your interests but is detrimental to the recipient, who is "blind" and uninformed about the issue at hand. Since only the person offering the advice is aware of his true intentions, the Torah writes, "And you shall fear your God" — for He can distinguish the real intent behind a person's actions.

Later in the *parashah*, the Torah commands us, "Stand up before the aged and give respect to the elderly; you shall fear your God — I am Hashem" (19:32). Rashi explains that a person might think that no one will know if he pretends not to see an elderly man, thereby obviating the need to stand up for him. Therefore, the Torah writes, "And you shall fear your God," Who knows the true motivation behind a person's actions.

In *Parashas Behar*, there are three additional places where the Torah writes in conjunction with specific mitzvos, "And you shall fear your God." Although Rashi was careful with every word he wrote, each time this phrase appears he explains that only the person himself can discern the underlying motivation for his action. This is why the Torah felt the need to write, "And you shall fear your God."

With this in mind, we can gain a deeper understanding of the concept of *yirah*. *Yirah* can be found in the recesses of the mind and in the rationale behind a person's actions. The gauge to measure one's *yiras Shamayim* is specifically those mitzvos that only Hashem knows about. Amazingly, all five of the aforementioned mitzvos are between man and his fellow. It is possible to give

> "*The gauge to measure one's yiras Shamayim is specifically those mitzvos that only Hashem knows about.*"

a pious impression to the world, while deep down harboring ulterior motives rooted in personal desires. These mitzvos are the true test of whether *yiras Shamayim* governs one's interpersonal relationships.

Such tainted thoughts are possible even with regard to mitzvos between man and Hashem. A person might buy a beautiful *esrog* so that others will think he is meticulous in his performance of mitzvos, while spending substantially less than he can afford when it comes to the performance of mitzvos that no one will know about. In contrast, a person who has true *yirah* will perform mitzvos objectively, without consideration of his own interests or other people's favorable comments.

(*Alei Shur*, Vol. II, p. 500)

❋ ❋ ❋

LOOKING OUT FOR INNOCENCE

בְּצֶדֶק תִּשְׁפֹּט עֲמִיתֶךָ
With righteousness shall you judge your fellow (19:15).

There are two forces that influence all of a person's actions: his *yetzer hatov* and his *yetzer hara*. Each person's every action can theoretically be placed on a spiritual scale to determine whether the intention behind the action is positive or negative. However, human beings only perceive external actions and are not privy to the internal causes behind those actions. Therefore, the Torah commands us, "With righteous shall you judge your fellow." Rashi cites *Chazal* (*Shavuos* 30a) who explain this mitzvah as referring not to the judges of a *beis din*, but rather to the judgment that takes place in the courtroom of one's mind: we are to judge others' actions favorably.

A person who excels at judging his friend favorably will truly want his friend to emerge innocent of any questionable action. He will therefore go to great lengths to find some sort of rationalization that will interpret that action in a positive light. A case in point is the well-known story related by *Chazal* (*Shabbos* 127b):

A man hired himself out for three years. At the end of those three years, on Erev Yom Kippur, he approached his employer and requested his wages. The employer replied that he had no money.

"Give me produce," the worker said. The employer replied that he had none.

"Give me land." The employer replied that he had none.

"Give me livestock."

"I have none."

"Give me pillows and blankets." Once again the employer responded that he had none.

The worker slung his bags over his shoulder and dejectedly made his way home.

After Succos, the employer arrived at his worker's home along with three donkeys laden with food, drink, and other delicacies. They ate and drank together, and the employer gave the worker his wages. Then, he began to pepper him with questions. "When you asked for payment and I said I had no money, what did you think?"

"I thought that a good business venture had arisen and you had invested all your money."

"When you requested livestock and I replied that I had none, what did you think?"

"I thought that perhaps you had rented your animals out to other people."

"When you asked for land and I said that I had none, what did you think?"

"I thought that it might be leased to others."

"When you asked for produce and I replied that I have none, what did you think?"

"I thought that you had not yet tithed them."

"When you requested pillows and blankets and I said that I had none, what did you think?"

"I thought that perhaps you had consecrated all your possessions to Hashem."

"That is exactly what happened!" the employer exclaimed. "I consecrated all my possessions because of my son Hurkanos, who did not learn Torah, and when I came to the Rabbis in the South they released me from all my vows. Just as you judged me favorably, may Hashem judge you favorably as well."

We see to what extent a person can go to absolve his friend of guilt. Each rationalization of the worker to justify his employer's behavior was quite farfetched. Yet he *wanted* to believe that his employer was innocent, and he therefore searched with "a good eye" for some sort of reason that would prove that his employer's behavior was influenced by the yetzer hatov and not the yetzer hara.

Unfortunately, people tend to focus on other people's faults while ignoring their positive qualities. The mitzvah to judge people favorably is an exercise that allows us to search for the good in others at all costs. This exercise should extend into all areas of our lives. If we make an effort to search for and focus on the good qualities of others, our marriages, our children's *chinuch*, and every relationship we have will improve tremendously.

(*Alei Shur,* Vol. II, pp. 206-207)

> "Each rationalization of the worker to justify his employer's behavior was quite farfetched. Yet he wanted to believe that his employer was innocent."

❊ ❊ ❊

DO NOT BOTTLE UP RESENTMENT

לֹא־תִשְׂנָא אֶת־אָחִיךָ בִּלְבָבֶךָ הוֹכֵחַ תּוֹכִיחַ אֶת־עֲמִיתֶךָ
וְלֹא־תִשָּׂא עָלָיו חֵטְא

Do not hate your brother in your heart; rebuke your friend and do not bear a sin because of him (19:17).

There are two reasons why a person might hate someone else. A person might feel hatred toward another when he sees him transgressing a sin. Although this would seem to be a valid reason for hatred, the Torah tells us that the observer may not hate the transgressor; instead, he must rebuke him for his misdeed. If he fails to rebuke him, the Torah considers it as if the observer himself committed the transgression, and he will be punished accordingly. Accordingly, the *passuk* can be explained, "Even if you see your friend sin, you should not hate him. Rather, you should rebuke him, for if you do not, you will bear the sin!"

The second possible reason for hatred is when a person feels hurt by another person's actions. It does not make a difference if he was hurt physically, emotionally, or monetarily; the Torah tells him that he should not bottle up the resentment inside. He must approach the offender and discuss the motive for his actions, giving him the opportunity to explain or excuse himself. If he hides the hatred inside his heart, he is placing a sin upon the offender, because he may not know the gravity of his actions or he might miss out on the opportunity to ask for forgiveness. According to this explanation, the *passuk* means, "If you were hurt by another, do not keep your hatred inside your heart. Rather, speak to him and discuss the reason behind his actions so that the transgressor does not end up with a sin."

> *"It is much easier to continue hating someone, even for years on end, than to speak to him directly and ask him why he acted the way he did."*

It is much easier to continue hating someone, even for years on end, than to speak to him directly and ask him why he acted the way he did. It is very hard for the person who feels slighted to initiate a conversation that will give the offender the ability to excuse himself, thereby circumventing any reason for hatred. Yet we should speak up and discuss our feelings so that we can ultimately fulfill the obligation stated in the following *passuk*: "You shall love your fellow as yourself."

(*Shiurei Chumash, Parashas Kedoshim* 19:17, based on Ramban)

❋ ❋ ❋

THE EXTENT OF ACCOUNTABILITY

וְאֶת־הַבְּהֵמָה תַּהֲרֹגוּ
And you shall kill the animal (20:15).

Toward the end of *Parashas Kedoshim* the Torah tells us that if a man lives with an animal, not only is he put to death, the animal is also killed (20:15). Rashi explains that although the animal did nothing wrong and does not deserve to die, it is killed because it caused a person's demise. It goes without saying that if a person, who can differentiate between good and bad, causes his friend to transgress an *aveirah*, he will be punished.

In a similar vein, Rashi continues, the Torah commanded *Bnei Yisrael* upon entering Eretz Yisrael to destroy all the places and trees where idols were worshiped. Why did the trees deserve to be punished? The answer is the same as above; they were the cause of transgression, and therefore had to be destroyed. We learn from here that if a tree, which cannot see or hear, is punished because it caused a sin, how much more so is a person held accountable if he causes his friend to transgress an *aveirah* and stray from the path of life to the path of death.

Rav Wolbe once spoke to Rav Meir Chodosh about the possibility of expelling certain troublemakers from the yeshivah. Rav Chodosh commented that it might not be the troublemakers who needed to be expelled. Rather, perhaps some of the "good boys" needed to be thrown out. He explained that no one would be influenced by the behavior of the troublemakers, since everyone looked down upon them. However, there was a greater chance that boys in the yeshivah would emulate the "good boys" who learned well yet did not come to *davening*, since the students looked up to them. The above Rashi describes quite clearly the severity of one who causes his friend to stray from the true path.

We all find ourselves in situations and places where we are among other Jews, both religious and secular, who look up to us. They scrutinize our actions and define for themselves, on that basis, the proper behavior of a religious Jew. We bear the great responsibility of ensuring that no one is turned away from the path of life because of our actions. However, the opposite also holds true. If a person is turned *toward* the path of life because of our actions, we have created a *kiddush Hashem*. This is such a great mitzvah that its dividends can be received only in the World to Come!

(*Shiurei Chumash, Parashas Kedoshim* 20:15)

פרשת אמור
Parashas Emor

MEIS MITZVAH, CHAI MITZVAH

לְאָבִיו וּלְאִמּוֹ לֹא יִטַּמָּא

He shall not contaminate himself to his father and his mother (21:11).

If we were to give a heading to this week's *parashah*, that heading would be "*kavod*" — honor. The *parashah* delineates numerous forms of *kavod*, which pertain to Hashem, the *kohanim*, the *kohen gadol*, the *korbanos*, Bnei Yisrael, and the Yamim Tovim. The tremendous amount of *kavod* befitting a Jewish person can be gleaned from the halachos of *meis mitzvah:* a Jew who dies and has no one to attend to his burial.

In contrast to all other *kohanim*, the *kohen gadol* is commanded to continue performing the *avodah* in the *Beis HaMikdash* even after the death of a parent. Rashbam (10:3) explains that he must set aside his own feelings and continue the *avodah* because a cessation of the *avodah* would be a disgrace to Hashem. Nevertheless, if a *kohen gadol* comes upon a *meis mitzvah* while on his way to perform the *avodah* even on Yom Kippur, he must take the time to bury the dead person. The fact that the body of a *tzelem Elokim* is lying in disgrace without anyone to tend to it overrides even the *avodah* of the *kohen gadol* on Yom Kippur.

If so much *kavod* is required for a *meis mitzvah*, then how much more *kavod* is owed to a "*chai mitzvah*": a living Jew who has no one to nurture and tend to him. Indeed, *Chazal* tell us (*Berachos* 19b), "*Kavod haberiyos* is so important that it even overrides a negative commandment of the Torah."

Who can be classified as a "*chai mitzvah*"? One example is a child who learns Torah but has no one to guide him. When a person is born, he is likened to a wild donkey. The aim of *chinuch* is to turn this wild donkey into a *mentsch*: "*Let one who is [like] a wild donkey be reborn as a man*" (*Iyov* 11:12). Yet we cannot expect a child to be reborn if there is no "midwife" to "deliver" him. Even if a child learns well in school, *derech eretz* and *yiras Shamayim* do not simply evolve by themselves. In addition to the Torah he is taught, every child needs someone to nurture and guide him.

Chinuch is a skill, one that requires much foresight and consideration. The interesting thing is that most parents think they have mastered this skill! Another interesting phenomenon regarding *chinuch* is that while some results of *chinuch* are recognizable immediately, others can only be seen many years down the road. For example, a child who misbehaves in school and is yelled at or slapped might not repeat that misdemeanor ever again. However, the real litmus test of successful *chinuch* is how the child behaves when he is 30 years old. *Chinuch* must always be implemented with an eye to the future, and a spur-of-the-moment response generally does not take into account the long-term effects.

> "*The real litmus test of successful chinuch is how the child behaves when he is 30 years old.*"

Every encounter we have with our children has the ability to affect them — positively or, God forbid, negatively — for many years to come. Indeed, *chinuch* is a time-consuming job, but there is no better investment of time than the time one spends cultivating a child into the *tzelem Elokim* he is meant to be.

(*Shiurei Chumash, Parashas Emor* 21:1,10; *Igros U'Kesavim* Vol. II, pp. 179-180)

❋ ❋ ❋

WHERE THERE IS HOLINESS, THERE IS HONOR

וְהָיוּ קֹדֶשׁ
So they must remain holy (21:6).

We say in *davening*, "Holy, holy, holy is Hashem, the Master of all Legions." Hashem is entirely holy since He is completely removed from all physicality. Nevertheless, He gave us a means for recognizing His greatness: "The entire world is filled with His glory." Hashem revealed Himself through the creation of this most awe-inspiring universe, and this revelation is referred to as "*kavod*," glory. Indeed, the *passuk* states, "All that is called by My name is for My glory; I have created it, formed it, and made it" (*Yeshayah* 43:7).

We can glean from here that wherever there is *kedushah* there is also an element of *kavod*. Since every person has been infused with a holy *neshamah* and therefore possesses a level of *kedushah*, this *kedushah* in turn necessitates that one conduct himself with a certain amount of *kavod*.

The connection between *kedushah* and *kavod* is made abundantly clear in *Parashas Emor*. The *parashah* begins with the *kedushah* of the *kohanim* and the halachic aspects of *kavod* that their *kedushah* demands. It continues with the *kedushah* of the *korbanos*, Hashem's *kedushah*, and the *kedushah* of Shabbos and Yom Tov, imparting the halachos of *kavod* that relate to each of these *kedushos*. The *parashah* ends with the story of the "*mekalel*" — the son of the Egyptian who cursed Hashem.

The root of the word "*kavod*" is "*kaveid*," heavy or serious. The polar opposite of *kavod* is "*klalah*," curse, which stems from the word "*kal*," light. When one behaves with seriousness toward another person, he has shown him *kavod*, while if he makes light of another person he may end up cursing him.

The Gemara (*Kedushin* 40b) tells us, "One who eats in the marketplace can be compared to a dog. Some say that he has disqualified himself from acting as a witness in *beis din*." Rashi explains that someone who eats in the public marketplace has demonstrated that he does not care about his *kavod*, and he will not be embarrassed to do something that will render him ineligible to act as a witness.

What is so terrible about eating in the marketplace? As long as the food is kosher and he made a *berachah*, what could be the problem? Although such behavior is not forbidden outright, it displays a lack of refinement and sensitivity. One who eats in the marketplace is lacking *kavod*, which can be defined as "an outward conduct that is necessitated by the reality of an inner *kedushah*." The cognizance of the holy *tzelem Elokim* inside himself requires a person to act accordingly.

> "*Kavod* can be defined as 'an outward conduct that is necessitated by the reality of an inner *kedushah*.'"

Rambam (*Hilchos Dei'os*, Chapter 5) describes the refined manner in which a *talmid chacham* should conduct himself. We might find it hard to understand what is so terrible if a person lacks this extra dose of refinement. *Yeridas hadoros*, coupled with the influence of the behavior of the nations around us, has clouded our perception of the *kedushah* that resides within each and every one of us. It is this *kedushah* that necessitates *kavod*.

(*Alei Shur*, Vol. II, pp. 225-226)

❋ ❋ ❋

FROM ONE RELATIONSHIP TO ANOTHER

וּבְקֻצְרְכֶם אֶת־קְצִיר אַרְצְכֶם . . . לֶעָנִי וְלַגֵּר תַּעֲזֹב אֹתָם

When you reap the harvest of your land ... for the poor and the proselyte you shall leave them (23:22).

This *parashah* recounts the different holidays that occur throughout the year. Juxtaposed with the mention of these Yamim Tovim is the Torah's warning that when we harvest our fields, we should not forget to leave various parts of the field for the poor. Rashi (23:22) quotes *Chazal*, who ask, "Why does the Torah deem it appropriate to place this *passuk* between the different holidays: Pesach and Shavuos on one side, and Rosh Hashanah and Yom Kippur on the other? To teach you that a person who gives charity from his field properly is considered to have built the *Beis HaMikdash* and brought sacrifices there."

What is the correlation between giving charity and bringing sacrifices in the *Beis HaMikdash*? The former is a mitzvah between man and his fellow man, while the latter is a matter solely between man and Hashem. *Chazal* are hinting to us that the closeness to Hashem effected by a sacrifice can also be achieved by giving *tzedakah* properly.

> "The same traits that impact our relationship bein adam lachaveiro also impact our relationship bein adam laMakom."

The same traits that impact our relationship *bein adam lachaveiro* also impact our relationship *bein adam laMakom*. *Chazal* tell us (*Mishnas Rabbi Eliezer* 7), "One who is ungrateful to his friend will ultimately be ungrateful to Hashem." What does a person's lack of appreciation to his friend have to do with *"frumkeit"*? Traits that are present in interpersonal relationships are automatically active in a person's interaction with Hashem as well.

This concept is also true with regard to a person's positive character traits. The Gemara says (*Succah* 49b), "It is certain that a person who does acts of kindness is one who fears Hashem." What do acts of kindness have to do with a person's fear of Hashem? The answer is that they both sprout from the same root.

This can be understood through an analogy. The heart can be compared to a closed room that has doors and windows. When a person is in a closed room he sees nothing. However, if he opens a window he sees both people and the sky. Similarly, a person who practices kindness is someone who has opened the window of his heart to see others, and when the window is open he is no longer focused solely on himself, so he sees the sky (i.e., Hashem) as well.

The words "*yirah*" (fear) and "*re'iah*" (seeing) share the same root, because when a person "sees" Hashem he comes to fear Him.

A person cannot interact with Hashem in a respectful manner while disregarding the way he acts with his fellow man, and vice versa. The manner in which he acts in one of his relationships will automatically find expression in his behavior in other relationships.

(*Shiurei Chumash, Parashas Emor* 23:22; *Alei Shur*, Vol. I, p. 92)

✿ ✿ ✿

LET NOTHING GET IN THE WAY

עַל הַמְּנֹרָה הַטְּהֹרָה יַעֲרֹךְ אֶת־הַנֵּרוֹת לִפְנֵי ה' תָּמִיד

On the pure Menorah he should arrange lamps before Hashem continually (tamid) (24:4).

Rashi explains that "*tamid*" does not mean that the *Menorah* must be lit at all times. Rather, it means that Aharon must light the *Menorah* every single night. Ramban adds that we deduce from the word "*tamid*," which connotes something constant, that the *Menorah* is to be lit even on Shabbos and even when the *kohen* is in a state of impurity.

> "A *masmid* is not necessarily one who learns Torah day and night. Rather, it is a person who sets definite times for Torah study."

We can glean from this *passuk* the appropriate definition of a "*masmid*," which comes from the root "*tamid*." A *masmid* is not necessarily one who learns Torah day and night. Rather, it is a person who sets definite times for Torah study. It is not the quantity of the Torah study that is important, but the consistency. The true *masmid* is one who sets aside fixed times for his learning, day in and day out, even on Shabbos and even when it's difficult for him to do so.

Sometimes situations arise in which even a person who has fixed times for his Torah, *tefillah*, or *avodas Hashem* must rearrange his schedule to fit the occasion. For example, *Chazal* tell us that one must interrupt his study of Torah to fulfill a mitzvah that cannot be performed by anyone else (*Yoreh De'ah* 246:18). This rule applies even when the mitzvah arises during the specific time that one has allotted for learning. Nevertheless, he should attend to this interruption in the most time-efficient manner possible, enabling himself to return to his schedule of *avodas Hashem*.

If we have a set time for work, and a set time for meals, then all the more so should we have set times for *avodas Hashem*. If we are hesitant to let anything get in the way of the times designated for work and for meals, then we certainly should not let anything get in the way of the times we have designated (or will designate) for *avodas Hashem*.

(*Shiurei Chumash, Parashas Emor* 24:2; *Alei Shur*, Vol. II, p. 322)

פרשת בהר-בחקותי
Parashas Behar-Bechukosai

WHAT SHEMITTAH AND SHABBOS HAVE IN COMMON

כִּי תָבֹאוּ אֶל־הָאָרֶץ אֲשֶׁר אֲנִי נֹתֵן לָכֶם וְשָׁבְתָה הָאָרֶץ שַׁבָּת לַה׳

When you enter the land that I give you, the land should rest a Shabbos for Hashem (25:2).

Parashas Behar begins with the mitzvah of *Shemittah*: "When you enter the land that I give you, the land should rest a *Shabbos for Hashem*." Rashi explains that "for Hashem" means for the sake of Hashem. He adds that we find this exact wording in the *Aseres Hadibros* (*Shemos* 20:10) with regard to the weekly Shabbos: "And the seventh day shall be a *Shabbos for Hashem*." What connection is there between Shabbos and *Shemittah*?

The Raavad, in his introduction to *Baalei Hanefesh*, notes that numerous mitzvos share a common denominator: they demonstrate that Hashem is in charge of the world, and we are not. Both *Shemittah* and Shabbos fall under this category of mitzvos. During *Shemittah* we desist entirely from working the land, and all the produce that grows during this year is free for the taking. The land is not ours; it belongs to Hashem.

Likewise, on Shabbos we are commanded to refrain from performing the 39 *melachos*. What these *melachos* have in common is that they are all acts of creation. On Shabbos, we demonstrate that we are ceasing to create, for Hashem is the sole Creator of the world.

Shemittah is an infrequent and uncommon mitzvah, since it occurs only once every seven years and applies only in Eretz Yisrael. On the other hand, Shabbos occurs weekly and is relevant in every location in the world. It is not merely a day off from work and an opportunity to spend time with family and friends; it is an entirely different perspective on life.

> "Shabbos is not merely a day off from work and an opportunity to spend time with family and friends; it is an entirely different perspective on life."

Shabbos helps us to internalize that Hashem runs the world, and we are simply His caretakers. It is not *our* world into which Hashem has to gain entrance. Rather, it is Hashem's world that we have the *zechus* of entering, and therefore we must faithfully follow His precepts.

(Shiurei Chumash, Parashas Behar 25:2)

❊ ❊ ❊

YOUR BROTHER'S INTERESTS

אַל־תִּקַּח מֵאִתּוֹ נֶשֶׁךְ וְתַרְבִּית וְיָרֵאתָ מֵאֱלֹהֶיךָ וְחֵי אָחִיךָ עִמָּךְ

Do not take from him interest and increase, and you shall fear your God; and let your brother live with you (25:36).

We are prohibited from lending money with interest. Rashi explains that because of the uniqueness of this prohibition, the

Torah adds an exhortation, "and you shall fear your God." Not only does a person have a natural inclination to charge interest, he is also inclined to excuse his actions with the rationalization, "My money is lying idle with my friend when it could be reaping dividends." Therefore, the Torah warns, "and you shall fear your God."

Why are we forbidden to charge interest? After all, the very same money could have been invested or put into a bank account; lending it to a fellow Jew causes one to lose that additional income.

When a person's brother needs financial help, he does not take into account losses that might result from coming to his brother's aid. The lender should have the same outlook when lending money to any Jew in need, and this act of *chessed* should be performed without any thought of remuneration. By contrast, the Torah tells us, "You may charge interest to a gentile" (*Devarim* 23:21; see Ramban, ibid. 20).

The *passuk* concludes, "and let your brother live with you." Ramban explains this to mean that if you did charge interest, you must return the interest to the borrower, so that he will be able to live adequately. If we are commanded to ensure that our fellow Jew has an adequate material life, how much more so must we ensure that he has the ability to live an adequate spiritual life. If a fellow Jew is having difficulty with any aspect of *Yiddishkeit* — from its basic precepts to understanding a commentary on the Gemara — we are obligated to offer our assistance.

> "We must relate to our fellow Jews no differently from the way we would relate to our closest relatives, both in material and spiritual matters. What would one not do for a sibling?"

Every Jew is a brother or sister. We must relate to our fellow Jews no differently from the way we would relate to our closest relatives, both in material and spiritual matters. What would one not do for a sibling? Let's bear this in mind the next time we are asked to do a *chessed*.

(*Shiurei Chumash, Parashas Behar* 25:36)

❃ ❃ ❃

THE END DOES NOT JUSTIFY THE MEANS

אַחֲרֵי נִמְכַּר גְּאֻלָּה תִּהְיֶה־לּוֹ

After he has been sold, he shall have redemption (25:48).

In *Parashas Toldos*, Yitzchak Avinu wished to bless Esav. Yitzchak therefore commanded Esav to prepare a delectable meal for him so that he would be in the proper mood to impart the blessing. Rivkah, however, was determined that Yaakov be the recipient of the great bounty of Yitzchak's blessing. While Esav was outside searching for an animal to prepare for his father, Rivkah commanded Yaakov to go to the sheep, "and take *for me* from there two choice young goats, and I will make of them delicacies for your father, as he loves" (*Bereishis* 27:9). The words "for me," Rashi explains, tell us that she was not stealing the two sheep. They belonged to her, since Yitzchak had obligated himself in his marital contract to provide her with two kid goats every day.

Rivkah implied that had the sheep not belonged to her she would not have commanded Yaakov to bring them to her. What, then, would have become of the blessings? *Klal Yisrael's* entire future hinged on these blessings, and Rivkah knew that. What bigger mitzvah could there be than procuring the *berachos* for those who rightfully deserved them and thereby ultimately providing for their survival throughout the ages?

The answer is that one may not transgress a commandment in the process of performing a mitzvah. Our

> "One may not transgress a commandment in the process of performing a mitzvah."

Sages refer to such a mitzvah as a "*mitzvah habaah ba'aveirah*"; a mitzvah that comes as a result of an *aveirah*. Furthermore, the Gemara teaches that a blessing said over a stolen item is in reality an act of blasphemy (*Bava Kamma* 94a). If the goats had not belonged to Rivkah, the importance of the blessings would not have justified the means of obtaining them.

This idea is expressed in this *parashah* as well. If a Jew were to become impoverished, he might sell himself as a slave to a non-Jew. Should this occur, the Torah commands his relatives to redeem him immediately from bondage lest he become assimilated into non-Jewish culture. Rashi (25:50) explains that the Torah is referring to an era when the Jewish people have dominion over the gentiles. Nevertheless, the Torah commands that the slave be redeemed via monetary compensation; he should not be forcibly removed from his master's possession (ibid. v. 48).

Do we not have an obligation to save him from his master and avert the prospect of assimilation? What could possibly be forbidden in such a dire situation? The answer is that despite the fact that this is a matter of life and death in the spiritual arena, we are not allowed to use deceitful methods to obtain the desired results. The Torah is telling us that even in such a situation, the end does not justify the means.

(*Shiurei Chumash, Parashas Behar* 25:50; *Shiurei Chumash, Parashas Toldos* 27:9)

❊ ❊ ❊

WALKING IN TORAH

אִם־בְּחֻקֹּתַי תֵּלֵכוּ

Im b'chukosai teileichu —
If you walk in My statutes (26:3).

Rashi explains this *passuk* as an exhortation to toil in the study of Torah. Why is Torah study referred to as "*teileichu*," walking? Shouldn't the Torah have written, "*Im b'chukosai tilmedu*" — if you *study* My *chukim*?

The study of Torah is unique in that it is always possible to delve deeper and deeper into the Torah's wisdom. The more one toils over a *maamar Chazal*, the more insightful it becomes. As a person grows older, the very same statement that he might have already studied in his youth can take on a whole new meaning. As he continues to age and become wiser, he will be amazed when he once again studies the same passage and perceives newfound profundity within the Torah's timeless words. It is for this reason that Hashem termed the toil of Torah "walking." A person can constantly stride deeper and deeper into the Torah, all the while gaining greater perception of its infinite wisdom.

A similar *passuk* appears in *Parashas Acharei Mos* (18:4): "And you shall guard My statutes to *walk in them*." Rashi explains that a person should not say, "I have already studied the Torah, and therefore I will now go study the wisdom of the nations." If a person constantly "walks" and delves deeper into the wisdom of the Torah, he will never claim that he is finished with Torah study.

> *"A person can constantly stride deeper and deeper into the Torah, all the while gaining greater perception of its infinite wisdom."*

Even with regard to *chukim* the Torah writes that one should "walk" and toil. Although we cannot understand the full reason for these mitzvos, there are aspects that we can comprehend. The more we apply ourselves, the more we will succeed in tapping into the vast wisdom contained within each word of the Torah.

(*Shiurei Chumash, Parashas Bechukosai* 26:3)

❃ ❃ ❃

NEITHER CASUAL NOR RANDOM

וְאִם־תֵּלְכוּ עִמִּי קֶרִי וְלֹא תֹאבוּ לִשְׁמֹעַ לִי

And if you behave with Me "keri" and you refuse to heed Me (26:21).

We read in the *Tochachah*, "And if you behave with Me '*keri*' and you refuse to heed Me, I will add another blow upon you" (*Bamidbar* 26:21). Rashi tells us that the word "*keri*" comes from the same root as the word "*mikreh*," which means "casually." The

Tochachah comes as a result of behaving casually with regard to *avodas Hashem*, performing the mitzvos some of the time, while neglecting them at others.

> "*The Tochachah comes as a result of behaving casually with regard to avodas Hashem, performing the mitzvos some of the time, while neglecting them at others.*"

Rambam (*Hilchos Taanis* 1:1-3) offers a different explanation for the word "*keri.*" In the beginning of the halachos pertaining to fast days, he writes: "There is a positive commandment to cry out and blow trumpets at the advent of any trouble that befalls the populace . . . However, if they do not cry out nor blow the trumpets, but rather say that what has occurred is due to natural circumstances, and that this calamity has come merely by chance . . . then the calamity will lead to other calamities. In regard to this it is written in the Torah, 'And if you behave with Me "*keri*" and you refuse to heed Me, I will add another blow upon you.'" Rambam understands "*keri*" to mean "by chance." If a person perceives all of Divine Providence to be random coincidence, he is guilty of behaving toward Hashem in a manner of "*keri*," and the terrible punishment for such behavior is delineated in the subsequent *pesukim* of the *Tochachah*.

Tumah — spiritual impurity — is also described as "*keri.*" According to Rashi's explanation, the manifestation of spiritual impurity is the casual performance of *avodas Hashem*. Rambam adds another dimension of spiritual impurity: failing to notice the hand of Hashem and instead attributing all occurrences to natural causes.

Both explanations are true. Nothing happens by chance; each and every event is carefully orchestrated by the Creator Himself. Our *avodas Hashem*, too, should not be performed casually or by chance. We are His servants at all times, and our performance of His mitzvos should reflect that: day or night, rain or shine.

(*Shiurei Chumash, Parashas Bechukosai* 26:21)

ספר במדבר
Sefer Bamidbar

פרשת במדבר
Parashas Bamidbar

NOT JUST A CENSUS

שְׂאוּ אֶת־רֹאשׁ כָּל־עֲדַת בְּנֵי־יִשְׂרָאֵל
Take a census of the entire assembly of the Children of Israel (1:2).

The process of counting *Bnei Yisrael* described in this *parashah* differs drastically from the election tallies or censuses that take place in our time. In the electoral process it makes no difference whether a professor or an illiterate placed the ballot, because the purpose of the voting is not to place a spotlight on the individual; the aim is simply to identify which party has accumulated the greatest sum total of votes. Similarly, the purpose of a census is to determine the total count of people in any specific area. The counting of *Bnei Yisrael*, on the other hand, was carried out as a manifestation of Hashem's *Hashgachah Pratis* and love for each Jew. Rashi tells us, "Because of His affection for them, He counts them at all times" (1:1).

The Torah instructed Moshe, Aharon, and all the leaders of the tribes to be present during the process of the counting. Since this census was performed by counting each individual's half-shekel donation, would it not have sufficed for a collector to go around and collect the money? Why did the leaders of the nation have to give of their precious time to be involved in this process?

This census was meant to be an uplifting experience: *"Se'u es rosh Bnei Yisrael"* — lift up the heads of *Bnei Yisrael* (1:2). The only way the counting could be performed was if the greatest men of the generation would take interest in the individual.

Ramban explains that there was even a more compelling reason that necessitated the presence of Moshe and Aharon. *"Additionally, he who comes and introduces himself before the foremost prophet and his brother, the holy one of Hashem, has gained merit and life ... It is a merit to be counted by Moshe and Aharon because they will look at them favorably and pray that Hashem have compassion on them ..."* When each person came to give his half-shekel, Moshe would ask him his name and then bless him that he succeed in his endeavors.

The Gra said that during the era of prophecy there was no need for anyone to try to determine his own unique purpose in life. He would simply ask the prophet, and the prophet would tell him what he was supposed to do and how to go about doing it. A person who came before Moshe, the greatest of all prophets, would merit an even more inspiring encounter. Moshe would penetrate into the deepest recesses of each person's soul in order to give him an appropriate blessing for success. Afterward, Aharon and the leader of his *shevet* would also bless him individually. Such a process uplifts and encourages a person significantly.

> "Every person has a unique combination of strengths and circumstances that distinguish him from anyone else who has lived or will ever live."

It is crucial that every person know that he is important: "Each and every person must say, 'The world was created for me'" (*Sanhedrin* 37a). Every person has a unique combination of strengths and circumstances that distinguish him from anyone else who has lived or will ever live. He was born to specific parents, lives in a particular era and place, and was given certain talents because he has an *avodah* that he, and only he, can accomplish. The entire creation is waiting for him to achieve what is incumbent upon him.

If a person is not conscious of his own importance, he cannot begin his *avodah* in Torah. As an introduction to *Kabbalas HaTorah*, Hashem told *Bnei Yisrael*, "And you will be for Me a kingdom of priests (i.e., dignitaries)" (*Shemos* 19:6; see Rashi). Every Jew is a dignitary with responsibilities and an elevated status, no different from a dignitary in a government. It was with these feelings that *Bnei Yisrael* prepared themselves to receive the Torah, and it would be beneficial for us to try to emulate these feelings as well.

(Shiurei Chumash, Parashas Bamidbar 1:1; Alei Shur, Vol. I, p. 168)

❈ ❈ ❈

MY STUDENT, MY CHILD

וְאֵלֶּה תּוֹלְדֹת אַהֲרֹן וּמֹשֶׁה בְּיוֹם דִּבֶּר ה' אֶת־מֹשֶׁה בְּהַר סִינָי.
וְאֵלֶּה שְׁמוֹת בְּנֵי־אַהֲרֹן . . .

"And these are the offspring of Moshe and Aharon on the day that Hashem spoke to Moshe on Har Sinai. These are the names of the sons of Aharon . . ." (3:1-2).

Rashi notes that although the first *passuk* also mentioned the offspring of Moshe, in the subsequent *pesukim* only the children of Aharon are enumerated. He explains that a person who teaches his friend's child Torah is considered to have begot him. Aharon's children are listed as if they were Moshe's offspring, since he taught them Torah.

A teacher must be devoted to a student as if the student were his own child. Likewise, a student should perceive his teacher as a parent. Elisha referred to his *rebbi*, Eliyahu HaNavi, as "*Avi, Avi*" — my father, my father. *Chazal* (*Moed Katan* 26a) tell us that he repeated "*Avi*" a second time because he felt that Eliyahu was not only like a father but also like a mother.

Rav Yerucham Levovitz once showed Rav Dovid Povarsky a bloody napkin. Rav Yerucham explained that he had coughed up blood because he was extremely worried about his son. He added that he had never worried about a student to the extent that he had coughed up blood, and he was therefore concerned that he had not properly fulfilled his obligation as a *rebbi*. This comment notwithstanding, Rav Yerucham was known to be greatly concerned about his students' welfare. When one of his students was accused of spying and was in great danger, Rav Yerucham worried so much that when he woke up the next morning his beard had turned white!

Not only did Rav Yerucham care for his disciples as he cared for his children, his disciples felt as if he were their father. When Rav Wolbe arrived at the yeshivah in Mir, Poland, he met a student who had been learning in the yeshivah for a few years. The student told Rav Wolbe that he was 2 years and 3 months old, because exactly 2 years and 3 months ago he met Rav Yerucham for the first time and was "reborn"!

> "*To be able to positively impact a disciple, one must care for him as he would care for his own flesh and blood.*"

To be able to positively impact a disciple, one must care for him as he would care for his own flesh and blood. And if one wishes to gain from a mentor, he must trust that his *rebbi* or teacher has the best of intentions, just like a father or mother.

(*Shiurei Chumash, Parashas Bamidbar* 3:1)

פרשת נשא
Parashas Nasso

WHAT HAPPENED TO HER CAN HAPPEN TO YOU, TOO

אִישׁ אִישׁ כִּי־תִשְׂטֶה אִשְׁתּוֹ . . . אִישׁ אוֹ־אִשָּׁה כִּי יַפְלִא לִנְדֹּר נֶדֶר נָזִיר לְהַזִּיר לַה'

Any man whose wife shall go astray (5:12) ... A man or woman who shall disassociate himself by taking a nazirite vow of abstinence for the sake of Hashem (6:2).

In this *parashah*, the Torah delineates the laws of the *sotah* — a woman who is suspected of immorality — and the laws of the *nazir*, a person who has accepted upon himself a temporary "code of holy conduct" including abstention from wine. Rashi (6:2), citing *Chazal*, asks why the Torah juxtaposes these two mitzvos. He answers that the Torah is implying that a person who sees a *sotah* in her state of degradation should abstain from wine, since wine can bring one to immorality.

We tend to think that witnessing the degradation of a *sotah* would automatically arouse feelings of repugnance toward her degree of corruption. However, the Torah tells us that our reaction should be more profound. When we see another Jew's transgression, we must take the proper precautions so that *we* do not end up committing the same misdeed. One might ask, "Why? What does her misconduct have to do with me?" The answer is that what happens to another person can also happen to you. If she slipped, then it is quite possible that you might slip, too. Therefore, the Torah warns us to take the necessary precautions lest we follow the wayward conduct of the *sotah*.

The first step in preventing such behavior is contemplating what brought this woman to her level of decadence. Such situations do not usually happen suddenly; they evolve over the course of time. Someone visited her, they had a drink together, and one thing led to another. This behavior must be nipped in the bud, necessitating an abstention from wine and accepting upon oneself to become a *nazir*.

> "If going somewhere, doing something, or talking to someone invariably causes us to sin, then we must set up concrete boundaries that prevent this behavior."

If this idea is true when witnessing another person's transgressions, it holds true all the more regarding one's own transgressions. There is generally a process that leads up to a sin, and we must take the proper precautions to ensure that we halt this process in its tracks. If going somewhere, doing something, or talking to someone invariably causes us to sin, then we must set up concrete boundaries that prevent this behavior. Abstaining from these activities parallels the *nazir*'s abstention from wine, and enables one to reach a high level of *kedushah*.

(*Shiurei Chumash, Parashas Nasso* 6:2)

פרשת בהעלותך
Parashas Beha'alosecha

THE TONGUE: THE DOORWAY TO ONE'S INTERIOR

קַח אֶת־הַלְוִיִּם מִתּוֹךְ בְּנֵי יִשְׂרָאֵל
Take the Levi'im from among the Children of Israel (8:6).

After participating in the sin of the golden calf, the firstborn lost their elevated status and were replaced by the Levi'im. The Levi'im were then commanded to shave all their hair as part of their purification process, in anticipation of their newfound spiritual level. Rashi explains the reason for this unique procedure: "The Levi'im were assigned [to their position] as an atonement for the firstborn who worshiped idols. Idol worship is referred to as a sacrifice of the dead, and a *metzora* is referred to as 'dead.' Therefore, Hashem required them to shave their hair the same way a *metzora* must shave his hair" (8:7). Why must a *metzora* shave all the hair on his body?

Rav Yerucham Levovitz explains that *every* aspect of a person's physical makeup was created for a specific reason. Esav was "entirely [hairy] like a woolen shawl" (*Bereishis* 25:25). This alluded to his corresponding spiritual character: his evil personality. Dirt gets caught between the hairs of a wooly garment, as opposed to a smooth garment, from which dirt easily slides right off. Esav was caught up in his sinful desires, and the filth of transgression was heavily embedded and entangled in his personality. Yaakov, on the other hand, was referred to as a "smooth-skinned man" (ibid. 27:11). This describes not only the physical appearance of his body, but also his corresponding spiritual state: he was pure and unsullied by desire and sin.

Since hair represents sin, the shaving performed by a *metzora* was most fitting. *Tzaraas* is a spiritual punishment inflicted upon a person who speaks *lashon hara*. The Gemara (*Sotah* 42a) tells us that there are four groups of people who will not merit basking in the Divine Presence. The last group mentioned is those who constantly speak *lashon hara*, which is referred to as evil, as it says (*Tehillim* 5:5), "Evil will not dwell with You." But the tongue is merely the doorway to the inside of the body; if a person's inside is evil, that will be manifested by his tongue. When a *metzora* purifies himself from his affliction, which was caused by the *lashon hara* he spoke, he must rid his entire body of hair, symbolizing the evil inside him.

It is difficult to wean oneself from speaking *lashon hara*. A person might refrain from speaking gossip for an entire day, but the next day he will likely end up "paying interest" and speak twice as much as usual. He simply closed his mouth the first day, but he did not treat the root of the problem: the evil that lies inside him. A person who is filled with evil will inevitably make his interior known by way of his disparaging speech.

> "A person might refrain from speaking gossip for an entire day, but the next day he will likely end up 'paying interest' and speak twice as much as usual."

It is not enough to simply make a decision not to speak *lashon hara*. A person has to acquire and maintain a positive outlook toward others. There was a woman in Stockholm, where Rav Wolbe had lived, about whom he declared, "It was impossible to speak *lashon hara* in her presence." When she heard someone speak negatively about another person, she would say, "If that is the case, then we must help him. How can we help him?" If a person maintains such an attitude, he will never come to speak derogatorily about someone else.

The next time we have an urge to speak *lashon hara*, let us think how we can possibly help that person instead. In time, this will help us acquire a "good eye" (*Avos 2*:13) and ultimately effect a positive change on our entire personality.

(*Shiurei Chumash, Parashas Beha'alosecha 8:7*)

❊ ❊ ❊

LOCATION, LOCATION, LOCATION

עַל־פִּי ה' יִסְעוּ בְּנֵי יִשְׂרָאֵל וְעַל־פִּי ה' יַחֲנוּ

According to the word of Hashem would Bnei Yisrael journey, and according to the word of Hashem they would encamp (9:18).

The Torah describes *Bnei Yisrael*'s travels in the desert, which were orchestrated by the cloud that rested above the *Mishkan*. When the cloud began to move, *Bnei Yisrael* packed their bags and followed suit, and wherever the cloud stopped, they unpacked and pitched their tents. Sometimes the cloud stayed in the same place for years on end, while other times, the cloud would resume its journey after merely a few days, or even a single night.

Sforno (9:17-22) explains that by way of this description, the Torah is recounting the greatness of *Bnei Yisrael*. They traveled through the desert exactly as Hashem wished, despite the many hardships involved. At times, they might have camped in a terribly uncomfortable place, yet they would remain there until the cloud moved despite their intense desire to camp elsewhere. Alternately, they might have stopped at an oasis that provided abundant food for them and their animals, but they would move on as soon as the cloud lifted, even if it was after only a few days.

[Scorners, liars, flatterers, Me mockers] cannot see G-d's Presence

Sforno's explanation can be understood with regard to the spiritual realm as well. Even we can sense that certain places have more spirituality, or are more conducive to spirituality, than others. Likewise, in the desert, there were times when *Bnei Yisrael* camped in a veritable spiritual oasis where *avodas Hashem* was easier, but they might have been pressed to move on after a few days. Conversely, at times they camped in an area devoid of any spirituality, where they encountered much difficulty in their *avodas Hashem* and in overcoming their *yetzer hara*. Nevertheless, they would remain there as long as Hashem willed.

This idea should be integrated into our own lives as well. Often, a person senses that *Hashgachah* has placed him in a specific location or situation. Sometimes he feels that this is to his benefit, while at other times it seems that it is to his detriment, since it might be extremely difficult to properly serve Hashem in that location. However, he should know that if Hashem put him in a specific situation, then he must serve Hashem to the best of his ability under the circumstances. If he senses that his *avodas Hashem* is easier, he should take advantage of the opportunity afforded him. If, on the other hand, he senses that his *avodah* is more difficult, he must exert himself to overcome his *yetzer hara* and accomplish as much as he can.

> "If Hashem put a person in a specific situation, then he must serve Hashem to the best of his ability under the circumstances."

It is Hashem Who decides where each person will be. We are not supposed to run away from the location where we were placed, nor can we ignore it. If a person is facing difficulties in his *avodah* that he feels are connected to his place of residence, he should seek the advice of a rav. He might be surprised to hear that he should remain there and face the challenges that Hashem has designated for him.

(*Shiurei Chumash, Parashas Beha'alosecha* 9:17)

❈ ❈ ❈

THE STRENGTH OF A LION

וְהָאסַפְסֻף אֲשֶׁר בְּקִרְבּוֹ הִתְאַוּוּ תַּאֲוָה
And those who were gathered felt a craving (11:4).

Rashi explains that the *passuk* is referring to the *Eirev Rav*, who attached themselves to *Bnei Yisrael* at the time of the Exodus. The *Eirev Rav* consisted of Egyptians who were circumcised by Yosef and distanced themselves from the idol-worshiping Egyptian populace. This unique group of people lived in their own cities for hundreds of years, until the time of *Yetzias Mitzrayim*, when they decided to join the Jewish people. They followed the Jews into the barren wilderness — truly a praiseworthy endeavor. However, ultimately, they were the driving force behind the fiasco in this *parashah*.

Often, a person has the willpower to start great things, but he gives up in the middle because he lacks the ability to maintain the momentum. The journey on which the *Eirev Rav* embarked reflected true greatness, but their resolve eventually broke down, and they began to focus on having their desires fulfilled. The *passuk* (*Tehillim* 24:3) asks: "Who will *ascend* the mountain of Hashem; who will *stand* in His holy place?" After a person *ascends* to a higher spiritual plateau, he faces an additional challenge: *standing firm* and maintaining his newfound level.

At *Akeidas Yitzchak*, Hashem asked Avraham, "*Please* withstand this test" (*Bereishis* 22:2). Rashi explains why Hashem had to "plead" with Avraham: "Please withstand this trial so that they should not say that the first [nine] trials were nothing." Even if Avraham would not withstand the trial, why would that invalidate the first nine trials that he did withstand?

Our Sages tell us, "If someone begins a mitzvah, we tell him to complete it" (*Yerushalmi Rosh Hashanah* 1:8). This is the concept of *shleimus*, completeness. Rav Yisrael Salanter said that a person is not obligated to become a *gadol*, but he is obligated to become a *shaleim* — a complete person.

Rav Yerucham Levovitz compares this concept to a pot with a hole. Such a utensil is not "a pot with a hole"; it is not a pot at all.

Had Avraham not passed his final test, there would have been a "hole" in his service of Hashem, which would have nullified all of his previous tests as well.

"Be bold as a leopard, swift as an eagle, quick as a deer, and strong as a lion to do the will of your Father in Heaven" (*Pirkei Avos* 5:23). Rav Yerucham explains that *Chazal* delineated the faculties a person needs in order to bring a task to completion. To begin an endeavor one must be bold. Then, he needs to be swift as an eagle in order for the plan to be launched. The next imperative is to be "quick as a deer," because if he acts lethargically, he will not succeed. Finally, when completion is near, the strength of a lion is necessary to be able to cross the finish line. This last aspect is the hardest of all.

> "When someone is learning a masechta, the last two pages are the hardest ones to finish."

The Chazon Ish said that when someone is learning a *masechta*, the last two pages are the hardest ones to finish. The *yetzer hara* despises completion, and a person needs the strength of a lion to overcome this obstacle.

(*Shiurei Chumash, Parashas Beha'alosecha* 11:4)

❊ ❊ ❊

THE REBBI-TALMID IMPERATIVE

וְאָצַלְתִּי מִן־הָרוּחַ אֲשֶׁר עָלֶיךָ וְשַׂמְתִּי עֲלֵיהֶם

And I will increase some of the spirit [of prophecy] that is upon you and I will place it upon them (11:17).

Bnei Yisrael complained about their monotonous diet of *mann* and petitioned Moshe Rabbeinu to supply them with meat. Moshe relayed their complaints to Hashem and added that he did not have the ability to lead the nation by himself. Hashem responded that he should gather seventy elders from *Bnei Yisrael* who would assist him in the role of leadership: "And I will increase some of the spirit [of prophecy] that is upon you and I will place it upon them." Rashi explains that at that time Moshe was similar to a candle. Even if many candles are lit from a single candle, the flame is not diminished. Likewise, even though Hashem "kindled" the prophecy of the seventy elders from Moshe, this did not at all decrease Moshe's level of prophecy.

Hashem could certainly have given prophecy to each of the seventy elders individually. Why did He choose to make Moshe the conduit for it? The answer is that Torah has to be transmitted from *rebbi* to *talmid*. By observing and studying under a *rebbi*, a student grows in his own spirituality. Similarly, the chassidic approach to *avodas Hashem* is based on a connection to a *tzaddik* (the Rebbe). Rav Yisrael Salanter also endorsed this idea, since he felt that a student's growth is directly proportional to the *yiras Shamayim* of his *rebbi*.

> "By observing and studying under a rebbi, a student grows in his own spirituality."

Sadly, many people today lack a connection to a spiritual guide. It is crucial to develop such a connection, for Torah learning is of utmost importance to a person's spiritual growth, and Torah can only be transmitted from *rebbi* to *talmid*.

(Shiurei Chumash, Parashas Beha'alosecha 11:17)

✽ ✽ ✽

TOLERANCE: AN ESSENTIAL VIRTUE

וְהָאִישׁ מֹשֶׁה עָנָו [עָנָיו] מְאֹד מִכֹּל הָאָדָם אֲשֶׁר עַל־פְּנֵי הָאֲדָמָה
Moshe was exceedingly humble (anav), more than any person on the face of the earth (12:3).

At the end of this *parashah*, the Torah recounts how Aharon and Miriam spoke about their brother Moshe. In the face of their criticism, "Moshe was exceedingly humble (*anav*), more than any person on the face of the earth." Rashi translates "*anav*" as "modest and tolerant." Moshe tolerated their criticism and did not grow angry.

Tolerance is an essential virtue in all of our interpersonal relationships. The Alter of Kelm writes, "How great it would be if we could habituate ourselves to act with tolerance, for it is the root of all *middos* and qualities and the source of serenity."

In addition to the tolerance a person must show toward others, one must also be tolerant of himself. We are all seeking to grow and become better people, but we constantly encounter difficulties. Sometimes we feel that the *yetzer hara* is out to stop us at all costs, sometimes we lose our drive to continue, and sometimes we forget where we are headed. A person who lacks patience in his *avodas Hashem* will give up or get depressed, and there is nothing more detrimental to *avodas Hashem* than depression.

> "A person who lacks patience in his avodas Hashem will give up or get depressed, and there is nothing more detrimental to avodas Hashem than depression."

We think, *If only I would be able to daven the entire Shemoneh Esrei with kavanah, my whole day would look different.* Or, *If only I would be able to rectify my negative middos, I would be a different person altogether.* Although these musings might be true, we must bear in mind an important Midrash. *Chazal* tell us (*Shemos Rabbah* 34:1) that Hashem does not expect from a person more than he can handle. Hashem knows our limitations and the impediments that stand in our way, and He does not expect us to turn around our lives in a day, a week, a month, or a year — and sometimes even many years. We must remember that a person who "grabs" too much will be left with nothing, while one who grabs a little will retain what he has grabbed (*Rosh Hashanah* 4b).

The Vilna Gaon expresses this idea in his explanation of the following *passuk* (*Mishlei* 19:3), "A man's foolishness corrupts his way, and his heart rages against Hashem." Sometimes a person begins studying Torah or serving Hashem and then stops because it has grown too difficult. He feels that Hashem is not assisting him in his endeavors, and he becomes angry at Hashem for abandoning him. This person caused his own downfall, however, since he jumped ahead too quickly in his *avodah* and did not pace himself properly. Had he slowed his pace, Hashem would have assisted him in his *avodah*.

Tolerance is not merely a virtue to be exercised once we realize that we have not accomplished all that we planned. It is a *middah* that we must utilize when charting our course of action. If we realize our limitations and are truly cognizant of our present spiritual level, we will succeed in advancing in our *avodas Hashem* at the proper pace, thereby achieving positive, lasting changes.

(*Alei Shur,* Vol. II, pp. 214-217)

Parashas Shelach

THE MUSSAR PERSPECTIVE

שְׁלַח־לְךָ אֲנָשִׁים
Send forth men, if you please (13:2).

Why is the episode with the spies juxtaposed with Miriam's *lashon hara* and subsequent *tzaraas*? Rashi (13:2) explains that the spies saw what happened to Miriam, yet they did not apply the *mussar* to themselves. The Torah later refers to these spies as great people, but Rashi, quoting *Chazal*, refers to them as *resha'im*, because they did not take the incident to heart. The defining aspect of *mussar* is to understand that not only is one meant to see everything that he observes, but he is also supposed to learn something from everything that occurs.

A person can relate to current events in two different ways. He can think to himself, *It's so terrible to hear about all the wars and suffering going on in the world.* Alternatively, he can look at these events from a more personal perspective: *Soldiers and civilians are being killed and wounded. How does this affect me, and what am I doing about the situation?* The second approach can be referred to as the *mussar* perspective.

A person must approach Torah learning through the eyes of *mussar* as well. It is possible for one to learn the entire Torah without it affecting his lifestyle in the minutest way. He may have studied the different concepts and laws, but they did not "speak to him," nor did he relate to them. Through the study of *mussar*, however, one becomes accustomed to relating personally to everything he studies.

> "It is possible for one to learn the entire Torah without it affecting his lifestyle in the minutest way."

Without the constant study of *mussar*, one is not affected on a personal level by what goes on around him. Rashi tells us that such a person, no matter how great he is, is referred to as a *rasha*. A few minutes a day of *mussar* study can change our outlook — and indeed, our life.

(*Shiurei Chumash, Parashas Shelach* 13:2)

❋ ❋ ❋

NO BECHIRAH

וַיַּעֲלוּ בַנֶּגֶב וַיָּבֹא עַד־חֶבְרוֹן
*And they ascended in the south,
and he arrived at Chevron (13:22).*

Included in the narrative of the spies is an account of their travels through the Land of Israel. "And *they* ascended in the south, and *he* arrived at Chevron." Rashi explains that although all of the spies traveled into the south, Calev was the only spy to arrive at Chevron. He purposely made this detour, since he wanted to *daven* at the burial place of the *Avos* that he not be persuaded by the other spies to join their scheme.

It is difficult to understand the impetus for Calev's detour. If he was aware of the fact that the spies were scheming, and he knew that he did not want to join them, why could he not simply decide that he would not agree to their plan? Why did he feel the need to visit Me'aras Hamachpeilah to *daven* that he achieve what he had already determined was the proper course of action? Why was a firm resolution not enough to prevent him from being lured into their plot?

The answer is that one should never rely on his own *bechirah* when faced with the possibility of transgression, for he can never be sure that he will indeed make the correct decision. Instead, he should always view himself as if he has no *bechirah* at all and will certainly succumb to the *aveirah*. Such a mindset will push him to do everything in his ability to prevent himself from entering the problematic situation in the first place. Calev did not want to rely on his own resolution not to join the other spies, and he therefore prayed for Heavenly assistance that he not be persuaded to join them.

> "One should never rely on his own bechirah when faced with the possibility of transgression, for he can never be sure that he will indeed make the correct decision."

Often, we visit certain places, associate with certain people, or bring certain items into our homes that have the ability to inflict spiritual damage. We excuse these actions with the belief that, due to our steadfast morals, we will not be affected negatively. However, this is not the proper approach. Our *avodah* is to do everything possible to make sure we do not have to face a *nisayon* in the first place.

(*Shiurei Chumash, Parashas Shelach* 13:22)

❈ ❈ ❈

PROPPED UP WITH TRUTH

בָּאנוּ אֶל־הָאָרֶץ . . . וְגַם זָבַת חָלָב וּדְבַשׁ הִוא . . . אֶפֶס כִּי־עַז הָעָם הַיֹּשֵׁב בָּאָרֶץ וְהֶעָרִים בְּצֻרוֹת . . . אֶרֶץ אֹכֶלֶת יוֹשְׁבֶיהָ הִוא וְכָל־הָעָם אֲשֶׁר־רָאִינוּ בְתוֹכָהּ אַנְשֵׁי מִדּוֹת

We arrived in the land . . . and indeed it flows with milk and honey . . . However, the natives are mighty, the cities are fortified . . . the land devours its inhabitants and all those who reside there are giants (13:27-32).

When the spies returned from Eretz Canaan, they described the land in less than glowing terms. "*We arrived in the land . . . and indeed it flows with milk and honey . . . However, the natives are mighty, the cities are fortified . . . the land devours its inhabitants and all those who reside there are giants.*" But if they wanted to paint a dismal picture, why did they preface their tirade with, "indeed it flows with milk and honey"? Rashi explains that a falsehood that does not contain at least a minimal amount of truth cannot endure. The spies purposely mentioned something true about the Promised Land, so that the rest of their lies would be believed.

Chazal (*Shabbos* 104a) say that *sheker* does not have the ability to endure. Because *sheker* is not a reality, it cannot become a reality. It might take 10, 20, or even 30 years before the lie is proven false, but eventually the truth will become clear. *Sheker*'s only chance of survival is if it props itself up with truth.

The various ideologies that have surfaced over the course of history are all based upon some aspect of truth. For example, communism was established to ensure social justice, which is a truthful concept. However, we are all witness to the terrible oppressiveness and deceit that were the hallmark of communism in Russia and other countries. The *sheker* feeds off the truth on which it was founded.

Chazal (*Sanhedrin* 98a) tell us that Mashiach will arrive in a generation that is either completely righteous or completely wicked. We can understand why a completely righteous generation should merit Mashiach, but why would Mashiach reveal himself to a generation that is full of deceit? Rav Yerucham Levovitz explains that in a generation in which there is not even an iota of truth, the *sheker* will automatically be proven false and eradicated, thereby facilitating Mashiach's arrival.

> "The falseness that abounds today is almost palpable, and at a certain point it simply exposes itself."

To a certain extent, this concept has become a reality in our days. Over the past few generations, there has been a marked increase in the number of Jews who have found their way back to their roots — a veritable "*teshuvah* movement." The falseness that abounds today is almost palpable, and at a certain point it simply exposes itself. Then, people can discover the truth of Hashem's Torah shining in all its brilliance.

(*Shiurei Chumash, Parashas Shelach* 13:27)

❖ ❖ ❖

THE ULTIMATE PURPOSE OF HEALTH, WEALTH, AND TRANQUILITY

וְאָמְרוּ הַגּוֹיִם אֲשֶׁר־שָׁמְעוּ אֶת־שִׁמְעֲךָ לֵאמֹר. מִבִּלְתִּי יְכֹלֶת ה׳ לְהָבִיא אֶת־הָעָם הַזֶּה אֶל־הָאָרֶץ אֲשֶׁר־נִשְׁבַּע לָהֶם וַיִּשְׁחָטֵם בַּמִּדְבָּר

The nations that heard of Your fame will say, "Because Hashem lacked the ability to bring this nation into the land that He promised them, He slaughtered them in the desert" (14:15-16).

When the spies returned with a derogatory report about Eretz Yisrael, Hashem threatened to wipe out *Bnei Yisrael* and create a new Jewish nation with Moshe Rabbeinu as its patriarch. Moshe succeeded in averting the fulfillment of this threat, however, by petitioning Hashem: "The nations that heard of Your fame will say, 'Because Hashem lacked the ability to bring this nation into the land that He promised them, He slaughtered them in the desert.'" In other words, wiping out *Bnei Yisrael* would result in a terrible *chillul Hashem*. Hashem responded, "I have forgiven [them] for the reason you said."

Before his death, Moshe castigated *Bnei Yisrael* regarding their transgressions in the desert and the numerous prayers he had to offer on their behalf. The Rashbam (*Devarim* 9:25) explains that Moshe was letting them know that they would not always be able to rely on such prayers. Moshe's prayers succeeded because *Bnei Yisrael* had not yet entered Eretz Yisrael, and at that time the possibility existed that the other nations would claim that Hashem lacked the ability to conquer the thirty-one kings of the land, which would constitute a *chillul Hashem*. However, once Hashem brought *Bnei Yisrael* into the Promised Land and systematically destroyed the nations inhabiting it, no longer would anyone be able to claim that Hashem's ability was lacking, and Moshe's method of prayer would be ineffective.

Every prayer must somehow be connected to creating *kiddush Hashem* or preventing *chillul Hashem*. Even when a person prays for the speedy recovery of someone who is ill, the intention should be that in this person's present situation he cannot properly serve Hashem, and his recuperation will lead to a greater degree of *kiddush Hashem*.

> *"Every prayer must somehow be connected to creating kiddush Hashem or preventing chillul Hashem."*

We are not on the spiritual level to ensure that all of our prayers are offered with perfect intentions, but we must still pray in every given situation. Nevertheless, we should bear in mind that the ultimate purpose of health, wealth, and tranquility is to have the ability to serve Hashem without any distractions, thereby glorifying His Name in this world. Often, if we dig deep enough, we will realize that this is the underlying impetus for our prayers. Bringing these thoughts to the forefront while praying might just make our prayers all the more effective.

(*Shiurei Chumash, Parashas Shelach* 14:16)

❈ ❈ ❈

TESHUVAH: A NEW PATH

כִּי־עַל־כֵּן שַׁבְתֶּם מֵאַחֲרֵי ה׳
*Because you have turned away
from the service of Hashem (14:43).*

When the spies returned with a derogatory report about the Land of Israel, and *Bnei Yisrael* mourned their bad fortune, the entire nation was severely punished: "You will all die in this desert. And your children will wander in the desert for forty years ... until you all die" (14:29-33).

In response to this devastating piece of news, *Bnei Yisrael* attempted to rectify their misdeed. "They arose early in the morning and ascended the mountain, stating, 'We will go to the land that Hashem has promised us, for we have sinned'" (v. 40). Moshe responded (vs. 41-42), "Why are you transgressing the word of Hashem — it will not succeed! Do not ascend, for Hashem is not in your midst!"

It seems that *Bnei Yisrael* did *teshuvah* and regretted their misdeed. Why, then, did Moshe say that Hashem was not in their midst, "because you have turned away from the service of Hashem" (v. 43)? As the subsequent *pesukim* show, Moshe was proven right, and we must therefore understand where *Bnei Yisrael* went wrong.

It is possible to err even when one intends to do *teshuvah*. A person might have the necessary components of repentance — remorse and a resolution to improve — but still overlook one vital aspect: he must know to what he is returning. *Teshuvah* means returning to comply with the will of Hashem.

The sin of the spies was that they distanced themselves from the word of Hashem. Though Hashem had already promised them that they would take possession of Eretz Yisrael, they wanted to "see for themselves" how this could be accomplished. Since they followed the "Laws of Nature" and the "way of the world," the spies were correct in their depressing assessment of the situation. However, they should have relied on Hashem's word, and in this aspect they failed.

When *Bnei Yisrael* wished to rectify their wrongdoing, they once again disregarded the word of Hashem by setting out to conquer

Eretz Yisrael. This was not the *teshuvah* that Hashem desired, however. He now wanted them to wander in the desert, and the first step in their process of *teshuvah* should have been to comply with His will. This was why Moshe was certain that they would not succeed in their endeavor.

The Gemara (*Menachos* 29b) tells us that this world was created with the letter *hei*. Just as the bottom of the *hei* is open, so, too, a person who wishes to sin and "leave this world" has an opening through which to do so. Additionally, the leg of the *hei* is suspended, leaving a "doorway" on the side, to allow penitents to enter. Why cannot a penitent return through the bottom, via the same route by which he left?

The Gemara answers, "because he will not succeed." The Gemara is, in essence, referring to the above insight regarding *teshuvah*. Bnei Yisrael erred when they said (14:3), "*Let us return to Egypt*," and now they sought to rectify their mistake by doing the exact opposite and proceeding onward to Eretz Yisrael. This attempt was comparable to attempting to return through the letter *hei* via the bottom opening. But *teshuvah* necessitates that one take a different approach and follow a new path.

(*Shiurei Chumash, Parashas Shelach* 14:41-43)

> "*Teshuvah necessitates that one take a different approach and follow a new path.*"

❊ ❊ ❊

ONE RUNG DOWN ON THE LADDER

וְהִקְרִיב הַמַּקְרִיב קָרְבָּנוֹ לַה׳ מִנְחָה

The one who brings his offering to Hashem shall bring a meal-offering (15:4).

Sforno writes (15:3, 20) that after the debacle with the spies, Hashem instituted additional mitzvos, including the commandment to bring flour and libation offerings as a supplement to the *korbanos*. Having distanced themselves from Hashem through their transgression, *Bnei Yisrael* were required to bring another sacrifice through which they could once again feel His closeness. Furthermore, sin disconnects the transgressor from the Source of all blessings; therefore, *Bnei Yisrael* were subsequently commanded to separate *challah* from their dough and give it to a *kohen* as a means of bringing blessing into their homes.

Two fundamental lessons can be gleaned from *Sforno*'s explanation. First, *every* sin lowers the perpetrator one rung on the spiritual ladder, which forces him to strive harder to regain his previous closeness to Hashem. After every sin, *Bnei Yisrael* needed yet another mitzvah to enable them to reclaim their former spiritual status.

Additionally, the Torah guides a person on whatever level he finds himself. Because the Torah is eternal, it contains within it the guidance needed to direct each and every individual. Every wrongdoing on *Bnei Yisrael*'s part brought them down another notch in their spiritual standing; nevertheless, the Torah "stepped down" with them and added a mitzvah for their benefit. In whatever situation or spiritual state a person finds himself, the Torah provides direction so that he will be able to live his life properly.

> "Every wrongdoing on Bnei Yisrael's part brought them down another notch in their spiritual standing; nevertheless, the Torah 'stepped down' with them and added a mitzvah for their benefit."

The Torah was given more than 3,000 years ago to act as our guiding light, and it continues to shine brightly today to each person on his individual level. There is no reason for one to feel depressed about his spiritual status, because the Torah invariably addresses his specific situation.

(*Shiurei Chumash, Parashas Shelach* 15:20)

פרשת קרח
Parashas Korach

HIDDEN MOTIVATIONS

וַיִּקַּח קֹרַח
Korach separated himself (16:1).

What was Korach's impetus for starting a fight with Moshe? Rashi (16:1) explains that he was jealous of his cousin Elitzafan, who was appointed *nasi* of the family of Kehas, a position Korach felt he rightfully deserved.

Rashi describes the scene of the argument: Korach gathered 250 distinguished men, and they wrapped themselves in *tallisos* that were completely dyed with *techeiles*. In this "costume" they approached Moshe and asked him if one is obligated to put a *techeiles* string on such a *tallis*. Moshe answered in the affirmative. They ridiculed this answer, contending that if one strand of *techeiles* exempts an entire garment, then certainly a garment that is completely colored with *techeiles* should be exempted, without the need for an additional strand of *techeiles*. Korach's understanding of this mitzvah was that everyone should in fact be required to don a *tallis* that is completely dyed with *techeiles*, but the Torah allows us to fulfill this obligation with a single string.

Following this line of reasoning, Korach claimed that there was no reason for Moshe and Aharon to elevate themselves above the rest of the populace. A leader, he reasoned, is only necessary if the entire nation is not on a high spiritual level. If that is the case, the leader — who is generally head and shoulders above the rest of the people — "exempts" the populace from their obligation to maintain a high level of spirituality. However, at the time that Korach's quarrel took place, the entire nation was maintaining a high level of spirituality, and he therefore felt that there was no need for a leader at all.

In response, Moshe held a test to demonstrate his and Aharon's elevated status. Aharon, Korach, and the 250 men would each bring an offering of incense, and a Heavenly fire would consume only one person's incense, while the rest of the contenders would perish. Korach was a smart man; what possessed him to agree to such a contest and to think that he would be the chosen one? Rashi (16:7) answers that he foresaw through prophecy that his descendant would be Shmuel HaNavi, who was equal to Moshe and Aharon. Korach assumed that he would be saved in the merit of Shmuel. However, he failed to see that it was only because his children repented that they merited such an illustrious descendant, while he himself perished due to his sins.

> "Korach's fight against Moshe stemmed from his feelings of jealousy, which generated his ideology regarding the mitzvos in general and the leader of the nation in particular."

This incident gives us an understanding of the hidden motivations that underlie our actions. Korach's fight against Moshe stemmed from his feelings of jealousy, which generated his ideology regarding the mitzvos in general and the leader of the nation in particular. Additionally, he solidified his position with the prophetic vision of a great future. These three factors led Korach to take action against

Moshe: (1) he had a philosophy; (2) he even had "proof" that he was right; yet (3) it was all rooted in a negative trait — jealousy.

The same three factors often compel us to act, as well. We might have ideas and ideals, and we might even have proof that we are following the correct path, but we must always realize that these ideas or actions are borne of our character traits. Before acting, and certainly before taking drastic measures, we should take time to think about the real impetus for our thoughts and deeds. If they are rooted in positive traits — kindness, compassion, and so on — then we know we are truly on the right path. However, if we suspect that they might be rooted in negative traits — jealousy, hatred, craving for honor, and the like — then we are better off admitting our faults and refraining from acting upon them.

(*Shiurei Chumash, Parashas Korach* 16:7; *Alei Shur,* Vol. I, pp.160-161)

❊ ❊ ❊

OUT OF THIS WORLD

וַיִּקַּח קֹרַח
Korach separated himself (16:1).

Rashi (16:1) asks the obvious question: What possessed Korach to argue with Moshe? He explains that Korach felt that the position of *nasi* should have been his, and he therefore envied his cousin Elitzafan ben Uziel, who received the appointment. As the *mishnah* in *Avos* (4:28) tells us, this jealousy literally "took him out of this world," and the ground swallowed him alive.

The Rambam explains the above *mishnah* as follows: "Jealousy, desire, and love of honor take a person out of the world. The reason for this is that possessing these three *middos*, or even a single one of them, inevitably causes a person to forfeit his *emunas haTorah*." It is clear that the Rambam understood "the world" mentioned in the *mishnah* as a reference to a person's *emunah*. Why do these three things cause a person to lose his *emunah*?

Jealousy — (*kinah*) — hinders a person's ability to perceive Divine Providence. If he would truly believe that everything Hashem does is calculated down to the very last detail, there would be no room for jealousy. How can one be jealous of what his friend has when he knows that Hashem specifically decided that he does not need or deserve that particular thing?

> "How can one be jealous of what his friend has when he knows that Hashem specifically decided that he does not need or deserve that particular thing?"

Emunas haTorah is belief in the fact that spirituality is a reality. **Desire** — (*taavah*) — stands diametrically opposed to one's ability to connect to spirituality. As the *Chovos HaLevavos* writes (*Shaar HaPrishus*, Chapter 2), the purpose of the Torah is "to enable one's logic to reign over his desires." Getting caught up in fulfilling physical desires detracts from one's ability to believe in spirituality as a reality.

Finally, he who pursues **honor** — (*kavod*) — is clearly lacking in his belief that true reward and punishment are allocated only in the next world. One who is cognizant of this fact does not feel the need to seek honor, because he knows that his actions will be aptly rewarded in due time. Moreover, as Rabbeinu Yonah writes (*Sefer HaYirah*), the honor one receives in this world might even detract from the reward he is meant to receive in the next world.

The Rambam tells us that a person's "world" is his *emunah*. In light of the above, one way to work on *emunah* is by diminishing our pursuit of jealousy, desire, and honor. This is easier said than done, since most things we do are connected to these *middos* in some way. Nevertheless, merely being aware of the detrimental effects of these *middos* is already a step in the right direction.

(*Alei Shur*, Vol. I, p. 102)

❈ ❈ ❈

THE CHOICE IS OURS

כִּי כָל־הָעֵדָה כֻּלָּם קְדֹשִׁים וּבְתוֹכָם ה' וּמַדּוּעַ תִּתְנַשְּׂאוּ עַל־קְהַל ה'

For the entire nation — all of them — is holy and Hashem is among them, and why do you exalt yourselves over the congregation of Hashem? (16:3).

This *parashah* begins with Korach criticizing Moshe and Aharon: "For the entire nation — all of them — is holy and Hashem is among them, and why do you exalt yourselves over the congregation of Hashem?" Moshe responds, "In the morning Hashem will make known the one who is His own and the holy one" (v. 5). Rashi cites a Midrash that explains the intent behind Moshe's choice of words. He was telling Korach that Hashem set definitive boundaries in the world. Just as Korach does not have the ability to change morning into night, so, too, he does not have the ability to change Hashem's appointment of Aharon as the *kohen gadol*.

The Midrash is informing us that the appointment of Aharon as *kohen gadol* was a "creation" no different from the creation of day and night. When Hashem places a person in a specific position, He molds the person to fit the position. It is impossible to change this mold.

This concept applies to each and every one of us. Hashem created each person with a unique character, and there is no way to alter it. *Chazal* tell us that one who is born under the *mazal* of *Maadim* will invariably spill blood (*Shabbos* 156a). He cannot change this innate characteristic, but he *can* channel it into a specific occupation: He can be a *shochet*, a *mohel*, a bloodletter, or a murderer. These options span the entire spectrum of occupations. A *mohel* spills blood for a vital mitzvah, while a murderer spills blood in sin. The *shochet* is somewhere in between, since slaughtering animals is not an obligatory mitzvah (one is not required to eat meat).

Parashas Korach / 283

Chazal tell us (*Bereishis Rabbah* 63:8) that when Shmuel HaNavi came to anoint David as king, he was concerned because David had a ruddy complexion — similar to that of Esav — which indicated a natural tendency to spill blood. Shmuel was relieved when he noticed David's fine-looking eyes, however, since they signified that he would spill blood only with the consent of the Sanhedrin: the "eyes" of the nation.

> "Every person is born with certain immutable tendencies, but those tendencies can be channeled in a number of different directions."

Every person is born with certain immutable tendencies, but those tendencies can be channeled in a number of different directions. The choice is ours: will we use these characteristics to create and build, or to destroy?

(*Shiurei Chumash, Parashas Korach* 16:5)

❋ ❋ ❋

NOT EVEN ONE DONKEY

וַיֹּאמֶר אֶל־ה׳ אַל־תֵּפֶן אֶל־מִנְחָתָם לֹא חֲמוֹר אֶחָד מֵהֶם נָשָׂאתִי וְלֹא הֲרֵעֹתִי אֶת־אַחַד מֵהֶם

And he said to Hashem, "Do not turn to their offerings; not even one donkey did I take from them, nor did I harm any of them" (16:15).

When Korach and his followers came to complain to Moshe about *Bnei Yisrael*'s leadership, Moshe told each of the 250 complainers to offer incense as a means of proving that the nation's leaders had been appointed directly by Hashem. Hashem's acceptance of one person's incense would indicate whom He had chosen.

The Torah tells us that Moshe *davened* to Hashem that He not accept their offerings: "And he said to Hashem, 'Do not turn to their offerings; not even one donkey did I take from them, nor did I harm any of them.'" Rashi explains that when Moshe traveled from

Midyan to Mitzrayim to redeem *Bnei Yisrael*, he rode on his own donkey rather than take one from *Bnei Yisrael*.

What would have been so terrible if he had taken a donkey to transport his family from Midyan? Was he not entitled to have his transportation sponsored by those he came to redeem and lead?

Moshe was declaring that he was free from any *negi'os*, from any bias, in his role as *Bnei Yisrael*'s leader, because he did not enjoy monetary benefit from his position. He could have declared that he put his life on the line for *Bnei Yisrael*'s sake or that he devoted immeasurable time and effort to them, which gave him the right to ask Hashem not to accept their offerings. However, the true test of a person's greatness is how he acts regarding money. Moshe was claiming that in his position as a leader he did not even take money for travel expenses, and he was therefore worthy of Hashem's backing.

> "Integrity in financial matters is one of the hallmarks of greatness."

Likewise, we find that when Moshe accepted the donations for the *Mishkan*, he wore clothing that had no pockets or seams, lest *Bnei Yisrael* think — even for a second — that he had taken some of the money for himself. He was so scrupulous in financial matters that he would not allow the slightest doubt to creep into anyone's mind that he had taken some of the funds allocated for the *Mishkan*.

Money is necessary in order to live. However, we must be sure that our money is earned honestly, for integrity in financial matters is one of the hallmarks of greatness.

(*Shiurei Chumash, Parashas Korach* 16:15)

❊ ❊ ❊

NO EXCUSE FOR MACHLOKES

וַתִּפְתַּח הָאָרֶץ אֶת־פִּיהָ וַתִּבְלַע אֹתָם וְאֶת־בָּתֵּיהֶם
וְאֵת כָּל־הָאָדָם אֲשֶׁר לְקֹרַח

The earth opened its mouth and swallowed them and their households, and all the people who were with Korach (16:32).

Not only were Korach and his cohorts swallowed alive, their wives and children also died in this extraordinary fashion. Rashi comments (16:27) that the gravity of this punishment helps us comprehend the severity of *machlokes*. While a Jewish court of law only punishes a man after he reaches the age of 13, and Heaven only punishes from the age of 20, *machlokes* is so serious an infraction that even infants perished as a result. Why did the children, who were in no way involved in the dispute, deserve to die together with their parents?

In the *Aseres Hadibros* we read, "Who visits the sin of fathers upon children to the third and fourth generations" (*Shemos* 20:5). *Sforno* explains that Hashem waits until the fourth generation to mete out punishment, because when four consecutive generations sin in the same manner, the sin becomes entrenched — part of the family's very personality — and there is no hope that they will ever do *teshuvah*.

Similarly, Korach's children were born into a situation of *machlokes*. The terrible quarrel raging around them had the power to leave an indelible impression even on the second generation, and to make contentiousness part of their nature. In addition, the knowledge that their father disagreed so adamantly with Moshe would cause them to forever doubt Moshe Rabbeinu's qualifications as a leader. Therefore, the only option was for them to perish along with their parents, thereby preventing the *machlokes* from continuing.

One of the 613 commandments is, "And one shall not be like Korach and his followers" (17:5). This commandment, which prohibits one from causing *machlokes*, applies even when a person has good intentions and acts for the sake of Heaven. In fact, a person must be especially careful when he acts "*l'shem Shamayim*," because he might think that the truth of his cause gives him license to do as he pleases.

The *mishnah* (*Avos* 5:20) states, "Any dispute that is for the sake of Heaven will endure … Any dispute that is not for the sake of Heaven will not endure." Rav Yisrael Salanter explains this *mishnah* homiletically. When two businessmen argue, at the end of the day they will make amends and drink a beer together. However, when a person feels that he is arguing for the sake of Heaven, his quarrel can never end, for how can he give in when Heaven's honor is at stake? Such a *machlokes* will endure forever!

> "When a person feels that he is arguing for the sake of Heaven, his quarrel can never end."

Any *machlokes*, even one that is motivated by the best of intentions, can have terrible repercussions. The Alter of Kelm writes that Korach must have had truly lofty intentions, for if he did not, the pans he used to sacrifice the incense would not have been converted into plating for the *Mizbei'ach*. Despite his lofty intentions, however, the *machlokes* caused the demise of his entire family. If so, can there be any cause that does justify *machlokes*?

(*Shiurei Chumash, Parashas Korach* 16:27, 17:2, 17:5)

פרשת חקת
Parashas Chukas

GAAVAH: CLOSING THE CIRCUIT OF SIN

וְלָקַח הַכֹּהֵן עֵץ אֶרֶז וְאֵזוֹב וּשְׁנִי תוֹלָעַת וְהִשְׁלִיךְ אֶל-תּוֹךְ שְׂרֵפַת הַפָּרָה

And the kohen shall take cedar wood, hyssop, and wool dyed scarlet with the dye of a worm, and throw [it] into the fire of the burning heifer (19:6).

Rashi, in his explanation of the mitzvah of *Parah Adumah*, illustrates how each aspect of this mitzvah correlates to and rectifies the sin of the golden calf. The cedar is the tallest of all trees and the hyssop is the lowest, symbolizing that the haughty person who sinned should lower himself to the level of a hyssop and a worm, and he will be forgiven.

The Torah is informing us that sin begins with *gaavah*. A similar idea is conveyed in the Torah's description of how *Bnei Yisrael* complained about the *mann* and demanded that they be fed meat.

Hashem sent them quail as a punishment, and said that they would eat it "until it comes out of your noses and you are disgusted with it, for you have disgusted Hashem Who is in your midst" (11:20). Rashi explains that Hashem was telling them that were it not for the fact that He dwelled in their midst, they would not have become conceited and sinned. It was their haughtiness that brought them to sin and ultimately led to their downfall.

If it were possible for a person to completely rid himself of *gaavah*, he would never come to sin. Our Sages (*Derech Eretz Zuta* 6) enumerate seven traits that bring a person to sin, the foremost of which is *gaavah*. These traits can be compared to an electric circuit; only when there is a connection is there light. Likewise, without these traits there is no circuit or current that arouses one to sin.

Without *gaavah* it is impossible to sin. Rabbeinu Yonah (*Shaarei Teshuvah* 1:27) refers to *gaavah* as the plow of transgression — it cultivates sin and causes it to sprout.

Although one must adhere to every halachah, he should be wary of taking on stringencies. If abiding by a stringency will cause him to become conceited about his high level of spirituality, then he is better off without it. It was because *Bnei Yisrael* were on such a high spiritual level — they merited having Hashem's *Shechinah* reside in their midst — that they became haughty and subsequently sinned.

All this relates to one's own trait of *gaavah*. With regard to the *gaavah* of others, however, we must take an entirely different approach. *Chazal* (quoted in Rashi to 12:5) tell us that we may praise someone partially when he is present and completely when he is not present. This is not because we are worried that the subject of our praise will become conceited; rather, the issue is that effusive praise borders on flattery, which is prohibited. Rav Yisrael Salanter said that although we must "flee" from honor, when it comes to another person we have to "pour on" the honor in great quanti-

> "Although we must 'flee' from honor, when it comes to another person we have to 'pour on' the honor in great quantities."

ties. Similarly, although we should refrain from indulging our own desires and cravings, we should try to provide our friends with all types of delicacies.

The fact that *gaavah* is an impetus for sin should only be a concern with regard to our personal striving for greatness. With regard to others, although we must be concerned for their spiritual well-being, we should not deprive them of pleasure due to such concerns.

(*Shiurei Chumash, Parashas Chukas* 19:6; *Shiurei Chumash, Parashas Beha'alosecha* 12:5)

❈ ❈ ❈

INSPIRING OTHERS THROUGH OUR ACTIONS

יַעַן לֹא־הֶאֱמַנְתֶּם בִּי לְהַקְדִּישֵׁנִי לְעֵינֵי בְּנֵי יִשְׂרָאֵל

Because you did not believe in Me to sanctify Me before Bnei Yisrael (20:12).

Rambam in *Sefer Hamitzvos*, wherein he enumerates the 613 mitzvos, includes the mitzvah of *"V'nikdashti b'soch Bnei Yisrael* — and I will be sanctified amidst *Bnei Yisrael"* (*Vayikra* 22:32). He explains that this is a commandment to sanctify Hashem's Name by publicizing true *emunah* in the world. This mitzvah is so significant, in fact, that we are obligated to sacrifice our lives for this purpose, which means that it is one of the central objectives of our lives.

This mitzvah, commonly referred to as *kiddush Hashem*, can be defined as conducting oneself in a way that his actions arouse others to realize their responsibilities and connection to their Creator. How can one's actions cause others to become cognizant of their obligations to Hashem? An example of this phenomenon can be found in this *parashah*.

Hashem commanded Moshe to speak to the rock in order that it should give forth water. Moshe erroneously understood that he was supposed to hit the rock to achieve such an outcome. After he hit the rock, Hashem chastised him, saying, "Because you did not believe in Me to sanctify Me before *Bnei Yisrael* …" Had Moshe spoken to the rock instead of hitting it, Hashem would have indeed been sanctified. People would have reasoned that if a simple rock that cannot speak or hear and does not require sustenance heeds Hashem's commandments, how much more so must *we* heed His commandments. This incident could and should have brought others to recognize their obligation toward Hashem. Since it did not effect such results, Moshe and Aharon were punished (Rashi, ibid.).

This mitzvah of *kiddush Hashem* is incumbent upon each and every one of us. People are constantly scrutinizing those who abide by the Torah, and we must be aware of this and concerned about the impression that we make on them. This applies all the more to a *talmid chacham*, since people feel that he epitomizes everything Judaism stands for. When his actions pass their inspection, he has created a *kiddush Hashem*, for his actions have spurred others to realize how they should be acting and have led them to emulate his conduct. The opposite is also true, however. When one's actions cause others to distance themselves from Hashem and from those who lead their lives in accordance with his statutes, he has created a *chillul Hashem*.

> "People are constantly scrutinizing those who abide by the Torah, and we must be aware of this and concerned about the impression that we make on them."

Specifically in our generation, when both non-Jews and Jews are observing us with a critical eye, our duty to sanctify Hashem's Name is compounded. All of our actions must inspire others to be conscious of the way they relate to Hashem's commandments.

(*Alei Shur,* Vol. I, pp. 49, 50, 241)

❈ ❈ ❈

THE DANGER OF PASSING THROUGH A FOREIGN LAND

נַעְבְּרָה־נָּא בְאַרְצֶךָ
Let us pass through your land (20:17).

In an attempt to shorten the final leg of *Bnei Yisrael*'s journey to Eretz Yisrael, Moshe sent messengers to the king of Edom requesting permission to pass through Edom on the way to the Promised Land. The king of Edom refused to grant permission, however, and *Bnei Yisrael* were forced to take a more circuitous path. Thereafter, the Torah writes, "And Hashem spoke to Moshe and Aharon on Hor Hahar near the border of Edom, saying, 'Aharon shall be gathered to his people'" (20:23-24). Rashi explains why the Torah emphasizes that this conversation took place near the border of Edom: Since *Bnei Yisrael* allied themselves with the wicked Esav (Edom), they lost a righteous man (Aharon).

> *"Just speaking the language of the populace introduces certain negative influences, for language expresses a nation's most profound characteristics and ideologies."*

All *Bnei Yisrael* wanted was to pass through the land of Edom. Why, then, did Hashem refer to this as an act of alliance with Edom?

We do not truly understand the danger of living among other nations. We are so used to living in *galus* that we do not even realize the extent to which the people around us influence our lives. We mimic their actions, copy their way of thinking, and absorb their culture. Just speaking the language of the populace introduces certain negative influences, for language expresses a nation's most profound characteristics and ideologies.

Bnei Yisrael merely requested permission to pass through a foreign land, but the danger of such an action was so great that they lost one of their greatest leaders as a result of the request.

We will live in *galus* until Mashiach comes, but we need to be aware of the negative effect of our environment so that we can take steps to minimize it.

(*Shiurei Chumash, Parashas Chukas* 20:23)

❋ ❋ ❋

MISTAKEN IDENTITY

וַיִּשְׁמַע הַכְּנַעֲנִי מֶלֶךְ־עֲרָד יֹשֵׁב הַנֶּגֶב כִּי בָּא יִשְׂרָאֵל ... וַיִּלָּחֶם בְּיִשְׂרָאֵל

And the Canaanite, the king of Arad, who dwelled in the south, heard that Yisrael had come ... and he fought with Yisrael"
(21:1).

Shortly after Aharon passed away, *Bnei Yisrael* were attacked by one of the nations living in Canaan. The Torah tells us, "And the Canaanite, the king of Arad, who dwelled in the south, heard that Yisrael had come ... and he fought with Yisrael." Rashi explains that these attackers were in fact the Amalekites, who lived in the southern portion of Canaan. The Torah refers to them as Canaanites because they masqueraded as Canaanites, with the intention of rendering ineffective *Bnei Yisrael's tefillos* to "defeat the Canaanites," since they were actually Amalekites.

We see from here that one must be clear about the subject of his prayers. Rabbi Akiva Eiger was once asked to *daven* for someone who was ill. After *davening*, he sent back a message that he had not been answered, so it would be worthwhile to verify that there was no mistake made in the name given to him. Indeed, after some clarification, it was discovered that he had been given the wrong name!

Now, we must appreciate that, even if our prayers are not answered in the manner we desire, *tefillah* is not merely a means of obtaining something that we are lacking. *Tefillah* is a thrice-daily exercise in *emunah*, when we train ourselves to recognize that there is no one else to whom we can turn, for Hashem is the only One Who can truly help us. This is an end in itself, regardless of whether we get what we are praying for.

This answers a legitimate question about how *tefillah* works. What right do we have to *daven* for wisdom, health, wealth, or anything else we might be lacking if Hashem put us in that predicament in the first place?

> "By recognizing that everything comes from Hashem, we become worthy of His assistance, and then we have the ability to improve any situation."

By recognizing that everything comes from Hashem, we become worthy of His assistance, and then we have the ability to improve any situation. Each *tefillah* has the ability to strengthen our *emunah* — if we realize that the only One Who can help us is Hashem.

(*Shiurei Chumash, Parashas Chukas* 21:1; *Alei Shur,* Vol. II, p. 348)

פרשת בלק
Parashas Balak

SEEING IS PERCEIVING

וַיְהִי בַבֹּקֶר וַיִּקַּח בָּלָק אֶת־בִּלְעָם וַיַּעֲלֵהוּ בָּמוֹת בָּעַל
וַיַּרְא מִשָּׁם קְצֵה הָעָם

And it was in the morning, and Balak took Bilaam and brought him up to the heights of Baal, and from there he saw the edge of the nation (22:41).

After Bilaam arrived in Moav, Balak prepared him to curse *Bnei Yisrael*: "And it was in the morning, and Balak took Bilaam and brought him up to the heights of Baal, and from there he saw the edge of the nation." Why did Balak feel the need to show Bilaam the Jewish nation? Couldn't Bilaam have cursed them from the comfort of his office? The Ramban explains that Balak specifically led Bilaam to a place where he would be able to see *Bnei Yisrael* with his own eyes, because a person is deeply affected by what he sees. The success of the curse depended on the impression that seeing *Bnei Yisrael* would make upon Bilaam's heart.

We find a similar phenomenon with Moshe Rabbeinu. When *Bnei Yisrael* left Mitzrayim, Amalek came out to greet them with sword in hand. Yehoshua gathered a group of men who would wage war, while Moshe went to the top of the mountain to *daven* for their success. There, too, the Ramban (*Shemos* 17:9) points out that Moshe specifically chose a spot from which he would be able to see those below (and they would be able to see him), because this would positively affect his prayers.

True awareness is only achieved when a person sees something before his eyes. If one wants to truly feel the pain and suffering of a poor person, he should go to his house and view his dire living conditions.

Even if we cannot see something with our eyes, we still have the ability to "see" it in our mind's eye. Picturing an event in our mind will affect us and enhance our *emunah* far more profoundly than merely reading about the event in a *sefer*. Indeed, *Chazal* tell us (*Pesachim* 116b) that on the *Seder* night we are supposed to see ourselves as if we left Mitzrayim. If we can re-create and depict in our minds the Exodus, then we can succeed in truly feeling as if we too left Mitzrayim.

Rav Wolbe often quoted *Kuzari*, who writes that imagination was given to us as a tool to conjure up pictures of our rich past, such as the *Akeidah*, *Maamad Har Sinai*, and the *Beis HaMikdash*. Seeing something, whether with our eyes or in our minds, allows us to fully appreciate it.

(*Shiurei Chumash, Parashas Balak* 22:41)

❃ ❃ ❃

THE ENEMY'S PRAISE

כִּי־מֵרֹאשׁ צֻרִים אֶרְאֶנּוּ וּמִגְּבָעוֹת אֲשׁוּרֶנּוּ הֶן־עָם לְבָדָד יִשְׁכֹּן

From the tops of rocks I perceive them and from hills I see them, a nation that will dwell in solitude (23:9).

There was no prophet who described *Bnei Yisrael*'s essence better than Bilaam. Ramban writes (22:20) that Hashem specifically wanted a non-Jewish prophet to bless *Bnei Yisrael*. Similarly, *Chazal* tell us (*Avodah Zarah* 3a) that when Hashem will reward *Bnei Yisrael* in the future, all the nations of the world will protest that *Bnei Yisrael* are undeserving, since they failed to perform the mitzvos of the Torah. Hashem will respond that the gentiles themselves will testify to *Bnei Yisrael*'s vigilance in guarding the Torah's precepts. Lavan will testify that in 20 years of employment, Yaakov did not take a single item that was not his. Nevuchadnetzar will testify that Chananyah, Misha'el, and Azaryah refused to prostrate themselves before the idol, and so on. Here, too, Hashem wants our enemies to testify to our righteousness.

David HaMelech says (*Tehillim* 92:12), "When those who would harm me rise up against me, my ears listen." Rav Yisrael Salanter commented that when an enemy speaks, we must listen. If our enemy says that we are righteous, we can be certain that we are truly righteous. However, if he says something negative, then we know we have fallen short of the ideal, as the *passuk* says, "When Hashem favors a man's ways, even his enemies will make peace with him" (*Mishlei* 16:7). Hashem derives satisfaction, as it were, from the praises sung by our enemies, for there is no truer praise.

How does Bilaam describe *Bnei Yisrael*? "From the tops of rocks I perceive them and from hills I see them, a nation that will dwell in solitude." Rashi explains that Bilaam looked into *Bnei Yisrael*'s origins — the patriarchs and matriarchs — and

> "*Hashem derives satisfaction, as it were, from the praises sung by our enemies, for there is no truer praise.*"

found that their foundation is rock solid. Every action of our forefathers was done with the intention of creating a spiritual nation, one that would "dwell in solitude." We are to be so totally removed from the other nations that the Torah forbids us to even praise them or their possessions.

Bilaam perceived that the intention of the *Avos* was to build a nation that would dwell in solitude. Even when living among other nations, we must bear in mind that Bilaam's description is our very essence.

(*Shiurei Chumash, Parashas Balak* 23:9)

❋ ❋ ❋

SIN IS TO BE FORGOTTEN

וַיָּשֶׁת אֶל־הַמִּדְבָּר פָּנָיו
And he turned his face toward the desert (24:1).

After Bilaam failed in his attempts to curse *Bnei Yisrael*, he hit upon another plan: "And he turned his face toward the desert." Rashi quotes the Targum, who explains that Bilaam's intention was to mention *Bnei Yisrael*'s transgressions, thus causing Hashem to "remember" those transgressions. This would lay the groundwork for a curse to be successfully placed on *Bnei Yisrael*. Therefore, "he turned his face toward the desert" — he mentioned the desert, the place where *Bnei Yisrael* worshiped the golden calf.

We find a similar concept in the Torah's discussion of the laws of the *sotah*. The Torah refers to the *sotah*'s offering as a "*mazkeres avon*" — a remembrance of her sin. If she is guilty, her sin is remembered, and the *sotah* water enters her body and wreaks havoc on it.

Remembering a sin can be dangerous for another reason, too. Great scholars have asserted that when a person recites *viduy* on Yom Kippur, he should not spend too much time thinking about each individual sin. If he begins reliving his transgression, he might, God forbid, think to himself — even subconsciously — that he enjoyed what he did. In such a situation, remembering the sin will cause him to desire it once again, and the *viduy* will turn into a cause for punishment.

When a person distances himself from his transgression to the point where thoughts of the *aveirah* he committed do not even cross his mind, he can rest assured that he has been forgiven for that *aveirah*. In a similar vein, the *mishnah* in *Pirkei Avos* (2:2) tells us that it is good for a person to busy himself with both Torah and *derech eretz*, for together they cause "sin to be forgotten."

Although David HaMelech declares, "My sin is before me at all times" (*Tehillim* 51:5), one must be on an extremely high spiritual level to be able to continually remember his sins. Even such a person should probably not be constantly thinking about his sins. Rather, the *passuk* is teaching us that one should be careful at all times to avoid the type of situation that brought him to sin in the first place.

> "Proper teshuvah for a transgression should not include a detailed analysis of the sin."

Proper *teshuvah* for a transgression should not include a detailed analysis of the sin, for the more one thinks about his sin, the more susceptible he becomes to repeating his mistake.

(*Shiurei Chumash, Parashas Balak* 24:1)

❈ ❈ ❈

NOTHING GOES TO WASTE

וַיִּצָּמֶד יִשְׂרָאֵל לְבַעַל פְּעוֹר

And Yisrael cleaved [to the idol] Baal Pe'or (25:3).

Idol worship, in general, is difficult to understand. Although we can comprehend how people might attribute godly characteristics to celestial bodies like the sun, moon, and stars, we cannot fathom what they hoped to gain by prostrating themselves before a slab of wood. The worship of the Baal Pe'or idol is particularly baffling:

Rashi explains that the worshipers would expose themselves and defecate before the idol. What could possibly be the logic or philosophy behind such worship?

Rav Yitzchak Hutner explained that this ideology is a manifestation of pessimism. It was the worshipers' way of declaring that actions have no real purpose; at the end of the day, everything is worthless. Whether one eats a succulent steak or a gorgeous red apple, the end result is that everything turns into excrement.

Such an outlook is diametrically opposed to the Torah. The Torah teaches us that every action has the ability to build, and nothing goes to waste. Even excrement could be used as fertilizer, as it contains essential life-giving nutrients that help develop a new crop. Everything in this world has a purpose, and nothing is wasted or totally lost.

Bilaam declared (23:10), "Who can count the dust of Yaakov?" Rashi explains that there is no limit to the mitzvos that *Bnei Yisrael* perform with earth. We are prohibited from plowing a field with an ox and a donkey yoked together, and from planting mixtures of seeds (*kilayim*). We are commanded to use the ashes of the red heifer to purify those who came in contact with a dead person, and the test of the *sotah* was performed with a mixture that contained earth. *Bnei Yisrael* are able to elevate even something as lowly as dirt, by using it to perform mitzvos, attain purity, and restore harmony to the home of the *sotah*.

"Bnei Yisrael are able to elevate even something as lowly as dirt."

This concept is discussed in *Mesilas Yesharim*, who writes that *kedushah* is the ability to transform the mundane into the spiritual. *Chazal* tell us that giving food and drink to a *talmid chacham* is tantamount to offering a sacrifice and a wine libation, because a *talmid chacham* channels every action toward spirituality. Indeed, the *mishnah* (*Mikva'os* 9:5) refers to *talmidei chachamim* as "*bana'im*" — builders — because they are the true builders of the world.

(*Shiurei Chumash, Parashas Balak* 25:3)

פרשת פנחס
Parashas Pinchas

NO SWEET REVENGE

פִּינְחָס בֶּן־אֶלְעָזָר בֶּן־אַהֲרֹן הַכֹּהֵן הֵשִׁיב אֶת־חֲמָתִי מֵעַל בְּנֵי־יִשְׂרָאֵל בְּקַנְאוֹ אֶת־קִנְאָתִי בְּתוֹכָם

Pinchas, the son of Elazar, the son of Aharon HaKohen, turned back My anger from Bnei Yisrael when he zealously avenged Me among them (25:11).

Rashi explains that when Pinchas killed the transgressors, he avenged that which was appropriate for Hashem Himself to avenge.

Hashem is referred to as a "God of vengeance" (*Devarim* 5:9). What does it mean that Hashem "takes revenge"? The vengeance of Hashem is manifest when He eradicates evil from the world. The term "God of vengeance" is therefore an apt description, because He wants nothing more than for evil to be eradicated. Pinchas's act of vengeance paralleled Hashem's attribute of vengeance, since it was carried out with a single intention: to rid *Bnei Yisrael* of evil. It was not a desire for "sweet revenge" that galvanized Pinchas into action, but rather his purity of heart. Similarly, Hashem does not take revenge in the colloquial sense; rather, He eliminates evil by destroying the transgressors.

It is for this reason that *Chazal* tell us (*Yoma* 22b), "A *talmid chacham* who does not take revenge like a snake is not a true *talmid chacham*." A *talmid chacham* is one who cleaves to Hashem and emulates the attributes by which He is defined. "*Ohavei Hashem sin'u ra*" (*Tehillim* 97:10) — those who love Hashem despise evil, and those who despise evil do everything in their power to eradicate it from society. One who is apathetic to the evil being perpetrated around him cannot be considered a true *talmid chacham*.

With this approach we can understand why Hashem is meticulous in meting out punishment to those closest to Him, even for the slightest infraction. The righteous wish to purify themselves, and Hashem aids them through punishment in ridding them of even the minutest trace of evil. Likewise, many of our nation's leaders were very exacting when it came to disciplining their closest students. When Hagar became pregnant immediately after her marriage to Avraham, she looked down upon Sarah Imeinu, who had not yet merited a child. The Torah tells us that Sarah subsequently persecuted Hagar. Because Hagar was a close disciple of Sarah, Sarah felt the need to rid her of negative traits, and was therefore very strict with her.

> "Because Hagar was a close disciple of Sarah, Sarah felt the need to rid her of negative traits, and was therefore very strict with her."

Rav Yerucham Levovitz once grabbed a student and pulled him out of the *beis midrash* because of a misdemeanor. Some time later, he took that *bachur* as a husband for his own daughter!

Both Sarah Imeinu and Rav Yerucham (and all the great leaders in between) were not "taking revenge" because they felt slighted on a personal level; they were propelled solely by the desire to rid their disciples of their negative character traits. It is this form of "revenge" that characterizes Hashem and those who follow in His ways.

(*Shiurei Chumash, Parashas Pinchas* 25:11; *Shiurei Chumas, Parashas Lech Lecha* 16:6)

❋ ❋ ❋

IN THE MERIT OF RIGHTEOUS WOMEN

אֵלֶּה פְּקוּדֵי מֹשֶׁה וְאֶלְעָזָר הַכֹּהֵן . . . וּבְאֵלֶּה לֹא־הָיָה אִישׁ מִפְּקוּדֵי מֹשֶׁה וְאַהֲרֹן הַכֹּהֵן אֲשֶׁר פָּקְדוּ אֶת־בְּנֵי יִשְׂרָאֵל בְּמִדְבַּר סִינָי

These are the ones counted by Moshe and Elazar HaKohen . . . And of these there was no man of those counted by Moshe and Aharon in the Sinai desert (26:63-64).

Bnei Yisrael are counted once again in this *parashah*: "These are the ones counted by Moshe and Elazar HaKohen . . . And of these there was no man of those counted by Moshe and Aharon in the Sinai desert." Rashi comments that the Torah emphasizes "There was no man" because the women were still alive at the time of the second counting. They did not participate in the sin of the spies, for while the men accepted the slanderous report regarding Eretz Yisrael, the women cherished the land. This was demonstrated by the daughters of Tzelafchad, who came to Moshe requesting that they be allocated a portion of land in Eretz Yisrael.

Women were always at the forefront of great events mentioned in the Torah. *Chazal* tell us that in the merit of righteous women our

> "Women were always at the forefront of great events mentioned in the Torah."

forefathers were redeemed from bondage in Mitzrayim (*Sotah* 11b). Similarly, when *Bnei Yisrael* stood ready to accept the Torah at Har Sinai, the women were placed first in Hashem's command to Moshe: "So shall you say to the *daughters* of Yaakov and relate to the *sons* of Yisrael" (*Shemos* 19:3). It was the women who cherished Eretz Yisrael and thereby merited entering the land, while their male counterparts perished in the wilderness. In contrast to those who believe that women have an inferior spiritual status, the Torah clarifies for us their true level of greatness.

Rashi (27:7) tells us that the eyes of Tzelafchad's daughters "saw" what Moshe's eyes did not "see." Their request precipitated Hashem's commandment to Moshe regarding what should be done with the estate of a man who dies and leaves only daughters. It was in the merit of these wise women that *Bnei Yisrael* were taught the laws pertaining to inheritance. Once again, we see the greatness the Torah ascribes to women.

There is another lesson to be gleaned from the daughters of Tzelafchad: They are yet another example of the emphasis the Torah places on the importance of each individual. Their simple request, which demonstrated an intense spiritual desire, brought them honor in the eyes of their generation and all future generations, since Hashem recorded their dialogue in the Torah. Every individual has the potential to leave his mark!

(*Shiurei Chumash, Parashas Pinchas* 26:64, 27:5)

❋ ❋ ❋

PUTTING THE GUEST AT EASE

פָּרִים בְּנֵי־בָקָר שְׁלֹשָׁה עָשָׂר

Thirteen young bulls (29:13).

At the end of this *parashah*, the Torah tells us that *Bnei Yisrael* brought 13 cows as sacrifices on the first day of Succos. With each successive day of the Yom Tov, the number of cows steadily decreased. On the second day, only 12 cows were offered on the *Mizbei'ach*, and so on, until the last day, when only seven cows were brought. The Midrash writes that the Torah is teaching us the proper procedure (*derech eretz*) for hosting a guest. Just as the sacrifices decreased in number day after day, so, too, there should be a steady decline in the type of food one offers a guest. The first day a guest should be served fattened fowl, the following day he should be served fish, and on subsequent days he should be served meat, then legumes, and then vegetables (Rashi, 29:36).

Why is this the proper way to treat a guest? At this rate, in another few days the guest won't be given anything to eat! Rav Avraham Grodzinski explained that the Torah is teaching us how to make a guest feel comfortable. The first few days, he is served lavish meals in the dining room, at the table reserved for Shabbos. Afterward, he is cajoled into joining the family in the kitchen and eating the same food as the rest of the household. This is the *derech eretz* to which the Midrash was referring — slowly but surely closing the gap between the guest and the host, until the guest feels at home and even part of the family.

Other areas of *chessed* also require some level of tact to ensure that the beneficiary is left with a good feeling, as the following anecdote demonstrates. Reuven was in dire straits, but was too embarrassed to accept a monetary donation or loan. His good friend Shimon devised a plan to help him out. While in the company of Reuven, Shimon acted nervous and uneasy, and when Reuven asked what was wrong, Shimon explained that an elderly man whom he used to visit had passed away and entrusted him with a large amount of money to distribute to those in need. Shimon added that he was afraid to carry around so much money, and he did not know how to go about distributing

> *"The meaning of true chessed is helping a fellow Jew in a way that will make him feel comfortable and at ease."*

it. Reuven smiled broadly and told him to stop worrying, for right now he was tight on money and could use the amount Shimon was carrying. When Shimon handed over the money, Reuven felt that he was doing his friend a real favor!

Whether one is hosting a total stranger or helping out a good friend, the meaning of true *chessed* is helping a fellow Jew in a way that will make him feel comfortable and at ease.

(*Shiurei Chumash, Parashas Pinchas* 29:36; *Alei Shur,* Vol. II, p. 204)

פָּרָשַׁת מַטּוֹת-מַסְעֵי
Parashas Matos-Masei

PUNISHMENT IS NOT SWEET REVENGE

וַיְדַבֵּר ה' אֶל־מֹשֶׁה לֵּאמֹר. נְקֹם נִקְמַת בְּנֵי יִשְׂרָאֵל מֵאֵת הַמִּדְיָנִים אַחַר תֵּאָסֵף אֶל־עַמֶּיךָ. וַיְדַבֵּר מֹשֶׁה אֶל־הָעָם לֵאמֹר הֵחָלְצוּ מֵאִתְּכֶם אֲנָשִׁים לַצָּבָא וְיִהְיוּ עַל־מִדְיָן לָתֵת נִקְמַת־ה' בְּמִדְיָן

*And Hashem spoke to Moshe, saying, "Take revenge on behalf **of Bnei Yisrael** from the Midyanim and afterward you will pass away." And Moshe spoke to the nation saying, "Separate from yourselves men for the army so they may inflict the vengeance **of Hashem** against Midyan" (31:1-3).*

Rashi explains that one who acts against *Bnei Yisrael* is in effect acting against Hashem. Moshe therefore declared that the revenge against Midyan was being carried out for Hashem's sake, as if Midyan had acted against Hashem Himself.

Bnei Yisrael are Hashem's ambassadors in this world, for they bring knowledge of Him to the entire world. Just as an assault against a country's ambassador is regarded as an attack against the country, one who rises up against *Bnei Yisrael* has risen up against the Creator of the world Himself.

The revenge against Midyan was not the type of revenge that is described by the *Mesilas Yesharim* as "sweeter than honey." Rather, revenge in the Torah refers to an act of purging evil from the world, from a nation, or even from a single perpetrator (see *Parashas Balak*). All of the Torah's punishments are merely a way of cleansing the evil from the transgressor. Other nations claim that the Torah's punishments are rooted in revenge, as the *passuk* states (*Shemos* 21:24), "An eye for an eye, a tooth for a tooth." However, *Chazal* tell us that "an eye for an eye" means that one must pay monetary reparations for the damage caused.

Giving a murderer a lifetime jail sentence is a lot closer to an act of revenge than the Torah's punishment for murder. Those who are killed by *beis din* still have a portion in the World to Come. They were not put to death because of an attitude of "We'll show him." Rather, their death is a form of cleansing, which allows them entry into the World to Come — the ultimate goal of every Jew.

A parent must not punish a child with the intention of taking revenge. Sometimes a parent tells his child to do something, and the child defiantly ignores the parent, or even says no. Another common — and embarrassing — occurrence is when a child acts out in front of others. The parent is personally offended, and quickly metes out a "fair" punishment, which is often merely revenge in disguise. In this respect, there is no difference between taking revenge against one's friend and one's child; punishment solely for the sake of payback is forbidden. The infraction must be dealt with, but only with the desire to correct the misdemeanor, not to heal one's wounded ego.

> "There is no difference between taking revenge against one's friend and one's child; punishment solely for the sake of payback is forbidden."

Someone was once talking to Rav Abba Grossbard and said something offensive. Some time later, the offender needed a letter of recommendation from Rav Grossbard. Rav Grossbard tried to decline with all types of excuses, saying, "Do you really need it?" and, "I do not write letters." It was obvious that Rav Grossbard was not truly offended, but was deliberately avoiding the request so that the offender would realize that he had acted improperly. This tactic was successful, and the offender asked for forgiveness. This is the proper method of "punishment."

(*Shiurei Chumash, Parashas Matos* 31:3; *Alei Shur*, Vol. I, p. 260)

❋ ❋ ❋

UNLAWFUL GAINS

וַיֵּצְאוּ מֹשֶׁה וְאֶלְעָזָר הַכֹּהֵן וְכָל־נְשִׂיאֵי הָעֵדָה לִקְרָאתָם
Moshe, Elazar the Kohen, and all the leaders of the assembly went out to meet them (31:13).

When the soldiers returned from war with Midyan, Moshe Rabbeinu, Elazar HaKohen, and the princes of the *shevatim* all went out to greet them. Rashi explains that some youngsters had run to grab a portion of the abundant spoils, and Moshe Rabbeinu and the other leaders personally went out to prevent this from happening. When there was a suspicion that someone was stealing, Moshe did not rely on sending a messenger to investigate. He felt it was necessary to stop such behavior himself.

"*Throughout Chumash, we see the great vigilance that our forefathers displayed when it came to matters that involved other people's property.*"

Throughout *Chumash*, we see the great vigilance that our forefathers displayed when it came to matters that involved other people's property. Avraham's animals traveled with a muzzle, lest they graze in someone else's field. Yaakov lived in Lavan's house for more than 20 years, and did not take a single item from his house. When Moshe collected funds for the building of the *Mishkan*, he wore a specially tailored garment that had no pockets or seams, lest anyone suspect that he had taken some of the money for himself.

One Yom Kippur before *Ne'ilah*, the Chofetz Chaim stood in front of the *aron kodesh* and spoke. He said that twice in *Ne'ilah* we state, "So that we may refrain from the *oshek* of our hands" (referring to money taken unlawfully). Stealing is a very grave sin. Since *Ne'ilah* is a time to make a *kabbalah*, we should resolve that if we have in our possession any money that belongs to another person we will return it immediately after Yom Kippur.

Stealing is a terrible *aveirah*, and yet we do not even have an idea of what is included in this prohibition. Rav Yisrael Salanter would urge people to study the third section of *Choshen Mishpat*, which deals with interpersonal monetary matters. Rav Wolbe heeded this call and instituted that the *kollel* that learned in his *beis hamussar* should study those specific halachos. If we want to be sure that we do not unknowingly transgress the laws of *gezel*, we need to study these halachos and gain a more comprehensive understanding of them.

(Shiurei Chumash, Parashas Matos 31:13)

❊ ❊ ❊

CAUSING THE SUN TO SHINE

מַכֵּה־נֶפֶשׁ בִּשְׁגָגָה
One who takes a life unintentionally (35:11).

Toward the end of *Sefer Bamidbar* we are told the laws regarding one who kills a person accidentally: He must flee to a city of refuge and remain there until the death of the *kohen gadol*. In *Parashas Va'eschanan* we read how Moshe Rabbeinu designated three cities in Eretz Yisrael as *arei miklat*: "Then Moshe set aside three cities on the bank of the Jordan toward the rising sun (*mizrichah* shamesh)" (Devarim 4:41). Chazal (Makkos 10a) explain "mizrichah shamesh" homiletically. Some explain that Hashem was telling Moshe, "Cause the sun to shine for the murderers." Others explain that Hashem was commending Moshe on a job well done: "You have caused the sun to shine for the murderers." This was the very last mitzvah Moshe performed before he passed away.

The greatest prophet dedicated his last hours on earth to causing the sun to shine for dejected people. The truth is that his entire life was devoted to this cause. The first story the Torah tells us about Moshe, when he was growing up in Pharaoh's palace, is: "He went out to his brethren and observed their suffering" (Shemos 2:11). From the beginning until the end, Moshe's life was a continuous saga of caring for the downtrodden and causing the sun to shine for them.

This concept encapsulates our *avodah* in the realm of *bein adam lachaveiro*. Indeed, *Chazal* teach, "Rabbi Yochanan said, 'One who shows the white of his teeth [i.e., his smile] to his friend does more than one who gives him milk to drink'" (*Kesubos* 111a). Uplifting another person emotionally is more important than providing for his physical needs.

"Uplifting another person emotionally is more important than providing for his physical needs."

"Rav Masya ben Charash said, 'Initiate a greeting to every person'" (*Avos* 4:20). Responding to a greeting is an act of *derech eretz*, while initiating a greeting is much more than that: It is an act that truly lights up another person's life. Everyone craves and appreciates the interest that another person shows in him. Even a baby responds warmly to a smile; he gurgles and his face lights up. Conversely, if he receives a stern look, he immediately starts to cry.

Smiles do not cost anything, yet they give so much. Why not distribute them more freely?

(*Alei Shur,* Vol. I, pp. 190, 191)

❧ ❧ ❧

SELF-UNDERSTOOD RESPONSIBILITY

וְיָשַׁב בָּהּ עַד־מוֹת הַכֹּהֵן הַגָּדֹל

He shall dwell there until the death of the kohen gadol (35:25).

Why must a murderer stay in an *ir miklat* until the *kohen gadol* dies? What is the connection between the *kohen gadol* and the person who kills someone else accidentally?

The *kohen gadol* should have prayed that such a tragedy not occur during his lifetime. Since he did not, the length of the murderer's confinement in the *ir miklat* is determined by the life span of the *kohen gadol* (Rashi, 35:25).

Nowhere in the Torah do we find that it is the responsibility of the *kohen gadol* to pray for the welfare of the entire *Bnei Yisrael*, nor do we find mention of such a *tefillah* in the prayer text that the *kohen gadol* recited on Yom Kippur. It must be that this responsibility is patently obvious and self-understood. One who is chosen as the *kohen gadol* has been appointed guardian of *Bnei Yisrael*, and a guardian is responsible for the welfare of all his charges.

Anyone who occupies a position in which he is entrusted with the care of others has a responsibility to pray for their welfare. Whether one is a rabbi, teacher, manager of a company, or (even more so) a parent, he must pray for his charges. If he fails to pray for their welfare, he has not merely been derelict in his duty; he is also, to a certain extent, responsible for any tragedy that may befall them.

Rav Wolbe was certain that whatever he achieved in the area of Torah was in the merit of his mother's constant prayers. She would pray for him as often as 10 times a day. There is no limit to the number of prayers that we can offer on behalf of our children. We can never say, "We've prayed enough."

> *"There is no limit to the number of prayers that we can offer on behalf of our children."*

There is no set *nusach* of *tefillah* given to us by *Chazal* with which to *daven* for our children. It is up to each parent to come up with a personal prayer and pray from the depths of his or her heart. The *tefillos* can and should be adjusted to each particular situation or challenge that the child might be facing.

Davening for the success of one's children is so vital that it might very well be the most important aspect of raising our children. Although our children were placed in our care, it would be a grave mistake to think that their *chinuch* is entirely in our hands. The same holds true for anyone who is in a position to influence others. The very best way to influence them positively and safeguard them from harm is by offering heartfelt *tefillos* on their behalf.

(*Zeriyah U'Binyan Bechinuch*, pp. 34, 35)

❋ ❋ ❋

A TREASURE IN THE FRUIT

וְלֹא תְטַמֵּא אֶת־הָאָרֶץ אֲשֶׁר אַתֶּם יֹשְׁבִים בָּהּ אֲשֶׁר אֲנִי שֹׁכֵן בְּתוֹכָהּ כִּי אֲנִי ה' שֹׁכֵן בְּתוֹךְ בְּנֵי יִשְׂרָאֵל

Do not defile the land in which you dwell, in whose midst I reside, for I am Hashem Who resides in Bnei Yisrael" (35:34).

The Torah commands, "The land shall not be sold forever, because the land belongs to Me; for you are sojourners and residents with Me" (*Vayikra* 25:23). *Sforno* explains that although the *passuk* (*Tehillim* 115:16) states, "The heavens are the heavens for Hashem and the land He gave to mankind," nevertheless, Eretz Yisrael is not included in that declaration. Eretz Yisrael still belongs to Hashem, and we are mere sojourners in His land.

Accordingly, our entire foothold in Eretz Yisrael is merely a *kinyan peiros* — the ability to eat the fruits of the land, while the ground itself remains in the possession of Hashem. This idea is emphasized in the words of *Al HaMichyah*. We thank Hashem "for the desirable, good, and spacious land that You were pleased to give our forefathers as an inheritance, **to eat from its fruit and to be satisfied from its goodness**." Our ownership of the land is limited to eating its produce.

The ability to eat the produce of Eretz Yisrael is in truth a very meaningful gift. In *Al HaMichyah* we ask Hashem to return us to Eretz Yisrael and allow us to "eat from its fruit and to be satisfied from its goodness." Some *poskim* (see *Tur Orach Chaim* 208) maintain that these words should not be said, because the reason that we desire to return to the Promised Land is not for the material benefits of the land's produce. Rather, we yearn to return to our land in order to fulfill the mitzvos that can only be performed in Eretz Yisrael.

However, the Bach (ibid.) asserts that these words should be said, and he bases his opinion on a *passuk* in this week's *parashah*: "Do not defile the land in which you dwell, in whose midst I reside, for I am Hashem **Who resides in Bnei Yisrael**" (35:34). He explains that when *Bnei Yisrael* refrain from sinning, Hashem literally resides inside the land. When they ate the fruit of the land, they were, so to speak, ingesting the *Shechinah*! Accordingly, the *Shechinah* resided inside of *Bnei Yisrael*!

> "When Bnei Yisrael ate the fruit of Eretz Yisrael, they were, so to speak, ingesting the Shechinah!"

Should the land become contaminated with sin, the *Shechinah* that resided in the land departs. Subsequently, when the fruit that draws its nutrients from this impure land is eaten, the impurity will be transferred into the one eating the fruit, thereby ejecting the *Shechinah* from his body, too.

When we say *Al HaMichyah* we are expressing our yearning to once again merit to eat from the fruits of Eretz Yisrael that are imbued with the *Shechinah*, which will transform our physical bodies into an abode for the *Shechinah*. The produce of the land is actually the conduit for *hashraas haShechinah* — which is the very reason we were given the land.

With this, we can understand an interesting Gemara. *Chazal* ask (*Sotah* 14a) why Moshe Rabbeinu had such a great desire to enter Eretz Yisrael: "Was he interested in eating its fruit or becoming satisfied from its goodness? Rather, he wanted to perform the mitzvos that are connected to the land and can only be performed there."

Chazal specifically focused on eating the fruits of the land because they are a means of connecting to Hashem. *Chazal* were wondering: Could it be that Moshe needed the land's fruit to connect to Hashem? Even without ingesting the fruit, Moshe had achieved a level where he had turned his body into an abode for the *Shechinah*!

During the Three Weeks, we mourn the destruction of the *Beis HaMikdash* and our *galus* from Eretz Yisrael. Understanding the value of the fruits of Eretz Yisrael gives us added appreciation for just what we are missing, and will hopefully give us added impetus to utter a heartfelt prayer for the much-needed *Geulah Sheleimah*.

(*Alei Shur*, Vol. I, pp. 282, 283)

ספר דברים
Sefer Devarim

Rabbi Kagan wrote Chofetz Chayim
He also wrote Mishnah Brurah, which codifies
Shulchan Aruch to today's life
He wrote altogether 24 books
Born 1840, died 1934, mostly in Poland
(part of Belarus now)

פרשת דברים
Parashas Devarim

THE MOTOR OF HISBONENUS

עַמִּי לֹא הִתְבּוֹנָן

My nation did not contemplate (hisbonan) (Haftarah, Parashas Devarim, Yeshayah 1:3).

In the *haftarah* of this *parashah* we read how Yeshayahu HaNavi lamented, "My nation did not contemplate (*hisbonan*)." The fact that he began his prophecy with this allegation shows just how essential *hisbonenus* is. What exactly is *hisbonenus*, and why is it so important?

The Ramchal (*Derech Eitz Chaim*) reveals the secret behind *hisbonenus*. The Torah is likened to a fire, and its every word is like a coal. If left untended,

> *"The Torah is likened to a fire, and its every word is like a coal. If one fans the coals by toiling to understand the Torah, each coal will burst into a fiery flame."*

Parashas Devarim / 317

a coal will glimmer slightly at best. However, if one fans the coals by toiling to understand the Torah, each coal will burst into a fiery flame. In addition, a person is endowed with the ability to reach awesome levels of spiritual comprehension, but this can only be accomplished if he "ignites the fire" through *hisbonenus*.

Ramchal says that the world was specifically created in this fashion to allow for free will. If everything would be crystal clear at first glance, and we would immediately comprehend the absolute truth of the Creator of the world and the Torah, we would never sin. The *yetzer hara* would have no dominion whatsoever, for we would recognize how every mitzvah is a treasure and how every sin is literally a disaster. In order to balance the scales, Hashem created a world where true knowledge is like a smoldering coal that has the potential to turn into a fiery blaze. Man must choose whether to ignite it or allow it to remain a dim coal.

With this in mind, we can understand how the need for *hisbonenus* plays a fundamental role in the purpose of creation. *Hisbonenus* is the motor that triggers a person's *seichel* to properly comprehend things, which aids him in his war against the *yetzer hara*. The more clarity he has in his role in this world, the less interest he has in sinning.

Hisbonenus is the ability to focus on an idea and objectively contemplate a topic with the intention of integrating the knowledge into one's own life. It means taking Torah and *mussar* ideas that we might already know — but only as a smoldering coal — and turning them into a roaring fire that will burn its way into our minds and hearts. In addition, *hisbonenus* is the tool a person must use to truly get to know himself. If he objectively contemplates his actions and life goals, he can arrive at realizations that will change his path in life for the better.

(*Alei Shur,* Vol. I, p. 89)

פרשת ואתחנן
Parashas Va'eschanan

GREATNESS IS MEASURED BY KINDNESS

אַתָּה הַחִלּוֹתָ לְהַרְאוֹת אֶת־עַבְדְּךָ אֶת־גָּדְלְךָ

You have begun to show Your servant Your greatness (3:24).

"For I am Hashem Who does **kindness**, judgment, and charity in the land, and it is these things that I desire" (*Haftarah*, Tishah B'Av).

This *parashah* commences with Moshe's prayer that Hashem allow him to enter Eretz Yisrael: "You have begun to show Your servant Your greatness and Your strong hand ... please allow me to cross over the Jordan so that I should be able to see the good land" (3:24-25). Rashi explains that "Your greatness" refers to Hashem's attribute of kindness. We can deduce from here that performing acts of kindness is one of the defining characteristics of greatness.

Chazal tell us that Avraham Avinu personified kindness. Why was this trait chosen to define his essence, as opposed to the trait of *emunah*, which he epitomized? After all, Avraham was the first person to refer to Hashem as the Master of the world, and through his hospitality he continuously brought others to recognize their Creator.

The answer is that Avraham's *emunah* was the impetus for his kindness. The popular belief of the idol worshipers during Avraham's era was, "Yes, there might be a God, but He is so great and lofty that He does not get involved with, or even care about, what goes on in our lowly world." Avraham Avinu, the greatest man in his generation, refuted this notion through his many acts of kindness: He established an inn for wayfarers, and he himself provided for their every need.

Avraham proved that true greatness is measured by one's kindness to others. Hashem's greatness lies in the very fact that He takes an interest in our lowly world, sustains us, and cares for our every need. Avraham's belief in Divine Providence caused him to understand the parameters of true greatness.

It was only due to his kindness that Avraham was able to influence others positively: through his inn, he caused others to proclaim the Name of Hashem. Someone who is in a position of authority cannot expect to influence others without performing acts of kindness for them. We say in *Shemoneh Esrei*, "He bestows beneficial kindness and is the Owner of everything." Rav Yerucham Levovitz comments that we can homiletically infer from this that a person who performs acts of kindness has the ability to "acquire" (i.e., influence) others.

> "A person who performs acts of kindness has the ability to 'acquire' (i.e., influence) others."

Rav Wolbe was once informed that the local townspeople planned to rent an auditorium and bring a noted lecturer to address women on the importance of family purity. Rav Wolbe told them that this was not the correct way to influence the women, because those who were not interested would not attend. Instead, they should offer a donation to young brides (most of whom had been orphaned during the Holocaust), and this act of kindness would make them more receptive to what was being taught. The townspeople disagreed, so Rav Wolbe went to the Chazon Ish to ask who was right, and the Chazon Ish concurred with him.

(*Shiurei Chumash, Parashas Va'eschanan* 3:24; *Shiurei Chumash, Parashas Vayeira* 21:33)

❈ ❈ ❈

SO FAR, YET SO CLOSE

כִּי מִי־גוֹי גָּדוֹל אֲשֶׁר־לוֹ אֱלֹקִים קְרֹבִים אֵלָיו כַּה׳ אֱלֹקֵינוּ בְּכָל־קָרְאֵנוּ אֵלָיו

For which is a great nation that has God close to it as Hashem, our God, whenever we call out to Him? (4:7).

The *Yerushalmi* (*Berachos* 9:1) relates that a group of students once asked their *rebbi* to explain the following *passuk*: "For which is a great nation that has God close to it as Hashem, our God, whenever we call out to Him?" Hashem is singular, so why is the word "close" (*kerovim*) written in the plural form?

The *rebbi* explained that the Torah is telling us that Hashem is close in many different ways. Although idols seem close, in reality they are as distant as can be. A person might carry his deity in his hand, but he can cry and scream until he turns red and the idol will still not hear him. In contrast, Hashem appears to be distant, but there is nothing closer than He. From the earth to the first heaven is a journey of 500 years, and the journey from there to each subsequent heaven is also 500 years (*Pesachim* 94b). Despite this great distance, when a person merely whispers his prayers, Hashem hears him as if he were whispering into Hashem's ear. Could there be anything closer than that?

An idol appears close because it is a tangible, physical form; our senses help us perceive it as a reality. Though we no longer crave idol worship, each generation has its own form of idolatry garbed in a unique attire. Rav Eliyahu Dessler writes that in our time the obsessive drive for materialism can be compared to idol worship. When a person gets so caught up in the desire for material comfort that he forgets there is a spiritual reality, he has forgotten Hashem and is in a sense guilty of idolatry.

The above Gemara describes Hashem as appearing very distant from us here on earth. What does this mean? Does not the *passuk* say, "Hashem's glory fills the earth"?

The Gemara is describing the spirituality of the Creator in comparison to our physical world. He is so far removed from our physical comprehension that we have difficulty perceiving Him. We are restricted by our physicality; without the aid of our senses we have difficulty discerning spirituality in general and His presence in particular. Recognizing the great distance between our physicality and His spirituality is the key to realizing just how close Hashem is. He is not bound by physicality, and He is as close to our lips as a confidant's ear is to our mouth.

"A person who prays should envision the *Shechinah* standing before him" (*Sanhedrin* 22a). This is the very essence of prayer, realizing that we are praying to Someone Who listens to us as if we were standing right before Him. How are we, who are so involved with and limited by physicality, supposed to rise above our nature and recognize the existence of spirituality? That is the purpose of the Torah. The Torah, the mitzvos, and the *tefillos* were given to us as tools to propel us toward spirituality.

> "Hashem, Whom we perceive to be very distant, is closer to us than anything else."

Our *avodah* is to come to the realization that no matter how close materialism appears to be, it remains distant from a person's essence. It does nothing toward building his *penimiyus:* the reason he was put here on earth. On the other hand, Hashem, Whom we perceive to be very distant, is closer to us than anything else.

(*Maamarei Yemei Ratzon,* pp. 352-354)

❊ ❊ ❊

THE CLEAREST PROOF OF HASHEM'S EXISTENCE

כִּי מִי־גוֹי גָּדוֹל אֲשֶׁר־לוֹ אֱלֹקִים קְרֹבִים אֵלָיו כַּה' אֱלֹהֵינוּ בְּכָל־קָרְאֵנוּ אֵלָיו

For which is a great nation that has God close to it as Hashem, our God, whenever we call out to Him? (4:7).

The very first time Hashem revealed Himself to Moshe, He commanded him to tell *Bnei Yisrael* that he had been sent by Hashem to redeem them. "What should I tell them when they ask me Your Name?" Moshe queried. Hashem responded, "I shall be as I shall be" (*Shemos* 3:14).

Ramban's explanation sheds some light on this enigmatic exchange. Moshe was asking for the Name of Hashem that would unequivocally convey to *Bnei Yisrael* Hashem's existence and providence. Hashem responded that there is absolutely no reason why *Bnei Yisrael* should inquire as to His Name. The clearest proof of His existence is the fact that "I shall be" with them in their times of suffering; they simply have to call out and I will answer them. There is no need for any other evidence.

The most obvious proof of the existence of our Creator is the fact that whenever *Klal Yisrael daven* to Hashem, He answers them. This idea is found in this *parashah*: "For which is a great nation that has God close to it as Hashem, our God, whenever we call out to Him?" (4:7). Though we might not be on the spiritual level to always have our personal *tefillos* answered, like the righteous people of past and present generations, there is an aspect of this

> "*The most obvious proof of the existence of our Creator is the fact that whenever Klal Yisrael daven to Hashem, He answers them.*"

truth that we, too, can recognize. The Ibn Ezra explains the above *passuk* to mean, "For which great nation has God Who is close to it, Who always answers them regarding any request for wisdom?" In other words, Hashem answers any request for help in the spiritual arena (provided that it is reasonable).

Parashas Va'eschanan / 323

It is not enough to simply want to succeed in growing spiritually; it is not even enough to sit down and learn. We have to ask Hashem for help in achieving our goals. It is an established fact that these *tefillos* are always answered.

(*Maamarei Yemei Ratzon*, p. 35)

❋ ❋ ❋

ENVY: THE ANTITHESIS OF FAITH

וְלֹא תַחְמֹד אֵשֶׁת רֵעֶךָ וְלֹא תִתְאַוֶּה בֵּית רֵעֶךָ שָׂדֵהוּ וְעַבְדּוֹ וַאֲמָתוֹ שׁוֹרוֹ וַחֲמֹרוֹ וְכֹל אֲשֶׁר לְרֵעֶךָ

And do not desire your friend's wife, and do not covet your friend's house, his field, his servant, his maidservant, his ox, his donkey, or anything that belongs to your friend (5:18).

The Ibn Ezra (*Shemos* 20:14) presents a question that many ask: How can the Torah command us with regard to an emotion? How is it possible to prevent one from desiring in his heart a beautiful person or object?

He answers with a parable: An astute peasant who catches a glimpse of a beautiful princess will not desire her hand in marriage, because he knows that there is no possibility in the world for such a marriage to take place. Similarly, every intelligent person must acknowledge that a beautiful wife or desirable possessions are not granted to a person because of his brains or brawn. Rather, they are allocated by Hashem to whomever He chooses. Therefore, a person who understands that Hashem did not wish to give him that particular spouse or object will automatically refrain from desiring what belongs to another. Moreover, he will realize that no amount of scheming will help him obtain the desirable item; it is out of reach to even a greater degree than the princess is to the peasant.

A person who has true *emunah* cannot possibly covet another's possessions. Many people have difficulty with such an explanation, because their *emunah* and *bitachon* end when it comes to practical application. Some people claim to have *bitachon* in Hashem, but if a competitor opens a business across the street from them, they panic. "But do not you have *bitachon*?" a friend might ask. To which they will retort, "Of course I have *bitachon* — but at the end of the day he is going to take away my livelihood!" Their *bitachon* lasts until it is put to a real-life test.

> "Some people claim to have bitachon in Hashem, but if a competitor opens a business across the street from them, they panic."

The Ibn Ezra understood that *emunah* is not a matter of theory; it must be tested in order to be proven true. Yaakov Avinu lived with the belief that everything he had was allotted to him by Hashem, and therefore it was incumbent upon him to look after his possessions to the greatest extent possible. When it came to a real-life test, he extended himself to reclaim some forgotten vessels (*Bereishis* 32:25; see Rashi), for if Hashem gave them to him, then they served a purpose. Likewise, living with the realization that whatever Hashem gave a person is his, and what He did not give him cannot possibly be his, precludes one from desiring the possessions of his friends and neighbors.

(*Shiurei Chumash, Parashas Yisro* 20:14)

❊ ❊ ❊

THE MUSSAR INTUITION

וְעָשִׂיתָ הַיָּשָׁר וְהַטּוֹב
You shall do what is upright and good (6:18).

Chazal tell us (*Makkos* 24a) that the *navi* Chavakkuk found a single underlying *middah* that encompasses the entire Torah. That *middah* is *emunah*, as the *passuk* states (*Chavakkuk* 2:4), "And the righteous will live with his *emunah*." In a similar vein, Rabbi Akiva declared, "Love your friend like yourself; this is an all-encompassing rule of the Torah."

There are a number of other instances where we find that *Chazal* looked for an all-encompassing trait that encapsulates the entire Torah. Why did they deem it necessary to place all of the mitzvos in a single category? Because it is possible to perform all of the mitzvos and still lose sight of the ultimate purpose behind the commandments. *Chazal* highlighted the common denominator of all the mitzvos so that we could bear in mind our ultimate goal.

> *"It is possible to perform all of the mitzvos and still lose sight of the ultimate purpose behind the commandments."*

This same idea applies to *tikkun hamiddos*. Human beings have countless *middos*, each of which has innumerable components. Yet at times we can identify an underlying principle that encompasses the entire spectrum of self-improvement. The Chazon Ish had a unique approach to this subject (*Emunah U'Vitachon* 4:1):

"The origin [of all *middos*] can be traced to a single negative and a single positive *middah*. The negative *middah* is 'allowing life to run its natural course.' One who does this will succeed, without any effort, in perfecting each and every one of the negative *middos*. He will perfect the traits of irascibility, haughtiness, and revenge. He will not lack even a single negative *middah*!

"The single positive *middah* is an ironclad resolution to choose one's *mussar* intuition as opposed to the instinct of desire. From such a vantage point one has the ability to fight all the negative *middos* at once."

Every person is endowed with a "*mussar* intuition," which whispers to him exactly how to behave. This intuition is no less natural than the instinct to fulfill one's desires. A person's *avodah* is simply to favor his *mussar* intuition over his instinctive desires. In essence, the positive *middah* to which the Chazon Ish is referring is the *middah* of *yashrus* (uprightness).

The Ramban in this *parashah* alludes to this idea. The Torah tells us, "*V'asisa hayashar v'hatov*" — You shall do what is upright and good (6:18). The Ramban explains that although the Torah mentions numerous commandments that are related to good *middos*, it cannot dictate every single aspect of proper behavior. Therefore, the Torah gave us an all-encompassing mitzvah to conduct ourselves with *yashrus* — the type of behavior we should choose even without being specifically commanded by Hashem.

Perfecting our *middos* is a lifelong *avodah*. However, if we can go to the source and rectify the root of all *middos*, our job will be that much easier.

(*Alei Shur,* Vol. II, pp. 180-182)

פרשת עקב

Parashas Eikev

SMALL ACTIONS MAKE BIG PEOPLE

וְהָיָה עֵקֶב תִּשְׁמְעוּן
V'hayah eikev tishma'un (7:12).

Rashi translates "*eikev*" literally, to mean a heel. He explains that if we heed the mitzvos that people tend to trample upon with their heel, Hashem will bestow upon us the many *berachos* enumerated subsequently in the *parashah*. It is the small actions that garner great blessings.

The same concept applies to *aveiros*. The Gemara (*Avodah Zarah* 18a) relates that the daughter of Nakdimon ben Gurion was once walking, and two Roman noblemen took note of her manner of walking. "Look how beautiful this young girl's footsteps are!" one commented to the other. When she overheard their comment, she immediately placed even more emphasis on her manner of walking, and she was severely punished by Heaven. *Chazal* tell us that this story helps us understand a *passuk* in *Tehillim* (49:6), "The sin of my heel will surround me."

It is the seemingly small and insignificant *aveiros*, which a person "treads upon with his heel," that surround him at the time of judgment. In fact, the Midrash tells us that both Moshe Rabbeinu and Dovid HaMelech were tested specifically with small actions to see if they were fit to become leaders of *Bnei Yisrael*.

Why are small actions so crucial, to the point that they have the power to activate great blessing or, God forbid, trigger terrible punishment? Why are they the litmus test for determining true greatness?

Grandiose deeds are not testimony to one's benevolence, nor is refraining from several *aveiros* indicative of one's fear of Heaven. Often, big mitzvos are accompanied by pomp, which makes it easier to perform them. A person might more readily donate $10 million to a charitable institution that will put his name on their building than give a significantly smaller donation to an organization that will send him no more than a simple receipt.

Similarly, one might have a guilty conscience when it comes to serious *aveiros*, while he feels not a twinge of regret when speaking during *davening* or committing other *aveiros* that seem insignificant to him. Therefore, the Torah

> *"One might have a guilty conscience when it comes to serious aveiros, while he feels not a twinge of regret when speaking during davening or committing other aveiros that seem insignificant to him."*

was not so "concerned" about serious *aveiros*, since a person's conscience usually prompts him to avoid those *aveiros* and to do *teshuvah* if he transgressed. It is the small *aveiros*, which people trample on daily and for which they never repent, that remain with a person until the Day of Judgment. It is only great people who are meticulous with every small action.

Chazal tell us that a person who purifies himself slightly in this world is purified tremendously in the World to Come (*Yoma* 39a). Let us take a small step in purifying ourselves by deciding to be

meticulous in an area that we have trampled upon until now. Here, too, small actions are imperative. Do not take upon yourself something that you know will backfire due to its difficulty. Small steps and small actions make big people.
(*Alei Shur,* Vol. II, p. 189)

❋ ❋ ❋

FROM THE HAND OF THE CREATOR TO YOUR MOUTH

מָה ה׳ אֱלֹקֶיךָ שֹׁאֵל מֵעִמָּךְ כִּי אִם־לְיִרְאָה אֶת־ה׳ אֱלֹקֶיךָ

What does Hashem, your God, ask of you? Only that you should fear Hashem, your God (10:12).

R' Meir would say, "A person is obligated to make 100 blessings every day, as the *passuk* states, 'What (mah) does Hashem, your God, ask of you?'" [Do not read the word as "mah" (what) but rather as "me'ah" (100).] (*Menachos* 43b).

The purpose of our *avodah* is to bring us to fear Hashem, as the *passuk* states: "What does Hashem, your God, ask of you? Only that you should fear Hashem, your God." *Chazal* reveal a specific way to reach this objective: the recitation of *berachos* on a daily basis. How does a person's recitation of blessings bring him to fear Hashem?

In order for a person to fulfill his obligation, he must mention both Hashem and His Kingship in *every single berachah*. If he said "*Melech*" — the King — but left out the word "*ha'olam*" — of the world — he has not fulfilled his obligation, for a king without a kingdom cannot be considered a king. Therefore, every single blessing contains recognition of the Heavenly Kingship. Many *berachos* continue, "the Creator of …," which gives us another opportunity to strengthen our *emunah* with the knowledge that He is the One Who created the universe and all that it contains. If a person would reflect on the blessings instead of mumbling without thinking, 100 blessings a day would be more than sufficient to imbue him with *yiras Shamayim*.

The Gemara (*Yerushalmi Berachos* 6:1) states, "It is written, 'Hashem's is the earth and its fullness, the earth and its inhabitants.'

A person who derives any benefit from this world before the mitzvos [i.e., *berachos*] permit it is guilty of *me'ilah* [utilizing consecrated property for personal use]. Rav Abahu said, 'The world is similar to a holy vineyard [whose grapes one is required to redeem]. What must be done in order to redeem the world's pleasures? One must make a *berachah*.'"

This gives us a new outlook on the entire world. According to the first explanation in the Gemara, the world is comparable to a sacrifice whose blood must be sprinkled in order to permit the *kohanim* to partake of the animal. The world is holy, and we are forbidden to indulge in its pleasures before making a *berachah*, which permits us to enjoy them (despite the fact that they still retain their holiness — as does the analogous sacrifice).

According to the second explanation, the *berachah* acts as "redemption" for the pleasure. We "give" the *berachah*, so to speak, in return for the pleasure (thereby removing the holiness from the pleasure, just as the holiness is removed from the vineyard after the redemption process). Both explanations are based on the idea that this world is in reality *kodshei Shamayim*, and it was given to us as a catalyst to bless Hashem. One hundred *berachos* a day give us 100 opportunities to realize that we live in a holy world, and we must not indulge before we bless the Creator.

> "One hundred berachos a day give us 100 opportunities to realize that we live in a holy world, and we must not indulge before we bless the Creator."

As with all aspects of growth, one cannot work on too much at once. Let us try to concentrate on the *berachah* of "hamotzi lechem min ha'aretz." Instead of mumbling it automatically, picture in your mind stalks of wheat swaying in the breeze, and acknowledge the fact that the bread came to you from the Hand of the Creator.

(*Alei Shur*, Vol. II, pp. 314, 315)

❊ ❊ ❊

HASHEM RECIPROCATES OUR ACTIONS

וְהָיָה אִם שָׁמֹעַ תִּשְׁמְעוּ אֶל־מִצְוֺתַי

"And if you listen, you will listen (shamo'a tishme'u) to My mitzvos" (11:13).

Rashi explains the seemingly superfluous wording of the *passuk* as follows: "If you listen to the previous commandments, then you will listen to the subsequent commandments. Likewise, the Torah writes (8:19), 'If you forget, you will forget,' implying that if you begin to forget, you will end up forgetting everything, as [*Chazal*] state, 'If you forsake me [the Torah] for one day, I will forsake you for two days.'"

The *Yerushalmi* brings a parable to convey this idea. When two friends part, and one walks eastward while his friend walks westward, after a day of walking they are two days' distance apart. Similarly, if a person forsakes the Torah, the Torah will distance itself from that person. When he wishes to return to the Torah, he will not find it where he left it, and he will have to toil twice as hard to reconnect to the Torah.

The same concept applies to *tefillah*. Rashi in *Maseches Berachos* (4b) cites another *Yerushalmi*, which describes a person who fails to *daven Shemoneh Esrei* immediately after reciting the *Shema* and its blessings. This person can be compared to the friend of a king who knocked on the palace door, but turned around and left before receiving a response. When the king opened the door and saw that his friend had departed, he turned around and left as well. A person should draw Hashem close with praises of *Yetzias Mitzrayim* and He will come close; while Hashem is close, the person should request his needs. If we draw Hashem close, He will reciprocate, whereas if we turn around and distance ourselves, He will conduct Himself in a similar fashion.

Ramban (*Shemos* 3:13) quotes a Midrash that encapsulates this idea. Hashem told Moshe to tell *Bnei Yisrael* that He reciprocates their actions. If they open their hands to give *tzedakah*, Hashem will open His storehouses and bestow great bounty upon them.

We are the determining factor in our relationship with Hashem. If we distance ourselves from Him, He will respond in kind, while if we attempt to come close to Him, He will draw close to us, in proportion to the amount of effort we expend in achieving this goal.

We must take great care not to forsake Torah study or *tefillah*, especially when we are on vacation. One missed day translates into two days of work to regain what was lost. Not a single day should pass entirely devoid of *tefillah* or Torah study. The more effort we put into maintaining our relationship with Hashem, the closer Hashem will draw to us.

(*Maamarei Yemei Ratzon,* pp. 364-366)

✣ ✣ ✣

THE GOLDEN RULE OF CHINUCH

וְלִמַּדְתֶּם אֹתָם אֶת־בְּנֵיכֶם לְדַבֵּר בָּם

And you shall teach them to your children [so that they will] discuss them (11:19).

What should be our objective in the *chinuch* of our children?

The answer can be found in this *parashah*. In the second paragraph of *Krias Shema* we read, "And you shall teach them to your children [so that they will] discuss them" (11:19). The Ramban notes that we were already commanded to do this in the first paragraph of *Shema*, as the *passuk* states, "And you shall instruct your children about them and you shall discuss them when you sit in your house. . ." (6:7). What is the Torah adding in the second paragraph?

In the first paragraph of *Shema* the Torah focuses on the studying of the father: "And *you* shall discuss them when *you* sit in your house. . . ." The second paragraph adds that we should teach our children in a manner that will cause *them* to discuss the Torah at all times. Additionally, the first paragraph commands us to "*instruct our children*" — i.e., tell them about all the mitzvos — while in the second paragraph we are commanded to "*teach* them to our children." This implies that the Torah we transmit should not merely be stated; rather, it should be communicated with clarity, in a manner that enables our children to understand the reasons behind the mitzvos.

Our objective is to create a situation in which our children will discuss the Torah on their own. This is accomplished by the father conveying Torah ideas and values to his children with clarity and proper explanation. It is specifically the father who has an exceptional ability to help his children forge a relationship with Hashem.

Consequently, it is imperative that there always be a positive relationship between father and child. "It is forbidden for one to impose excessive fear in his house" (*Gittin* 6b). While children are still young, the mindset in the home must be focused on the future. The parents must ensure that the atmosphere in the home does not provoke fear or other negative emotions, lest these harmful impressions culminate in the child's forsaking his parents' way of life in his adolescent years.

> "Even if a child complies with his father's demands, the father should not fool himself into thinking that he has been mechanech his child for the long term."

Chazal teach us the golden rule of *chinuch* (*Shabbos* 32a): "Even though the Rabbis stated that a person must say three things in his house on Erev Shabbos, they must be said pleasantly, so that his words will be accepted." Things that are not stated softly and with patience are simply not accepted. Even if a child complies with his father's demands, the father should not fool himself into thinking that he has been *mechanech* his child for the long term.

Demands that appear reasonable to a parent might be perceived by a child as completely irrational. Therefore, even if a child fails to comply with a parent's request, there is no need for immediate punishment. Rather, the parent should reiterate his request with quiet determination.

The summer and other vacations throughout the year offer a rare opportunity for parents to spend extra time bonding with their children. Investing some thought into how to make the most of this opportunity goes a long way toward building the child's future.

(*Alei Shur,* Vol. I, pp. 260, 261)

פרשת ראה
Parashas Re'eh

THE DANGER OF WANTING TO MAKE A GOOD IMPRESSION

וּפֶן־תִּדְרֹשׁ לֵאלֹהֵיהֶם לֵאמֹר אֵיכָה יַעַבְדוּ הַגּוֹיִם הָאֵלֶּה אֶת־אֱלֹהֵיהֶם וְאֶעֱשֶׂה־כֵּן גַּם־אָנִי

Lest you seek out their gods, saying, "How do these nations serve their gods — and I will do the same myself" (12:30).

In this *parashah*, as in numerous other places, the Torah warns, "Lest you seek out their gods, saying, 'How do these nations serve their gods — and I will do the same myself.'" Why did Hashem deem it necessary to warn the Jewish people not to stray after the gods of the surrounding nations — something the Torah itself (Rashi to 29:16) describes as "repulsive as excrement"?

Rav Yerucham Levovitz explains that the practice of flattering wicked people stems from an internal drive to find favor in other people's eyes. Even if one were to meet a deranged person, he would hope to make a favorable impression during the encounter. Moreover, if there were somebody — even on the other side of the world — who he knew did not view him in a favorable manner,

> "*The practice of flattering wicked people stems from an internal drive to find favor in other people's eyes.*"

he would endure sleepless nights and go to great lengths to rectify the situation. Similarly, when *Bnei Yisrael* passed through the idol-worshiping nations, they too wished to find favor in the eyes of their neighbors. What better way could there be to find favor in their eyes than to worship their gods?

This is the force that drives people to pursue the newest styles and fads, even if those were concocted by foolish people, so that they not be looked down upon by their colleagues and peers. This force can be very dangerous, for it can cause a person to disregard mitzvos or halachos for fear of becoming an object of derision.

Halachah mandates (*Yoreh Dei'ah* 268:2) that someone who wishes to convert to Judaism must be told, "Do you not know that currently *Bnei Yisrael* are scorned and mocked?" If he answers, "I know, and I am not worthy," he is accepted immediately. His answer indicates that he recognizes the essence of *Bnei Yisrael* and acknowledges that it is worthwhile to pursue his goal, despite any scorn he might encounter.

No one wishes to be considered a fool. However, our Sages (*Eduyos* 5:6) tell us that it is better for a person to be considered a fool in the eyes of the world his entire life, than to be considered a fool for even one moment in the eyes of Hashem! Styles and fashions, newspapers and songs that are antithetical to Torah values have no place in our homes and offices. The drive to be "one of them" could, God forbid, cause a person to neglect Torah laws, and we must nip this in the bud lest it bring disaster in its wake.

(*Maamarei Yemei Ratzon*, pp. 272, 273)

✣ ✣ ✣

FOCUSING INWARD

כִּי עַם קָדוֹשׁ אַתָּה לַה' אֱלֹהֶיךָ
For you are a holy nation unto Hashem (14:21).

Sifrei gives an interesting interpretation of these words: "Make yourself holy with regard to things that you permit. Even if you are of the opinion that a specific thing is permitted, when you find yourself in the company of those who forbid it, you should not permit it in their presence."

If we had to describe what is wrong with permitting something in the presence of those who forbid it, we would probably explain that such behavior is improper because one is disregarding the feelings of those who act stringently. Moreover, his actions might even cause them to abandon their stringency.

However, it is clear from *Sifrei* — which states, "Make *yourself* holy" — that the focus of this teaching is not on the others who act stringently; rather, it is on the person himself. *Sifrei* is revealing to us that *kedushah* involves applying to oneself that which one perceives around him. When one finds himself in the company of those who are more scrupulous, this should arouse in him a desire to emulate them, at least for the duration of the time he spends in their presence.

> "When one finds himself in the company of those who are more scrupulous, this should arouse in him a desire to emulate them."

In a similar vein, *Chazal* tell us, "One who sees a *sotah* in her state of degradation should abstain from wine" (*Sotah* 2b). The Torah is telling us that instead of denouncing the perpetrator and the terrible transgression committed, one should direct his focus inward and concentrate on ensuring that he himself never commits such a sin.

This is the criticism that *Chazal* (*Bamidbar Rabbah* 16:5) level against the *meraglim,* the spies. Although they had seen what happened to Miriam when she spoke derogatorily about Moshe Rabbeinu, they failed to apply the lesson to themselves.

The Baal Shem Tov would say that everything we see is to be taken as a message from Hashem as to how we ourselves appear. If we see something, it means that we are meant to glean a lesson from it. Instead of getting annoyed at the fellow who double-parked his car, we should think of the many instances when we are guilty of similar behavior (even if not to the same degree of insolence). This not only helps to improve one's character, it also yields numerous benefits in one's relationships.
(*Alei Shur,* Vol. I, p. 137)

❊ ❊ ❊

TICKET TO THE WORLD TO COME

עַשֵּׂר תְּעַשֵּׂר אֵת כָּל־תְּבוּאַת זַרְעֶךָ הַיֹּצֵא הַשָּׂדֶה

You shall tithe all the crops of your field (14:22).

Rav Moshe Feinstein declared that just as one must give a tenth of his money to those who are financially less fortunate, so, too, he should give a tenth of his time to those who are spiritually less fortunate. There are numerous sources that delineate the importance of bringing other people closer to the service of Hashem.

Rabbeinu Yonah (*Shaarei Teshuvah* 3:158) writes, "Now contemplate the great obligation we have to sanctify Hashem, for the primary reason that Hashem sanctified us with His Torah and mitzvos and singled us out as His nation is so that we should sanctify Him and fear Him; and it is only proper that those who sanctify Him should be sanctified themselves."

With this in mind, we can understand an astounding statement made by the *Chovos HaLevavos* (*Shaar HaBitachon,* Chapter 6): "A person is not worthy of meriting the reward of *Olam Haba* solely through the performance of good deeds. Rather, he becomes worthy before God with two additional things after the good deed, the first of which is instructing people regarding the service of Hashem and guiding them to do good."

The *Chovos HaLevavos* implies that even if a person fulfilled all the mitzvos of the Torah, with the exception of the one stated above, he is not worthy of meriting the reward of the next world! We can understand this when we bear in mind Rabbeinu Yonah's words. The purpose of the mitzvos is to sanctify Hashem's Name in this world. A person who fails to cause Hashem's Name to be sanctified in the eyes of others is lacking the most essential aspect of the mitzvos.

> "A person who fails to cause Hashem's Name to be sanctified in the eyes of others is lacking the most essential aspect of the mitzvos."

Elsewhere (*Shaar Ahavas Hashem*, Chapter 6), the *Chovos HaLevavos* implies that a person who limits his *avodas Hashem* to himself will certainly receive reward. Yet, he continues, the reward will not come close to the reward of a person who also helps others in their *avodas Hashem*. He compares these two types of people to two merchants who each bought numerous pairs of shoes for $10 each. The first merchant sold one pair of shoes for $100, 10 times the original price, netting a total profit of $90. The second merchant sold shoes for a mere $20, but he sold thousands of pairs. Despite the fact that the first merchant netted a much greater profit on the shoes that he sold, the second merchant earned thousands of dollars more than the first merchant. Likewise, although a person who spends his entire life focusing on his own spirituality will certainly earn significant reward for his self-perfection, it cannot compare to the reward merited by a person who also helped others grow in their spirituality.

Rambam writes that the final redemption will only come about after *Bnei Yisrael* do *teshuvah*. Let us take an active part in this *teshuvah* process. Our demeanor, in the realm of both *bein adam laMakom* and *bein adam lachaveiro*, should be such that those who see us think, *I, too, wish to be like that.* When we have a chance to say a kind word to those spiritually less fortunate, and certainly if we have the opportunity to impart to them some of the beauty and truth of the Torah, we should do so. It is a small action, but it earns infinite reward!

(*Maamarei Yemei Ratzon,* pp. 454, 455)

❈ ❈ ❈

GIVE HIM WHAT *HE* LACKS

כִּי־יִהְיֶה בְךָ אֶבְיוֹן ... כִּי־פָתֹחַ תִּפְתַּח אֶת־יָדְךָ לוֹ וְהַעֲבֵט תַּעֲבִיטֶנּוּ
דֵּי מַחְסֹרוֹ אֲשֶׁר יֶחְסַר לוֹ

If there shall be a destitute person among you ... you shall surely open your hand and lend him money, as much as he needs; whatever he is lacking (15:7-8).

Rashi explains: "Lend him" — if he does not want to accept a present, then give him money in the form of a loan. "As much as he needs" — but you are not commanded to make him wealthy. "Whatever he is lacking" — even a horse to ride upon and a servant to run before him. "*He* is lacking" — this refers to a wife.

There is no rule of thumb when it comes to *chessed*. A person who would like to work on becoming a true *baal chessed* must listen and look out for what the recipient is truly missing. The Torah states that we must find the pauper a wife, and she must certainly be someone who is suitable for his personality. So, too, we must address the rest of his material needs and deal with them in a manner that befits his stature and individual nature.

Let us try to picture the situation in which this formerly affluent man finds himself. He must move out of his mansion and into a humble dwelling. He has lost all his gold and silver to his creditors. He can handle that, but there is one thing that he simply cannot bear: He has lost his fancy car and he must make his way around by foot or via public transportation. He leaves his house and returns home feeling humiliated. Such a person would not have the audacity to ask that we supply him with a car; however, we ourselves should be able to understand that this is what he truly lacks. From a practical perspective, those who need food or medical treatment might take precedence in receiving our charity. Nevertheless, should we have the ability, we would be obligated to provide this formerly affluent man with the car that he so sorely misses.

If one would invest effort into recognizing what this man is lacking, instead of getting angry that he has the chutzpah to complain about his mode of travel when there are people crying for bread, we would look to lighten his burden. We probably will not be able to provide him with a "horse to ride on and a servant to run before him," yet if we truly understand him, we can comfort him that, with Hashem's help, he will soon return to his former prominence.

> "Some people speak about their problems, while others not only do not speak about them, they are not even aware that they exist."

There are many different types of deficiencies. One person might need monetary help, while another needs advice. Someone else does not have a job, while yet another person requires medical or spiritual assistance. Some people speak about their problems, while others not only do not speak about them, they are not even aware that they exist. Before working on actually assisting others, we must first determine what type of assistance they truly need.

(*Alei Shur,* Vol. II, pp. 198, 199)

פרשת שופטים
Parashas Shoftim

**FROM BLUEPRINT TO
PRACTICAL APPLICATION**

שֹׁפְטִים וְשֹׁטְרִים תִּתֶּן־לְךָ בְּכָל־שְׁעָרֶיךָ
*You should establish judges (shoftim) and
policemen (shotrim) in all the gates
of your cities (16:18).*

Rashi explains that *shoftim* are those who set guidelines, and *shotrim* are the people assigned to ensure that the populace follows those guidelines. The process of construction is also twofold. An architect designs a building, and the contractor then executes the practical application of these construction plans. Music follows this same pattern, with a composer writing a song and an orchestra bringing the song to life.

The mitzvos and laws of the Torah are the blueprint that establishes guidelines, while *mussar* is the practical application that shows us how to follow these guidelines. Throughout the generations we were given different *mussar* "instructions." The prophets laid the foundations, the *Tanna'im* authored *Pirkei Avos*, the *Amora'im* designated the portions of Talmudic *aggadah* to deal with this topic, and what was left was clarified masterfully by the Torah leaders who followed.

> "The mitzvos and laws of the Torah are the blueprint that establishes guidelines, while mussar is the practical application that shows us how to follow these guidelines."

Halachah revolves around the mitzvos themselves, while *mussar* revolves around the person who heeds the mitzvos. Different situations and locations necessitate different obligations: moving to Israel, for example, may require one to perform the mitzvos related to farming the land. Similarly, times of war or difficulty require one to strengthen himself in mitzvos more than he does during times of serenity. Even during trying times, a person who learns *mussar* will acclimate to the situation and act accordingly.

Rambam (*Shemoneh Perakim*) writes, "An *adam hashaleim* — a person achieving spiritual perfection — must constantly review his traits, weigh his actions, and examine his character each and every day." The cornerstone of *mussar* is a daily regimen of *mussar* study. It is axiomatic that a person who studies *mussar* day in and day out will improve his character — often without even being conscious of such a transformation. Rav Yisrael Salanter writes that one who studies *mussar* for even a few minutes a day will, in due time, grow to surpass his peers in the manner in which he acts and the way he thinks.

(*Alei Shur,* Vol. I, pp. 87-88)

❈ ❈ ❈

YOU BE THE ONE TO SMILE FIRST

לֹא תַכִּיר פָּנִים
Do not show favoritism (16:19).

Rashi explains this commandment as a warning to a judge not to act harshly toward one litigant and kindly toward the other. "He should not make one [litigant] stand while the other sits, because when one sees the judge honoring his opponent, he becomes disoriented." How can a litigant, who was well prepared when he stepped into court, lose track of his claims? This happens as a result of the judge's *hester panim* (loosely translated as dislike or disapproval; the opposite of *he'aras panim*). Being the recipient of *hester panim* clouds one's thoughts and weakens his mental defenses.

Every person wants to feel that others take an interest in him, and every person has the ability to display *he'aras panim* to others and show them the approval they so intensely desire. However, it often happens that two people display *hester panim* because they lack an understanding of each other. They might reside in close physical proximity, but their relationship remains distant and even bitter.

The underlying reason for these feelings might just be in the fact that each person is waiting for the other to initiate the relationship. A teacher might be waiting for his student to come forward with his questions and concerns, while the student is waiting for the teacher to reach out to him. This is true with regard to any relationship. Each person thinks there is something preventing the other person from nurturing the relationship; the days go by and the chasm between them widens. In truth, all that is lacking is the realization that each and every person is required to display *he'aras panim*, and not to ignore the people around him or wait for them to promote the relationship.

How great are our Sages, who encapsulated this idea in a mere few words: "You should [be the one to] initiate a greeting to every person" (*Avos* 4:20).

Babies, in particular, are sensitive to the expressions on the faces of people around them. When a baby encounters a smiling person, his face lights up and he gurgles excitedly, but if he sees a frown he will start to cry. Who knows which is more important for the proper development of a child — nourishment in the form of food or nourishment in the form of *he'aras panim*? One thing is certain: a child who grows up without any *he'aras panim* is like a plant that grows without any sunlight. There is no possibility that he will be emotionally healthy.

> "Who knows which is more important for the proper development of a child — nourishment in the form of food or nourishment in the form of he'aras panim?"

A few well-placed words of greeting contain awesome power. Even a mere smile has the ability to light up another person's day. Smile at your neighbor, friend, spouse, or colleague. You might very well affect his day in a way you would never have believed.

(*Alei Shur,* Vol. I, p. 191)

❊ ❊ ❊

THE GIFT OF THE PRESENT

תָּמִים תִּהְיֶה עִם ה׳ אֱלֹקֶיךָ
You shall be wholehearted with Hashem your God (18:13).

The Torah instructs us, "You shall be wholehearted with Hashem your God." Rashi explains that one should follow Hashem unquestioningly, rather than try to investigate what the future will bring. Whatever Hashem decrees upon a person, he should accept wholeheartedly, and then he "will be with Him and be His portion."

Human nature is such that a person thinks much more about the future than about the present. His imagination runs wild with the unlimited possibilities and opportunities that the future might bring. But the Torah instructs us not to spend our time contemplating or worrying about the future. Instead, we should let life run the course set by Hashem and accept wholeheartedly everything that happens.

Nor should one focus excessively on the past. Shlomo HaMelech states, "Do not say, 'How was it that former times were better than these?' since that is not a question prompted by wisdom" (*Koheles* 7:10). *Chazal* (*Yalkut Shimoni*, *Shmuel* I, on the above *passuk*) tell us that Yiftach in his generation paralleled Shmuel in his generation, and one must follow the judge of his generation. One should not spend his time reminiscing about former glorious times, for focusing on the past rather than on the present is not a worthwhile pursuit.

The past can often be viewed with greater clarity than the present, because the past has already occurred, and one can clearly identify his past accomplishments. In contrast, the present is murky, since one cannot know what the outcome of his current actions will be. One might prefer to dwell on the concrete accomplishments of

"*Do not worry about the future, and do not live in the past — make the most out of every day as it presents itself.*"

the past rather than concentrate on his present actions. Shlomo HaMelech therefore informs us that it is not wise to escape to the chambers of one's memory and live in the past.

The Torah teaches us not to be concerned about the future, nor to long for the past. Rather, one should focus all his efforts toward investing into the present. *Chazal* (*Rosh Hashanah* 16b) tell us that Hashem judges a person according to his present state, since the present encapsulates the past and is the seed of the future.

Do not worry about the future, and do not live in the past — make the most out of every day as it presents itself.

(*Maamarei Yemei Ratzon*, pp. 31, 32)

❊ ❊ ❊

ROUSING OUR INNER STRENGTHS

כִּי הָאָדָם עֵץ הַשָּׂדֶה
For man is like a tree of the field (20:19).

In the *haftarah* of *Parashas Shoftim* we read, "Awaken, awaken, (*uri, uri,*) don your strength, Tzion" (*Yeshayah* 52:1). The Targum translates the *passuk* slightly differently: "Reveal, reveal, don your strength, Tzion."

At times people experience *giluy* (clarity), while at other times they experience *hester* (confusion). In certain situations the confusion can be so great that a person is not even aware of his inner strengths until he is awakened and made aware of them by someone else. The Targum explains that the "awakening" mentioned in the *passuk* is, in reality, a mere revelation of inner strengths, which had previously gone unnoticed.

A person is similar to a tree, as it is written, "For man is like a tree of the field." The seed of a fruit contains the entire physical design of the tree that it is able to produce: the type of fruit and leaves, the height of the tree and its color. Yet none of this is discernible when looking at the actual seed: the fruit's pit. It is only after the tree grows that all the features inherent in the seed become revealed. Similarly, every person contains astounding qualities and strengths that are meant to become revealed over the course of his lifetime. However, he differs from a tree in that there is no guarantee that all his features will be revealed, and sometimes it takes an outside source to inspire and reveal his latent strengths.

> "Ideally, people should be similar to ants and not need outside assistance in arousing their innate qualities and characteristics."

The first *passuk* in the *parashah* commands us, "You shall appoint judges and officers for yourself in all your cities" (16:18). The Midrash states, "This refers to the verse (*Mishlei* 6:6), 'Lazy one, go to an ant; see its ways and gain wisdom.' Though it has no leader, officer, or ruler, it prepares its bread in the summer and hoards its food at harvest time." In other words, *Bnei Yisrael*'s need for judges and officers seems to be a less-than-ideal situation. Ideally, people should be similar to ants and not need outside assistance in arousing their innate qualities and characteristics.

Our job is to reveal the many qualities hidden inside us and use them in our *avodas Hashem*. Before a person begins to learn *mussar* and starts focusing on his negative traits, it is absolutely imperative that he be fully cognizant of his positive qualities. The first step in improving ourselves is acknowledging our awesome potential!

(*Maamarei Yemei Ratzon*, p. 77)

פרשת כי תצא

Parashas Ki Seitzei

THE DANGER OF VENTURING OUT

כִּי־תֵצֵא לַמִּלְחָמָה עַל־אֹיְבֶיךָ...
When you go out to war against your enemies ... (21:10).

Almost every time the Torah mentions the word "*yetziah*" — going out — our Sages explain it in a derogatory way. "And Dinah the daughter of Leah *went out* to see the girls of the land" (*Bereishis* 34:1; see Rashi). Why did the Torah specify that Dinah was the daughter of Leah, as opposed to the daughter of Yaakov? Since Leah also acted indiscreetly by "going out" (ibid. 30:16), Dinah was referred to as the daughter of Leah. Likewise, regarding the man who cursed Hashem the Torah states, "And the son of a Jewish woman *went out* ... and cursed Hashem" (*Vayikra* 24:10-11). In this case, he went out of his world (Rashi, ibid.). Finally, in the debacle of Korach and his cohorts, the Torah writes (*Bamidbar* 16:27), "And Dasan and Aviram *went out* upright at the entrance of their tents." Rashi comments, "They were standing arrogantly, with the intention to speak blasphemously and curse."

Yet we also find the term *yetziah* interpreted in a positive light. The Torah writes about Yaakov (*Bereishis* 28:10), "And Yaakov *went out* from Be'er Sheva." Rashi explains, "When a *tzaddik* leaves a town, he leaves a void behind him. When he lives in their midst he is their splendor and glory, and when he leaves they lose that splendor and glory." Why does the Torah generally regard "going out" as something negative, and how did Yaakov's departure differ from the other instances mentioned above?

The answer can be found in this *parashah*. "When you go out to war against your enemies . . . and you take captives, if you should see among the captives a beautiful woman and you desire her, you may take her for a wife" (21:10-11). Rashi explains that the Torah permitted such a marriage because otherwise the soldiers would marry these women in a forbidden manner.

Our Sages tell us that only completely righteous men went out to war; someone who transgressed even a rabbinic prohibition was told not to go in battle (*Sotah* 44b). If so, Rav Yechezkel Levenstein asks, why are we concerned that such spiritual giants would come to desire a non-Jewish woman to the degree that had the Torah not permitted him to marry her, he would have disregarded this commandment and fulfilled his desires in any case?

> **"These righteous warriors left the confines of their safe havens and ventured into unknown territory. Doing so left them vulnerable to the lures and temptations that lurked outside their homes."**

The answer lies in the *passuk* "When you go out to war." These righteous warriors left the confines of their safe havens and ventured into unknown territory. Doing so left them vulnerable to the lures and temptations that lurked outside their homes.

Before a person departs from his regular routine, he must take a moment to contemplate if what he plans to do or the place he wishes to visit will affect him negatively. This is why the Torah relates to most instances of "going out" in a derogatory fashion. It is only with regard to a *tzaddik* like Yaakov Avinu that the Sages explained his departure in a positive light. No matter where Yaakov Avinu found himself, he was able to retain the spiritual level that he maintained at home. When he left his town, it was the people left behind who suffered a spiritual loss.

This is the level that we all should strive to emulate. But until we reach that point, we should consider whether it is truly necessary to visit or travel through a place that may affect us in a way we never imagined.

(*Shiurei Chumash, Parashas Vayeitzei* 28:10)

❊ ❊ ❊

TWIN BROTHERS OF THE KING

כִּי־קִלְלַת אֱלֹקִים תָּלוּי

For a hanging person is a disgrace to God (21:23).

The book of *Iyov* begins with a dialogue between Hashem and the Satan, which, as Rashi tells us, took place on Rosh Hashanah. Hashem asked the Satan, "Have you noticed My servant Iyov? There is no one like him in the entire land: a pure, upright man who fears God and abstains from bad." The Satan retorted that Iyov acted this way because all was well with him: "Send out Your hand and destroy all that he has [and let us see] if he does not curse You" (*Iyov* 1:8-11).

We see from this story that the judgment of Rosh Hashanah revolves around the extent to which a person overcame the impediments and *nisyonos* that threatened to hinder his service of Hashem.

"*The judgment of Rosh Hashanah revolves around the extent to which a person overcame the impediments and nisyonos that threatened to hinder his service of Hashem.*"

The Satan was

claiming that Iyov could not be considered the ultimate *tzaddik* since he had not faced and overcome trials; therefore, his verdict was that he be tested with *nisyonos*. The judgment for us, who constantly face *nisyonos*, focuses on the extent to which we overcome those *nisyonos*.

Some people feel that they are not on the level to overcome the *nisyonos* that confront them. They may despair and grow depressed, or, alternatively, reassure themselves that all will be fine because their lowly state absolves them of the need to overcome *nisyonos*. The first step in the *teshuvah* process is eliminating these thoughts. We must uproot the feelings of despair and the notion that on our level we "cannot accomplish."

In this *parashah* the Torah commands us, "If a man commits a sin whose judgment is death, he shall be put to death, and you shall hang him on a gallows. Do not leave his body hanging … for a hanging person is a disgrace to God" (21:22-23). Rashi explains that leaving a body hanging would be a disgrace to Hashem Himself, because people (and specifically *Bnei Yisrael*) are made in His image. Rashi elucidates this idea with a *mashal*: Identical twins took different paths in life. One brother became a king, while the other became a thief and was hanged. Everyone who saw the thief hanging mistakenly thought that it was the king who was hanging. Even in a situation where a man committed a capital offense and was punished by hanging, he still retains his Divine image and is considered "a twin brother of the King."

Every person has an element of *kedushah* inside him; he must merely believe and admit that it exists. Absorbing this belief is the first step in the process of *teshuvah*. Rather than despair for the *aveiros* one has accumulated, he should recognize that his true essence is *kedushah*. This recognition will bring a person to abandon his negative patterns of behavior and return to Hashem and to a life of *kedushah*.

(*Maamarei Yemei Ratzon*, p. 66)

✻ ✻ ✻

THE CLOD OF EARTH THAT CAN RISE TO THE LEVEL OF ANGELS

כִּי יִקָּרֵא קַן־צִפּוֹר לְפָנֶיךָ בַּדֶּרֶךְ בְּכָל־עֵץ אוֹ עַל־הָאָרֶץ

If a bird's nest happens to be before you on the road, on any tree or on the ground (al ha'aretz) (22:6).

The Torah describes the mitzvah of *shiluach haken* as follows: "If a bird's nest happens to be before you on the road, on any tree or on the ground (*al ha'aretz*), and the mother is sitting on the chicks or eggs, do not take the mother along with the young. Send away the mother and then take the young" (22:6-7).

The Gemara (*Chullin* 139b) asks: Since the *passuk* stresses that the nest was found on the ground, if one finds a nest atop a person's head, is he also obligated to fulfill the mitzvah of *shiluach haken*? The Gemara answers that he is obligated, since we find another *passuk* (*Shmuel II* 15:32) that states, "And earth (*adamah*) upon his head." Rashi explains that since the Torah chose to use the word "*adamah*" as opposed to "*afar* (dirt)," we can infer that earth does not lose its connection to the ground even if it is detached from the ground and placed upon a person's head. If so, it must be that the human being himself is considered earth.

This fascinating Gemara grows even more interesting. The Gemara asks, "Where does the Torah allude to Moshe [even before he was born]? In the verse, 'Since he is but flesh' [in Hashem's declaration that He would destroy the world with a flood]." Rashi explains that the word "*b'shegam* (since he is but)" has the same numerical value as Moshe. Moreover, the generation of the Flood was given 120 years to repent, and Moshe lived to the age of 120.

What is the Gemara conveying to us with these two enigmatic statements? The first statement stresses the lowliness of man; even after being created he still remains "a clod of earth." The second statement stresses the diametric opposite: the greatness of man.

Despite the fact that he "is but flesh," man has the ability to rise to the level of the angels — as Moshe did. His origin is lowly, but his potential is unlimited.

> *"Despite the fact that he 'is but flesh,' man has the ability to rise to the level of the angels — as Moshe did."*

This idea sheds light on the Gemara's next statement as well. "Where does the Torah allude to Haman? 'Is it from the tree [from which I told you not to eat that you ate?]' (*Bereishis* 3:11)." The tree of knowledge was the root of all evil. However, Haman succeeded in taking evil to an entirely new level. Because a single person failed to bow down to him, he schemed to annihilate an entire nation! Once again, we perceive the unlimited potential of man — this time harnessed for evil.

The Gemara then continues: "Where is Mordechai hinted to in the Torah? *Meira dachya*" (the Targum's translation of *mar dror*, the first of the spices used in the incense) (*Shemos* 30:23). The incense was burned in privacy, with no one watching. Similarly, Mordechai personified the *middah* of *tznius:* doing what is right without fanfare. Esther also exemplified the *middah* of *tznius*, since after she became queen, she did not reveal her nationality.

There is yet another common denominator between Mordechai and the incense. The smoke caused by the burning of the incense would rise upward, like a pillar, without dispersing to the sides. So, too, Mordechai stood ramrod straight and did not bow to Haman and the evil he espoused. It was these two traits — *tznius* and an unswerving adherence to the Torah's standards — that effected the miracle of Purim.

Man's ability is unlimited. Harnessing our awesome potential toward the service of Hashem not only brings us closer to Him, it also has the ability to bring redemption to His entire nation.

(*Daas Shlomo Geulah,* pp. 187, 188)

❈ ❈ ❈

ABOMINABLE BY VIRTUE OF ITS EXISTENCE

לֹא־יִהְיֶה לְךָ בְּבֵיתְךָ אֵיפָה וְאֵיפָה גְּדוֹלָה וּקְטַנָּה. אֶבֶן שְׁלֵמָה וָצֶדֶק יִהְיֶה־לָּךְ, אֵיפָה שְׁלֵמָה וָצֶדֶק יִהְיֶה־לָּךְ לְמַעַן יַאֲרִיכוּ יָמֶיךָ עַל הָאֲדָמָה אֲשֶׁר־ה' אֱלֹקֶיךָ נֹתֵן לָךְ. כִּי תוֹעֲבַת ה' אֱלֹקֶיךָ כָּל־עֹשֵׂה אֵלֶּה, כֹּל עֹשֵׂה עָוֶל. זָכוֹר אֵת אֲשֶׁר־עָשָׂה לְךָ עֲמָלֵק בַּדֶּרֶךְ בְּצֵאתְכֶם מִמִּצְרָיִם...

And you shall not keep in your house two measures — one large and one small. You should have a complete and just weight, a complete and just measure, so that you merit longevity on the land that Hashem has given to you. For it is an abomination to Hashem your God all who do this — all who act corruptly. Remember what Amalek did to you on the way when you left Egypt ... (25:14-17).

Rashi explains the juxtaposition of the commandment to have honest measures with the commandment to remember our encounter with Amalek: "If you are dishonest with your weights and measures — fear an attack from your enemy, for it is written, 'Deceitful weights are an abomination to Hashem ... The wicked one comes [and attacks]...' (*Mishlei* 11:1-2)."

What did Shlomo HaMelech in *Mishlei* add to the Torah's exhortation not to conduct business with faulty weights? Rabbeinu Yonah (*Mishlei*, ibid.) writes that this *passuk* is informing us that even if a person does not use faulty weights in his business dealings, the very presence of dishonest measures in his house is an abomination to Hashem. The Gra adds that even if he weighs the merchandise with a faulty measure and then compensates for the difference, he has not acted in accordance with Hashem's will, for "Hashem desires [specifically] a complete weight."

Parashas Ki Seitzei

Using deceitful weights causes a person to distance himself from Hashem. Such an object, even if it remains untouched, has no place in one's home, because the mere fact that he owns an item used for deceit is an abomination in the eyes of Hashem. Particularly in our society, where so many abominations abound, even if one were to bring them into his home *without using them*, it would still constitute a violation of this principle.

(*Alei Shur*, Vol. II, p. 463)

> "The mere fact that one owns an item used for deceit is an abomination in the eyes of Hashem."

❈ ❈ ❈

THE CASUAL APPROACH

אֲשֶׁר קָרְךָ בַּדֶּרֶךְ
That he happened upon you on the way (25:18).

This *parashah* ends with an account of how Amalek attacked *Bnei Yisrael* shortly after they left Mitzrayim. "Remember what Amalek did to you on the way, as you left Mitzrayim. *Asher **karcha** baderech*. . ." (25:17-18). Rashi, in his second explanation of the word "*karcha*," writes that it is a derivative of the word "*mikreh*" (chance). Amalek related to all events as happenstance, and they attacked *Bnei Yisrael* with the intention of indoctrinating them with this mentality.

> "Amalek related to all events as happenstance, and they attacked Bnei Yisrael with the intention of indoctrinating them with this mentality."

Such a perception of current events is antithetical to the Torah view, which is that nothing happens by coincidence, and *every event is deliberately planned and calculated by the Creator*. We are expected to perceive Hashem's *Hashgachah* in this world and to understand the messages He wishes to convey through the events He sets in motion.

There is yet an additional aspect of "*mikreh*" personified by Amalek that stands in opposition to *avodas Hashem*. *Mikreh* is also defined as "casualness." In *Parashas Bechukosai* Hashem warns us, "And if you walk with Me *b'keri*... I too will walk with you with a fury of *keri*" (*Vayikra* 26:21-28). Rashi translates these *pesukim* as follows: "If you walk with Me casually — i.e., occasionally — I will also deal with you casually. One must be consistent in his *avodas Hashem* and not merely serve Hashem at his convenience."

The *Ohr HaChaim* and the *Avi Ezri* both explain that Hashem generally metes out punishment measure for measure so that one can recognize from the punishment what he must rectify. If *Bnei Yisrael* walk with Him casually, however, He too will reciprocate and punish them casually — i.e., with a punishment that seemingly has no connection to their transgression. This will allow them to relate to the punishment as a coincidence, rather than recognize why they are being punished.

We should aim to replace this casual approach to *avodas Hashem* with a more consistent one, and to recognize the messages Hashem continually sends us rather than ascribe things to chance.

(*Maamarei Yemei Ratzon*, pp. 143-146)

❊ ❊ ❊

THE FIERY COVENANT

זָכוֹר אֵת אֲשֶׁר־עָשָׂה לְךָ עֲמָלֵק בַּדֶּרֶךְ בְּצֵאתְכֶם מִמִּצְרָיִם

Remember what Amalek did to you on the way when you were leaving Mitzrayim (25:17).

Rashi (25:18) tells us that Amalek cut off *Bnei Yisrael*'s *milahs* and threw them toward the heavens. What exactly does this mean?

The Zohar writes that the letters of the word "*Bereishis*" also spell out "*bris eish*" — a fiery covenant. A covenant is what joins two — often conflicting — interests, and unites them into a single force. Through the mitzvah of *bris milah*, *Bnei Yisrael* succeed in creating such a covenant. Their performance of this mitzvah unites physicality with spirituality, body with soul, and man with his Creator.

Amalek, on the other hand, stands in stark contrast to this unique characteristic of *Klal Yisrael*. *Chazal* tell us that the head of their patriarch, Esav, is buried in Me'aras Hamachpeilah alongside some of the greatest people who ever lived. How did he merit such an awesome honor?

In his head, Esav was as lofty as our *Avos*, and his comprehension of the Creator was on par with theirs. However, he lacked one thing: the ability to fuse body and soul. He did not translate his knowledge into action, and his lofty level of spirituality remained in his head without ever being integrated into the rest of his body.

By throwing the *milahs* heavenward, Amalek wished to demonstrate their forefather Esav's trait. They lived their lives with a partition separating the physical and the spiritual, and they had no interest in uniting the two. They took the *bris milah* — the symbol of the unification of body and soul — and threw it heavenward.

> "The avodah of a Jew is to take knowledge of the spiritual and translate it into physical actions."

The *avodah* of a Jew is to take knowledge of the spiritual and translate it into physical actions. There is no better time to do this than the month of Elul, for during this month Hashem draws closer to us with the anticipation that we will draw closer to Him. Even the smallest step toward this end generates a tremendous amount of *siyatta diShmaya*.

(*Shiurei Chumash, Parashas Ki Seitzei* 25:18; *Shiurei Chumash, Parashas Toldos* 26:34)

פרשת כי תבוא

Parashas Ki Savo

GRATITUDE CREATES LOVE

וְאָמַרְתָּ אֵלָיו
And you shall say to him (26:3).

"Hashem said to Moshe, 'I have a wonderful present in My treasure-house called Shabbos; go and tell Bnei Yisrael about it.' R' Shimon ben Gamliel said that from this we can deduce that one who gives a child a present must notify his mother" (*Beitzah* 16a).

When parents are aware that someone gave their child a present, they realize that the benefactor loves them, and this in turn causes feelings of love and camaraderie among Jewish people (Rashi, ibid.).

Although charity should be given secretly so as not to embarrass the recipient, with regard to a gift, the Torah specifically wants the beneficiary to know who the giver is. This is because the purpose of a present is to promote good feelings between people.

> "Although charity should be given secretly so as not to embarrass the recipient, with regard to a gift, the Torah specifically wants the beneficiary to know who the giver is."

Rav Yerucham Levovitz explains that *hakaras hatov* is not "extra credit." It is an obligation with accompanying halachos, and a person who does not take the time to appreciate and reflect on another's generosity has in essence "stolen" from him.

Hakaras hatov is applicable not only to humans. We find sections of the Torah that delineate the appreciation that Hashem shows to those who honor Him. In *Parashas Nasso*, the Torah lists the *korban* of each and every *nasi*, even though they were all identical. Ramban (*Bamidbar* 7:2) explains that Hashem honored the *nesi'im* because they honored Him. Similarly, we find that Hashem said, "Pinchas turned back My wrath from *Bnei Yisrael*; therefore I will give him a covenant of peace" (ibid. 25:11-12).

This trait is relevant to inanimate objects as well. Hashem told Moshe that Aharon should hit the water and the earth to initiate the first three plagues, because the water protected Moshe when he was placed in the Nile River as a baby, and the earth covered the Egyptian that he smote. It made no difference to the water and dirt who hit them; the difference was felt by Moshe alone.

Someone who recognizes and appreciates when another person does him a favor realizes that his friend loves him. "Just as water reflects a face, one's heart reflects another's heart" (*Mishlei* 27:19). The love is reciprocated, and friendship reigns. Conversely, where *hakaras hatov* is absent, love and friendship also cease. Be it a relationship of spouses, co-workers, parent and child, or teacher and student, if appreciation is not shown, the love between them will disintegrate — and possibly devolve into hatred.

How do we integrate *hakaras hatov* into our personality? We read in this *parashah* with regard to the mitzvah of *bikkurim* that one must give his first fruits to the *kohen*. "And you should come to the *kohen* that is in your generation and you should say to him ..." (26:3). Rashi explains that he must say it explicitly, to show that he is not *kafuy tov* — ungrateful. The Torah is telling us that *hakaras hatov* must be expressed and not hidden in one's heart.

Let us try to express our appreciation to those who help us, even in small ways. The storekeeper who helps us find just what we requested, the mailman, the waiter who serves us our food, even the janitor — all of them deserve recognition and a kind word (regardless of the fact that they are being paid). To the degree that we recognize, and express our appreciation for, other people's kindness, we will be able to feel friendship and love toward them.

(*Alei Shur,* Vol. II, pp. 278-280)

❊ ❊ ❊

VIDUY: HONORING HASHEM

בִּעַרְתִּי הַקֹּדֶשׁ מִן־הַבַּיִת
*I have removed the holy things
from the house (26:13).*

Among the numerous mitzvos mentioned in this *parashah* is the mitzvah of *bi'ur* and *viduy maasros*. On Erev Pesach after the third year of the seven-year *shemittah* cycle, we are commanded to properly allocate any of the third-year tithes that might have remained in our possession. The Torah commands that along with the allocation one must also recite *viduy*, a "confession" that he has properly performed all of the relevant mitzvos associated with the giving of the tithes.

Teshuvah, which includes true remorse over one's actions and a serious commitment to refrain from repeating those actions in the future, must also be accompanied by *viduy* — a verbal confession. What is the purpose of this *viduy*? Once a person regrets his transgressions and makes a serious commitment to refrain from such actions in the future, what more does the *viduy* accomplish?

Furthermore, *Chazal* say, "Whoever slaughters his *yetzer hara* and recites *viduy* is considered by the Torah as if he has honored Hashem both in this world and in the next world" (*Sanhedrin* 43b). When Yehoshua attempted to convince Achan to confess his sin of taking from the consecrated booty, he told him, "My child, please give honor to Hashem the God of Yisrael and confess to Him" (*Yehoshua* 7:19). How does one honor Hashem with a verbal confession?

> "When a person commits an aveirah, he imagines or believes that Hashem does not see him perpetrating the misdeed, almost as if he has hidden himself from his Creator."

More than a sin causes Hashem to distance Himself from the transgressor, it causes the transgressor to distance himself from Hashem. When a person commits an *aveirah*, he imagines or believes that Hashem does not see him perpetrating the misdeed, almost as if he has hidden himself from his Creator. The way to rectify such behavior is with the recitation of *viduy*. We declare, "For the sin that we have sinned *before You*." We acknowledge that not only were You, Hashem, watching us when we sinned, but at the same time You even continued to bestow upon us the physical capacity that was used to commit the offense. A person who acknowledges this truth and removes the partition that separates himself from his Creator has honored Hashem.

Prior to *viduy* we beseech Hashem, "Please accept our prayers and do not ignore our entreaties." We no longer want to pretend that Hashem ignores our actions; we are acknowledging His supervision. With this in mind, our recitation of *viduy* should take on a whole new dimension. It should be recited with a feeling of connection to Hashem, similar to the way one recites *Shema* or the first *berachah* of *Shemoneh Esrei*. In essence we are declaring that Hashem is with us at all times, and we are expressing our true desire to stop pretending that He fails to take notice of our deeds. Such a *viduy* will certainly be accepted by Hashem.

(*Maamarei Yemei Ratzon,* pp. 89-91)

❈ ❈ ❈

THE POWER OF A MENTAL PICTURE

הַסְכֵּת וּשְׁמַע
Imagine and hear (27:9).

In conjunction with the covenant that *Bnei Yisrael* would make with Hashem to perform the commandments of the Torah, Moshe tells *Bnei Yisrael* the following: "*Haskeis u'shema*, Yisrael, today you have become a nation to Hashem your God and you shall heed the voice of Hashem" (27:9-10). *Sforno* explains, "'*Haskeis*' — picture in your mind; '*u'shema*' — and contemplate; 'And you shall heed the voice of Hashem' — when you picture this and understand it, then you will undoubtedly heed the voice of Hashem."

According to *Sforno*, the Torah is revealing to us that picturing Torah concepts in our mind can aid us in our fulfillment of the mitzvos. For example, we are commanded on Pesach to feel as if we ourselves left Egypt. This includes conjuring up a picture of this momentous occasion. We should imagine the pillar of fire that illuminated the area, as well as the awe-inspiring procession led by Moshe and Aharon — each family surrounded by 90 donkeys laden with bounty, all marching out of Mitzrayim in an incredible display of Hashem's might. The same concept applies to the commandment not to forget the revelation at Har Sinai.

Picturing these events, which defied all the laws of nature, is not merely a fulfillment of a specific mitzvah; it is an essential part of our *emunah*. A person's *emunah* in *Yetzias Mitzrayim* and his belief that the Torah came from Hashem is not complete until he has depicted and contemplated these occurrences in his mind. Conjuring

> "*We should imagine the pillar of fire that illuminated the area, as well as the awe-inspiring procession led by Moshe and Aharon — each family surrounded by 90 donkeys laden with bounty, all marching out of Mitzrayim in an incredible display of Hashem's might.*"

up a picture gives life to these events, and this simulated experience can make an indelible impression on a person's life.

Imagining these events is an activity that can be performed anytime and anywhere. Picture the *Beis HaMikdash*, *Akeidas Yitzchak*, *Yetzias Mitzrayim*, Har Sinai, or any of the numerous momentous occasions in our rich history. Take a few minutes to let your imagination fill in as many details as possible. The more time you invest, the more real the event becomes.

This simple exercise has the power to strengthen one's *emunah*, and can also aid one's preparation for Rosh Hashanah. A true "picture" of Hashem as the King over the entire world will make it easier to accept His sovereignty during the Yamim Nora'im.

(*Alei Shur,* Vol. II, p. 274)

פרשת נצבים-וילך
Parashas Nitzavim-Vayeilech

FILLING THE FULL VESSEL

פֶּן־יֵשׁ בָּכֶם אִישׁ אוֹ־אִשָּׁה . . . אֲשֶׁר לְבָבוֹ פֹנֶה הַיּוֹם מֵעִם ה׳ אֱלֹקֵינוּ . . . לְמַעַן סְפוֹת הָרָוָה אֶת־הַצְּמֵאָה

Perhaps there is among you a man or a woman ... whose heart turns away today from being with Hashem, your God ... thereby adding the watered upon the thirsty (29:17-18).

"Come and see how Hashem's attributes differ from those of a human being. A vessel formed by a human being has the ability to store items only when it is empty. In contrast, Hashem's vessel has the ability to store only when it is full, as it is written, 'If you listened [to the Torah], you will listen,' but if you have not listened [in the past], you will not listen [in the future]" (Succah 46a).

Parashas Nitzavim-Vayeilech / 365

A person completely void of Torah is not a vessel that can retain Torah. The Torah tells us (29:17-18), "Perhaps there is among you a man or woman . . . whose heart turns away from Hashem . . . And when he hears the words of these curses he will bless himself in his heart, saying, 'Peace will be with me though I walk as my heart sees fit,' thereby adding the watered upon the thirsty."

Ramban explains that if a person indulges a desire to transgress, even though his soul had previously been satiated ("watered") and did not crave sin, his soul will now "thirst" to transgress that sin once again. His desire will grow to the point where he will begin thirsting to transgress *aveiros* that until now did interest him. *Chazal* tell us (regarding immorality) that the more a person satisfies his desire, the hungrier he gets (*Sanhedrin* 107a).

How can a person ensure that he does not fall into the terrible cycle described by Ramban? Through the performance of mitzvos. We were given 613 mitzvos, which dictate how we spend every hour of our lives. These mitzvos fill up our bodies and souls and prevent any unwanted desires from creeping into our minds.

> "There is no better way for a person to prepare for the Yamim Nora'im than by filling himself with extra Torah and mitzvos."

There is no better way for a person to prepare for the Yamim Nora'im than by filling himself with extra Torah and mitzvos. An extra minute spent learning in the *beis midrash*, or a short phone call to a lonely soul, does not merely garner an additional mitzvah. It fills up our souls, thereby forming a vessel that can hold more Torah and mitzvos, and prevents unwanted thoughts from penetrating our hearts and minds.

(*Alei Shur*, Vol. I, pp. 200-202)

❃ ❃ ❃

MITZVOS: FUSED INTO OUR PHYSICAL MAKEUP

כִּי הַמִּצְוָה הַזֹּאת אֲשֶׁר אָנֹכִי מְצַוְּךָ הַיּוֹם לֹא־נִפְלֵאת הִוא מִמְּךָ וְלֹא־רְחֹקָה הִוא. לֹא בַשָּׁמַיִם הִוא . . . כִּי־קָרוֹב אֵלֶיךָ הַדָּבָר מְאֹד בְּפִיךָ וּבִלְבָבְךָ לַעֲשֹׂתוֹ

For this commandment that I command you today is not hidden from you, nor is it distant from you. It is not in the heavens. . . . For, it is very near to you; in your mouth and in your heart to perform it" (30:11-14).

This *parashah* contains a wondrous declaration: "For this commandment that I command you today is not hidden from you, nor is it distant from you. It is not in the heavens. . . It is not on the other side of the ocean. . . . Rather, it is very near to you; in your mouth and in your heart to perform it."

While the Ramban explains that these *pesukim* refer to the mitzvah of *teshuvah*, Rashi asserts that they refer to the Torah. Despite the great distance that separates Hashem from His creations, we have the ability to bridge this gap through the Torah that is near to us. All of the mitzvos given to us are performed by the physical body, not by the *neshamah*. The *Aseres Hadibros* begin with "*Anochi Hashem*" and end with commandments warning us to refrain from killing, adultery, and coveting. The intent is that the Torah should penetrate every part of our bodies.

Additionally, the Torah does not explicitly refer to the next world. The *Kuzari* explains that since our purpose is to connect to Hashem, the Torah does not say, "If you do this, after you die I will bring you to a place of pleasure." Rather, the Torah says, "And you will be for Me a nation and I will be for you a God; and I will guide you." The purpose of the Torah is to bring us close to Hashem in this world.

The mitzvos, although they are spiritual, become part and parcel of the physical makeup of those who perform them. The Gemara (*Menachos* 43b) relates that David HaMelech entered the bathhouse and cried out, "Woe unto me that I stand bare of all my mitzvos!" — i.e., *tefillin*, *tzitzis*, and *mezuzah*. When he remembered his *bris milah*, however, he was relieved. Since one is not even allowed to think about holy things in a bathhouse, it is certainly not a place to perform mitzvos. If so, why was David HaMelech so troubled by his lack of mitzvos?

The answer is that when David realized that he was bare of mitzvos, it occurred to him that the mitzvos he performed were obviously not a part of him. Once he remembered the *bris milah* that was imprinted upon his body, however, he was comforted, for he understood that the mitzvos are not mere actions; they become fused into the very makeup of a person.

> "The mitzvos are not mere actions; they become fused into the very makeup of a person."

If we would realize just how close we could come to Hashem through the mitzvos we perform, we would have a completely different outlook on life. This is especially true during Elul, when we are given an extra dose of Heavenly assistance.

(*Maamarei Yemei Ratzon*, pp. 378, 379)

❊ ❊ ❊

RETURN!

כִּי־קָרוֹב אֵלֶיךָ הַדָּבָר מְאֹד בְּפִיךָ וּבִלְבָבְךָ לַעֲשׂתוֹ

"For this matter is very near to you — it is in your mouth and in your heart to be accomplished (30:14).

Ramban explains that this *passuk* is referring to the mitzvah of *teshuvah*, which literally means to return. If the mitzvah is to return, we must know to where we are returning.

Regarding the verse (*Tehillim* 112:1) "Praiseworthy is the man who fears Hashem," the Gemara (*Avodah Zarah* 19a) states, "Is only a man praiseworthy ...? Rav Amram says in the name of Rav: Praiseworthy is he who does *teshuvah* while he is a man." Rashi explains that "while he is a man" refers to when he is young and in his prime. In other words, he recognizes his Creator before he reaches old age.

The *teshuvah* described here is not an act of penitence that is associated with sin. Rather, a person who is not cognizant of his Creator has unquestionably strayed from the path that he was meant to follow. When he "recognizes" Hashem, he has in essence aligned himself with the type of life he is supposed to live, and it is to this *teshuvah* that the Gemara is referring.

A person whose *emunah* in Hashem and His Torah is ingrained in him with complete certainty is a person who truly recognizes Hashem. Eliyahu HaNavi demanded this feeling of certainty from his generation: "Until when will you vacillate? If Hashem is God then follow Him, and if the baal [is god] then follow him" (*Melachim I* 18:21). It was with this goal of instilling *emunas Hashem* into the hearts of his audience that Eliyahu performed a miracle, causing a fire to come down from the heavens and devour his sacrifice.

Recognizing Hashem in one's heart translates into a certain type of behavior as well. When Tamar was sentenced to death because of allegedly illicit relations, she sent a message to Yehudah: "Please recognize to whom this signet ring, garment, and staff belong" (*Bereishis* 38:25). Rashi explains that she was entreating him to recognize his Creator and not cause three people (Tamar and her unborn twins) to be killed. Only a person who is truly cognizant of his Creator has the strength to pass such a test and admit to his involvement despite the great embarrassment that entailed.

> "It is to our advantage that Rosh Hashanah precedes Yom Kippur, since the entire Mussaf of Rosh Hashanah is based on clarifying Hashem's Oneness and Kingship."

When doing even the most basic *teshuvah*, we must be aware that we are returning to Hashem and recognizing Him. It is to our advantage that Rosh Hashanah precedes Yom Kippur, since the entire *Mussaf* of Rosh Hashanah is based on clarifying Hashem's Oneness and Kingship. Once our faith in Hashem has been reinforced, we have the ability to approach Yom Kippur, for we know to Whom we are returning.

Instilling this *emunah* into our hearts will also help us recognize exactly where we stand. We will realize from Whom we have distanced ourselves and how distant we are as a result of our actions, which will arouse within us a desire to once again come close to

Hashem. The impetus for our sins was our desire, and our desire is also what prompts us to do *teshuvah*.

"He who comes to be purified is assisted, and he who comes to defile himself, the door is opened for him" (*Yoma* 38b). If we truly desire to better ourselves, we will be assisted in achieving this goal. If, upon introspection, we find that we are still to some degree in the category of those who are "coming to defile themselves," then we must redirect our desires. This is accomplished by instilling *emunah* in our hearts.

Let us take some time to think about our Creator. Cognizance of Hashem will elicit our true desires and allow us to correctly perform this wonderful mitzvah of *teshuvah*.

(*Alei Shur*, Vol. II, pp. 435-437)

✣ ✣ ✣

YES, YOU CAN CHOOSE

הַחַיִּים וְהַמָּוֶת נָתַתִּי לְפָנֶיךָ הַבְּרָכָה וְהַקְּלָלָה וּבָחַרְתָּ בַּחַיִּים
"Life and death I have placed before you — blessings and curses — and you shall choose life" (30:19).

The most elementary aspect of *bechirah* is that people have the ability to choose not to sin, thereby saving themselves from death in this world and the next. Throughout the generations there have been various forms of heresy, but our generation has reached an all-time low in this regard: We do not even believe that we have free will. Courts of law absolve murderers from responsibility for their crimes because of psychological disorders and the like. We have absorbed some of this mentality, and many of us believe that we are compelled to sin. Do we believe that it is possible to live from Yom Kippur to Yom Kippur, or even a single day, without sinning?

> "Do we believe that it is possible to live from Yom Kippur to Yom Kippur, or even a single day, without sinning?"

370 / RAV WOLBE ON CHUMASH

We must realize that we are responsible for our actions, and ultimately it is we and only we who will have to answer for them. Integrating this idea into our lives can aid us in our *avodas Hashem*, since the very knowledge that a person has the ability to choose to uphold the Torah gives him the strength to overcome his *yetzer hara* when temptation beckons.

(*Alei Shur*, Vol. II, p. 41)

פרשת האזינו
Parashas Ha'azinu

GROWTH MUST ORIGINATE WITHIN

יַעֲרֹף כַּמָּטָר לִקְחִי
May My Torah drip like the rain (32:2).

In what way is Torah similar to rain? Rav Yerucham Levovitz explains that rain dampens the soil and creates a fertile environment for the seeds planted within, but the actual growth of the plant comes from inside the seed itself. Similarly, although the Torah prepares and cultivates a person for spiritual growth, a great portion of the growth must originate from inside the person himself.

Rabbeinu Yonah writes (*Shaarei Teshuvah*, 2:26), "If a person does not arouse himself, how will *mussar* help?" A person has to spur himself to growth by properly digesting what he has heard or read.

We might make a similar observation regarding Succos. The Yom Tov of Succos has the potential to be one of the most spiritually uplifting times of the year — if we allow it to be. We sit in makeshift "clouds of glory" surrounded by Hashem's Divine protection, and we rejoice in the recent forgiveness we attained on Yom Kippur. Succos, and the rest of the Yamim Tovim of Tishrei, climax with Simchas Torah, a day specifically designated as a spiritual rendezvous between Hashem and *Klal Yisrael*. *Chazal* tell us that Hashem, so to speak, says, "Your parting is difficult for Me! Please set aside one more day so that I can enjoy you."

"Sukkos has the potential to be one of the most spiritually uplifting times of the year."

The opportunity for spiritual growth that Succos affords us is immense. If we fail to arouse ourselves, though, we might leave the succah just as we entered it.

(*Shiurei Chumash, Parashas Haazinu* 32:2; *Alei Shur,* Vol. II, p. 415)

פרשת וזאת הברכה
Parashas V'Zos HaBerachah

MOSHE: ROLE MODEL OF PERFECTION AND PURITY

וַיָּמָת שָׁם מֹשֶׁה עֶבֶד־ה׳...
"And Moshe, the servant of Hashem, passed away ..." (34:5).

Rashi (*Bamidbar* 30:2) quotes an interesting statement of *Chazal*. *Sifrei* writes that just as Moshe prophesied with the words "So said Hashem," the other prophets also prophesied with those same words. Yet Moshe was superior to all other prophets, because he also prophesied with the words "*Zeh hadavar* — *This* is the word [that Hashem commanded]." Whenever the word "*zeh*" (this) is mentioned in the Torah, it refers to something tangible that can be pointed to with one's finger. This is what *Sifrei* means when it says that Moshe prophesied with the words "*This* is the word." While other prophets saw only ambiguous visions, Hashem spoke to Moshe with total clarity, to the extent that he was able to "point" to the words that Hashem had spoken.

Why did Moshe merit such precise visions while the other prophets had to contend with vague prophecies? Moshe is referred to as a "servant of Hashem." He completely subjugated himself before Hashem, to the point that he became like "a tool in the hands of a craftsman": his every action personified the will of Hashem.

Additionally, the Midrash (*Devarim Rabbah* 11:10) tells us that when it came time for Moshe to take leave of this world, his *neshamah* refused to leave his body. In most human beings, the *neshamah*, which originates from the heavens, has to force itself to stay inside its bodily encasement, which is replete with negative characteristics. This was not the case with Moshe Rabbeinu. He elevated and purified his body to the point that he resembled an angel, and his *neshamah* did not wish to part from him.

Moshe did not merely purify his physical body; he also reached the pinnacle of perfection in his *middos*. For an entire week he refused to become the redeemer of *Bnei Yisrael*, lest his older brother feel slighted. How could such a concern warrant a refusal to take the entire nation out of Egyptian bondage? The answer is that Moshe had such refined *middos*, if there was even the faintest possibility of slighting his brother, then he considered himself unworthy to become the redeemer.

It was this self-perfection and subjugation to Hashem that brought Moshe to the level where he was able to perceive Hashem "*b'aspaklaria hame'irah*" — with total clarity. Every negative trait creates a separation between a person and his Creator, and the more separations there are, the less the person is able to perceive Hashem. Moshe, who perfected every one of his traits to the fullest, was able to perceive Hashem and His word with the utmost lucidity, for there was only one separation between himself and Hashem: he was human. Only such a person had the ability to bring down Hashem's Torah and *Shechinah* from the heavens to this world. Moshe, who had elevated himself *above his nature*, was able to become a conduit through which countless miracles, which defied the laws of nature, could be performed.

Though we are far from reaching the perfection and purity attained by Moshe, his personality must be inscribed in our minds so that we recognize the extraordinary greatness that man can reach. The Alter of Kelm, who lived in the era in which Darwin propagated his theory about the origin of man, said, "It is fine for Darwin to say that man originated from monkeys, because he never encountered an 'adam' — a true person. However, I, who saw Rav Yisrael Salanter, know that a person does not originate from a monkey!" Realizing our greatness and the heights that we can reach is imperative in our drive toward truly fulfilling the will of Hashem.

(*Shiurei Chumash, Parashas Matos* 30:2; *Alei Shur,* Vol. II, pp. 74-76, 79)

> "The Alter of Kelm said, 'It is fine for Darwin to say that man originated from monkeys, because he never encountered an "adam" — a true person. However, I, who saw Rav Yisrael Salanter, know that a person does not originate from a monkey!"

מועדים
Festivals

Elul

אֱלוּל

TREMBLING FROM JOY

Rav Avraham Grodzinski, Rav Wolbe's father-in-law, offers a penetrating insight into the proper attitude toward the month of Elul. He cites the Tur (*Orach Chaim* 581), who quotes *Pirkei D'Rabbi Eliezer*: "On Rosh Chodesh Elul, Hashem told Moshe to ascend the mountain in order to receive the second *Luchos*. They sounded a *shofar* in the camp ... 'Moshe has ascended the mountain,' lest the nation stray after idol worship [again] ... Therefore, *Chazal* instituted that every year we blow the *shofar* from Rosh Chodesh Elul to warn *Bnei Yisrael* to do *teshuvah*, as it is written, 'Is the *shofar* sounded in a city and the people will not tremble?'" (*Amos* 3:6).

It is difficult to understand the trembling mentioned in conjunction with the *shofar*. When *Bnei Yisrael* were notified that they were going to receive the second set of *Luchos*, they should have been overjoyed. Not only did this proclamation indicate that Hashem had forgiven them for the sin of the golden calf, it also heralded their receiving the entire Torah, something that even the *Avos* did not merit. Where do fear and trembling fit into the picture?

Bnei Yisrael recognized the awesome joy associated with receiving the *Luchos*, and they trembled out of fear that one day they might lose this intense pleasure. They had already seen how a single sin caused them to fall from the pinnacle of spirituality, and they feared a repeat of that. This is the trembling associated with Moshe's ascension, and it is also the fear instilled by the *shofar* each and every year, for Elul presents an opportunity that simply cannot be missed.

On Rosh Hashanah, Hashem apportions life and the keys to all physical and spiritual success. On Yom Kippur, a person has the ability to rid himself of a year, or even years, of transgressions. Is there a greater joy than this? A person must delight in this wondrous opportunity and tremble lest it slip through his fingers. This fear is what propels a person to do *teshuvah* so that he, too, can gain from this treasure chest of the Days of Awe.

> *"On Yom Kippur, a person has the ability to rid himself of a year, or even years, of transgressions. Is there a greater joy than this?"*

How does a person go about doing *teshuvah*? Hillel said (*Avos* 1:14), "If I am not for myself, who will be for me?" Rabbeinu Yonah explains that if a person does not arouse himself, no amount of *mussar* will help him. It is possible to listen to many *mussar* discourses and to read through many *mussar sefarim* and gain almost nothing. A person should read a line in a *mussar sefer* and see if he can relate to what is written. If his actions are not in tandem with what he has read, he must contemplate the reason behind this laxity and ponder whether there is anything he can do to improve.

Along with Elul comes a fear — not a fear laced with dread, but a fear arising from joy over the tremendous opportunity that is knocking at our door. Hashem has so much to give us; we need merely arouse ourselves so that we become worthy of receiving it.

(*Toras Avraham*, p. 193; *Alei Shur*, Vol. II, p. 415)

ראש השנה

Rosh Hashanah

A POSITIVE JUDGMENT, GUARANTEED

> *Rava says, if one overlooks others' transgressions [toward him], Hashem will overlook all his sins, as the passuk states, "He pardons sin and overlooks transgression." For whom does He pardon sin? For he who overlooks [another's] transgression"* (Rosh Hashanah 17a).

This Gemara teaches us a phenomenal way to achieve a favorable judgment on Rosh Hashanah. If Hashem were to meticulously count a person's many transgressions over the course of the year, he would very likely not emerge unscathed. However, *Chazal* revealed to us that Hashem's judgment reflects the way we treat others. If we are offended by another person, and we overlook his misdemeanor instead of being quick to retaliate, we have in effect saved ourselves from punishment. This obligates us to put special emphasis on our interpersonal relationships during this time of year.

> *"If we are offended by another person, and we overlook his misdemeanor instead of being quick to retaliate, we have in effect saved ourselves from punishment."*

It is not only the judgment aspect of Rosh Hashanah that requires us to improve our *middos*. Accepting upon ourselves His Heavenly Kingship also necessitates a *middos* upgrade. *Chazal* say (*Devarim* 33:5), "'And He was King in Yeshurun.' When? 'When the leaders gathered together and the tribes of Yisrael were united.'" Rabbi Shimon bar Yochai said this is analogous to a man who took two boats, tied them together, and built a palace upon them. As long as the boats stayed tied together, the palace remained standing. Once they separated, the palace collapsed. Likewise, as long as *Bnei Yisrael* remain united, Hashem has a foundation on which His Kingship can rest (*Sifrei, V'Zos HaBerachah*).

If Hashem is to be our King, then we must be His nation: a united nation. Especially during this time of year we must go out of our way to befriend others, love our fellow Jews, and pursue peace at all costs.

When saying *Kedushah*, there is a *minhag* to look to the right and left before saying, "*Kadosh, Kadosh, Kadosh.*" This is because we declare in the *Kedushah*, "We will sanctify His Name in this world just as the angels sanctify Him in the Heavens." The angels dwell in complete harmony and therefore sanctify Hashem with total unity. If we are to sanctify Hashem just as they do, we must be sure that we are at peace and in complete harmony with everyone around us. Therefore, we turn to the right and to the left to confirm that we live in harmony with those around us. If this is the case every time we say *Kedushah*, how much more so does it apply on Rosh Hashanah!

As Rosh Hashanah approaches, we have these two significant reasons to make an extra effort to overcome our negative *middos* and emphasize our positive traits. Although at other times of the year we might decide to work on each *middah* individually and at a slower pace, we do not have that luxury during Elul and the Yamim Norai'm. We must distance ourselves from anger, hatred, jealousy, and bearing a grudge. Before *Shacharis* we should accept upon ourselves to love our fellow Jews and overlook their offenses, which is a sure way to guarantee a positive judgment.

(*Alei Shur,* Vol. II, pp. 430, 431)

❋ ❋ ❋

PRESCRIPTION FOR INSCRIPTION

Rav Yisrael Salanter said that if a person wants to ensure that he will be signed and sealed for life on Rosh Hashanah, he should see to it that he is needed by many people. Since such a person plays a pivotal role in this world, Hashem will make sure that he continues to live, for the sake of the people who need him.

If a person would see someone lying in the street in a pool of his own blood, he would certainly run to save his life. When we see thousands of Jews who are dying spiritually, how can we not try to save as many of them as possible? When a person who lives a Torah-true life observes his brethren who are ignorant of the beauty of such a lifestyle, his heart will surely pulsate with a desire to bring them closer to Hashem and His Torah.

> "We cannot simply serve Hashem in our little corner and block out the rest of the world."

We cannot simply serve Hashem in our little corner and block out the rest of the world. If we have tasted some of the sweetness of Torah, we must share it with others who have not yet enjoyed this privilege. This is one way to become needed by others and ensure a sweet new year.

There is always someone who knows less than you about *Yiddishkeit* and could gain immensely from your knowledge. A Shabbos invitation, a telephone call, or a sincere inquiry as to his well-being has the power not only to make an indelible impression on another Jew, but also to ensure an inscription in the book of life!

(*Alei Shur,* Vol. II, p. 424)

❋ ❋ ❋

ROSH HASHANAH: DAYS OF JOY

The *navi* depicts the emotional first Rosh Hashanah experienced by the remnants who returned from the Babylonian exile. Everyone gathered in the streets and requested that Ezra HaSofer read from the Torah, and he proceeded to read and explain the Torah and mitzvos in a clear and concise fashion. This caused *Bnei Yisrael* to weep copiously, for they realized how far they had strayed from Hashem and His commandments. However, Ezra and Nechemiah encouraged them, "Today is sacred to Hashem your God; do not mourn and do not weep … Eat delicacies and drink sweet beverages and send portions to those lacking, for today is sacred to our Master. Do not be despondent, because the enjoyment of Hashem is your strength" (*Nechemiah* 8:1-12).

The tears shed by those penitent Jews upon hearing the Torah's commandments indicated their sincere regret for their wayward actions. If so, why did Ezra and Nechemiah cut short their heartfelt *teshuvah*?

The answer to this question lies in the crucial difference between Rosh Hashanah and the subsequent days of Aseres Yemei Teshuvah. A person who studies the *tefillos* of Rosh Hashanah will find that there is no mention of *viduy* or regret for recalcitrant behavior. That is because the *teshuvah* of Rosh Hashanah is not aimed at individual transgressions. Rather, the focus is on accepting the yoke of Heaven with genuine happiness. On Rosh Hashanah, "The enjoyment of Hashem is our strength." After blowing the first blasts of the *shofar* we declare, "*Praiseworthy* is the nation who knows the *shofar* blasts"; "In Your Name *they will rejoice* all day long and through Your righteousness *they will be exalted*." We specifically choose *pesukim* of rejoicing, for there is no greater delight than accepting upon oneself the yoke of Heaven.

> "If the days of Rosh Hashanah were not days of judgment, it would be appropriate to dance from sheer joy when reciting Aleinu."

If the days of Rosh Hashanah were not days of judgment, it would be appropriate to dance from sheer joy when reciting *Aleinu*.

Obviously, there is a gravity that comes along with this awesome day of judgment, but at the same time, we should bear in mind that there is no greater joy than serving Hashem and having the opportunity to develop a relationship with Him.

(*Alei Shur*, Vol. II, p. 434)

❊ ❊ ❊

RESISTANCE ON ROSH HASHANAH

The *avodas hayom* of Rosh Hashanah is "to confuse the *Satan*" (see *Rosh Hashanah* 16b). In other words, we are to contest the erroneous assumption that the *yetzer hara* is made of steel and there is no way to overcome it. In all of the *tefillos* of Rosh Hashanah that revolve around the final redemption, one thing becomes clear: Evil is not an invincible entity. When Hashem reveals His glory, "all evil will dissipate like smoke." Our objective is to leave Rosh Hashanah with a firm belief that the evil in the world can and will be destroyed, and that the evil within us — the *yetzer hara* — can also be vanquished. It might take time, but with Hashem's help and with the strength of the Torah we can conquer the *yetzer hara*.

Interestingly, on Rosh Hashanah itself the *yetzer hara* often manages to arouse feelings of rebellion inside us. A person might feel, for example, that it is more difficult to concentrate on the Rosh Hashanah *tefillos* than on those of a regular weekday. Why is it that on the day when Hashem reveals Himself most clearly, we find it most difficult to connect to Him?

This phenomenon can be explained as follows. *Chazal* tell us (*Shabbos* 88a) that when *Bnei Yisrael* stood at Har Sinai, Hashem lifted the mountain above their heads to force them to accept the Torah. Subsequently, *Bnei Yisrael* could always excuse a laxity in their performance of mitzvos with the fact that they had been forced to accept the Torah, since accepting something with a gun to one's head cannot be considered a completely genuine acceptance. (The Gemara concludes that in the days of Mordechai and Esther, *Bnei Yisrael* accepted the Torah again, this time wholeheartedly.)

It is clear from *Chazal* that a forced acceptance can sometimes engender feelings of rebellion. In contrast, when one accepts something willingly, feelings of rebellion are not aroused.

If one feels forced into *davening* on Rosh Hashanah, he might feel resistance when he stands in shul. However, if one approaches the *tefillos* with a sense of joy that he has the opportunity to accept upon himself the yoke of Hashem, he will not experience any resistance.

> "If one feels forced into davening on Rosh Hashanah, he might feel resistance when he stands in shul."

We certainly have sufficient reason to rejoice, as we express throughout the *tefillos* on Rosh Hashanah: "That He has not made us like the nations of the world and not made our portion like the portion of their masses." "*Praiseworthy* is the nation who knows how to blow the *shofar*; Hashem, they will walk *in the light of Your countenance!*" "*In Your Name* they will *rejoice* all day and in your justice they will be *exalted.*"

If we approach Rosh Hashanah with a positive outlook, knowing that there is nothing greater than accepting Hashem's Kingship, we will *b'ezras Hashem* merit a year filled with spiritual and material bounty.

(*Maamarei Yemei Ratzon*, pp. 388, 389)

יוֹם כִּפּוּר

Yom Kippur

FREEDOM FROM THE EVIL MASTER

Chazal tell us that there are three books opened on Rosh Hashanah: "Those who are completely righteous are immediately signed and sealed for life. Those who are completely wicked are immediately signed and sealed for death. Those who are in between hang in the balance until Yom Kippur; if they are found meritorious they are inscribed for life, and if they are not found meritorious they are inscribed for death" (*Rosh Hashanah* 16b).

Whether a person is "righteous" or "wicked" depends on the amount of mitzvos and *aveiros* he has performed; the righteous have more mitzvos than *aveiros*, while the wicked have more *aveiros* than mitzvos. That is the standard explanation of the Gemara.

The Alter of Kelm challenges this explanation, however. Since the Gemara states that one who fails to observe even a Rabbinic commandment is called wicked, how can the litmus test for righteousness be dependent on the proportion of mitzvos to *aveiros*? It is very possible that one might have more mitzvos than *aveiros*, and still be considered a *rasha* because he failed to observe a Rabbinic commandment!

It must be, says the Alter, that "righteous" and "wicked" in the above context do not refer to the amount of mitzvos or *aveiros* one has amassed. Rather, it describes a person's standing with regard to *teshuvah*. One who is close to performing *teshuvah* is righteous, and one who is distant from *teshuvah* is wicked. Even if one has performed numerous sins, if in his heart he bemoans his lowly spiritual state and has a sincere desire to improve, in Heaven he is included in the book of the righteous.

> "Even if one has performed numerous sins, if in his heart he bemoans his lowly spiritual state and has a sincere desire to improve, in Heaven he is included in the book of the righteous."

According to this explanation, who are "those who are in between," who are neither completely righteous nor completely wicked? A person is either close to the performance of *teshuvah* or far from it; he cannot be near and far at the same time.

The answer can be found in the *Selichos* recited on Erev Rosh Hashanah (*Selichah* 28):

"[Man] serves two masters during the course of his life. He does the will of his Creator or of his [evil] inclination, as he pleases. It is good to embrace his Creator at all times, for then he is a servant who is free of his [evil] master."

While it is true that man serves his Creator — he learns Torah, *davens*, and performs mitzvos and acts of kindness — he also serves his evil inclination. When he finishes his learning session and sits down to eat, or goes to sleep, or spends time with friends, he wishes to take a break from his spiritual responsibilities and do as he pleases. Most of us can relate to this desire to "have the best of both worlds."

This is an apt description for "those who are in between." Such a person might regret his laxity in Torah study and his lack of concentration during *davening*, and in these spiritual areas he is close to *teshuvah*. Yet in those areas where "he serves his evil inclination," he is far from *teshuvah*, for it does not occur to him that he has anything to rectify.

Our *avodah* on Yom Kippur is to recognize that "it is good to embrace his Creator *at all times* for then he is a servant free from his evil master." Attaining the spiritual level where every aspect of one's life is geared toward serving one's Creator is a lifelong endeavor, but it all begins with recognizing that we have only one true Master. This recognition is not only the cornerstone of *teshuvah*, it is also the key to true freedom.

(*Maamarei Yemei Ratzon*, pp. 226-229)

❊ ❊ ❊

THE BATTLEFRONT OF BECHIRAH

Rambam (*Hilchos Teshuvah* 5:2) writes that any person who desires perfection can reach a level similar to that of Moshe Rabbeinu, while someone who desires evil can descend to a level similar to that of Yeravam ben Nevat. The *decision* to strive for perfection –or, conversely, to sink to the lowest levels — can be made in a matter of minutes. However, the actual process of reaching one's goal spans many years. It is impossible for a person to transform himself from a *rasha* to a *tzaddik* in one day. Although every person has *bechirah*, it is not realistic for him to think he can exercise his *bechirah* to the extent that he can do a 180-degree turn in one moment.

Rav Eliyahu Dessler explains the concept of *bechirah* ingeniously. When two countries wage war, the objective of each country is to conquer the entire territory that is presently under the dominion of the rival country. However, the actual battle takes place on only one front. By the time the battle is over, one country has expanded its territory while the other has lost part of its territory — and the battle then moves to a point deeper in the vanquished territory.

The war between the *yetzer hatov* and *yetzer hara* is no different. Most of our actions are not a product of *bechirah* because they are not at the battlefront. A person performs many mitzvos and good deeds without choosing to perform them; rather, they are dictated by his upbringing or his intrinsic nature. Likewise, there are many *aveiros* that a person does without even realizing that they are wrong; it is simply a result of the way he was educated. His *nekudas habechirah* — point of free will — is at one specific location: the point where what he knows to be true clashes with what he imagines is true (although deep down he knows that it is not).

For example, many people speak *lashon hara* without even realizing that there is anything wrong with the way they are speaking. The *yetzer hara* will not try to convince those people to be *mechallel Shabbos*, however, since they have been habituated from their youth to keep Shabbos, and the *yetzer hara* has no chance of gaining a foothold in this area.

A person's *nekudas habechirah* is not stagnant. Every time he conditions himself to perform a particular mitzvah, he gains ground against the *yetzer hara* and moves the battle to a point deeper in enemy territory. From then on, the *yetzer hara* will no longer try to convince him to disregard this mitzvah, because it is no longer a challenge for him to perform it. This mitzvah now enters the domain of the *yetzer hatov*, which can now venture to conquer more territory by defeating the *yetzer hara* on the battleground of a more difficult mitzvah. The opposite holds true for one who conditions himself to perform an *aveirah*.

It follows that the level of one's upbringing merely determines his battlefront: his *nekudas habechirah*. The *nekudas habechirah* of a person who grew up among righteous people will be in the finer aspects of each mitzvah, while the *nekudas habechirah* of one who grew up among criminals will be much more basic. For such a person, stealing is a way of life; it does not occur to him that there is anything wrong with it. His *bechirah* might come into play when he has to decide whether to murder his victim or merely take his money and let him go.

We must approach Yom Kippur with this idea in mind. There might be many aspects of Torah and mitzvos in which we feel that we are deficient. However, our *teshuvah* must begin with the *aveiros* that are within our realm of *bechirah*. For example, a person who *davens* every day without any concentration cannot change this pattern in one moment. Instead, he must try to rectify this problem gradually. If he feels that it is in his ability to concentrate while he recites *Birchos HaTorah*, then he should start with that.

This is why Rav Yisrael Salanter said that a person should make a small, practical — but ironclad — *kabbalah* before Rosh Hashanah. After he has identified his *nekudas habechirah*, a *kabbalah* will help him condition himself in a small aspect of his *avodas Hashem* and conquer territory from the *yetzer hara*. He will have won this battle — and he will have moved closer toward winning the war.

"*After one has identified his nekudas habechirah, a kabbalah will help him condition himself in a small aspect of his avodas Hashem and conquer territory from the yetzer hara.*"

(*Alei Shur,* Vol. II, pp. 39, 40)

❊ ❊ ❊

THREE PATHWAYS OF TESHUVAH

We find three different aspects of *teshuvah* described by the Targum:

1) "Return, Yisrael, to Hashem your God" (*Hoshea* 14:2). The Targum translates this as, "Return, Yisrael, *to the fear* of your God."

2) "Take words with you and return to Hashem" (ibid. 14:3). This is translated as, "Bring with you words of confession and return *to the service* of Hashem."

3) "Wash yourselves, purify yourselves" (*Yeshayah* 1:16). The Targum explains this to mean, "Return *to the Torah*."

The literal meaning of the word "*teshuvah*" is to return, for the entire concept of *teshuvah* is to return and become closer to Hashem. How does a person accomplish such a feat? How can he bring himself closer to his Creator? He can do this in any of three ways, as demonstrated by the above *pesukim*: by returning to the fear of Hashem,

Yom Kippur / 391

by returning to the service of Hashem, or by returning to the Torah.

Torah is not only the elixir of life, it is also the most foolproof way of combating the *yetzer hara*. As *Chazal* tell us (*Kiddushin* 30b), Hashem declares, "I created the *yetzer hara*, and I created the Torah as its antidote." If a person contemplates the motivations for his *aveiros*, he will find that every one of them is rooted in a laxity in some area of Torah study. He might be able to trace his *aveiros* to the fact that he has not established a set time for Torah study, or perhaps that he settles for a superficial understanding of what he studies. Perhaps he has not studied the applicable halachos, or he has not reviewed what he learned. It is possible, too, that he should be spending time learning *mussar* or even studying the *siddur* (from which one can glean fundamentals of *emunah* and *bitachon*), and he has not taken the time to do so. There is no better day to do "*teshuvah* to Torah" than Yom Kippur, the day we received the Torah in the form of the second set of *Luchos*.

> "Torah is not only the elixir of life, it is also the most foolproof way of combating the yetzer hara."

The *teshuvah* mentioned in conjunction with service of Hashem is achieved by internalizing the proper attitude toward performing mitzvos. Most mitzvos are aimed at purifying, sanctifying, and elevating our bodies from the physical to the spiritual. The constant performance of the mitzvos, day after day, leaves small but indelible impressions upon our bodies. However, there is one catch: The performance of mitzvos only leaves these impressions when one pays attention to what he is doing. *Avodas Hashem* performed by rote, even if it is done for many years, will leave a person on the same spiritual plane he started from. Doing *teshuvah* by performing mitzvos with a sense of purpose is another way to return to Hashem.

"Returning to the fear of Hashem" means returning to the *study* of the fear of Hashem. Of all the areas of Torah, the one the *yetzer hara* expends special effort to prevent people from studying is *mussar*, whose focus is fear of Hashem. The *yetzer hara* knows just how powerful this study is, and he wages his war accordingly. A person's *teshuvah* must therefore include allotting time for the study of *mussar*.

All three forms of *teshuvah* mentioned above are viable ways of coming closer to Hashem. There is no time more conducive to making a *cheshbon hanefesh* and doing *teshuvah* than during Aseres Yemei Teshuvah in general and on Yom Kippur specifically.

(*Alei Shur,* Vol. II, pp. 442-444)

❋ ❋ ❋

THE POWER OF THE DAY IS IN YOUR HEART

Ramban (*Vayikra* 23:28) points out that in the Torah portion that discusses Shabbos and Yom Tov, the terminology of "*b'etzem hayom hazeh*," in the midst of this very day, is used only with regard to the Yamim Tovim of Yom Kippur and Shavuos. With regard to Yom Kippur, Ramban explains that *Chazal* tell us that this terminology reflects the fact that the day *itself* has the ability to effect atonement.

Yom Kippur is unique as a Yom Tov in that there is no mitzvah requiring a physical action. On Rosh Hashanah we blow the *shofar*, on Succos we take the *arbaah minim* and sit in the *succah*, and on Pesach we eat matzah. Yom Kippur, on the other hand, is a day that largely depends on the way one feels in his heart. Repentance, which comprises feelings of regret and a genuine commitment to leave one's misdeeds behind, is effective to the degree that one's heart truly experiences these feelings. The day itself has a special potency, but we must also do *teshuvah* in our hearts. (This is perhaps the reason that some people have difficulty properly connecting to this holiest day of the year.)

This same idea holds true for the Yom Tov of Shavuos. There is no physical mitzvah pertaining to the day; our *avodah* on Shavuos is to renew our commitment to Torah study and mitzvah observance.

> "The power of Yom Kippur and Shavuos cannot be accessed with our hands, only with our hearts."

Yom Kippur and Shavuos are two days that, if utilized properly, can significantly change a person for the better. But the power of those days cannot be accessed with our hands, only with our hearts.

(*Shiurei Chumash, Parashas Emor* 23:38)

ENVELOPED BY THE SUCCAH

Chazal tell us (*Succah* 2a) that a *succah* taller than 20 *amos* is invalid, and one who sits inside it does not fulfill his obligation. The Torah commands us to sit in a *succah*, "So that your generations *will know* that I caused *Bnei Yisrael* to reside in *succos* when I took them out of Mitzrayim" (*Vayikra* 23:43). The Gemara infers from this that a person can only fulfill his obligation when he knows that he is residing in a *succah*. When the *succah* is higher than 20 *amos*, one's eyes do not notice the *s'chach* and he therefore does not know that he is sitting in a *succah*.

What does this mean? It is hard to believe that one would not be aware that he is sitting in a *succah* simply because the *s'chach* is outside his field of vision!

What *Chazal* mean is that even though one *knows* he is in a *succah*, he is missing the added dimension of awareness afforded by his vision.

With this in mind, we can explain the following *passuk*: "And you *shall know* today and take to your heart that Hashem is the God in the Heavens above and on the earth below" (*Devarim* 4:39). The Torah used similar wording with regard to both the mitzvah of *succah* and the obligation to "know" Hashem, and *Chazal* revealed to us that "knowing" refers to a level of certainty achieved with the aid of one's physical senses. If so, one's level of knowledge that there is a God must parallel the level of knowledge needed to fulfill one's obligation of *succah*. A person is therefore required to attain an awareness of Hashem that is tangible; the *baalei mussar* refer to this as *emunah chushis*.

The mitzvah of *emunah* requires even more than this, however. While it is incumbent even upon gentiles to know that there is a God — as the Torah tells us regarding the Egyptians (*Shemos* 14:4), "And Mitzrayim will know that I am Hashem" — only *Bnei Yisrael* are expected to have *emunah*.

Emunah is the ability to address Hashem directly: "Blessed are You, Hashem." It is the ability to believe that when one *davens*, Hashem literally stands opposite him and hears every single word he utters. It is the ability to recognize Hashem in all of a person's bodily functions, in all of nature, and in all of history. It is the ability to acknowledge that we are completely surrounded by Hashem at all times.

> "*Emunah is the ability to recognize Hashem in all of a person's bodily functions, in all of nature, and in all of history.*"

Succos affords us an opportunity to contemplate these ideas. The Vilna Gaon said that the mitzvah of *succah* is unique in that it totally envelops a person. The *succah*, which symbolizes Hashem's "clouds of glory," reminds us not only of the Divine Providence *Bnei Yisrael* merited in the desert, but also of the Divine Providence each of us merits every single day.

(*Alei Shur*, Vol. II, p. 296; *Daas Shlomo*, unpublished manuscript)

❊ ❊ ❊

CELEBRATING OUR UNIQUE REPRIEVE

> "Although there is a mitzvah to rejoice on all of the festivals, there was an added degree of celebration in the Beis HaMikdash during the festival of Succos, as it is written, "And you shall rejoice before Hashem for seven days" (Rambam, Hilchos Lulav 8:12).

Succos is referred to as "the time of our rejoicing." This extra measure of happiness comes in the wake of the Days of Awe and the forgiveness we achieved then.

The Gemara (*Succah* 53a) relates that during the *Simchas Beis Hasho'eivah*, "The pious elders would say, 'Praiseworthy are [the years of] our youth since they did not embarrass our latter years,' while the penitent elders would say, 'Praiseworthy are our latter years because they atoned for the years of our youth.' Both of them would declare, 'Praiseworthy is one who has not sinned, and he who has sinned should repent and he will be forgiven.'" In other words, the essence of happiness is purification from sin. This is the *simchah* that each of us celebrates on Succos on a personal level.

"The essence of happiness is purification from sin."

Purification from sin is also a reason for rejoicing on a communal level. The Gemara (*Sotah* 9a) tells us that Hashem does not mete out retribution upon a nation until their "quota is filled." When a nation's "quota is filled," it means that they have become entrenched in sin to the extent that it has become part of their very nature. Once they have reached this point, there is no hope that they will ever repent, and as a result they are destined for destruction (see *Sforno, Shemos* 34:7).

In contrast, Hashem does not allow *Bnei Yisrael* to become rooted in sin. Every year *Bnei Yisrael* do *teshuvah* during the Days of Awe, and on Yom Kippur Hashem forgives them for their wrongdoings, wiping their slate clean. The other nations never enjoy such a reprieve, however, since they do not have the Yamim Nora'im.

Our rejoicing on Succos celebrates the perpetuity of *Bnei Yisrael*, which is an unparalleled source of happiness.

(*Alei Shur,* Vol. II, p. 451)

Simchas Torah
שמחת תורה

IN PREPARATION FOR SIMCHAH

The *Kuzari* enlightens us as to the proper way of rejoicing on Yom Tov: "Our Torah is divided between fear [of Hashem], and love and joy; bring yourself close to Hashem with all of these means. Your subjugation to Hashem on a day of fasting does not cause a greater closeness than your *simchah* on Shabbos and Yom Tov — as long as the *simchah* is with *kavanah* and a complete heart. For just as supplications require thought and *kavanah*, *simchah* in the performance of His mitzvos and the study of His Torah requires thought and *kavanah* as well. Recognize what good He has bestowed upon you [by giving you the mitzvos], for it is as if you have been invited into His residence and to dine at His table... and if the *simchah* brings one to song and dance — that is *avodah* and *dveikus* to Hashem!"

True *simchas Yom Tov* can only be achieved if one fully comprehends the message of the *Kuzari*. *Simchah* is the medium through which one's closeness to Hashem finds expression. When a person is firm in his *emunah* of Hashem, *simchah* and even song and dance follow. These are a means of serving Hashem and a way of attaining *dveikus*.

This description of *simchah* is quite distant from the way *simchah* is used in the vernacular. We must be extra careful on Simchas Torah not to get caught up in frivolous merriment that has nothing to do with Hashem and His mitzvos. If we are fortunate, we can draw a wealth of *emunah* and inspiration from the dancing. Our song and dance can arouse a strong connection to our Creator, creating an intense, lasting desire to strive toward spirituality and purity of heart. This is the way Torah-true *simchah* should look!

How foolish are those who view days of *simchah* as opportunities to "let go." A person must prepare for *simchah* precisely as he would prepare for any fundamental aspect of *avodas Hashem*. *Simchah* requires thought and *kavanah* just as *davening* and fasting do.

(*Alei Shur,* Vol. I, p. 48)

> "Simchah requires thought and kavanah just as davening and fasting do."

חֲנֻכָּה

Chanukah

LIGHTING THE TRUE CHANUKAH FLAME

During a difficult period in Rav Wolbe's yeshivah he went to see the Chazon Ish. The Chazon Ish told him that a person has to jump into the sea and keep walking until the water is up to his neck, and then the sea will split. In other words, man must do everything he can if he wishes to merit *siyatta diShmaya*. If he does not utilize his abilities to their fullest extent, how can he expect to receive Heavenly assistance that is beyond his ability? This concept is manifest in a number of places in the Torah.

In *Parashas Vayeishev*, Potiphar's wife tried unrelentingly to seduce Yosef. One fateful day, when no one was home besides Yosef, Potiphar's wife made another attempt. According to one opinion in *Chazal* (*Sotah* 36b), Yosef was ready to capitulate, and at that moment his father's image appeared to him and warned of the dire consequences should he sin. If at that moment Yosef had not been on the spiritual level to merit such a revelation, he would not have seen it. It was only because up until that point he had done everything in his ability to prevent himself from sinning that he merited Heavenly assistance in the form of his father's image. (For this reason, one cannot say, "Had my father appeared to me before I sinned, I, too, would have refrained." Had he resisted temptation as Yosef did, he, too, would have merited having his father's image appear to him!)

Another such example is the splitting of the sea. *Chazal* tell us that Nachshon ben Aminadav jumped into the sea and walked until the water reached his nostrils, and only then did the water split. Because he walked until he could walk no more, he merited the *siyatta diShmaya* needed to split the sea.

This concept is, in essence, the message of Chanukah. The Bach (*Orach Chaim* 670) writes that the *kohanim* were lax in their performance of the *avodah* in the *Beis HaMikdash*; measure for measure, the Greeks issued an edict that forbade the *avodah*: offering sacrifices and lighting the *Menorah*. Moreover, they defiled all the oil that was to be used for the *Menorah*. Only after the Chashmona'im showed that they were willing to sacrifice their lives for the sake of reclaiming the *avodah* in the *Beis HaMikdash* did they merit Heavenly assistance in this area. A handful of *kohanim* defeated a mighty army; they were able to re-enter the *Beis HaMikdash*, where they found a single intact flask of oil; and a day's worth of oil burned miraculously for eight days. Therefore, *Chazal* established these days of Chanukah as days of "praise and thanks to Hashem" — a time when we must strengthen our *avodah*.

> "It is the person who, in honor of Chanukah, learns with vigor during his set time for Torah study, or davens a tefillah with extra concentration, who has lit the true flame of Chanukah."

Pesach revolves around *Yetzias Mitzrayim*, Shavuos around *Matan Torah*, Rosh Hashanah around *yirah*, Yom Kippur around purity, Succos around *simchah*, and Chanukah around *chizuk* — strengthening our *avodah*. It is the person who, in honor of Chanukah, learns with vigor during his set time for Torah study, or *davens* a *tefillah*

with extra concentration, who has lit the true flame of Chanukah.
(*Daas Shlomo*, unpublished manuscript)

❊ ❊ ❊

THE UNIQUENESS OF THE CHANUKAH MIRACLE

On Chanukah we light the menorah to commemorate the miracle of the flask of oil, which contained enough oil to burn in the *Beis HaMikdash* for one night but burned for eight consecutive days. Many overt miracles occurred in the *Beis HaMikdash* on a daily basis (see *Pirkei Avos* 5:7). What was the special significance of this miracle that motivated *Chazal* to institute an entire holiday to commemorate it?

In order to understand the uniqueness of the miracle of the oil, we must gain a deeper understanding of Chanukah.

We find a contrast between the holidays of Purim and Chanukah. We celebrate Purim through eating and drinking, while we celebrate Chanukah by offering praise and thanksgiving to Hashem (i.e., the recitation of *Hallel*). Why do we observe these two festivals so differently? The Bach (*Orach Chaim* 670) explains that in the period leading up to the Purim miracle, the Jewish people sinned in a physical way, by indulging at the feast of Achashverosh. Therefore, they were threatened with a decree of physical annihilation. To rectify their sin of physical indulgence, they deprived their bodies through fasting, thereby averting the decree of death.

In the era preceding the miracles of Chanukah, the Jewish people's service of Hashem deteriorated, which in turn caused the assimilation of the Hellenists into Greek culture. The Greeks then issued a decree forbidding the *avodah* in the *Beis HaMikdash*. Through the *mesirus nefesh* of the Chashmona'im to guard the Torah and its commandments, they merited to find an intact flask of oil, which miraculously burned for eight days. The oil symbolized not only the neglected *avodah* that was the reason for the decree; it also symbolized the *mesirus nefesh* the Chashmona'im demonstrated, which helped them regain their original lofty level.

When there is a weakening in our service of Hashem, He brings a decree against us measure for measure, in order that we recognize the reason we are being punished. When we are *moser nefesh* in that specific area where we were negligent and regain our previous spiritual level, we merit a miracle that brings salvation. Once we have done all that is humanly possible, Hashem helps us with the final step, which is out of the realm of nature: a miracle.

After the Chashmona'im risked their lives for the sake of strengthening the service of their Creator, Hashem performed a miracle and the oil lasted for the entire eight days. This is the deeper meaning behind the miracle of the oil that we celebrate on Chanukah: It symbolizes the strengthening of our performance of mitzvos, which ultimately leads to redemption.

> *"At least once over the course of Chanukah, when we want to sit back and relax because it is Chanukah, we should instead stand up and accomplish — because it is Chanukah."*

Chanukah is a time for intensification of our service of Hashem. At least once over the course of Chanukah, when we want to sit back and relax because it is Chanukah, we should instead stand up and accomplish — because it is Chanukah.

(*Alei Shur,* Vol. II, pp. 455-457)

פורים / Purim

TZNIUS: MUCH MORE THAN A MODE OF DRESS

The first of the spices used in the preparation of the *ketores* is "*mar dror*" — pure myrrh. Targum translates these words as, "*meira dachya*," and the Gemara discerns in them a reference to Mordechai. This is not merely a play on words; it is also a reference to one of Mordechai's defining character traits: *tznius*. The *ketores* was burned in the *Kodesh HaKodashim* with only the *kohen gadol* in attendance. Even on a daily basis, when the *ketores* was burned outside the *Kodesh HaKodashim*, the *kohanim* would disperse from the courtyard to allow it to burn in private. Similarly, Mordechai was a paradigm of *tznius*.

What exactly is *tznius*? *Tznius* is much more than a mode of dress; it involves behaving and speaking in a modest and unassuming manner. The concept of *tznius* should envelop all aspects of a person's life.

The Gemara tells us, "Blessing rests only on something that is hidden from the eye" (*Taanis* 8a). An endeavor that everyone knows about often does not succeed.

During World War II, when Rav Wolbe was in Stockholm, he opened a *beis midrash*. No one knew about his plans until they actually materialized. Had people known about his intentions, he later explained, someone would have given him advice, another person would have hindered him for another reason, and he never would have succeeded.

This concept is evident from a number of stories in the Torah. Yehudah and Tamar's progeny were conceived in a seemingly inappropriate way, since the conception of the forebear of Mashiach must occur inconspicuously and not amid fanfare and pomp. Rivkah received a prophecy that Esav wanted to kill Yaakov. However, she simply told Yitzchak that she wanted to send Yaakov away because she was disgusted with the local marriage prospects, never revealing that she had been privy to other information via a prophecy.

Rav Wolbe used to say that he always wanted to write a book containing 20 biographies: 10 of Torah luminaries, and 10 of world leaders. The purpose, he explained, would be to show how in all moral aspects our Torah leaders surpassed world leaders. A prime example was the world-renowned professor of theology, Albert Schweitzer. He was a well-rounded man; he was a priest, a university professor, and a musician. When Schweitzer was in his 30's he heard about the lack of medical services in third-world countries, and despite great opposition he gave up his prestigious positions and went to study medicine. He then traveled to Africa, where he set up a clinic to help the needy natives — something truly remarkable for a man of his stature. However, every step of the way he chronicled his accomplishments.

That cannot be said about the Chazon Ish, one of the great Torah giants of the previous generation, who helped countless orphans and widows with their financial and emotional problems. His door was constantly open to anyone and everyone in need — but we only know

> "*The Chazon Ish's door was constantly open to anyone and everyone in need — but we only know these stories because the people he helped related them to others.*"

these stories because the people he helped related them to others. This attribute of *tznius* can be found in all Torah luminaries; they do what has to be done without fanfare and without taking credit. This is the true embodiment of the *passuk* (*Michah* 6:8) "You should walk modestly — with *tznius* — with your God."

This is how we connect and feel close to Hashem, despite Hashem "hiding" His face.

(*Alei Shur* II, p. 469; *Shiurei Chumash, Parashas Vayeishev* 38:26; *Shiurei Chumash, Parashas Toldos* 27:42)

❈ ❈ ❈

HAMAN'S FANTASY WORLD

Megillas Esther depicts two diverse worlds — the world of Haman and the world of the Jewish people — and the interaction between them. Haman's world was dominated by fantasy. Immediately upon being promoted to his position of prominence, he enacted two new laws: Everyone must bow down to a statue of his likeness, and they must bow down to Haman himself. When Mordechai refused to bow down, Haman was overcome with rage, to the point that he wished to annihilate an entire people because of one person's insubordination. Such acts and feelings are born of fantasies and desires, and are not the product of clear, logical thinking.

There are numerous other illustrations of Haman's delusional thinking in the *Megillah*. Even after the decree of annihilation went into effect and Mordechai's fate was "signed and sealed," Haman was still infuriated by Mordechai's refusal to bow. He gathered all of his advisers and friends and asked them to devise a plan to rid him of this thorn in his side. They advised him to build a gallows 50 cubits high and hang Mordechai on it in view of the entire city. Why was he so set on killing an already marked man? What honor did he expect to gain by building a towering gallows?

Haman's fantasies and imagination caused him to believe that this would be the greatest act of revenge and would bring him tremendous honor. This obsession spurred him to make a nocturnal visit to the king and gain permission to hang Mordechai. Upon Haman's arrival, the king asked him what should be done to someone the king wished to honor. His imagination led him to believe that out of the millions of people in Achashverosh's kingdom, he was the only one deserving of honor. He answered that such a person should be paraded in the streets in royal clothes and a crier should proclaim, "So should be done to the one whom the king wishes to honor!" This was the ultimate honor he could envision for himself.

Even the invitation to the royal party prepared by Esther boosted Haman's ego without good reason. Was it not common practice for the governing hierarchy to convene and discuss various issues? Yet in Haman's mind, everything that happened revolved around his greatness and prominence. He lived in a world of complete fantasy.

The Jewish people crossed paths with this world when they partook of the party thrown by Achashverosh. Until then, they had lived in a world that spurned fantasy. But because they indulged at Achashverosh's banquet, Haman was given free rein to do as he wished — and he wished to annihilate the entire Jewish nation.

Haman's scheme gave the Jewish people a clarity of perception that had not been achieved by the exhortations of all 48 prophets, who had called upon them in the past to repent. Threatened with annihilation, the Jewish people realized that they had no part in a world that was built on fantasies. They understood that the only true "light" is the light of the Torah, and real pleasure lies in the performance of mitzvos and the bond that we have with Hashem. This realization was so strong that it brought them to reaccept the Torah — this time out of pure love of Hashem.

> "*Threatened with annihilation, the Jewish people realized that they had no part in a world that was built on fantasies.*"

Purim is a day that grants us the ability to perceive the fantasy of the world in which most people live. It allows us to uproot ourselves from such an existence and replant ourselves in the world of truth: the legacy of the Jewish people.

(*Daas Shlomo Geulah*, pp. 199, 200)

❈ ❈ ❈

IN SEARCH OF TRUE PLEASURE

Mesilas Yesharim (Ch. 1) writes that man was created to have pleasure — and not just any pleasure, but "to delight in Hashem and have pleasure from the radiance of His *Shechinah*." *Chazal* tell us that in the World to Come there is no eating or drinking; rather, the righteous sit with crowns on their heads and derive pleasure from the radiance of the *Shechinah*.

Pleasure is what dominates a person's existence from the time of his birth through all of eternity, and it is the deciding factor behind all of our actions. But what gives a person pleasure? Different people find pleasure in different things, and the things that give a person pleasure are the litmus test for determining who he is. Even if most of one's pleasure is derived from physical gratification, does he also, from time to time, obtain enjoyment in the spiritual arena? Does he delight in performing a kindness for another person, in connecting to Hashem through prayer, in the profundity of *Chazal* or an ingenious Torah thought? This is a question every person should ask himself.

> "Pleasure is what dominates a person's existence from the time of his birth through all of eternity, and it is the deciding factor behind all of our actions."

One of the lessons that we can glean from the story of Purim is to look for pleasure in the right places. *Chazal* tell us that the three days of fasting that Esther instituted had another purpose aside from enabling the Jews to pray with more feeling. The fast was meant to counteract the physical pleasures they enjoyed when they participated in Achashverosh's party. As the Gemara states (*Megillah* 12a), the decree to kill the Jews came in the wake of their participation in that party. If all the food was kosher and no one was forced to drink anything, what could possibly be so terrible about partaking in the festivities? Why were all of Shushan's Jews slated for annihilation as a result of that party?

Instead of seeking to derive pleasure from the spiritual realm and thereby gain eternity, the Jews sought to derive pleasure from physical sources, immersing themselves in a hedonistic party. Only after they fasted and put physical pleasures in the proper perspective did they merit salvation from their enemies.

"And the Jews had light, happiness, joy, and honor" (*Esther* 8:15). *Chazal* tell us that this refers to the light of Torah, the happiness of Yom Tov, the joy of *bris milah*, and the honor of *tefillin* (*Megillah* 16b). The Jews reached to a new perception of what pleasure is, and they acknowledged that true light, happiness, joy, and honor are obtained through Torah and mitzvos.

We ask of Hashem, "Please make the Torah pleasurable (*v'haarev*) in our mouths." The word "*v'haarev*" — make pleasurable — shares the same root as the word "*hisareiv*" — to blend in — because the things one finds pleasurable blend into his very essence and make-up. Although we are flesh and blood and are therefore automatically connected to physical pleasures, we should strive to integrate the Torah into our flesh and blood. This will enable us to enjoy the greatest pleasures possible!

(*Daas Shlomo Geulah*, pp. 207-210)

❊ ❊ ❊

THE POWER OF PURIM

Chazal (*Shir Hashirim Rabbah* 1:18) tell us that the violation of Rabbinic commandments carries a more severe punishment than the violation of commandments written in the Torah. Rav Yerucham Levovitz explains the rationale behind this idea. The more a person can relate to a concept or idea, the more it obligates him. It is easier for us to relate to the commandments and restrictions that were enacted by the Rabbanim, not only because the reasons behind them are more comprehensible to us, but also because the people who instituted them lived in a more recent era than the one in which the Torah was given. Therefore, these mitzvos obligate us to a greater degree, and neglecting them carries a greater punishment.

If *mitzvos d'Rabbanan* carry a greater punishment, it follows that their fulfillment yields greater results, for the fact that we can relate to the mitzvah means that we can gain more from it. Therefore, it is quite possible that we can gain more from Purim, which is *d'Rabbanan*, than we can gain from other *Yamim Tovim*, even though they are *d'Oraisa*. Additionally, the *Arizal* teaches that the name "Yom Kippurim" indicates that Yom Kippur is "a day *like* Purim" — i.e., Yom Kippur is secondary to the day of Purim. Another sign of the spiritual loftiness of Purim is the fact that a *sefer* in *Tanach*, a *masechta* of Gemara, and a plethora of mitzvos and customs are dedicated solely to this day.

> "It is quite possible that we can gain more from Purim, which is d'Rabbanan, than we can gain from other Yamim Tovim, even though they are d'Oraisa."

The miracle of Purim was the very last miracle recorded in *Tanach* that happened to *Bnei Yisrael*. The uniqueness of this miracle lies in the fact that it occurred during a time of *galus* and *hester panim*, which means that we can glean from Purim everything we need to know in order to weather the subsequent days of *galus* and *hester panim*.

When Achashverosh gave his ring to Haman, allowing Haman to do to the Jews as he pleased, the Jewish people were able to see through the prevailing *hester panim* and realize that it was Hashem Who had brought upon them the decree of annihilation. This realization was more successful in causing them to do *teshuvah* than all the prophets' exhortations had been. Moreover, when they merited salvation, they felt Hashem's loving Hand penetrating through the *hester panim*, which prompted them to reaccept the Torah wholeheartedly.

The Yom Tov of Purim helps us to become more aware of Hashem despite the *hester panim* of *galus*. If we prepare ourselves properly, and internalize the message of the miracle of Purim, we can reap the spiritual benefits of this unique day.

(*Daas Shlomo Geulah*, pp. 201, 202)

❋ ❋ ❋

TWO WAYS TO KNOW HASHEM

Shlomo HaMelech counsels us, "If you seek it like silver and you search for it like a treasure, [only] then will you understand the fear of Hashem and will you find *daas Elokim* (knowledge of Hashem)" (*Mishlei* 2:4-5). What is this *daas Elokim* for which we are searching?

Rav Yeruchom Levovitz explains that the main objective of *Krias Yam Suf* was not the awesome Divine revelation caused by the miraculous splitting of the sea. Rather, Hashem wished to surround *Bnei Yisrael* with perils from all sides to force them to acknowledge that there was no natural way out of their predicament. Such a situation would compel them to turn to Hashem. When *Bnei Yisrael* directed their focus toward Hashem, He responded by splitting the sea simply as a means of extracting them from their predicament.

In a similar vein, Sarah Imeinu was not merely barren; she was physically unable to bear children, as she did not even have a womb. Hashem created her in such a manner so that she and Avraham would realize that the laws of nature left no possibility for them to have a child, and they would be forced to invest all their efforts in petitioning Hashem. The subsequent miracle of Sarah's bearing a child was merely to release her from her difficulty. In summation, Divine Providence often removes all viable options in order to redirect our focus, so that instead of turning to outsiders for help we are forced to turn our gaze inward and come to the realization that only Hashem can help us.

> "*Divine Providence often removes all viable options in order to redirect our focus, so that instead of turning to outsiders for help we are forced to turn our gaze inward and come to the realization that only Hashem can help us.*"

With this introduction, says Rav Wolbe, we can gain an understanding of what *daas Elokim* is: It is a heartfelt sense of clarity that the Creator exists, beyond any shadow of a doubt.

Purim / 411

How can one attain this *daas Elokim*? There are two possible ways. The first, as mentioned above, is by coming to the realization that salvation can only be achieved through Hashem. *Chazal* tell us (*Megillah* 14a), "Greater was the removal of the signet ring [from Achashverosh to Haman] than the 48 prophets. While none of the prophets succeeded in causing *Bnei Yisrael* to repent, the [decree written by Haman after the] removal of the signet ring succeeded in bringing them back to the proper path." Despite the many foreboding prophecies they had heard, *Bnei Yisrael* always thought that there was a way out other than *teshuvah*. However, when faced with Haman's threat of annihilation, they could not ignore their impending doom. This brought them to the realization that there was no natural way out and salvation could only come from Hashem.

The second way of attaining *daas Elokim* can be gleaned from the Radak on the *passuk* "I had said I would not see Hashem" (*Yeshayah* 38:11). He quotes Rav Saadya Gaon, who explains that "seeing Hashem" is a reference to giving thanks. The Radak concurs, explaining that "perceiving Hashem is thanking and praising Him and contemplating His ways." Someone who possesses the trait of *hakaras hatov* sees Hashem in every single thing He has given him. He appreciates the many gifts he receives, and he thanks Hashem for each one of them. In this way, he sees Hashem in every aspect of his life.

The Purim miracle occurred after *Bnei Yisrael* acknowledged that the only way out was with Hashem's help. This internal revelation was so powerful that it propelled them to new spiritual heights and was the impetus for renewing their acceptance of the Torah. They had gained a new appreciation of the Torah and mitzvos, as *Chazal* explain with regard to the *passuk* "The Jews had light, happiness, joy, and honor" (*Esther* 8:15): "Light refers to the Torah, happiness refers to Yom Tov, joy refers to the mitzvah of *bris milah*, and honor refers to the mitzvah of *tefillin*" (*Megillah* 16b). While we might have difficulty seeing the light of the Torah or the honor of *tefillin*, Mordechai and his generation, after being forced to turn inward and perceive Hashem internally, attained *daas Elokim* and were able to tap into the *pnimiyus* of the Torah and mitzvos.

Ramban (*Shemos* 24:11) writes that whenever there was a great revelation of the *Shechinah*, *Bnei Yisrael* celebrated with food and drink. Perhaps the mitzvah of feasting on Purim was enacted by *Chazal* as a celebration of the revelation attained by Mordechai and his generation, and the possible revelation that can be achieved every year when we revisit this wondrous time.

(*Daas Shlomo Geulah*, pp. 211-214)

A DIFFERENT TYPE OF PESACH CLEANING

The month of Nissan in general, and the Yom Tov of Pesach in particular, are times that are auspicious for *geulah* (redemption). One aspect of this redemption is the ability to redeem ourselves from enslavement to the *yetzer hara*. As with all good things, however, to merit any level of redemption one must prepare properly. How do we do that? The answer can be found in the Torah's description of the first *Korban Pesach*.

Prior to the redemption from Mitzrayim, Moshe Rabbeinu commanded *Bnei Yisrael*, "**Draw** [forth] and **take** for yourselves one sheep for your families" (*Shemos* 12:21). Would it not suffice to simply say, "Take for yourselves a sheep"? The beginning of the *passuk*, "Draw [forth]," seems to be superfluous. *Chazal* explain that there was a deeper intention behind Moshe's commandment. He was telling *Bnei Yisrael* that before performing the mitzvah of *Korban Pesach*, they must first sever their connection to *avo-*

dah zarah. Moshe was implying, "**Withdraw** yourselves from idol worship, and only then **take** a sheep for the *Korban Pesach*."

Each one of us has a personal "*avodah zarah*." It might be a negative *middah*, or a bad habit that we have yet to overcome. *Avodah zarah* also manifests itself in the numerous forms of addiction that abound nowadays. We must shake off this yoke of evil in order to make ourselves worthy of redemption.

What should one do if he has no idea which *avodah zarah* he "worships"? The answer can be gleaned from the mitzvah of *bedikas chametz*. The Gemara tells us that the search must be performed with a candle, since the *passuk* says, "A man's soul is the **candle** of Hashem, which **searches** the chambers of his inner self" (*Mishlei* 20:27). The Gemara deduces from this *passuk* that another search must also be performed with a candle: the search for chametz. Yet the connection between the search for chametz and the above *passuk* is more profound. Just as we search for chametz in our homes, we must also search the chambers of our hearts for any spiritual chametz. We must reflect on our *middos* and attitudes in order to enable us to pinpoint the "idol worship" inside of us.

The days leading up to Pesach give us an opportunity for some serious soul-searching. A generous amount of time is spent cleaning for Pesach. The searching, scrubbing, and cleaning we do should inspire us to mentally search, scrub, and clean the chambers of our heart. Performing this spiritual exercise not only makes us worthy of redemption from the *yetzer hara*, it is also the preparation needed to merit the final redemption!

(*Daas Shlomo*, unpublished manuscript; see also *Alei Shur*, Vol. II, p. 389)

> "*The searching, scrubbing, and cleaning we do should inspire us to mentally search, scrub, and clean the chambers of our heart.*"

❈ ❈ ❈

NO PHILOSOPHICAL PROOF NEEDED

The *Kuzari* (authored by R' Yehudah Halevi in the 12th century) was written as a dialogue between a Jewish sage and the king of Kuzar, who was searching for spiritual fulfillment. After failing to be convinced of the authenticity of Catholicism or Islam, the king summoned this Jewish sage and asked him to describe the beliefs of the Jewish nation. The sage responded, "We believe in the God of Avraham, Yitzchak, and Yaakov, Who took us out of Egypt with miracles and wonders."

Why, the king wondered, did the sage describe Hashem as, "the One Who took us out of Egypt," in contrast to the representatives of other religions, who describe God as "the One Who created the world"? The sage answered that the other religions base their belief in God on philosophical conclusions. Nature itself is evidence to the existence of a Creator, and other religions therefore relate to God as the Creator of the world, for Creation is the foundation of their beliefs. The Jewish people have no need to resort to intellectual proofs, however, since they "saw" Hashem through the numerous miracles performed during *Yetzias Mitzrayim*. They refer to Hashem as the One Who took them out of Mitzrayim, which was an occurrence that they witnessed — as opposed to Creation, which was witnessed by no one.

Our *emunah* is not based on logic; it is an outgrowth of what we perceived with our own eyes. We "saw" Hashem when He took us out of Mitzrayim, when He gave us the Torah on Har Sinai, and when He sustained us in a barren desert with daily bread from the heavens. This is what the *sefarim* refer to as "*emunah chushis*" — belief that can be felt with the senses.

We can understand that this level of *emunah* was achieved by those who actually experienced the above miracles. But how can we, who live more than three millennia after those events took place, achieve a parallel level of *emunah*? The Torah, in its description of *Matan Torah*, addresses this issue. When Hashem descended upon Har Sinai, the mountain was consumed by fire, "and its smoke rose like the smoke of a furnace." *Chazal* tell us that the allegorical reference to a furnace was inserted so that one could relate to what had occurred.

Why is that important? We need to know that we received the Torah on Har Sinai, but why is how the mountain looked significant? What difference does it make? It makes a difference to us, because the way for those who were not present at Har Sinai to attain the level of *emunah* that was achieved back then is by reliving what occurred. And we can only relive it if we know exactly what transpired. We need to know that the mountain was shaking and that the smoke was rising as smoke rises from a furnace.

Elsewhere, the *Kuzari* writes that we should employ imagination to picture the awesome events of the past, such as *Yetzias Mitzrayim* and *Maamad Har Sinai*. Imagination is a powerful tool, one that can even effect changes in the natural world, as we find in the Torah regarding the staffs that Yaakov placed before the sheep (*Bereishis* Ch. 30). Likewise, imagination has the ability to enhance our level of *emunah*. The extent to which we are able to relive and "perceive" the occurrences mentioned in the Torah is dependent upon the extent that we are able to imagine them.

The *Chovos HaLevavos* mentions another way to achieve *emunah* similar to that which we experienced at Har Sinai. He writes (*Shaar HaBechinah* Ch. 5) that one should contemplate the survival of the Jewish people through the generations, because it is a wonder akin to the wonders of Har Sinai!

> "The survival of the Jewish people through the generations is a wonder akin to the wonders of Har Sinai."

The *Seder* night is the most opportune time of the entire year to inculcate *emunah* in our children. e must recount and relive *Yetzias Mitzrayim* in a way that they can relive it, too. Our aim is to create an atmosphere that lends to feeling as if "he himself went out of Mitzrayim." Moreover, the point mentioned by the Maharal is also referred to during the *Seder* when we recite, "In every generation they stand up against us to annihilate us, and Hashem saves us from their hands." Serious contemplation and discussion of these ideas on *Leil HaSeder* can bring us and our children to levels of *emunah* unattainable during the rest of the year.

(*Daas Shlomo*, unpublished manuscript)

✽ ✽ ✽

HASHEM ACTED ON MY BEHALF

On the night of the *Seder* we must inculcate within ourselves the ideas mentioned in the *Haggadah*, to the point that we feel as if we ourselves were redeemed from Mitzrayim. Although the *rasha* mentioned in the *Haggadah* shows interest in the discussion, he is considered wicked because he disassociates himself from the *avodah* of Pesach. "What is this *avodah* for you?" he asks. *Chazal* tell us that had he been in Mitzrayim he would not have been redeemed. Freedom must start with a sincere desire to be part of the process of redemption.

The Gemara tells us that even if a person does not have children or a wife, he must still ask himself the four questions. Why are questions such a crucial part of the *Seder*? Would not a mere recitation of the *Haggadah* suffice for one to fulfill his obligation of retelling the story of the Exodus?

A question reveals a person's inner feelings. The aim of the *Seder* is to arouse our interest in the discussion to the point that we are prompted to question the proceedings and inspired to identify with the redemption.

> *"Reciting numerous interpretations or expounding on the inferences of the unique wording of the Haggadah will not bring a person to this realization as much as paying close attention to the deeper meaning behind the overall process of redemption from Mitzrayim."*

Reciting numerous interpretations or expounding on the inferences of the unique wording of the *Haggadah* will not bring a person to this realization as much as paying close attention to the deeper meaning behind the overall process of redemption from Mitzrayim. A person who follows the story attentively from start to finish will be aroused to feel that "Hashem acted on *my* behalf when *I* left Mitzrayim."

(*Alei Shur,* Vol. II, p. 394)

❈ ❈ ❈

THE FREEDOM OF MATZAH

The Torah refers to Pesach as *Chag HaMatzos*, the festival of ma-tzos, while *Chazal* refer to it as *Z'man Cheiruseinu*, the time of our freedom. The Maharal (*Gevuros Hashem* Ch. 51) writes that the reason matzah is called *lechem oni* is that it contains only flour and water, the two basic ingredients of bread, with no additional ingredients. This bread is similar to the poor man who possesses nothing but himself. What does this mean for us?

The Gemara relates (*Berachos* 17a) that Rav Alexandri would include a small statement in his prayers: "It is revealed and known before You that our will is to fulfill Your will. What prevents us? The yeast in the dough [the *yetzer hara*] and our subjugation to foreign dominion." Why is the *yetzer hara* called "the yeast in the dough"? Yeast is an outside factor that causes the dough to rise more than it would have risen by itself. Likewise, the *yetzer hara* inflates the innate *middos* found inside every person beyond their proper limits.

For example, every person needs a certain amount of self-respect. In fact, one who eats in the marketplace has disqualified himself from giving testimony in *beis din*, since, "If he does not care about his own honor, he certainly will not care about another's honor" (*Kiddushin* 40b). However, the *yetzer hara* inflates a person's need for honor and causes him to seek honor at every opportunity.

Similarly, jealousy is an essential trait, for without it no one would marry or build a house (see *Mesilas Yesharim* Chapter 11). Once again, however, the *yetzer hara* inflates this trait of jealousy until it encompasses everything the neighbor owns.

Desire is also a positive trait. One who lacks this *middah* would not be able to fulfill the mitzvah of eating matzah, since it would be considered *achilah gasah* (overeating). The problem is that the *yetzer hara* pumps up a person's desire. Instead of remaining a means to an end, desire becomes an end in and of itself, transforming man into a pleasure-seeker.

As a result of the *yetzer hara*'s work, when a person grows older and takes a good, honest look at himself, he might be astounded to discover that the persona he has cultivated for himself is totally foreign to his true self.

All this relates to the *yetzer hara* that dwells inside a person. The Gra (*Even Sheleimah* 4:19) explains that there is yet another, external *yetzer hara* that we must contend with. This is the *yetzer hara* of being subjugated to foreign dominion. We live among the nations, and we are influenced by their way of life. For example, we feel the need to keep up with the latest fashions, lest we be looked upon as a relic from the past. It is astounding to think that some tailor in Paris can fashion a garment, and within a week the entire world feels compelled to wear the product of his imagination!

If we could succeed in uprooting external foreign influences and bursting the internal bubble of inflated *middos*, we would experience a true sense of freedom.

> "Just as matzah is free of all outside influences, true freedom can only be experienced when one purges himself of all outside influences."

This is the meaning behind the Maharal's explanation of why matzah is referred to as bread of poverty. We eat matzah during the time of our freedom, because just as matzah is free of all outside influences, true freedom can only be experienced when one purges himself of all outside influences and perceives himself honestly. This is what we strive for on the *Chag HaMatzos*.

(*Kuntress Kol HaTorah*, Vol. 61, pp. 57, 58)

❖ ❖ ❖

WHY THE FOCUS IS ON PHARAOH

It is interesting to note that when the Torah describes *Yetzias Mitzrayim*, there is a much greater focus on Pharaoh than on *Bnei Yisrael*. Much of the story of the redemption focuses on the 10 plagues, which were primarily aimed at subduing Pharaoh.

In the earlier generations (including the *Dor Haflagah*, Nimrod, and the people of Sodom), there were people who acknowledged the Creator yet intentionally rebelled against Him. If they truly comprehended His Omnipotence, how is it possible that they intentionally rebelled against Him? In a similar vein, Rashi (*Bereishis* 6:6) explains that although Hashem was planning to destroy mankind in the Flood, He was "consoled" by the fact that He created man down on earth and not in the heavens, for had man been created in the heavens he would have convinced even the angels to rebel! *Chazal* reveal to us the arrogance of man: he wishes to remain independent at all costs. Even if he were to dwell in the heavens, he still would not subjugate himself to the Creator Who rules over heaven and earth.

A mere few days after *Bnei Yisrael* heard the Ten Commandments from Hashem Himself, they made the golden calf. It is easier to worship something that was created with one's own hands than to worship Hashem, Who created man and demands his subservience. After they sinned, Hashem told Moshe Rabbeinu, "I have seen this nation and they are a stiff-necked nation" (*Shemos* 32:9). The root of the sin was not idol worship, but stubbornness.

This explains why the earlier generations acknowledged Hashem and rebelled against Him. Since they recognized His greatness, they had trouble subjugating themselves to a power that was so much greater than they were. Later generations, on the other hand, were not as cognizant of Hashem's true greatness, and did not feel threatened by His Omnipotence. They therefore did not feel the need to rebel.

The Torah focuses the story of the Exodus on Pharaoh and not on *Bnei Yisrael* because the years of bondage had taken a toll on *Bnei Yisrael*. They were broken in body and spirit, and they were waiting for redemption, so when Hashem revealed Himself, they willingly accepted His yoke. This was not the case with Pharaoh, who stated, "I do not know Who Hashem is" and "The Nile is mine and I created myself!" The plagues were therefore aimed toward systematically subduing Pharaoh by showing him Hashem's greatness.

Many people find that when they study Torah they are alert and focused, but when they *daven* they have difficulty concentrat-

ing and are constantly distracted by countless random thoughts. This is because when a person *davens* he is acknowledging that there is a Higher Power that controls everyone and everything, and automatically a feeling of rebelliousness rears its head. We must learn from Pharaoh that no matter how great a person thinks he is, he is still a mere creation, and he must humble himself before his Creator and submit to being His servant.
(*Daas Shlomo Geulah*, pp. 306, 307)

> "When a person davens, he is acknowledging that there is a Higher Power that controls everyone and everything, and automatically a feeling of rebelliousness rears its head."

❋ ❋ ❋

INSIGHTS ON THE HAGGADAH

"Because of this [the Pesach, matzah, and maror] Hashem acted on my behalf when I went out from Egypt." Rashi explains that we were redeemed in order to perform His mitzvos. Rav Yerucham Levovitz would say that people think they must make a *berachah* because they want to eat. However, the opposite is true. The reason we were created with the need to eat is so that we should have the opportunity to recite a *berachah*. Likewise, we do not perform these mitzvos because Hashem took us out of Mitzrayim; rather, the purpose of *Yetzias Mitzrayim* was to give us the opportunity to perform these mitzvos.
(*Alei Shur*, Vol. II, p. 390)

"In the beginning our forefathers were idol worshipers, but now Hashem brought us close to Him." Why does the *Haggadah* state, "*Now* Hashem brought us to His service"? Did not this occur more than 3,000 years ago, at the time of the redemption from Egypt?

The celebration of Pesach is not merely a commemoration of what occurred in the distant past. Rather, at the time of the redemption *Bnei Yisrael* experienced a Divine spiritual illumination, and every year on the night of the *Seder* there is a reoccurrence of that exact spiritual illumination. If we tap into this illumination, we can feel the same way as those who actually left Egypt on this night thousands of years earlier. It is with this aim that we recite the *Haggadah* on the Seder night.

(*Alei Shur,* Vol. II, p. 390).

"The Pesach sacrifice that our fathers ate when the Beis HaMikdash was standing; for what reason? Because Hashem passed over the houses of our fathers in Egypt." During the rest of the year we must be careful not to leap and jump in our service of Hashem, lest we fall flat on our faces. We must serve Hashem on a level that is appropriate to our spiritual standing. However, on Pesach we have an opportunity to grow by leaps and bounds.

Rashi (*Shemos* 12:11) explains why *Bnei Yisrael* were commanded to eat the Pesach sacrifice in a hurry: "Just as Hashem jumped and skipped over the houses of *Bnei Yisrael* when He slew the firstborn, so, too, you should 'jump and skip' [hurry] in your service of Hashem [eating the Pesach sacrifice]." When we experience the spiritual illumination of the *Seder* night, we can "jump" in our level of service of Hashem in a manner that is not possible on any other day of the year.

"When we experience the spiritual illumination of the Seder night, we can 'jump' in our level of service of Hashem in a manner that is not possible on any other day of the year."

(*Alei Shur,* Vol. II, p. 395)

ספירת העומר
Sefiras HaOmer

WHEN THE FLASH OF INSPIRATION WANES

Bnei Yisrael were at a spiritual low after the many years of bondage in *Mitzrayim*, and Hashem had to grant them holiness in order for them to be worthy of redemption. Through this act of benevolence, *Bnei Yisrael* climbed many rungs on the spiritual ladder in a very brief amount of time, reaching a spiritual zenith on the night before they were released from bondage.

Nevertheless, the Ramchal tells us that in the 49 days between *Yetzias Mitzrayim* and Shavuos, *Bnei Yisrael* extracted themselves from the 49th level of impurity and ascended to the 49th level of holiness. If they had reached great spiritual heights when they left Mitzrayim, why did they have to work for seven weeks to climb to a plateau on which they already stood?

The answer is that the tremendous level of greatness experienced at *Yetzias Mitzrayim* disappeared the following day. *Bnei Yisrael* then had to re-establish that level, this time through their own efforts.

For when Hashem dispenses a flash of inspiration, He then expects us to recreate that experience through our *avodas Hashem*.

In a similar vein, *Chazal* (*Chagigah* 12a) tell us that at the time of Creation the light was so intense that Adam was able to see from one end of the world to the other. However, because of the wicked, who would not be worthy of this light, Hashem "hid" it and set it aside for the righteous. If Hashem knew that He would hide it, why did He create it in the first place? Additionally, we know that a child in the womb experiences this otherworldly light. He is taught the entire Torah, only to forget it all when he is born. If a child forgets everything when he is born, what is the purpose of creating a spiritual utopia for him in his mother's womb?

Both of these questions can be answered with the above concept. Hashem gives a flash of inspiration that leaves an indelible impression, which enables us to subsequently achieve that spiritual level independently.

> "Hashem bestowed upon them a spiritual revelation, and then retracted it in order to allow them to work their way back up to that level of their own accord."

Many people feel a surge of inspiration, be it after the *Seder* night or following any other inspiring event. However, these feelings wane after a few days, and those who were so inspired might feel that they are back to square one. In reality, what happened is that Hashem bestowed upon them a spiritual revelation, and then retracted it in order to allow them to work their way back up to that level of their own accord. When a flash of inspiration disappears, there is no reason to feel despondent; rather, it should be the impetus for investing renewed efforts into our *avodas Hashem*.

❈ ❈ ❈

WHAT DO WE DO WITH OUR NEWFOUND FREEDOM?

Until the day following the seventh week you shall count fifty days, and you shall offer a new minchah to Hashem (Vayikra 23:16).

Rashi explains that the Torah refers to the *Korban Minchah* of Shavuos as a "new" offering because it is the first offering to be brought from the new crop of grain. Rashi continues that although the *Minchas HaOmer* was brought earlier (on the second day of Pesach), it is not reckoned as the first offering because it was brought from barley, as opposed to the rest of the *menachos*, which were brought from wheat.

There is one other *minchah* that was brought from barley: the *minchah* of a *sotah*. The word *se'arim* (barley) has a linguistic connection to *saarah* (hair). *Chazal* (*Bava Kamma* 50a) tell us that Hashem judges the righteous meticulously and punishes them for even an infraction the size of "a hairsbreadth." In other words, *se'arim* connote, and therefore arouse, Hashem's judgment.

A *sotah* brings a barley offering because her situation warrants Divine judgment. Is she guilty of adultery, and deserving of punishment via the bitter waters? Or is she innocent, and worthy of being blessed with beautiful children? In a similar fashion, *Bnei Yisrael* would bring a barley offering after the first day of Pesach. A day earlier, they experienced freedom from bondage — and this was true every year, because the Exodus was not a one-time event. Rather, we revisit and relive that momentous occasion each year on the *Seder* night, as per the commandment to feel as if we left Mitzrayim.

Since *Bnei Yisrael* were expected to relive *Yetzias Mitzrayim* on the first day of Pesach, there was a need to judge them the next day. How had they utilized their newfound freedom? Did it galvanize them into greater service of the Creator?

Though we no longer have the *Beis HaMikdash* and the *mena-*

chos, we do have the ability to experience freedom on the night of the *Seder*. Subsequently, we must examine how these feelings affected us. Do we have, or are we at least working toward, a greater level of *emunah*? Are we even a tad less enslaved to our *yetzer hara* and our desires? This is the lesson of the *Minchas HaOmer*.

> *"Though we no longer have the Beis HaMikdash and the menachos, we do have the ability to experience freedom on the night of the Seder."*

(*Shiurei Chumash, Parashas Emor* 23:16)

Shavuos שבועות

WHO IS SERVING WHOM?

Chazal tell us (*Avodah Zarah* 11a) that Onkelos, the nephew of the Roman caesar, converted to Judaism. In a desperate attempt to convince him to retract his decision, his uncle sent a group of soldiers to forcibly bring Onkelos back to Rome. However, Onkelos piqued their interest by quoting some *pesukim* from the Torah, and they were inspired to convert.

The caesar sent another group of soldiers, but this time with an explicit warning not to engage in any sort of conversation with Onkelos. As they led Onkelos away, he related an interesting observation he had made. In an army, a private holds a torch to light the way for the lieutenant, the lieutenant holds the light for the captain, the captain for the general, and the general for the king. "Does a king ever hold a torch to light the way for a common citizen?" he asked. The soldiers answered in the negative.

"Well," said Onkelos, "our King lights the way for *Bnei Yisrael*." He then quoted the *passuk* (*Shemos* 14:21), "And Hashem walked in front of them in the form of a cloud by day, to show them the way, and by night in the form of fire to light the way for them." They, too, converted.

What was so powerful about the message Onkelos conveyed? How did this brief insight sway the caesar's hardened soldiers? Onkelos offered them an entirely new perspective on the concept of religion and service of Hashem. From ancient times until this very day, people believe that they must honor God because life and death are in His hands, and according Him insufficient honor could lead to dire consequences. They view religion as merely a means to demonstrate their honor for God, and they hope that their demonstration of honor will benefit them in the long run, similar to the motivation to honor a king.

In Judaism, however, it is not the subject who lights the way for the King, but the King Himself Who lights the way for His subjects. The Torah is not a means of honoring Hashem; it is the torch that Hashem has handed us to light our way! Every mitzvah is a candle and the entire Torah is a light. This is not a poetic declaration; it is the reality of Torah for anyone who has toiled in its study and lived in accordance with its precepts.

A mitzvah that is performed properly causes a radiance that is palpable. It does not matter whether it is a mitzvah that purifies our body (such as refraining from forbidden foods) or one that perfects our character traits (such as the prohibitions regarding stealing and gossiping). There are mitzvos that illuminate our hearts with lofty feelings (*tefillin*, Shabbos, Yamim Tovim, and the Days of Awe, to name a few) and there are mitzvos that brighten our interpersonal relationships (such as the laws in *Parashas Mishpatim*). Each mitzvah is a torch that lights up our life with purpose and meaning, while the light generated through Torah study enters a person's mind and heart and paves the way to a new, meaningful outlook on life.

Through the mitzvos we perform, Hashem serves us, so to speak,

> *"In Judaism, it is not the subject who lights the way for the King, but the King Himself Who lights the way for His subjects."*

by illuminating our lives. If this concept has the power to cause gentiles to convert, it certainly has the ability to bring those who are already Jewish closer to Torah!

(*Olam HaYedidus,* pp. 97-100)

❊ ❊ ❊

EVERY PERSON WANTS TO CLIMB

It is possible to discern great things from the games that children play. Children love to climb on rooftops and up trees. When they are a bit older they enjoy hiking and climbing mountains. They dream of one day being able to fly a plane; flying high seems to be the greatest experience possible to children. The *Chovos HaLevavos* writes (*Shaar Avodas Elokim,* Ch. 9), "Hashem created us from nothing, with the desire that we be raised and uplifted to the level of those who are close to Him, entirely for our benefit." Since we were created in order to be uplifted, even young children strive to reach great heights.

This concept is, in essence, the explanation behind the need for the awe-inspiring revelation that *Bnei Yisrael* experienced at Har Sinai. The *passuk* states (*Shemos* 20:17), "And Moshe said to the nation, 'Do not fear [the noise, fire, and *shofar* blast] because Hashem has come *l'nasos es'chem.*'" Rashi translates "*l'nasos es'chem*" as: to make you great in the world, when the nations hear that He revealed Himself to you.

"*L'nasos*" means to uplift; the root of the word is "*nes*," which means a banner that is held high. The Ten Commandments could have been given in a more modest fashion, without all the thunder and fanfare. They were specifically given amid great ceremony, however, because the entire awe-inspring "presentation" was intended to raise and uplift *Bnei Yisrael*.

This comment of Rashi seems to contradict what we are told in a different *passuk*. Hashem tells Moshe (*Shemos* 19:9), "I am coming to you in a thick cloud so that the nation will hear when I speak to you and they will also believe in you." It would seem from this *passuk* that the purpose of the revelation was to ingrain *emunah* into *Bnei Yisrael*. How can we reconcile this paradox?

Both concepts are in truth one idea. In order for a person to be truly uplifted, he must first believe wholeheartedly in Hashem. It is not enough to merely recite the *Ani Maamin*s; we must truly live them. Hashem revealed Himself to the point where *Bnei Yisrael* stood "facing" the *Shechinah*, because it was necessary that they "experience" their *emunah* in order for them to be uplifted. When a person recognizes God's existence more fully, all of his actions change for the better. His eating is different, his sleeping is different, his interaction with others is different — and it goes without saying that his learning and *davening* are imbued with new life and spirit.

The Midrash (*Shemos Rabbah* 25:8) compares *Bnei Yisrael* to a stork that laid its eggs in the dirt, where they were trampled upon and ruined by passersby. The eggs were destroyed because the bird laid them on the ground; had she flown to a high place and laid them there, no one would have been able to destroy them. Similarly, when *Bnei Yisrael* are not cognizant of Hashem and they despair of reaching great heights, they "lay their eggs" (i.e., live their life) in the dirt, where all the passersby can destroy them.

When people hear about greatness and lofty levels of observance, they often sigh and say that these levels are not for them to aspire to. On Shavuos we must remember that we were given wings to soar, and we should make use of those wings to raise ourselves to new heights of *emunah*.

> "On Shavuos we must remember that we were given wings to soar, and we should make use of those wings to raise ourselves to new heights of emunah."

(*Daas Shlomo, Zman Matan Torahseinu*, pp. 370-374)

תשעה באב

Tishah B'Av

MOURNING THE INTERNAL DESTRUCTION

Nefesh HaChaim (*Shaar Aleph*, Chapter 4) offers a novel approach to understanding the *Beis HaMikdash* and its destruction. He writes that Hashem commanded, "Make for a Me a *Mikdash* so I can dwell within them" (*Shemos* 25:8). Hashem did not say, "So that I can dwell within *it*," but rather "within *them*," because He desires to dwell within each and every Jew. Every person can become a veritable *Beis HaMikdash*.

The *navi* (*Yirmiyah* 7:4) refers to the righteous as "the sanctuary of Hashem." The commandment to build an actual *Beis HaMikdash* was to facilitate an understanding of how our personal *Beis HaMikdash* should look. Actions carried out with pure and holy intentions and with the goal of creating an abode for Hashem in this physical world mirror the holy vessels of the *Beis HaMikdash*, which were prepared with the objective of creating a place in which the *Shechinah* would reside on Earth. When *Bnei Yisrael*'s behavior deteriorated to the point that they defiled their internal *Beis HaMikdash*, the external *Beis HaMikdash* automatically lost its viability and was destroyed.

When we mourn on Tishah B'Av and the days leading up to it, we are not merely mourning for the *Beis HaMikdash* that once stood in Yerushalayim. We are mourning the destruction of our internal greatness. Is there anyone who truly believes that he has the ability to turn himself into an abode for the *Shechinah*?

Bnei Yisrael have always produced great leaders who provide us with glimpses of true greatness. One such example is the Chofetz Chaim. His every action was measured and every word was weighed. He was a Torah giant, a paradigm of kindness and humility, and a paragon of *tefillah*.

Every Jew has the ability to reach a similar level, but one of the obstacles we face is the mindset that people are small and will always remain small. We must rid ourselves of this mindset, because it destroys our personal *Beis HaMikdash*.

We do not recite *Tachanun* on Tishah B'Av because the *passuk* refers to it as a *mo'ed*. We can understand why Succos is a *mo'ed*, but why is Tishah B'Av a *mo'ed*? Rav Yerucham Levovitz explains that there are *mo'adim* of *kiruv* (closeness) and *mo'adim* of *richuk* (distance). Tishah B'Av is a time for a person to contemplate just how far he is from Hashem. His every action has the ability to create an atmosphere suitable to house the *Shechinah*, but he does not believe for a second that he can achieve this goal.

> "One's every action has the ability to create an atmosphere suitable to house the Shechinah, but he does not believe for a second that he can achieve this goal."

Recognizing and acknowledging one's distance from Hashem is the first step in rebuilding our internal *Beis HaMikdash*. Once this is accomplished, the *Beis HaMikdash* in Yerushalayim will follow immediately. This is why *Chazal* say (*Taanis* 30b), "Whoever mourns Yerushalayim will merit seeing its joy."

(See also *Alei Shur*, Vol. II, pp. 411, 412)

❋ ❋ ❋

SPIRITUAL GROWTH IS NOT AUTOMATIC

An astounding *Chazal* (*Vayikra Rabbah* 26:2) puts the importance of good *middos* into perspective. In the days of David HaMelech, even the small children were so proficient in Torah that they were able to explain each law of the Torah in 98 different ways. Despite the generation's greatness in Torah, when they waged war against their enemies they suffered losses in battle, because the people spoke *lashon hara*. In contrast, the entire generation of King Achav worshiped idols, but since they refrained from speaking *lashon hara* they did not fall.

How could it be that the tremendous amount of Torah study in David HaMelech's time did not protect the generation from defeat? In addition, how were there gossipmongers in the times of David HaMelech? Does not Torah study automatically generate good *middos*?

With regard to spiritual growth nothing is automatic. A person who does not make a conscious effort to work on himself in a particular area will remain deficient in that area. It is evident from *Chazal* that a deficiency in *middos* is so significant that it overrides other mitzvos and tips the scales against the Jewish people.

Another example of the severe ramifications of a deficiency in *middos* is the destruction of the second *Beis HaMikdash*. *Chazal* tell us that although the people of that era studied Torah, performed mitzvos, and acted charitably, since they were guilty of *sinas chinam* the *Beis HaMikdash* was destroyed. All of the mitzvos they did could not compensate for their shortcomings nor prevent the calamity that bad *middos* precipitate. This brings us to the realization that we have no choice but to consciously invest effort in developing good *middos*. Such qualities do not simply happen by themselves, and when there are failings in this area, the consequences can be catastrophic, *chas v'shalom*.

Hatred has no place among the Jewish people — especially among those who spend their days immersed in Torah study. The *mishnah* (*Sanhedrin* 3:5) tells us, "What is an expression of hatred?

When, as a result of his hatred, one does not speak to another person for three consecutive days."

Our Sages tell us (*Yerushalmi Yoma* 1:1), "In every generation in which the *Beis HaMikdash* has not been rebuilt, it is as if the *Beis HaMikdash* has once again been destroyed." Our generation has not been cleansed of the hatred that caused the destruction of the *Beis HaMikdash*. During the days leading up to Tishah B'Av, and all the more so on Tishah B'Av itself, we should make a conscious effort to purge ourselves of *sinas chinam*, restore harmony to those relationships that we have neglected, and once again speak to those people whom we had resolved to ignore.

(*Daas Shlomo*, unpublished manuscript)

❊ ❊ ❊

MOURNING THE ABSENCE OF HASHEM'S GLORY

"All that Hashem created in His world was created solely for His glory" (*Avos* 6:11). Since Hashem's glory is the purpose of the entire creation, the *passuk* states, "The entire world is filled with His glory" (*Yeshayah* 6:3). Angels are always able to perceive this glory. Humans also had this ability to discern Hashem's glory: Adam HaRishon lived with this perception until he sinned, causing Hashem to conceal Himself to a great degree. *Bnei Yisrael* returned to this level when they stood at Har Sinai, only to lose it when they succumbed to sin and worshiped the golden calf. Consequently, the entire world became devoid of the palpable manifestation of Hashem's presence, for which it was created.

There was one place where Hashem's glory was clearly revealed: in the *Beis HaMikdash*. Hashem's presence was almost tangible there. A person would enter the *Beis HaMikdash* laden with transgression and depart completely cleansed, feeling spiritually uplifted, enveloped in a sense of holiness. This was a place that encapsulated the entire purpose of Creation. On Tishah B'Av this last bastion of Hashem's glory was destroyed.

Rambam writes (*Hilchos Taanis* 5:9) that it was the custom of the pious men of previous generations to only eat dry bread with salt and drink water on the eve of Tishah B'Av. They would feel as if they were in the presence of the body of a close relative who had passed away. Although even the greatest person is not mourned for more than 30 days nor eulogized for more than 12 months, we are still mourning the destruction of the *Beis HaMikdash* after nearly 2,000 years. The mourning renews itself every year as if the *Beis HaMikdash* were destroyed before our eyes. Every moment that there is an absence of Hashem's glory, which is the entire purpose of Creation, is a cause for mourning. The Me'iri writes that one must "arouse his heart to mourn" the destruction of the *Beis HaMikdash*, the distress of the *Shechinah*, and the misery of a world that did not fulfill its purpose.

> "Every moment that there is an absence of Hashem's glory, which is the entire purpose of Creation, is a cause for mourning."

We have a difficult task before us. Imagine a child who is born and raised in a prison. He leads a pitiful existence, yet even he finds meaning and joy in his life. When he is let outside to the prison courtyard for a few minutes a day, fettered in chains, and he observes the blossoming of the trees and hears the chirping of the birds, he thinks to himself that he lives in a wonderful world. When cigarettes are distributed once a week, he eyes them as though they are the greatest pleasure attainable. If one were to describe to him life outside the prison walls, he would have great difficulty comprehending such a world.

We are, in a sense, like this child. Do we have any comprehension of what a world with the *Beis HaMikdash* looked like? Can we picture the holiness and serenity that pervaded the lives of those who lived in that era? Do we even realize that we were created to bring glory to Hashem? The world was created for Hashem's glory, and this glory has been absent since the destruction of the *Beis HaMikdash*.

These are a few of the things that we must think about on Tishah B'Av. We should contemplate how the destruction of the *Beis HaMikdash* affects us, and if we find that it does not affect us in a significant way, then we should at least feel anguish that we are so disconnected.

(*Daas Shlomo*, unpublished manuscript)

✻ ✻ ✻

POINT OF CONNECTION

The twelfth *kinnah* we read on Tishah B'Av is titled "*O'hali asher taavta.*" This *kinnah* was composed by R' Elazar HaKalir, and each stanza concludes with a *passuk* that ends with the word "*poh*" (here). With this single word, R' Elazar HaKalir encapsulated the tragedy of the destruction of the *Beis HaMikdash*.

The *Kuzari* writes that the king of Kuzar asked an interesting question: Why is it that other religions, such as Islam, promise great reward in the next world, while the Torah makes hardly any mention of the reward that awaits us in the World to Come?

The sage answered that other religions cannot guarantee anything with regard to this world. All their promises are regarding the next world, since there is no way for a human to disprove such promises. In contrast, the Torah does not need to rely on promises that will be fulfilled only in the World to Come, since it has the ability to guarantee the way our lives will look in this world. The greatest guarantee is Hashem's declaration, "And I will be for you a God and you will be for Me a nation" (*Vayikra* 26:12). The Torah pledges that if we fulfill Hashem's commandments, we will have — and feel — a true connection to Hashem right here in this world.

This is what *Bnei Yisrael* lost with the destruction of the *Beis HaMikdash*. Hashem's *Shechinah* was here on earth for all to see, and when the *Beis HaMikdash* was destroyed we lost this closeness and the resulting sublime spiritual levels.

> *"It used to be obvious that true fulfillment and pleasure in life could only be achieved through closeness to Hashem, but we have since lost this clarity."*

This destruction grows more profound as the *galus* extends, since it becomes more and more difficult for us to comprehend how Hashem could truly be found in this mundane mortal world. It used to be obvious that true fulfillment and pleasure in life could only be achieved through closeness to Hashem, but we have since lost this clarity.

One of the early *Rishonim*, Rabbeinu Tam, writes that every person experiences "days of love, and days of hatred and despair."

Some days, our *avodas Hashem* seems to flow easily, while on other days we feel sluggish, and every aspect of *avodas Hashem* seems like a heavy burden. On days when we sense Hashem's closeness more strongly, it is easier for us to fulfill His dictates, while the opposite is true on days when we are less cognizant of His closeness.

The *Beis HaMikdash* was a point of connection. It was the site where the physical connected with the spiritual, and it was abundantly clear to all how they were intertwined. The *churban* caused the spiritual to be separated from the physical, and from then on it became increasingly difficult to discern spirituality here in this world. Nevertheless, despite the many years of exile and destruction, *Klal Yisrael* is still aware that Hashem does exist here. We simply need to make the effort to look for Him.

Tishah B'Av was given to us as an opportunity to contemplate just how far we have drifted from Hashem's *Shechinah*. Tishah B'Av is called a *mo'ed*, because we realize that despite all the destruction, Hashem can still be found right here on Earth.

May we merit the ultimate closeness to Hashem with the rebuilding of the *Beis HaMikdash* speedily in our days.

(*Daas Shlomo*, unpublished manuscript; *Alei Shur*, Vol. II, pp. 409-411)

Glossary

achilah gasah — gluttony.
Adam — the first man.
adam — Man; person.
adamah — earth.
Aggadah (pl. *aggados*) — homiletical, non-halachic teaching of the Sages.
ahavah — love.
ahavas habriyos — love of other beings.
ahavas Yisrael — love for other Jews; love of Jews.
Akeidah, Akeidas Yitzchak — the Binding of Yitzchak.
Al HaMichyah — the three-faceted blessing said after eating grains or certain fruits.
Amen, Yehei Shmei Rabba — Amen. May God's great name be blessed, a core response during Kaddish.
Amora'im — Sages cited in the Gemara.
anav — a humble person.
anavah — humility.
Ani Maamin — lit., *I believe;* refers to the 13 statements setting forth the fundamental principles of faith.
arbaah minim — the Four Species taken on Succos.
arei miklat — cities of refuge, where one who killed accidentally could find safe haven.
Aron — (in Mishkan) Holy Ark that housed the Tablets (*Luchos*).
aron kodesh — (in shul) the ark into which Torah scrolls are placed and kept.
Aseres Hadibros — The Ten Commandments.
Aseres Yemei Teshuvah — the Ten Days of Repentance between Rosh Hashanah and Yom Kippur.
Asher Yatzar — prayer said after performing bodily functions.
aveirah (pl. *aveiros*) — sin; transgression.
avodah — work; service (prayer).
Avodah Zarah — idol worship; idolatry.
avodas hamiddos — refinement of personal characteristics.
avodas Hashem — service of Hashem.
avodas hayom — the primary task of the day.
Avos — the Patriarchs; Abraham, Isaac, and Jacob.
b'ezras Hashem — with Hashem's help.
baal chesed (pl. *baalei chesed*) — one who does *chesed*; one who performs acts of kindness.
baal teshuvah — one who repents; one who returns to Torah-true Judaism.
baal (pl. *baalei*) *hanefesh* — one who wishes to do the proper thing even when it is not required by *halachah*.
baalei mussar — one who toils in the study of ethical conduct.
bachur (pl. *bachurim*) — young man; an unmarried young man, used to denote a student in a yeshivah.
bais hamussar — a center for introspection and self-improvement through the study of *mussar*.
bal tashchis — wasting food; one who wastes food.
baruch Hashem — lit., *blessed is Hashem;* thank Hashem; an

expression of appreciation of Hashem's goodness.

be'ezras Hashem — with Hashem's help.

bechirah — free will; the ability to make choices.

bedikas chametz — the search for *chametz* carried out on the night before the Pesach Seder.

bein adam lachaveiro — between man and his fellow.

bein adam laMakom — between man and G-d.

bein hazmanim — vacation time from yeshiva; intersession.

beis din — a Rabbinical court.

Beis HaMikdash (pl. Batei Mikdash) — the Holy Temple in Jerusalem.

beis midrash — a study hall where Torah is learned, often used as a synagogue as well.

berachah (pl. *berachos*) — blessing.

bikkurim — first fruits presented to a Kohen in the *Beis HaMikdash*.

Bircas Hamazon — Grace After Meals; the series of four blessings recited after eating bread.

Birchos Hashachar — blessings recited during the morning prayer service.

Birchos HaTorah — the blessings said before studying Torah.

bitachon — lit., *trust*; trust in G-d.

bizui ochlin — treating foods in a disrespectful way.

Bnei Yisrael — lit., *the Children of Israel;* the "children" of Israel (the Jewish people).

bris (*bris milah*) — circumcision of male infants, generally performed on the eighth day after birth.

Chag HaMatzos — lit., *the Festival of Matzos;* Pesach.

challah — 1. colloquially, loaves of soft wheat-bread traditionally eaten at a Shabbos meal. 2. the portion separated from the dough and given to a *Kohen* (today it is burnt).

chametz — leavened foods prohibited during the Passover Festival.

chamor — a type of donkey.

chanufah — flattery.

charoses — a dip into which the *maror* is dipped at the Seder. Made of wine, nuts, apples, and cinnamon, its color and consistency are meant to remind us of the bricks and mortar used by the Jewish slaves in Egypt.

chas v'shalom — G-d forbid; Heaven forbid.

Chazal — the Sages, of blessed memory.

chazzan — a cantor; one who leads the prayer service in the synagogue.

cheshbon hanefesh — spiritual accounting; accounting of one's deeds.

chessed — kindness; generous acts; lovingkindness; acts of benevolence; acts of beneficence.

chiddush (pl. *chiddushim*) — Talmudic or halachic novellae.

chillul Hashem — desecration of Hashem's Name.

chinuch — Jewish education; Torah education (of minors).

chitzoniyus — externality.

chizuk — encouragement.

chok (pl. *chukim*) — statute, a Biblical decree; a decree; a Midrashic teaching derived from the Torah.

Choshen — the Kohen Gadol's Breastplate.

Chumash — one of the Five Books of the Torah; the Five Books collectively.

Churban — 1. destruction. 2. (cap.) destruction of the Holy Temple. 3. the Holocaust.

chutz la'Aretz — anywhere outside of the Land of Israel.

d'Oraisa — of Biblical origin.

daas — full moral comprehension; knowledge.
daven — (Yiddish) to pray.
davening — (Yiddish) 1. praying. 2. prayers.
derech eretz — proper conduct; respect; courtesy.
din — a law; Jewish law; the attribute strict justice.
Dor Haflagah — Generation of the Dispersion.
dvar Torah (pl. *divrei Torah*) — a lesson from the Torah; a Torah thought.
dveikus — bonding with or clinging to God.
Eirev Rav — mixed multitude.
emunah — faith; belief in G-d; faithfulness.
emunas — belief in
emunas chachamim — belief in the advice of Torah scholars.
esrog — citron, one of the Four Species taken in hand during the Succos Festival.
Eitz Hadaas — the Tree of Knowledge in the Garden of Eden, from which Adam and Chavah were prohibited from eating.
ex nihilo — (Latin) something from nothing
frumkeit — (Yiddish) the state of being religious.
gaavah — arrogance; excessive pride.
gabbai — (Yiddish) person responsible for the proper functioning of a synagogue or other communal body; attendant of a tzaddik; attendant of a Chassidic Rebbe.
gadlus ha'adam — the inherent greatness of Man.
gadol (pl. *gedolim*) — 1. an adult according to halachah 2. an outstanding Torah scholar.
galus — the Jewish exile; (cap.) the Diaspora

Gehinnom — Hell.
gemilus chassadim — acts of loving-kindness.
Geonim — post-Tamudic sages; the Sages who lived between approx. 600 C.E. and 1,000 C.E.
ger — a convert.
geulah — redemption; (cap.) the Final Redemption.
Geulah Sheleimah — lit., *complete redemption*; the Final Redemption.
gezel — theft.
guf — the body; the physical component of Man.
hachnasas orchim — hospitality; inviting guests; a facility offering free lodging for guests.
haftarah — the selection from the Prophets read following the Torah reading on the Sabbath, Festivals, and fast days.
Haggadah — liturgy recited at the Pesach Seder.
hakaras hatov — 1. gratitude. 2. expressing gratitude.
Hallel — lit., *praise*; a prayer of praise and thanksgiving recited during prayer services on Rosh Chodesh and most Festivals and in the Haggadah.
hashavas aveidah — returning a lost object.
Hashgachah, Hashgachah Pratis — Divine intervention.
hashraas haShechinah — the immanence of the Divine Presence.
havtachah — promise; guarantee.
he'aras panim — a reference to Divine grace.
hefker — ownerless.
hester; hester panim — lit., *hidden; hidden face*; referring *to* when God hides His countenance
hisbonenus — meditation and introspection.

Glossary / 441

hishtadlus — one's own efforts; the required effort.

im yirtzeh Hashem — if G-d wills it; "If Hashem so wills it."

ir miklat — city of refuge, where one who killed accidentally could find safe haven

kabbalah — (l.c.) lit., *acceptance*; the act of taking on a specific action to elevate oneself spiritually; an obligation taken upon oneself. (u.c.) the body of Jewish mystical teachings.

kadosh — holy; holy one.

kavanah — positive attitude or intensity in prayer.

kavod haberiyos — the respect and dignity with which one should treat others.

kedushah — holiness; sanctity.

kehunah — the priesthood.

keilim — utensils.

ketores — the incense offered in the *Beis HaMikdash*.

Kiddush — the prayer said over wine, before the Friday evening or Saturday lunchtime Sabbath meal.

kiddush Hashem — doing something that brings honor to Hashem; sanctification of G-d's Name.

kinnah — jealousy.

Klal Yisrael — the community of Israel; the entire Jewish community, taken as a single entity; the Jewish nation.

Kodesh HaKodashim — Holy of Holies; the inner chamber of the Sanctuary.

kohen (pl. *kohanim*) — 1. a member of the priestly family descended in the male line from Aaron; *kohanim* performed a number of services in the Temple. Although there is no Temple today, there are still a number of laws pertaining specifically to *kohanim*. 2. a priest; members of the priestly caste.

kohen gadol — the High Priest who served in the *Beis HaMikdash*.

kollel — academy of higher Jewish study, usually for married men.

korban (pl. *korbanos*) — a sacrificial offering.

Korban Minchah — a Meal-Offering.

Korban Pesach — the Passover Offering.

Krias Shema — three paragraphs of the Torah recited twice daily, beginning with the words "*Shema Yisrael*, Hear, O Israel."

Krias Yam Suf — the splitting of the Reed Sea.

l'shem Shamayim — for the sake of Heaven.; selfless action for the sake of heaven.

Lashon Hakodesh — lit., the holy tongue; Biblical Hebrew.

lashon hara — lit., *evil speech*; derogatory or slanderous speech; gossip; harmful speech.

Leil HaSeder — the night of the Seder; i.e., the first night of Passover.

Levi'im — Levites; members of the Tribe of Levi.

limud haTorah — the learning or teaching of the Torah.

Luchos — tablets inscribed with the Ten Commandments; the Tablets of the Ten Commandments.

Maadim — lit., *times*; the Festivals.

machlokes — an argument; a dispute.

maggid — speaker or lecturer who uses stories to teach moral lessons.

makkos — the Ten Plagues.

malchus — kingship; royalty.

mamleches kohanim — *a kingdom of priests*.

mann — the manna that miraculously fell in the Wilderness for the Jews.

maror — bitter herbs; bitter herbs used at the Passover Seder.

masechta — tractate of Talmud.

mashal — a parable.

mashgiach — spiritual guide in a yeshivah; dean of students.

masmid — exceptionally diligent student.

Matan Torah — the Giving of the Torah at Sinai.

mazel — good fortune.

Me'aras Hamachpeilah — the Cave of Machpelah, burial place of Adam, Eve, Abraham, Sarah, Isaac, Rebecca, Jacob, and Leah.

mechallel Shabbos — 1. one who desecrates the Sabbath. 2. the desecration of the Sabbath.

mechanech — educator.

meis mitzvah — the mitzvah of arranging the burial in a case where there is no one else to do so.

melachah (pl. *melachos*) — labor; any of the 39 labors forbidden to be performed on the Sabbath.

Menorah — candelabrum used to hold the Chanukah lights.

mentsch — (Yiddish) all-around good person

menuchah — rest; peace of mind.

menuchas hanefesh — peace of mind; spiritual calm.

meraglim — the Spies who were sent by Moshe Rabbeinu to scout the land of Canaan.

mesirus nefesh — selfless devotion, even to the extent that one is willing to give his or her life to sanctify Hashem's Name; total and unlimited devotion.

metzora — one who suffers from the skin disease *tzaraas*, similar to leprosy.

mezuzah — small parchment scroll in a casing, affixed to a doorpost and containing the first two paragraphs of the *Shema* prayer.

middah (pl. *middos*) — character trait; attribute.

middah k'neged middah — measure for measure.

Middas HaChessed — the Divine attribute of Mercy.

mikdash — a temple.

mikdash me'at — lit., *miniature Beis HaMikdash*; a synagogue.

mikreh — by chance; happenstance.

minchah — a meal-offering; the afternoon prayer service.

Minchas Ha'Omer — the Omer Offering, brought on the second day of Passover.

minhag — custom.

minyan — quorum of ten men necessary for conducting a prayer service.

Mishkan — Tabernacle; the portable Temple used by the Jews during their sojourn in the Wilderness.

mizbe'ach — an altar; a sacrificial altar.

Mo'ed (pl. *Mo'adim*) — Festival.

mohel — one who performs a circumcision.

moser nefesh — self-sacrificing.

Mussaf — lit., *additional*; supplementary prayer service added to the morning services on Festivals.

mussar — ethical teachings geared toward self-refinement; reproof; reprimand; ethical teachings.

mussar shmuess — lecture on self-refinement.

nasi — a chief of the Twelve Tribes.

navi — a prophet; (cap.) one of the Books of the *Prophets*.

nazir — a Nazarite; one who has vowed, for a defined period, to refrain from cutting his hair and to abstain from (a) grapes and grape products and (b) contact with a grave or a corpse.

Ne'ilah — concluding prayer of Yom Kippur.

neder — a vow.

neshamah — the soul.

nesiah b'ol, nesiah b'ol chaveiro — lit., carrying the burden; empathizing with other and sharing their plight.

Nevi'im — Prophets, the Books of the Tanach including Yehoshua, Shoftim, Shmuel, Melachim, Yeshayah, Yirmiyahu, Yechezkel, and Trei Asar.

nevuah — prophecy.

nisayon (pl. *nisyonos*) — a test, esp. a spiritual test.

nosei b'ol — sharing [another person's] burden or yoke.

nusach —1. style of prayer service. 2. melody used during a prayer service.

Olam Haba — the World to Come

Olam Hazeh — lit., this world; the material world; the physical, lower world.

oved Hashem — a servant of G-d.

Parah Adumah — the Red Heifer.

parashah (pl. parashiyos) — the weekly Torah portion; Torah portion; parchment inscribed with Torah paragraphs and inserted into tefillin.

passuk (pl. *pesukim*) — a Biblical verse; verse in the Tanach or liturgy.

penimiyus — inward; internal.

poskim — halachic authority

rasha (pl. *reshaim*) — evil person; evil-doer; wicked individual.

rebbi (pl. *rebbeim*) — a male Torah teacher.

Rishonim — early commentators on the Talmud, 11th – 15th centuries; Rabbinic authorities of the post-Geonic era (11th – 16th c.).

Ruach HaKodesh — Divine inspiration; Divine Spirit.

ruchniyus — spirituality; spiritual growth.

s'chach —the roof of the succah, generally made from leaves, branches, or bamboo.

Sanhedrin — high rabbinical court in Jerusalem; supreme judicial body in the Holy Land during the Roman period, consisting of 71 ordained scholars.

savlan — one who is patient and forbearing.

savlanus — patience; forbearance.

seder — 1. order 2. study period. 3. set time, usually for learning. 4. (u.c.) Pesach-night ritual during which the Haggadah is recited. 5. an order of the *Mishnah* or Talmud.

Sefiras HaOmer — Counting of the Omer.

seichel — insight; intelligence; common sense; one's rational side.

Shabbos — the seventh day of the week, which G-d commanded us to keep holy.

Shacharis — morning prayer service.

shaleim — whole; complete.

shalom — peace; often said on meeting or leave-taking.

Shas — the Talmud.

Shechinah — Divine Presence; the spirit of the Omnipresent manifested on earth.

shechitah — ritual slaughter; the ritual manner in which an animal is slaughtered

shehakol — the blessing recited before eating foods that have no other specific blessing.

sheker — (n.) falsehood. (adj.) false.

sheleimus — wholeness; perfection.

shemittah — the Sabbatical year; the Sabbatical year, occurring every seventh year, during which the land is not worked. This law only pertains to the Land of Israel.

Shemoneh Esrei — lit., *18*; the prayer, originally eighteen blessings but now nineteen, that forms the central core of each weekday prayer service; the Shabbos *Amidah*.

Shevatim — the Twelve Tribes, the sons of Yaakov.

shevet — tribe.
shidduch — 1. match, esp. a marriage match. 2. proposed marriage match. 3. one's betrothed.
shiluach haken — the mitzvah of sending away the mother bird before taking the eggs or chicks.
shiur (pl. *shiurim*) — a Torah lecture.
shleimus ha'adam — lit., *completion of Man*; spiritual and ethical perfection.
shlita — acronym for "May he live a long and good life."
shmuess (pl. *shmuessen*) — (Yiddish) lecture on Torah topics; Torah discourse
shochet — ritual slaughterer; one who slaughters an animal in accordance with Jewish/Torah law.
shofar — the ram's horn blown on Rosh HaShanah.
Shoftim — the Book of Judges.
Shovavim — acronym for Shemos, Va'eira, Bo, Beshalach, Yisro Mishpatim, the first six Torah portions of Sefer Shemos. It refers to the period of the year during which these Torah portions are read, a time considered propitious for introspection and repentance.
shulchan — table. (cap.) the Golden Table in the Holy Temple.
siddur — prayer book.
simchah — joy.
sinas chinam — unwarranted hatred of one Jew for another; unwarranted hatred; causeless hatred.
siyatta diShmaya — Heavenly assistance; Divine Providence; help from Hashem.
sotah — a married woman suspected of infidelity. (cap.) the Talmudic tractate dealing with this issue.
succah (pl. *succos*) — booth in which Jews are commanded to dwell during Succos.

Succos — Tabernacles; the festival during which one dwells in a *succah* and takes the Four Species.
tahor — ritually pure.
tallis (pl. *talisos*) — four-cornered prayer shawl with *tzitzis,* worn during morning prayers.
talmid (pl. *talmidim*) — student.
talmid chacham (pl. *talmidei chachamim*) — lit., *the student of a wise person*; Torah scholar; accomplished Torah scholar; a person learned in Torah and Talmud; a Torah scholar.
tamei — ritually impure; spiritually defiled.
Tanach — acronym for **Torah, Neviim, Kesuvim**: the written Torah, including the Five Books of Moses, the eight books of Prophets, and eleven books of Writings.
Tannaim — the Sages who are quoted in the Mishnah.
techeiles — a unique blue dye; wool dyed with this dye; the blue thread of *tzitzis;* the blue dye used in *tzitzis*.
tefillah (pl. *tefillos*) — Jewish prayer.
tefillin — phylacteries, small black leather boxes containing parchment scrolls inscribed with Biblical passages, bound to the arm and forehead of adult Jewish males during the weekday morning prayer service.
teshuvah — 1. answer. 2. repentance.
tikkun hamiddos — perfection of one's character traits.
tochachah — rebuke; harsh rebuke; (cap.) the Admonition, in which the Torah foretells the punishments that will befall the Jews if they fail to heed the Torah.
Torah — the Bible; the 24 books of the Scripture; also refers collectively to

both the Oral and Written Torahs given to Moses on Mount Sinai.

treif — colloquial term for non-kosher.

tumah — moral degeneration; spiritual impurity; spiritual defilement.

tzaddik (pl. *tzaddikim*) — righteous male person.

tzaraas — a severe skin disease affliction that manifests itself (on people) as white or light-colored spots on the body.

tzedakah — compassion; charity.

Tzelem Elokim — lit., *image of G-d*; G-dly image; Man was formed in the image of G-d and therefore each human being is deserving of respect; the image of G-d.

tzibbur — congregation; the community as a whole.

tzitzis — the fringes on four-cornered garments worn by Jewish men and boys; a special garment made to enable one to wear such fringes.

tznius — modesty standard in speech, behavior, and dress.

Vaad, (pl. *vaadim*) — group; a *mussar* talk given to a small, select group.

viduy — confession recited on Yom Kippur and before death.

Yamim Nora'im — High Holy Days.

yashrus — uprightness.

yeri'os — coverings of the Tabernacle.

yetzer hara — evil inclination; connotes the negative impulse to behave contrary to the Torah's commandments.

yetzer [ha]tov — *good inclination.*

Yetzias Mitzrayim — the Exodus from Egypt.

Yiddishkeit — (Yiddish) Judaism; the Jewish way of life.

yirah — fear; awe of Hashem

yiras Shamayim — lit., *fear of Heaven*; connotes reverence for G-d, an all-pervasive attitude of piety.

Yovel — the Jubilee year.

zechus — privilege or merit.

zerizus — enthusiasm; urgency.

zocheh — to merit.